Study Abroad and the Second Language Learner

Also available from Bloomsbury

Second Language Acquisition in Action,
by Andrea Nava and Luciana Pedrazzini
Social Networks in Language Learning and Language Teaching,
edited by Avary Carhill-Poza and Naomi Kurata
Teaching Pragmatics and Instructed Second Language Learning,
by Nicola Halenko
The Interactional Feedback Dimension in Instructed Second Language Learning,
by Hossein Nassaji
The Production-Comprehension Interface in Second Language Acquisition,
by Anke Lenzing

Study Abroad and the Second Language Learner

Expectations, Experiences and Development

Edited by
Martin Howard

BLOOMSBURY ACADEMIC
LONDON • NEW YORK • OXFORD • NEW DELHI • SYDNEY

BLOOMSBURY ACADEMIC
Bloomsbury Publishing Plc
50 Bedford Square, London, WC1B 3DP, UK
1385 Broadway, New York, NY 10018, USA
29 Earlsfort Terrace, Dublin 2, Ireland

BLOOMSBURY, BLOOMSBURY ACADEMIC and the Diana logo are trademarks of Bloomsbury Publishing Plc

First published in Great Britain 2021
Paperback edition published 2022

Copyright © Martin Howard and Contributors, 2021

Martin Howard has asserted his right under the Copyright, Designs and Patents Act, 1988, to be identified as Editor of this work.

For legal purposes the Acknowledgements on p. xvi constitute an extension of this copyright page.

All rights reserved. No part of this publication may be reproduced or transmitted in any form or by any means, electronic or mechanical, including photocopying, recording, or any information storage or retrieval system, without prior permission in writing from the publishers.

Bloomsbury Publishing Plc does not have any control over, or responsibility for, any third-party websites referred to or in this book. All internet addresses given in this book were correct at the time of going to press. The author and publisher regret any inconvenience caused if addresses have changed or sites have ceased to exist, but can accept no responsibility for any such changes.

A catalogue record for this book is available from the British Library.

Library of Congress Cataloging-in-Publication Data
Names: Howard, Martin, 1972- editor.
Title: Study abroad and the second language learner : expectations, experiences and development / edited by Martin Howard.
Description: London ; New York : Bloomsbury Academic, 2021. | Includes bibliographical references and index.
Identifiers: LCCN 2020034766 (print) | LCCN 2020034767 (ebook) | ISBN 9781350104198 (hardback) | ISBN 9781350200630 (paperback) | ISBN 9781350104204 (ebook) | ISBN 9781350104211 (epub)
Subjects: LCSH: Second language acquisition. | Language and languages–Study and teaching–Foreign speakers. | Foreign study. | Students, Foreign–Services for.
Classification: LCC P118.2 .S884 2021 (print) | LCC P118.2 (ebook) | DDC 418.0071–dc23
LC record available at https://lccn.loc.gov/2020034766
LC ebook record available at https://lccn.loc.gov/2020034767

ISBN:	HB:	978-1-3501-0419-8
	PB:	978-1-3502-0063-0
	ePDF:	978-1-3501-0420-4
	eBook:	978-1-3501-0421-1

Typeset by Integra Software Services Pvt. Ltd.

To find out more about our authors and books visit www.bloomsbury.com and sign up for our newsletters.

Contents

List of Figures	vii
List of Tables	viii
List of Contributors	x
Acknowledgements	xvi

Study abroad and the second language learner: An introduction
Martin Howard   1

1. The legal framework of student mobility: How public law makes the Erasmus programme possible   *Luca Galli*   15
2. Should I stay or should I go? Factors that influence one's decision to participate in a student mobility programme
Katarzyna Ożańska Ponikwia and Angélica Carlet   33
3. Study abroad marketing and L2 self-efficacy beliefs
Emre Güvendir, Meltem Acar-Güvendir and Sinem Dündar   49
4. Close encounters of the third kind: Quantity, type and quality of language contact during study abroad
Jessica Briggs Baffoe-Djan and Siyang Zhou   69
5. Study abroad for secondary and higher education students: Differences and similarities in their interaction with the learning environment
Sofía Moratinos-Johnston, Maria Juan-Garau and Joana Salazar Noguera   91
6. Assessing the impact of educational support abroad on sojourners' interactional contacts, L2 acquisition and intercultural development
Ana Maria Moreno Bruna, July De Wilde, June Eyckmans and Patrick Goethals   115
7. The complex challenges of delivering a university-wide intercultural mentoring programme for study abroad students
Susan Oguro and Annie Cottier   137
8. Tapping into self-regulation in study abroad contexts: A pilot study
Kata Csizér, Mirosław Pawlak, Vanda Szatzker and Kitti Erdő-Bonyár   149
9. Structure and agency in the development of plurilingual identities in study abroad   *Josep M. Cots, Rosamond Mitchell and Ana Beaven*   165
10. Learning multiword expressions in a second language during study abroad: The role of individual differences   *Klara Arvidsson*   189

11 When in one's new country: Examining native-like selections in English at home and abroad *Victoria Zaytseva, Imma Miralpeix and Carmen Pérez-Vidal* 211

12 The role of transparency in grammatical gender marking among stay abroad learners of Spanish and French *Amanda Edmonds and Aarnes Gudmestad* 233

Index 254

Figures

6.1	Kolb's (1984) Experiential Learning Cycle	119
8.1	The Structure of the Questionnaire	155
11.1	Proportion of Different Adverbs Used in Oral Production	223
12.1	Targetlike Rates of Use for Individuals and the Group (Spanish Dataset)	243
12.2	Targetlike Rates of Use for Individuals and the Group (French Dataset)	245

Tables

2.1	Self-perceived L2 Proficiency – At-home vs. Stay Abroad Group	40
2.2	L2 Proficiency Test Scores – At-home vs. Stay Abroad Group	40
2.3	L2 Speaking Abilities – At-home vs. Stay Abroad Group	41
2.4	The Big Five Personality Questionnaire – At-home vs. Stay Abroad Group	42
2.5	Multicultural Personality Questionnaire – At-home vs. Stay Abroad Group	43
2.6	Trait Emotional Intelligence Questionnaire – At-home vs. Stay Abroad Group	43
3.1	Skewness and Kurtosis Values of the Pre-test and Post-test Scores according to the Factors	58
3.2	t-Test Results for the Pre-test and Post-test Scores	59
3.3	Listening Factor: Pre-test and Post-test Wilcoxon Signed Rankings Test Scores	59
3.4	Reading Factor: Pre-test and Post-test t-Test Results	59
3.5	Speaking Factor: Pre-test and Post-test Wilcoxon Signed Rankings Test Scores	59
3.6	Writing Factor: Pre-test and Post-test t-Test Results	60
3.7	Pre-test and Post-test Mean Values	60
5.1	Characteristics of the Interviewees	99
5.2	Main Codes and Themes Used in the Study	100
6.1	Descriptive Statistics for Pre- and Post-SA Results of L2 Vocabulary Size (LexTALE), L2 Pragmatic Competence (VKS) and Cultural Intelligence Scale Variables (E-CQS)	123
6.2	Participants' L2 Vocabulary Size (LexTALE), Pre- and Post-SA	124
6.3	Participants' Pragmatic Knowledge (VKS), Pre- and Post-SA	125
6.4	Participants' Cultural Intelligence Profile (E-CQS), Pre- and Post-SA	126
6.5	Popularity and Perceived Usefulness of the Tasks	127
6.6	Non-parametric Spearman's Rank-order Correlation (two-tailed) between Perceived Usefulness and Popularity of the Tasks	130
8.1	Cronbach Alpha Values for the Scales Included in the Tool	157
8.2	Proposed Constructs for Further Studies with Sample Items	158
8.3	Differences between the Hungarian and Polish Students with Respect to the Academic Dimension of the Learner-based Approach before, during and after Study Abroad	159
10.1	Information about the Participants and Test Scores from the Quantitative Study	197

11.1	Testing Times*	215
11.2	Frequency of Use of Impersonal Forms in Written Production	218
11.3	Excerpts from Learners' and NSs' Written Compositions Illustrating the Use of Impersonal Forms	218
11.4	Frequency of Correct and Incorrect Uses of 'Hold onto Customs' in Written Production	219
11.5	Frequency of Use of Adverbs Modifying Adjectives in Written Production	219
11.6	Examples of Adverbs Modifying Adjectives in Learner and NS Written Compositions	219
11.7	Frequency of Topic-related Verbs in Written Production I	220
11.8	Frequency of Topic-related Verbs in Written Production II	220
11.9	Frequency of Use of 'Another' and 'New' as Examples of L1 Transfer in Written Production	220
11.10	Frequency of Use of Deceptive Cognates and Literal Translation from L1 in Oral Production	221
11.11	Frequency of Use of L1 Transfer in Oral Production	222
11.12	Frequency of Use of Emphasis in Oral Production	223
11.13	Frequency of Use of Emphasis through '-ly' Adverbs in Oral Production	223
11.14	Frequency of Use of Delexicalized Verbs in Oral Production	224
11.15	Frequency of Use of Specific Verb Combinations in Oral Production	224
11.16	Descriptive Statistics for Written Lexical Proficiency: Mean Scores Obtained at T1, T2 and T3 for Learners ($n = 30$) and NSs ($n = 27$)	225
11.17	Descriptive Statistics for Oral Lexical Proficiency: Mean Scores Obtained at T1, T2 and T3 for Learners ($n = 30$) and NSs ($n = 25$)	225
11.18	Independent Samples t-Tests Comparing the NNS Written Lexical Mean Scores to Those of the NSs at T1, T2 and T3	226
11.19	Independent Samples t-Tests Comparing the NNS Oral Lexical Mean Scores to Those of the NSs at T1, T2 and T3	226
12.1	Background Information on Participants	239
12.2	Independent Variables	241
12.3	Mixed-effects Regression Model for Spanish Data	244
12.4	Mixed-effects Regression Model for French Data	245
12.5	Proportion of Modifiers Marked Overtly for Gender	248

List of Contributors

Meltem Acar-Güvendir is Associate Professor in the Department of Measurement and Evaluation in Education at Trakya University, Turkey. She received her PhD in Measurement and Evaluation in Education from Ankara University. Her research interests include student achievement, multilevel models, scaling and test development.

Klara Arvidsson is currently a lecturer in French at Dalarna University, Sweden. She received her PhD in French from Stockholm University. Her research interests include second language acquisition (SLA), the role of individual differences, idiomaticity and L2 learning in the study abroad (SA) context.

Ana Beaven is an English-language teacher at the University of Bologna Language Centre. She has a PhD in Applied Linguistics. Her main areas of interest are open educational resources and practices, intercultural language education, study abroad and virtual exchange. She has taken part in several European projects (WebCEF, CEFcult, RICH-Ed, SAREP) and was the coordinator of IEREST (Intercultural Education Resources for Erasmus Students and their Teachers).

Jessica Briggs Baffoe-Djan is Associate Professor of Applied Linguistics and Second Language Acquisition and Course Director of the MSc in Applied Linguistics and Second Language Acquisition at the Department of Education, University of Oxford. Her research focuses on SLA outside of formal language learning settings, such as in study abroad and English Medium Instruction contexts, with a particular focus on vocabulary acquisition and language learner strategies. Her work is published in key journals such as *Applied Linguistics* and *International Journal of Applied Linguistics*, and she sits on the executive committee of the British Association for Applied Linguistics (BAAL).

Angélica Carlet is Professor of English linguistics and Head of English in the Faculty of Education at Universitat Internacional de Catalunya (UIC), Barcelona, Spain. She holds a PhD in English philology and a master's degree in second language acquisition from the Universitat Autònoma de Barcelona (UAB). The influence of one's native language phonology in the acquisition of a second language constitutes the main area of her research interest along with the effect of formal instruction and stay abroad programmes on participants' oral skills. Her more relevant publications can be found at https://www.researchgate.net/profile/Angelica_Carlet/research.

Josep M. Cots is Professor of English and Applied Linguistics in the Faculty of Arts of the University of Lleida, where he teaches courses in pragmatics, discourse analysis, intercultural communication and multilingual education. His research focuses on applied discourse analysis, multilingualism and intercultural competence. He has been the lead researcher in several competitive funded research projects, and since 2002 his research has been awarded a total of fifteen grants from different institutions.

Annie Cottier (Dr. phil.) is a member of staff at UniBe International at the University of Bern, Switzerland. She is the programme manager of the MILSA programme (Mentoring Intercultural Learning through Study Abroad) and teaches intercultural learning workshops to MILSA participants. Her main research interests include intercultural learning, language and intercultural communication, cultural studies, cosmopolitanism and global literatures in English.

Kata Csizér, PhD, works at the Department of English Applied Linguistics, School of English and American Studies, Eötvös Loránd University, Budapest, Hungary. Her main field of research interest is socio-psychological aspects of second language learning and teaching as well as second and foreign language motivation. She is involved in a number of research projects mapping the foreign language learning processes of various groups of students including deaf learners. She is one of the co-editors of the *Palgrave Macmillan Handbook of Motivation for Language Learning* (Basingstoke, UK: Palgrave).

July De Wilde is Assistant Professor (tenure track) at Ghent University where she teaches courses on multilingual and multicultural communication, Spanish language and Spanish-American society and culture. Her research focuses on multilingualism, intercultural communication in professional settings, interpreter-mediated communication and language learning in multilingual contexts. She has published in various international peer-reviewed journals, including *Meta, Language and Literature, Journal of Language and Politics* and *Multilingua*.

Sinem Dündar is a research assistant in the Department of Foreign Languages at Trakya University, Turkey. She received her PhD in English Language Teaching from Çanakkale Onsekiz Mart University. Her research interests include discourse analysis, SLA and foreign language teaching methodology.

Amanda Edmonds is a *Maître de Conférences* at the Université Paul-Valéry Montpellier 3, where she teaches courses in linguistics and language didactics. Her research interests lie predominantly in the field of second language acquisition, and most of her research focuses on understanding vocabulary acquisition and interlanguage variation in French, English and Spanish as a second language. Recent research has been accepted for publication in journals such as *Language Learning* and *Applied Linguistics*.

Kitti Erdő-Bonyár has an MA degree in English Applied Linguistics from Eötvös Loránd University (ELTE); she graduated in 2018. In her MA thesis, she investigated the sources of Hungarian EFL (English as a Foreign Language) learners' English-speaking self-efficacy beliefs. She attended the first round of the Applied Linguistics

Scientific Students' Association conference at ELTE in 2018. Currently, she is an IT researcher at a recruitment agency. She helps multinational corporations to find the most talented IT professionals. Apart from end-to-end recruitment (contacting applicants, interviewing, assessing foreign language proficiency, etc.), she also keeps contact with business partners and conducts weekly calls and meetings.

June Eyckmans is Associate Professor of Applied Linguistics at Ghent University. She teaches courses on second language acquisition and TEFL pedagogy. Her research interests centre on SLA, with a special focus on L2 vocabulary learning. Her research into contextual language learning led her to the field of SA research and the development of a computer application (SALSA) to enhance students' integration during their sojourn abroad.

Luca Galli is Research Fellow in Administrative Law at the Center for Law and Pluralism of the Università degli Studi di Milano-Bicocca. He received a PhD in Administrative Law at the same university in 2018, with a thesis on human rights protection before the administrative judges. The topic of his latest research is in the area of the administrative management of migration, especially focusing on the role of the public administration in newcomers' integration.

Patrick Goethals is Associate Professor of Applied Linguistics at Ghent University, where he teaches courses on cross-linguistic pragmatics and Spanish language. His research interests centre on multilingualism in travel contexts, computer-mediated communication and computer-assisted vocabulary learning. He currently supervises PhD projects on SA research and multilingual computer-mediated communication.

Aarnes Gudmestad is Associate Professor in the Department of Modern and Classical Languages and Literatures at Virginia Polytechnic Institute and State University. Her research centres on the intersection of SLA and sociolinguistics. She examines the language variation and change of morphosyntactic structures in Spanish and French (e.g. grammatical gender, mood distinction, future-time reference). She is the co-editor of *Critical Reflections on Data in Second Language Acquisition* and has published articles in journals such as *Canadian Journal of Linguistics*, *Hispania*, *Journal of French Language Studies* and *Language Learning*.

Emre Güvendir is Associate Professor in the Department of Foreign Languages at Trakya University, Turkey. He received his PhD in Applied Linguistics from the University of California at Los Angeles. His research primarily focuses on investigating social, intercultural, individual and psychological factors related to language acquisition in both SA and foreign language learning contexts.

Martin Howard is Associate Dean (Global) in the College of Arts, Celtic Studies and Social Sciences at University College Cork. He is currently President of the Association for French Language Studies and was chair of the European COST

Action, Study Abroad Research in European Perspective (2016–20). He is editor of the journal, *Study Abroad Research in Second Language Acquisition and International Education*. His research interests are in SLA with special reference to study abroad, (socio)linguistic variation and the acquisition of French, sociolinguistics and Canadian studies.

Maria Juan-Garau is Full Professor in English Studies at the Universitat de les Illes Balears, where she teaches graduate and postgraduate courses on language learning in multilingual settings. Her research interests centre on language acquisition in different learning contexts, naturalistic or formal, with special attention to study abroad and content and language integrated learning (CLIL). Her work has appeared in international journals and edited volumes, including *Language Acquisition in Study Abroad and Formal Instruction Contexts* (Pérez-Vidal, 2014). She has also co-edited a book with Springer publishers, *Content-based Language Learning in Multilingual Educational Environments* (Juan-Garau and Salazar-Noguera, 2015), and is one of the co-editors of *Acquisition of Romance Languages* (Guijarro-Fuentes, Juan-Garau and Larrañaga, 2016).

Imma Miralpeix is Associate Professor at the Universitat de Barcelona, where she obtained her PhD in Applied Linguistics. Her main research interests include second language vocabulary acquisition, especially lexical development and assessment, and multilingualism. She is the author of several publications in these areas and has taken part in different funded projects on second language learning and teaching. Recent publications have appeared in *Language Teaching Research*, *International Journal of Bilingual Education and Bilingualism*, *Language Learning Journal* and the *Routledge Handbook of Study Abroad Research and Practice*.

Rosamond Mitchell is Emeritus Professor of Applied Linguistics at the University of Southampton, UK, and a Fellow of the UK Academy of Social Sciences. She trained as a teacher of languages in Dublin, Ireland, before working as a researcher and university lecturer in Stirling, Edinburgh and Southampton. Her main research interests include corpus-based approaches to SLA and foreign language education, including the linguistic and social impact of study abroad for advanced language learners. She is convenor of the 'Individual Differences' strand within the 2016–20 COST Action 'Study Abroad Research in European Perspective'.

Sofía Moratinos-Johnston is currently finishing her doctoral studies at the University of the Balearic Islands (UIB), where she is also a lecturer. Her PhD focuses on language learning motivation in different learning contexts: formal classroom instruction, CLIL and study abroad. Apart from her research at the UIB, she was also a visiting scholar in the Centre for Applied Linguistics, University of Warwick, and the School of Education, University of Birmingham. Her latest article is entitled 'Attitudes and Motivation in English Language Learning amongst Multilingual University Students in the Balearic Islands: The Effect of the L1 and Other Influential Variables' (*Journal of Multilingual and Multicultural Development*, 2018).

Ana Maria Moreno Bruna works as Research Assistant at the Faculty of Applied Linguistics at Ghent University, where she teaches courses in Spanish language and didactics and interpreting techniques. Her research interests centre on study abroad, second language acquisition, social network formation, intercultural communication and intercultural learning. She is currently preparing a PhD on intercultural and second language learning in the context of study abroad.

Susan Oguro (PhD) is Associate Dean (International) in the Faculty of Arts and Social Sciences at the University of Technology, Sydney, Australia. She teaches courses and supervises research students in the areas of languages education and intercultural communication. Her research interests and publications are in the fields of learning abroad and intercultural education; foreign and heritage languages curriculum and policy; and human rights education. Her most recent book is *Intercultural Interventions in Study Abroad* (Routledge, 2018).

Katarzyna Ożańska-Ponikwia is Associate Professor at the University of Bielsko-Biala, Poland. She holds a PhD in Applied Linguistics from Birkbeck, University of London, and habilitation in the field of Linguistics from Silesian University, Poland. Her main research interests include the relationship between higher- and lower-order personality traits and various aspects of bilingualism, SLA and L2 use. She is the author of two books entitled *Emotions from a Bilingual Point of View. Personality and Emotional Intelligence in Relation to Perception and Expression of Emotions in the L1 and L2* (2013) and *Personality and Emotional Intelligence in Second Language Learning* (2018), and many articles published in international journals in the fields of bilingualism and SLA.

Mirosław Pawlak is Professor of English at the Faculty of Philology, State University of Applied Sciences, Konin, Poland, and the Department of English Studies, Faculty of Pedagogy and Fine Arts in Kalisz, Adam Mickiewicz University, Kalisz, Poland. His main areas of interest are SLA theory and research, form-focused instruction, corrective feedback, classroom discourse, learner autonomy, learning strategies, motivation, willingness to communicate and pronunciation teaching. He is the Editor-in-Chief of the journals *Studies in Second Language Learning and Teaching* and *Konin Language Studies*, as well as the book series *Second Language Learning and Teaching* (Springer).

Carmen Pérez-Vidal is Chair Professor of Language Acquisition and English at Universitat Pompeu Fabra. Her PhD dealt with bilingual language acquisition in infancy. Since then her main research interests have included second/foreign language acquisition in SA learning contexts, immersion and CLIL, having published extensively on these topics. She has been head of the officially recognized Research Group 'Language Acquisition from Multilingual Catalonia' (ALLENCAM). Recent publications have appeared in *Language Teaching Research*, *International Journal of Bilingual Education and Bilingualism*, *Language Learning Journal* and the *Routledge Handbook of Study Abroad Research and Practice*.

Joana Salazar Noguera is Associate Professor at the University of the Balearic Islands, where she coordinates the MA in Modern Languages and Literatures. She has also taught at secondary education for eleven years and has published on the adequacy of EFL methodologies in the Spanish education context. Her most recent publications are a co-edited book entitled *Content-based Learning in Multilingual Educational Environments* (Juan-Garau and Salazar-Noguera (eds.) 2015, Springer) and an article entitled 'A Case Study of Early Career Secondary Teachers' Perceptions of Their Preparedness for Teaching: Lessons from Australia and Spain' (*Teacher Development*, 2017).

Vanda Szatzker is a philologist in English studies. She has received both her bachelor's and master's degree in English studies from Eötvös Loránd University in Budapest. During her BA studies, she specialized in English in business, while she focused on Applied Linguistics during the MA programme. Her research interest varies from the field of language policy, mainly focusing on the regulations related to children and young adults in Hungary, to language learner autonomy, the role of self-efficacy beliefs in language learning and psycholinguistics.

Victoria Zaytseva received her PhD in Applied Linguistics from the Universitat Pompeu Fabra (UPF) in 2016. Her research focuses on second language vocabulary acquisition with a special interest on context effects (formal instruction and study abroad). Within the last three years, she has taught courses in Linguistics, Translation and English at UPF, Universitat de Barcelona, Universitat Autònoma de Barcelona and Universitat Oberta de Catalunya. Recent publications have appeared in *Language Teaching Research*, *International Journal of Bilingual Education and Bilingualism*, *Language Learning Journal* and the *Routledge Handbook of Study Abroad Research and Practice*.

Siyang Zhou is a PhD candidate at the Department of Education, University of Oxford. She completed her master's degree at Cambridge University and was an English teacher in China. Her research focuses on SLA in the SA context, with a focus on language contact, social networks and formulaic language acquisition. Her research was awarded the Richard Pemberton Prize for the best postgraduate student presentation at the 2019 annual conference of the British Association for Applied Linguistics (BAAL).

Acknowledgements

This volume stems from the work of members and contributors to the European COST Action 15130, Study Abroad Research in European Perspective (SAREP). I am most grateful to the authors for their contributions to the volume, as well as the funding received in 2016–20 from COST (Cooperation in Science and Technology). I also wish to thank the anonymous reviewers for their time and expertise, as well as Becky Holland and Andrew Wardell and their colleagues at Bloomsbury.

Martin Howard
Cork, May 2020

Study abroad and the second language learner: An introduction

Martin Howard
University College Cork

Introduction

Situated at the interface between the fields of applied linguistics and international education, study abroad (SA) research has emerged as a significant independent sub-field in recent years, reflecting the growing research interest in the SA experience from diverse perspectives in tandem with ever-increasing participation in such education abroad. Those perspectives are wide-ranging extending to educational, intercultural, linguistic, personal and social development during a sojourn abroad, as we seek to better understand the link between study abroad and various facets of participant development. While study abroad is often held as offering optimal conditions for second language learning, participation has seen growing numbers of non-language specialists engage in study abroad such that they constitute a significant cohort among SA participants. Indeed, within the European Union's long-established Erasmus programme (see European Commission, 2017), the latter are in fact the majority relative to their language specialist counterparts, such that the field extends well beyond a focus on language learning to the nature of development at an educational, intercultural, personal, social, academic and professional level (see, e.g., Ogden, Streitwieser and Van Mol, 2020; Van Mol, 2014).

The focus of this volume predominantly extends to language learners, although the issues explored do not exclusively apply to such a group of participants but are indeed relevant to all participants, be they language specialists or not. Indeed, in the case of non-language specialists, many of them spend time in a country where a language other than their mother tongue may be the dominant language, such that language issues necessarily arise in their experience of study abroad in their temporary host community. Beyond language, other issues in the opportunities that study abroad offers equally apply to language and non-language specialists, such that many of the issues addressed in this volume will hold interest for both participant groups. While study abroad is increasingly promoted in higher education contexts, it can take various forms, such as a period of study at a partner institution abroad, a work experience or simply organized residence abroad as a period of time that the participant spends in another country, usually for educational, academic or professional reasons. As such, it is not exclusive to a higher education context but rather includes children and adolescents (see, e.g., Llanes and Muñoz, 2013), as well as adults who engage in study abroad in various capacities (see Forsberg Lundell and Bartning, 2015). While they constitute the participants, other stakeholders include SA organizers, programme staff and instructors in both the home and host institution contexts, parents or guardians, host families abroad and policy makers. Study abroad research therefore extends to a wide range of interested parties, and, indeed, the field is increasingly cognizant of the need to include their perspectives for a fuller understanding of and interaction on the issues at play (see Kinginger, 2008; Ogden, Streitwieser and Van Mol, 2020; Surtees, 2019).

Those issues are numerous, and this volume is an attempt to capture some recent research in the field which addresses some innovative areas of investigation and which complements the wealth of existing research in this highly buoyant field. Indeed, existing research has provided wide-ranging insights which, from a language perspective, have in the main focused historically on the nature of linguistic development during study abroad (see, e.g., Pérez-Vidal, 2014), but also since the early 2000s on individual factors at play in the participants' experience abroad, reflecting the social turn within the field of second language acquisition (SLA) (for an overview, see Kinginger, 2008, 2013a). From a language perspective, the field has highlighted the complexity of the SA experience, both at a personal level for the individual participant and in terms of language learning outcomes, whereby considerable individual variation is seen to prevail on both counts (see Freed, 1995a; Jensen and Howard, 2014). In other words, the experience is highly individualistic, in no way uniform across participants and dependent on a full range of personal, social and contextual factors at play, such that it is often seen to be difficult to draw definitive conclusions on the benefits of an experience abroad. In the case of second language learning in particular, the findings often contrast with the folk-belief that a stay abroad will lead to significant linguistic gains compared to learners who do not venture abroad. In other words, while gains can be made, they are by no means guaranteed, with considerable scope for further development remaining on the learners' return to their home classroom (see Hessel, 2020; Howard, 2009; Huensch and Tracy-Ventura, 2017; Huensch et al., 2019, on post-study abroad development).

Taken together, that body of research has undoubtedly served to drive the field forward since its inception following on Carroll's (1967) initial study, such that new questions necessarily emerge, some of which we address in the studies presented in this volume. If anything, we are increasingly cognizant that the issues are not restricted solely to the actual time spent abroad or the participants themselves, but rather include pre-study abroad and post-study abroad matters prior to and following on the participant's return to their home educational environment. Further, during the learners' time abroad, the issues are not restricted to language per se but extend beyond language to factors that complement and underpin such language learning, such as in terms of personal and social development, and the wide-ranging contextual factors that characterize the individual's experience abroad and which condition such development. Against this background, notwithstanding the importance of post-study abroad matters where some studies are beginning to emerge, such as in relation to long-term retention of linguistic gains (see Hessel, 2020; Huensch and Tracy-Ventura, 2017; Huensch et al., 2019), identity and learner reintegration issues (Benson et al., 2013; Jackson, 2019), this volume focuses more specifically on matters 'pre-' and 'during' study abroad. In so doing, an overriding theme is the link between folk-linguistic expectations of study abroad and experiences and development abroad. In the following, we outline some questions that arise, followed by a synopsis of the chapters which constitute the volume.

Study abroad expectations, experiences and development: Perspectives before and during study abroad

Within a higher education context, study abroad is often obligatory on the student's programme of study and where not is otherwise actively encouraged in various forms. For example, an optional semester or even full year abroad may be integrated within a programme of study, allowing the student to pursue educational courses at a host institution abroad while also engaging in the experience of living in another country. Such forms of a stay abroad are especially popular in Europe through the European Union's long-established Erasmus programme which has seen over three million participants since its inception in 1987 and which is overseen by various national Erasmus offices and institutional international offices in the home and host institutions. In a North American context, study abroad is often of shorter duration, frequently referred to as short-term study abroad, where students may spend a couple of weeks in another country, often in large groups from the same institution, with an organized daily programme of activities, including classes, led by a programme director who may be from the students' home university (see Kinginger, 2009; Plews and Misfeldt, 2018). Such short-term study abroad also extends to other participants across the world such as children and adolescents who participate in language courses abroad, often living with host families over a couple of weeks (see Llanes and Muñoz, 2009).

The choice to participate in study abroad is therefore a key initial question for participants and their families, as well as staff involved in the SA enterprise, with various questions underpinning such an overriding question. There is, for example, the question of the timing of study abroad, in relation to when to go. In the case of foreign language learning, the question relates to the learner's onset proficiency level and age whereby consideration may be given to an optimal time to adequately benefit from study abroad for language learning purposes. DeKeyser (2010), for example, notes the importance of having adequate linguistic resources in terms of developmental stage to cope with the input abroad, while Lafford and Collentine (2006) propose a threshold hypothesis whereby there may be a minimum onset proficiency level at which learners need to be. Equally important is the question of time per se in relation to the duration of study abroad. Serrano, Tragant and Llanes (2012), for example, find that fluency and lexis develop early on compared to grammatical skills which may require more time to evidence development (see also Davidson, 2010; Jensen and Howard, 2014). As we have mentioned, duration differs considerably across programmes, with the question arising as to how some components of the learner's language repertoire may be more or less sensitive to development depending on the duration of the stay abroad. The variety of SA opportunities also raises questions as to the type of SA programme to choose, such as a more organized study abroad or a freer type of programme that characterizes Erasmus studies, or indeed a work placement for older participants. Such programmatic issues equally extend to accommodation issues such as a host family, shared accommodation or living alone such as in a university residence (see Di Silvio, Donovan and Malone, 2014; Rivers, 1998).

Taken together, such issues therefore point to the important issues that underpin the very decision to study abroad and may be shaped by different expectations on all participant-stakeholders' part as to what is best, such as in terms of programmatic features and organization. Such issues constitute important questions where contemporary research can shine a lamp, providing important insights not solely for an academic audience but also for the diversity of participant-stakeholders involved.

Beyond programmatic and organizational issues, pre-study abroad issues also include student preparation matters where there is increasing awareness of the role of mentoring both pre-study abroad and during study abroad. Awareness of the potential of such preparation reflects the increased understanding that student mentoring is a significant resource that students can draw on in dealing with the various challenges that arise once abroad (see Borghetti, 2016; Jackson, 2015, 2018; Jackson and Oguro, 2018; Kinginger, 2011). Indeed, the existing literature overwhelmingly shows that the SA experience is not necessarily an easy one, with participants experiencing a diverse range of challenges from the personal and the social to the intercultural, as well as challenges underlying the language learning experience abroad (see Kinginger, 2008, 2013a). Pre-study abroad expectations as to the reality of experiences abroad are often only partially fulfilled with participants being disappointed with the oftentimes overly positive marketing message of widely available productive interactional language contact and subsequent language learning miracles. Such matters point to the pre-study abroad training that may serve to develop more realistic expectations on the part of learners as to what to expect abroad and aid them in enhancing their coping resources at various levels while also sensitizing them to the type of challenges that they may face at different levels. As mentioned earlier, the existing literature points to the considerable individualistic nature of an SA experience, such that learners differ in their experiences, while individuals also differentially embrace the opportunities available to them while abroad (Kinginger, 2008). An example in point relates to social networks and social integration which impact the learners' opportunities for language contact in terms of type of language activities and contact, quantity, frequency, intensity and interlocutor characteristics. Mitchell, Tracy-Ventura and McManus (2017) observe how social networks differ in their make-up in relation to co-nationals, other international students and host society members, with genuine social integration involving the latter not necessarily a given (see also Dewey et al.'s, 2013, work and Coleman's, 2013, concentric circles model). Pre-study abroad preparation serves therefore a critical role in our efforts to sensitize learners to such issues, and in so doing, lessen the gap between expectations and actual experiences at various levels. In sum, it is not a case of simply sending students abroad, but we are increasingly cognizant of factors that shape that experience and which can be integrated in a programme of pre-study abroad preparation. The issues, however, continue while the student is abroad.

As mentioned above, the scope of study abroad is wide-ranging, extending beyond language learning to personal, intercultural, social, academic and professional development. Given the predominant focus on language learning here, we especially consider matters in that area, but it is important to note that some of those matters equally extend beyond language learning per se such that they are also relevant to non-specialist language learners. Language learning is perhaps the most obvious reason to study abroad in the host language community, with folk-belief holding that it offers an optimal combination of naturalistic exposure with the learner's prior instructed learning (see DeKeyser, 1990). A wealth of existing studies within an SA context has explored the linguistic benefits of study abroad, in terms of the learner's general proficiency development such as through a CAF (complexity, accuracy, fluency) lens (see Juan-Garau, 2014; Juan-Garau, Salazar-Noguera and Prieto-Arranz, 2014), while others have explored specific components of the learner's linguistic repertoire and features therein, such as in relation to pronunciation (see Díaz-Campos, 2004; Mora, 2014), fluency (see Freed, 1995c; Leonard and Shea, 2017), lexis (see Ife, Vives Boix and Meara, 2000; Pizziconi, 2017), grammar (see Collentine, 2004; Howard, 2005b) and sociolinguistic and pragmatic competence (see Devlin, 2018; Howard, 2012; Ren, 2018). While there are certainly benefits, the benefits are not necessarily uniform, both across components and across learners. In the former case relating to how development may differ across components, existing findings suggest that grammar and pronunciation are more resistant to development, with gains more evident in the other areas, without necessarily reaching native speaker norms (see Howard, 2005a; Howard and Schwieter, 2018). In the latter case, relating to how development may differ across learners, the findings highlight the significant individual variation across learners (see Freed, 1995a; Jensen and Howard, 2014). On both counts, such findings have import for language instructors on the learners' return to the home classroom, highlighting learner needs in specific areas which may benefit from further instruction.

Against this background, the more social turn in SLA research since the early 2000s has highlighted the need to consider the learner's wider SA experience and how different social and contextual factors may shape the learner's development abroad (see Kinginger, 2008, 2013a). On this count, some of the pre-study abroad expectations and decisions we noted above are relevant, such as the type of SA programme and accommodation choice which may impact opportunities for target language (TL) contact. But such language contact also extends to the individual learner's resources to seize the contact opportunities available, such as in terms of developing social networks and input and interaction access and engagement. Again, individual variation is highly characteristic, with learners differing considerably in the extent to which they do so (see Kinginger, 2008; Mitchell, Tracy-Ventura and McManus, 2017; Wilkinson, 1998). The value of continued mentoring while abroad is therefore especially pertinent as a means of continuing to support learners in their efforts.

While such mentoring can offer support, it is also important to bear in mind that individuals also bring their own resources in terms, for example, of their motivation, attitudes, personality, identity, self-efficacy and self-regulation as individual factors at play. Some studies in the literature have addressed some such issues, seeking on the one hand to understand how such factors develop in their own right during study abroad and on the other hand exploring their correlation with the learner's linguistic development (see, e.g., Arvidsson et al., 2018, on personality; Cigliana and Serrano, 2016; Hernández, 2010, on motivation; Kinginger, 2013b, on identity; Isabelli-García, 2006, on attitudes). While their role may shape the language learning potential of study abroad, they constitute factors that are important to investigate in their own right as areas beyond language which are potentially ripe for development during a sojourn abroad. Indeed, existing studies demonstrate how such factors are not static but evolve over time (see Arvidsson et al., 2018; Tracy-Ventura et al., 2016). The scope of SA research is therefore wide-ranging, in no way limited to language learners and language learning but necessarily extends and applies to other learner types and other facets of development which may be related to language learning but which are deserving of investigation in their own right.

Against this background, the volume offered here presents a collection of studies which explore some of such issues relating to matters both pre- and during study abroad. We present a short outline of the volume subsequently, followed by a more detailed synopsis of the contributing chapters thereafter.

Outline of the volume

The studies presented are situated in a variety of SA contexts, in terms of both host and home communities, in relation to the target and source languages investigated and participant types. In relation to some of the issues highlighted, they offer complementary insights to existing research while also exploring new avenues of research on a number of counts. The volume opens with a chapter on the world's most famous SA programme, Erasmus, exploring the legislative mechanisms that allow such large-scale transnational mobility between participating countries within Europe. Following this initial chapter, from a pre-study abroad perspective two studies explore factors shaping the decision to engage in study abroad, one dealing with the impact of marketing (Güvendir, Acar-Güvendir and Dündar) and the other exploring the role of personality and linguistic proficiency factors (Ożańska-Ponikwia and Carlet). They reflect the need to better understand the reasons for SA uptake which is important not only for understanding the profile of students who go abroad but also in relation to the reasons as to why study abroad may not be for everyone. Thereafter, the focus is on matters during study abroad, although some maintain a pre-study abroad link in terms of understanding how pre-study abroad training may impact the experience abroad (Moreno-Bruna, De Wilde, Eyckmans and Goethals) and how pre-study abroad choices in relation to age of participation and accommodation type have consequences for the learner's experience abroad (Moratinos-Johnson, Juan-Garau and Salazar Noguera).

As noted, one of the key attractors of study abroad is the opportunities for so-called language immersion in a naturalistic context where masses of input are hypothetically available (see DeKeyser, 1990). While some existing research has previously explored language contact abroad, such as through different questionnaires (e.g. for the Language Contact Profile, see Freed et al., 2004, the Study Abroad Social Interaction Questionnaire, see Dewey et al., 2013), questions remain concerning the quality of language contact that might be especially fruitful for linguistic development. At a more global level, input questions also prevail in terms of the overall experience that different types of study abroad offer, such as in relation to the age profile of participants and accommodation, where younger participants dominate in home-stay contexts compared to other residence types. Such issues reflect the need to better understand the differential experiences of younger and older participants in different residence types which offer different opportunities for language engagement. The chapters by Briggs Baffoe-Djan and Zhou and Moratinos-Johnson et al. take such a focus on input and interactional experience.

Such input issues and overall experience abroad point to the need for learners to be active participants in contributing to shaping their language contact opportunities and general experiences. However, as we noted above, pre-study abroad preparation and mentoring during study abroad also have a role to play in making for a more productive experience abroad for learners in terms of coping and enhancing their engagement in the process. The role of tailored pedagogic interventions is also emerging as critical, with scope for greater consideration of the relationship between pedagogic design during study abroad and the learner's use of the language outside of the classroom (see Salaberry, White and Rue Birch, 2019). Mentoring and the impact of such mentoring, along with the role of pedagogic intervention on gains made abroad, is a further key area addressed here (see chapters by Oguro and Cottier, and Moreno Bruna, De Wilde, Eyckmans and Goethals).

The fourth area of focus relates to individual factors at play in terms of their potential for development during study abroad but also as factors that may impact language use, development and experience abroad. As noted above, while other research has explored a range of factors, two chapters here focus on the innovative areas of learner self-regulation, learner agency and plurilingual identities. While input opportunities are often seen as a key difference between a study abroad and at-home classroom context, such individual factors and how they develop also distinguish both learning contexts and are therefore critical to bear in mind in understanding the language learning experience abroad. For example, there is presumably scope for learners to develop specific identity characteristics at various levels as L2 learners and users but also as individuals which distinguish them as members of a different language community from their at-home counterparts. Indeed, given that international learner cohorts are diverse in languages of origin in the host university, interacting with members of oftentimes equally diverse host environments, the notion of plurilingual identity is especially timely in today's global world where English has attained the status of a global lingua franca (see Oakes and Howard, 2019). Such factors are explored in the chapters by Csizér and Pawlak and Cots, Mitchell and Beaven.

The final theme explored is a traditional and long-established one, namely linguistic development abroad, but with a focus on specific components and features of the learner's linguistic repertoire, namely lexis, on the one hand, which is seen as particularly conducive to development abroad, and grammar, on the other hand, which is held as less sensitive to development. While studies of such areas exist, the studies here by Arvidsson, Zaytseva, Miralpeix and Pérez-Vidal and Edmonds and Gudmestad offer insights into features underexplored in an SA context, namely formulaic language and grammatical gender marking, and thereby add further insights into the role of feature type in the learner's experience of linguistic development abroad.

Taken together, the chapters have as an overriding theme the dichotomy between stakeholder expectations, shaped and created by various external influences, and actual developmental experiences and outcomes abroad, equally shaped and created by various external influences, but also by learner-internal factors abroad which make for differential development in an SA context on various levels. In the following, we offer a more detailed synopsis of each chapter.

Synopsis of chapter contributions

The volume begins with a chapter by Luca Galli which offers legislative insight into the world's pre-eminent SA programme, namely the European Union's long-standing Erasmus programme which celebrated its thirtieth anniversary in 2017. Entitled 'The Legal Framework of Study Mobility: How Public Law Makes the Erasmus Programme Possible', the author provides a historical overview of the phases leading up to the establishment of the programme, followed by a look at the administrative and legal frameworks underpinning the programme at European and national levels. With the aim of education mobility across Europe providing equal rights for all irrespective of country, Galli then considers some legislative cases where such rights have been called into question. Taken together, the chapter offers crucial insight into the structures and efforts underpinning the world's most successful SA programme which has allowed more than three million participants to include an SA component to their educational studies.

While study abroad is actively promoted across educational institutions as a means of encouraging participants to enjoy the putative benefits of international experience within their studies, Katarzyna Ożańska-Ponikwia and Angélica Carlet offer a chapter entitled 'Should I Stay or Should I Go? Factors that Influence One's Decision to Participate in a Student Mobility Programme'. While study abroad is actively promoted, it is critical that we better understand factors that impact on students' decision to venture abroad as a means of understanding why some may be more reluctant to embark on such a venture. Based on a quantitative study of Spanish and Polish university students, the authors offer a comparison of students who have made the decision to go abroad and those who have not in relation to their personality traits, emotional intelligence and L2 proficiency measures. The findings point to personality traits as a key factor which distinguish the groups.

Emre Güvendir, Meltem Acar-Güvendir and Sinem Dündar continue the focus on pre-study abroad matters in their chapter entitled 'Study Abroad Marketing and L2 Self-efficacy Beliefs'. They present a quantitative study of Turkish students' reception of marketing material on a range of SA websites in relation to changes in the participants' self-efficacy beliefs. The findings highlight the impact of such marketing materials in impacting on the participants' beliefs, especially in relation to their speaking and listening skills, but also in relation to reading and writing skills, with increased self-efficacy scores emerging in the participants' responses on a self-efficacy questionnaire.

Having looked at some background issues surrounding pre-study abroad, the next chapters look at a number of issues within the SA context. The first of these concerns learner engagement with the TL in the host environment, reflecting the folk-belief that study abroad allows learners to be immersed in the TL and culture. The chapter entitled 'Close Encounters of the Third Kind: Quantity, Type and Quality of Language Contact during Study Abroad' by Jessica Briggs Baffoe-Djan and Siyang Zhou explores the critical question of learner engagement with the TL input and interactional opportunities in an SA context. While such opportunities may be potentially plentiful, the authors offer a range of thoughts on how to maximise the opportunities available so as to optimally benefit from the language contact opportunities available.

In their chapter entitled 'Study Abroad for Secondary and Higher Education Students: Differences and Similarities in Their Interaction with the Learning Environment', Sofía Moratinos-Johnston, Maria Juan-Garau and Joana Salazar Noguera address the issue of interactional opportunities from the perspective of study abroad at different education stages. In particular, they offer a qualitative comparison of SA experiences at secondary and higher education levels in different residence types, thereby exploring how learners engage with the different opportunities available to them as a function of education stage, age and residence type. The qualitative findings point to both similarities and differences in interaction experiences.

Following on the chapters by Briggs Baffoe-Djan and Zhou and Moratinos, Juan-Garau and Salazar Noguera, the next two chapters explore issues surrounding learner mentoring and pedagogic intervention in an SA context. The first, entitled 'Assessing the Impact of Educational Support Abroad on Sojourners' Interactional Contacts, L2 Acquisition and Intercultural Development' by Ana Maria Moreno Bruna, July De Wilde, June Eyckmans and Patrick Goethals, maintains a focus on learner engagement through L2 interaction. In particular, the authors consider how a pedagogical intervention can promote such engagement, leading to potentially enhanced linguistic and intercultural development. Their study is based on a quantitative comparison of two groups of Flemish university students in Spain with a view to investigating the potential impact of an online pedagogical intervention. The results point to some relative benefits of such an intervention, which have led the authors to develop SALSA, 'Study Abroad Language Support App'.

The next chapter, entitled 'The Complex Challenges of Delivering a University-wide Intercultural Mentoring Programme for Study Abroad' by Susan Oguro and Annie Cottier, maintains the focus on learner mentoring. The authors discuss the student and instructor experiences of a mentoring programme within the MILSA project, 'Mentoring Intercultural Learning through Study Abroad'. Reflecting its title, the chapter outlines a qualitative evaluation of the mentoring programme which points to the wide-ranging challenges involved in providing such a programme, in spite of the range of benefits that can ensue for both student and instructor participants alike, and which can substantially enhance the SA experience for all. While initial SA participants may have embarked on study abroad with underdeveloped support both prior to and during their sojourn abroad, the chapters by Oguro and Cottier and Moreno Bruna,

De Wilde, Eyckmans and Goethals offer evidence of the benefits to be accrued through such mentoring.

The next chapters switch the focus to developmental issues, firstly relating to individual factors shaping language learning and use in the first three chapters and then a focus on different facets of linguistic development per se in the two remaining chapters. In the case of individual development, Kata Csizér, Mirosław Pawlak, Vanda Szatzker and Kitti Erdő-Bonyár offer an initial study of self-regulation development in their chapter entitled 'Tapping into Self-Regulation in Study Abroad Contexts: A Pilot Study'. As a key factor in SLA, the authors test an instrument to measure the impact of different factors on self-regulatory processes during study abroad. Those factors relate to learner-, teacher- and technology-based factors in academic and social contexts which are predicted to shape such self-regulatory processes before, during and following study abroad. The findings point to differences in the influence of the different factors at play.

In their chapter entitled 'Structure and Agency in the Development of Plurilingual Identities in Study Abroad', Josep M. Cots, Rosamond Mitchell and Ana Beaven address the role of language identity. They do so through a plurilingual prism, reflecting the increasing multilingual nature of our contemporary global world whereby students encounter various languages across time and space in their everyday experiences during study abroad. Such encounters give rise to different language choices within their plurilingual repertoires, impacting on their identities as language users in their new but temporary host societies abroad. The authors offer insights into the study of such plurilingual repertoires and identities as a road map ripe for investigation within SA research.

Continuing with the issue of individual differences and factors at play, Klara Arvidsson offers a chapter on 'Learning Multiword Expressions in a Second Language during Study Abroad – The Role of Individual Differences'. As its title indicates, the chapter relates an aspect of linguistic development, namely multiword expressions to individual differences, whereby the author attempts to account for the individual variation at play in her Swedish university learners' lexical development in French as a second language through a qualitative lens. The study builds on the author's earlier quantitative investigation of the impact of quantity of TL contact which was not found to be at play. Rather, the more qualitative findings suggest that a psychological orientation, namely noticing, motivation, self-efficacy and self-regulation, in combination with varied and regular TL contact, offers more illuminating insights.

In their chapter entitled 'When in One's New Country: Examining Native-like Selection in English at Home and Abroad', Victoria Zaytseva, Imma Miralpeix and Carmen Pérez-Vidal continue the focus on lexical development, this time in the case of native-like selection among Spanish/Catalan university learners of English. The quantitative findings offer a comparison of the learners' development from the foreign language classroom to their residence abroad. Such development is gradual, with the learners enhancing the formality of their writing through the use of impersonal forms and fewer false cognates, while increasing their use of idiomatic intensifiers, lexicalized chunks and target-like adverbs.

Moving beyond lexis, the final chapter by Amanda Edmonds and Aarnes Gudmestad explores grammatical development. More specifically, as the title of their chapter suggests, 'The Role of Transparency in Grammatical-Gender Marking among Stay Abroad Learners of Spanish and French', the focus is on the challenging area for L2 learners of gender marking. Based on quantitative longitudinal written data analysis of British university learners of French and Spanish, the authors compare gender marking development across both languages. While the learners evidenced significant development, that development was constrained by the effect of TL and transparency, with a range of linguistic factors also found to condition the learners' variable use of the target-like variant.

Taken together, the chapters reflect recent directions within a number of innovative strands of SA research, reflecting the breadth of scope of such research and highlight how the field has advanced since Carroll's (1967) initial study and Freed's (1995b) seminal volume. While Carroll's work explored the linguistic benefits of study abroad using a general language proficiency test, and the studies in Freed's volume expanded the field to various dimensions of the learner's linguistic repertoire, such as in the areas of fluency and sociolinguistic development, the field has seen significant development which highlights the scope of current investigation, providing multifaceted insights of relevance to all involved.

References

Arvidsson, K., Eyckmans, J., Rosier, A., and Forsberg Lundell, F. (2018), 'Self-perceived Linguistic Progress, Target Language Use and Personality Development during Study Abroad', *Study Abroad Research in Second Language Acquisition and International Education*, 3 (1), 144–66.

Benson, P., Barkhuizen, G., Bodycott, P., and Brown, J. (2013), *Second Language Identity in Narratives of Study Abroad*, Basingstoke: Palgrave Macmillan.

Borghetti, C. (2016), 'Intercultural Education in Practice: Two Pedagogical Experiences with Mobile Students', *Language and Intercultural Communication*, 16 (3), 502–13.

Carroll, J. (1967), 'Foreign Language Proficiency Levels Attained by Language Majors Near Graduation from College', *Foreign Language Annals*, 1, 131–51.

Cigliana, K., and Serrano, R. (2016), 'Individual Differences in U.S. Study Abroad Students in Barcelona: A Look into Their Attitudes, Motivations and L2 Contact', *Study Abroad Research in Second Language Acquisition and International Education*, 1, 154–85.

Coleman, J. A. (2013), 'Researching Whole People and Whole Lives', in C. Kinginger (ed.), *Social and Cultural Aspects of Language Learning in Study Abroad*, 17–44, Amsterdam/Philadelphia, PA: John Benjamins.

Collentine, J. (2004), 'The Effects of Learning Contexts on Morphosyntactic and Lexical Development', *Studies in Second Language Acquisition*, 26 (2), 227–48.

Davidson, D. E. (2010), 'Study Abroad: How Long, and with What Results? New Data from the Russian Front', *Foreign Language Annals*, 43 (1), 6–26.

DeKeyser, R. (1990), 'Foreign Language Development during a Semester Abroad', in B. Freed (ed.), *Foreign Language Acquisition Research and the Classroom*, 104–19, Lexington, MA: D.C. Heath.

DeKeyser, R. (2010), 'Monitoring Processes in Spanish as a Second Language during a Study Abroad Program', *Foreign Language Annals*, 43, 80–92.

Devlin, A. M. (2018), 'The Interaction between Duration of Stay Abroad, Diversity of Loci of Learning and Sociopragmatic Variation Patterns: A Comparative Study', *Journal of Pragmatics*, 146, 121–36.

Dewey, D. P., Ring, S., Gardner, D., and Belnap, R. K. (2013), 'Social Network Formation and Development during Study Abroad in the Middle East', *System*, 41 (2), 269–82.

Di Silvio, F., Donovan, A., and Malone, M. E. (2014), 'The Effect of Study Abroad Homestay Placements: Participant Perspectives and Oral Proficiency Gains', *Foreign Language Annals*, 47 (1), 168–88.

Díaz-Campos, M. (2004), 'Context of Learning in the Acquisition of Spanish Second Language Phonology', *Studies in Second Language Acquisition*, 26, 249–74.

European Commission (2017), *Erasmus: Annual Report 2016*, Luxembourg: Publications Office of the European Union, retrieved from https://publications.europa.eu/fr/publication-detail/-/publication/b0250d33-fcce-11e7-b8f5-01aa75ed71a1/language-en/format-PDF (accessed 31 May 2019).

Forsberg Lundell, F., and Bartning, I. (eds.) (2015), *Cultural Migrants. Multiple Perspectives on Optimal Second Language Acquisition*, Bristol: Multilingual Matters.

Freed, B. (1995a), 'Language Learning and Study Abroad', in B. Freed (ed.), *Second Language Acquisition in a Study Abroad Context*, 3–33, Amsterdam/Philadelphia, PA: John Benjamins.

Freed, B. (1995b), *Second Language Acquisition in a Study Abroad Context*, Amsterdam/Philadelphia, PA: John Benjamins.

Freed, B. (1995c), 'What Makes Us Think That Students Who Study Abroad Become Fluent?' in B. Freed (ed.), *Second Language Acquisition in a Study Abroad Context*, 123–48, Amsterdam/Philadelphia, PA: John Benjamins.

Freed, B., Dewey, D., Segalowitz, N., and Halter, R. (2004), 'The Language Contact Profile', *Studies in Second Language Acquisition*, 26 (2), 349–56.

Hernández, T. (2010), 'The Relationship among Motivation, Interaction, and the Development of Second Language Oral Proficiency in a Study-abroad Context', *Modern Language Journal*, 94, 600–17.

Hessel, G. (2020), 'Overall L2 Proficiency Maintenance and Development among Returning ERASMUS Study Abroad Participants', *Study Abroad Research in Second Language Acquisition and International Education*, 5 (1), 119–52.

Howard, M. (2005a), 'On the Role of Context in the Development of Learner Language: Insights from Study Abroad Research', *ITL International Journal of Applied Linguistics*, 148, 1–20.

Howard, M. (2005b), 'Second Language Acquisition in a Study Abroad Context: A Comparative Investigation of the Effects of Study Abroad and Foreign Language Instruction on the L2 Learner's Grammatical Development', in A. Housen, and M. Pierrard (eds.), *Investigations in Instructed Second Language Acquisition*, 495–530, Berlin/New York: de Gruyter.

Howard, M. (2009), 'Short- versus Long-term Effects of Naturalistic Exposure on the Advanced Instructed Learner's L2 Development: A Case Study', in E. Labeau, and F. Myles (eds.), *The Advanced Learner Varieties: The Case of French*, 93–123, Bern: Peter Lang.

Howard, M. (2012), 'The Advanced Learner's Sociolinguistic Profile: On Issues of Individual Differences, Second Language Exposure Conditions, and Type of Sociolinguistic Variable', *The Modern Language Journal*, 96 (1), 20–33.

Howard, M., and Schwieter, J. W. (2018), 'The Development of Second Language Grammar in a Study Abroad Context', in C. Sanz, and A. Morales-Front (eds.), *The Routledge Handbook of Study Abroad Research and Practice*, 135–44, New York, NY: Routledge.

Huensch, A., and Tracy-Ventura, N. (2017), 'L2 Utterance Fluency Development before, during and after Residence Abroad: A Multidimensional Investigation', *The Modern Language Journal*, 101 (2), 275–93.

Huensch, A., Tracy-Ventura, N., Bridges, J., and Cuesta Medina, J. A. (2019), 'Variables Affecting the Maintenance of L2 Proficiency and Fluency Four Years Post-study Abroad', *Study Abroad Research in Second Language Acquisition and International Education*, 4 (1), 97–126.

Ife, A., Vives Boix, G., and Meara, P. (2000), 'The Impact of Study Abroad on the Vocabulary Development of Different Proficiency Groups', *Spanish Applied Linguistics*, 4 (1), 55–84.

Isabelli-García, C. (2006), 'Study Abroad Social Networks, Motivation, and Attitudes: Implications for Second Language Acquisition', in M. DuFon, and E. Churchill (eds.), *Language Learners in Study Abroad Contexts*, 231–58, Clevedon: Multilingual Matters.

Jackson, J. (2015), 'Becoming Interculturally Competent: Theory to Practice in International Education', *International Journal of Intercultural Relations*, 48, 91–107.

Jackson, J. (2018), 'Intervening in the Intercultural Learning of L2 Study Abroad Students: From Research to Practice', *Language Teaching*, 51 (3), 365–82.

Jackson, J. (2019), '"Cantonese Is My Own Eyes, and English Is Just My Glasses": The Evolving Language and Intercultural Attitudes of a Chinese Study Abroad Student', in M. Howard (ed.), *Study Abroad, Second Language Acquisition and Interculturality*, 15–45, Bristol/Toronto: Multilingual Matters.

Jackson, J., and Oguro, S. (eds.) (2018), *Intercultural Interventions in Study Abroad*, London/New York: Routledge.

Jensen, J., and Howard, M. (2014), 'The Effects of Time in the Development of Complexity and Accuracy during Study Abroad: A Study of French and Chinese Learners of English', *EuroSLA Yearbook*, 14, 31–64.

Juan-Garau, M. (2014), 'Oral Accuracy Growth after Formal Instruction and Study Abroad', in C. Pérez-Vidal (ed.), *Second Language Acquisition in Study Abroad and Formal Instruction Contexts*, 87–110, Amsterdam/Philadelphia, PA: John Benjamins.

Juan-Garau, M., Salazar-Noguera, J., and Prieto-Arranz, J. I. (2014), 'English L2 Learners' Lexico-grammatical and Motivational Development at Home and Abroad', in C. Pérez-Vidal (ed.), *Language Acquisition in Study Abroad and Formal Instruction Contexts*, 235–58, Amsterdam/Philadelphia, PA: John Benjamins.

Kinginger, C. (2008), 'Language Learning in Study Abroad: Case Studies of Americans in France', *Modern Language Journal Monograph Series*, 92, s1, 1–131.

Kinginger, C. (2009), *Language Learning and Study Abroad: A Critical Reading of Research*, Basingstoke: Palgrave Macmillan.

Kinginger, C. (2011), 'Enhancing Language Learning in Study Abroad', *Annual Review of Applied Linguistics*, 31, 58–73.

Kinginger, C. (ed.) (2013a), *Social and Cultural Aspects of Language Learning in Study Abroad*, Amsterdam/Philadelphia, PA: John Benjamins.

Kinginger, C. (2013b), 'Identity and Language Learning during Study Abroad', *Foreign Language Annals*, 46 (3), 339–58.

Lafford, B., and Collentine, J. (2006), 'The Effects of Study Abroad and Classroom Contexts on the Acquisition of Spanish as a Second Language: From Research to Application', in R. Salaberry, and B. Lafford (eds.), *The Art of Teaching Spanish: Second Language Acquisition from Research to Praxis*, 103–26, Washington, DC: Georgetown University Press.

Leonard, K., and Shea, C. (2017), 'L2 Speaking Development during Study Abroad: Fluency, Accuracy, Complexity and Underlying Cognitive Factors', *The Modern Language Journal*, 101, 179–93.

Llanes, À., and Muñoz, C. (2009), 'A Short Stay Abroad: Does It Make a Difference?' *System: An International Journal of Educational Technology and Applied Linguistics*, 37 (3), 353–65.

Llanes, À., and Muñoz, C. (2013), 'Age Effects in a Study Abroad Context: Children and Adults Studying Abroad and at Home', *Language Learning*, 63 (1), 63–90.

Mitchell, R., Tracy-Ventura, N., and McManus, K. (2017), *Anglophone Students Abroad: Identity, Social Relationships and Language Learning*, New York, NY: Routledge.

Mora, J. C. (2014), 'The Role of Onset Level on L2 Perceptual Phonological Development after Formal Instruction and Study Abroad', in C. Pérez-Vidal (ed.), *Language Acquisition in Study Abroad and Formal Instruction Contexts*, 167–94, Amsterdam/Philadelphia, PA: John Benjamins.

Oakes, L., and Howard, M. (2019), 'Learning French as a Foreign Language in a Globalised World: An Empirical Critique of the L2 Motivational Self System', *International Journal of Bilingual Education and Bilingualism*.

Ogden, A., Streitwieser, B., and Van Mol, C. (eds.) (2020), *Education Abroad: Leveraging International Research and Scholarship to Inform Practice*, Abingdon: Routledge.

Pérez-Vidal, C. (ed.) (2014), *Language Acquisition in Study Abroad and Formal Instruction Contexts*, Amsterdam/Philadelphia, PA: John Benjamins.

Pizziconi, B. (2017), 'Japanese Vocabulary Development in and beyond Study Abroad: The Timing of the Year Abroad in a Language Degree Curriculum', *The Language Learning Journal*, 45 (2), 133–52.

Plews, J., and Misfeldt, K. (eds.) (2018), *Second Language Study Abroad: Programming, Pedagogy, and Participant Engagement*, New York: Springer.

Ren, W. (2018), 'Developing L2 Pragmatic Competence in Study Abroad Contexts', in C. Sanz, and A. Morales-Front (eds.), *The Routledge Handbook of Study Abroad Research and Practice*, 119–33, New York: Routledge.

Rivers, W. (1998), 'Is Being There Enough? The Effects of Homestay Placements on Language Gain during Study Abroad', *Foreign Language Annals*, 31 (4), 492–500.

Salaberry, R., White, K., and Rue Birch, A. (2019), 'Language Learning and Interactional Experiences in a Study Abroad Setting. An Introduction to the Special Issue', *Study Abroad Research in Second Language Acquisition and International Education*, 4 (1), 1–18.

Serrano, R., Tragant, E., and Llanes, À. (2012), 'A Longitudinal Analysis of One Year Abroad', *Canadian Modern Language Review*, 68 (2), 138–63.

Surtees, V. (2019), '"As a friend, that's the one thing I always am very conscious not to do": Categorization Practices in Interviews with Peers in the Host Community', *Study Abroad Research in Second Language Acquisition and International Education*, 4 (1), 45–69.

Tracy-Ventura, N., Dewaele, J.-M., Köylü, Z., and McManus, K. (2016), 'Personality after the Year Abroad', *Study Abroad Research in Second Language Acquisition and International Education*, 1 (1), 107–26.

Van Mol, C. (2014), *Intra-European Student Mobility in International Higher Education Circuits. Europe on the Move*, Basingstoke: Palgrave Macmillan.

Wilkinson, S. (1998), 'On the Nature of Immersion during Study Abroad: Some Participants' Perspectives', *Frontiers. The Interdisciplinary Journal of Study Abroad*, 4, 121–38.

1

The legal framework of student mobility: How public law makes the Erasmus programme possible

Luca Galli
Università degli Studi di Milano-Bicocca

Introduction

The Erasmus programme is mainly considered an educational phenomenon, but as a tool of internationalization, it cannot be forgotten that it is, first of all, the result of political will and legislative choices. Its creation naturally passed through the introduction of its legislative framework, which reflected the recognition of education as a key factor for the progress of the European juridical system. On the other hand, the survival and improvement of the Erasmus programme depend on the evolution of this legislation and on the efforts of national public administrations to implement and enhance it. In addition, the courts, both national and European, play a key role in ensuring that all the public institutions involved in the Erasmus process act properly and in accordance with the spirit of cohesion, equality and mutual exchange that has underpinned the programme since its inception.

The aim of this chapter is to reveal how public law has allowed the circulation of millions of students through the Erasmus programme, playing a key role not only in student mobility but also in their ability to integrate in the local communities. In order to address this aim, the research is based on an analysis of how three main factors influenced, and still influence, the creation and the existence of the Erasmus programme: (i) legislative power; (ii) executive power and public administrations; and (iii) judicial power.

The following two sections will deal with the Erasmus legislative framework, from its birth to its latest evolution. Then, a section will be dedicated to the systems of public authorities that, operating on both European and national levels, carry out the implementation of the legislative framework. The final section before the conclusion will analyse some legal cases in order to clarify which other public actions, collateral to the Erasmus programme, might be undertaken to ensure a better integration of foreign students in the national context. Naturally, the starting point of this work must be the European legislation, administrative system and case law. Moving to the national level, the Italian legal system has been chosen as a research context, because recent debate has been brewing in Italian society regarding the possibility for foreigners to access public services on par with national citizens. The consequences of this debate have the potential to affect all kinds of foreigners' (including Erasmus students') rights and ability to integrate.

Teaching internationalism: The birth of an idea

According to tradition, Jean Monnet, one of the founding fathers of the European Union (who was called to build a new international reality from the ashes of the Second World War), said: 'If I were to start again, I would start with education' (Corbett, 2005; Grimonprez, 2014).[1] It is precisely to the immediate post-war period that the roots of understanding the relevance of educating youth about internationalism can be traced, along with the aim of making them better citizens of individual nations, Europe and the whole world (Corradi, 2015). Focusing our attention on the European context, first we should note that the topic of education was not explicitly included in the Treaties of Rome,[2] but it was left to the discretion of the Member States. Nonetheless, this did not preclude the spread of the need for a more European education, especially for university students, with the aim of completely forming the individual – both as a student and as a person – in order to implement the rise of a new supranational reality.

Against this background, mobility, border crossing and studying abroad in another European country were conceived as unique elements of personal growth. During this first phase (1950s–1960s), universities were the main promoters of international cooperation in higher education, drawing up agreements to allow the execution and recognition of studies abroad. To this end, several meetings between the rectors of European universities (especially Italian, French and German universities) took place reflecting the autonomy of universities to first determine and then implement equivalences between university courses in different nations (Corradi, 2015).

Nevertheless, the path towards Erasmus was not an easy one: not all European states were persuaded by the opportunity to share a common policy in the educational field. The immediate political challenge was to demonstrate that educational cooperation would not imply the standardization of different educational systems, leading to a complete loss of national competence and autonomy (Jones, 2017). In order to overcome resistance based on this opposition, the European Community clearly rejected the possibility of applying the harmonization principle, recognizing multiple times that the variety of educational systems constituted a precious resource that was essential for intercultural education (see the studies commissioned by the EEC [European Economic Community] in the 1970s, Dahrendorf, 1974; Masclet, 1975).

The political and academic communities' efforts finally led to an important result. Through the Resolution of the Council and of the Ministers of Education of 9 February 1976, there was a first, informal recognition that education fell within the remit of the European Community. The European education ministers agreed for the first time to establish a programme of close cooperation between the educational systems of the EEC. As one of their agreed priorities, the ministers decided to promote joint courses of study between universities and higher education institutions. Therefore, this act revealed the European Community's willingness to encourage the development of links between universities and to eliminate obstacles to the mobility of students, university teachers and research staff.

The Erasmus programme: Legal framework and evolution

The Resolution of the Council and of the Ministers of Education of 9 February 1976 was followed by ten years of practice and tests in order to demonstrate that the scheme could work despite the diversity of educational systems in the different Member States. During this period, the European Court of Justice (ECJ) was called upon to express its view on student mobility and the internationalization of education. In 1985, the *Gravier* case took place, concerning a French student who wished to pursue a course at a Belgian art school.[3] Gravier took the Belgian authority, the City of Liège, to court on the grounds that, as a European national, she should have been given a place on the same terms as Belgian students and not charged a higher fee as a foreign student. The court ruled that the imposition of a charge on students who are nationals of other Member States as a condition of access to university education, where the same fee is not imposed on students who are nationals of the host Member State, constitutes discrimination on grounds of nationality, contrary to the non-discrimination principle recognized by the Treaty of Rome. The free movement of students, which facilitates their education and preparation for a particular profession, can indeed be seen as a premise for the free movement of workers (Teichler and Jhar, 2001).[4]

The result of this case was to have a profound effect on the political discussions concerning the legal basis for the EU to promote and finance educational cooperation, highlighting the idea that the free movement of students was closely linked to the central pillars of the growing European system: the free movement of services, goods, capital and persons.

This long and tortuous path finally led to a defining moment for educational internationalization in the form of the Council decision of 15 June 1987. Through this act, the European Community Action Scheme for the Mobility of University Students, better known as the Erasmus programme, was adopted with the aim of achieving a significant increase in the number of university students spending an integrated period of study in another Member State. The Erasmus programme aimed to promote broad and intensive cooperation among universities in all Member States and, as a result, strengthen the interaction between the citizens of the different Member States, thus consolidating the concept of a People's Europe.[5]

Articles 128 and 235 of the Treaty establishing the EEC were recalled as the legal basis for this new programme. Looking at them closely, these rules did not directly concern education, but they allowed the Council to lay down general principles for implementing a common vocational training policy that would be able to support the development of the European economy and to take the appropriate measures to attain one of the objectives of the Community, even if the Treaty itself had not explicitly provided it with the powers necessary (Feyen and Krzaklewska, 2013).

Several complaints were lodged against the broad interpretation of the above-mentioned articles legitimizing the intervention of the Community in the educational field (Field, 1998; Lonbay, 1989; Murphy, 2003). Nevertheless, this interpretation was definitively confirmed by the ECJ, which was favourable to the extension of the supranational sphere of competence, anticipating the subsequent evolution of the Treaties. In this sense, *Commission v Council* upheld the legitimacy of the Council's decision of 15 June 1987:

> It must be held that the measures envisaged under the Erasmus programme do not exceed the limits of the powers conferred on the Council by Article 128 of the Treaty in the area of vocational training. [...] It follows that inasmuch as the contested decision concerns not only the sphere of vocational training but also that of scientific research, the Council did not have the power to adopt it pursuant to Article 128 alone and thus was bound, before the Single European Act entered into force, to base the decision on Article 235 as well. The Commission's first submission that the legal basis chosen was unlawful must therefore be rejected.[6]

In effect, it was only through the Treaty of Maastricht (art. 126, which is today art. 165 TFEU) that the topic of education finally found its place in the Community's core laws. According to the subsidiarity principle, Member States are responsible for curricula and the organization of education systems, while the Union should play a supporting, supplementary and coordination role. Overall, it explicitly stated that Union action shall be aimed at encouraging the mobility of students and teachers, inter alia by encouraging the academic recognition of diplomas and periods of study abroad (SA) (for a critique of the unused potential of art. 165 TFEU, see Grimonprez, 2014). Thus began one of the best-known European programmes, a programme that, according to certain researchers, can be considered the closest to citizens, offering concrete European experiences to students (Fenner and Lanzilotta, 2012).[7]

In the thirty years since its inception, the Erasmus programme has allowed more than three million students to cross national borders and receive grants while they study abroad.[8] However, the Erasmus programme does not solely have a didactic purpose and it is not only connected to the right to study; it also aims to expand the exchange of people to include the exchange of knowledge, cultures and experiences (for more about the benefits of the Erasmus programme beyond education, see Jacobone and Moro, 2015; Martínez-Usarraldea, Murillo Pausáb and García-López, 2017; Teichler, 2004a). The programme's success has also helped to shape higher education in Europe, alongside other projects, such as the launch of the Bologna Process in 1999 (*ex pluribus*, Corbett, 2006), which introduced comparable and compatible study degrees, and the establishment of the European Credit Accumulation and Transfer System (ECTS), which allows students to earn credits when studying abroad that can be applied to their degree at their home institution.[9]

Meanwhile, the programme has evolved and become an element of wider programmes. In the 1990s, it became part of the Socrates programme[10] (which not only aimed at promoting cooperation and mobility in the education field but also aimed at strengthening the European dimension of education at all levels, enhancing the knowledge of foreign languages, encouraging the use of new technologies and promoting equality), and in 2007, it merged into the Lifelong Learning Programme[11] (still aiming to improve education and supranational mobility at all levels, so as to enable people, at any stage of their life, to take part in stimulating learning experiences, as well as to develop education and training across Europe).

Therefore, European institutions have continued to promote mobility, which is understood as the principal tool for building a European area of education based on greater employment opportunities, lower poverty levels and, above all, the free movement of people and ideas: 'Mobility is important for personal development and employability; it fosters respect for diversity and a capacity to deal with other cultures. It encourages linguistic pluralism, thus underpinning the multilingual tradition of the European Higher Education Area and it increases cooperation and competition between higher education institutions.'[12] According to this logic, the last step was the creation of the Erasmus+ programme,[13] aiming to bring together all the previous European schemes in the fields of education, training, youth and sport, including the international aspects of higher education.[14] The programme features a strong international dimension in order not only to enhance the quality of European higher education but also to promote understanding between people and contribute to the sustainable development of higher education in the partner countries. In addition, the programme also aims to support broader socio-economic development of the countries involved by stimulating brain circulation through mobility actions.[15] All of this happens without prejudice: the programme promotes 'measures to combat discrimination based on sex, racial or ethnic origin, religion or belief, disability, age or sexual orientation. There is a need to widen access for members of disadvantaged and vulnerable groups and actively to address the special learning needs of people with disabilities in the implementation of the Programme'.[16]

In this new programme, mobility[17] is not limited to university students but also includes university staff and academics, students at all levels of education, entrepreneurs, athletes, etc. (on the importance of extending the Erasmus programme to categories other than university students, 'who are already very likely to feel European', see Kuhn, 2012, p. 994). Moreover, the Erasmus+ programme adds virtual mobility to physical mobility by involving a set of activities supported by information and communication technology, including e-learning, that realize or facilitate international collaborative experiences in a teaching and learning context.[18]

In conclusion, the decision to start a new programme is indicative of the Member States' faith in the Erasmus project, but it is not the only sign. Other signs are the increased funding allocated to it,[19] even in times of economic crisis, and the decision to expand the spatial dimension of exchange by opening it up to extra-European countries in order to make the Erasmus programme increasingly international. Indeed, the programme is open not only to Member States but also to the 'European neighborhood', thereby widening the circulation of people.[20] For these reasons, it seems that the goal of the Erasmus programme today is not only to create a European consciousness but to facilitate the overcoming of social and cultural barriers and border crossing, so as to make students 'citizens of the world'.[21]

Internationalization and public law: The role of universities and other public administrations

Over the past thirty years, public administrations have played a primary role in the realization of the Erasmus programme. First of all, we must reaffirm the influence of the universities, which have made a fundamental contribution to the birth of the Erasmus programme, by acknowledging the importance of student exchange and looking at it as an intercultural exchange with unique educational, scientific and social functions.[22] Even today, the power of the initiative is placed firmly in the hands of universities. Every institution that wants to engage in the Erasmus programme must ensure that foreign students attend courses cost-free (they pay tuition fees only in their home institutions), ensure the recognition of courses and exams attended by their own students at the universities with which they have an agreement, help students administratively and organize the reception and integration of foreign students, to whom they must also offer the opportunity to enhance their knowledge of the local language. All these duties are described in detail in the Erasmus Charter for Higher Education (ECHE),[23] an act released by the Commission and which an institution must abide by in order to participate, and they are reiterated in each Learning Agreement, meaning that they are included in every agreement concluded by two universities in relation to every single student engaged in an exchange, indicating the courses attended and their ECTS values.

On the other hand, as long as internationalization is seen as an enhancement of educational quality, universities have to take both reactive and proactive action. Participating in the Erasmus programme does not just mean receiving foreign students but also preparing domestic students to participate in international exchanges. Consequently, universities play a key role in promoting exchange agreements with foreign higher education institutions, and also by encouraging their own students to study abroad and providing foreign language courses and organizing lectures in different languages (first of all, English for the non-English-speaking countries) to attract and support foreign students but also to encourage their own students in the direction of international experiences (Pappa, Sflomos and Panagiaris, 2013).

Looking at the effectiveness of these tools, the literature on barriers to participation in the Erasmus programme suggests they need sharpening. First of all, despite what many perceive to be a pervasive amount of widely accessible information about mobility opportunities, a lack of information about the Erasmus programme and how it works is still perceived by students as an important factor inhibiting their participation (Vossensteyn et al., 2010). Moreover, other recognized obstacles to student mobility concern uncertainty about the quality of education abroad, expected difficulties related to credit recognition, incompatibility of academic calendars, lack of language skills, lack of study programmes in English and lack of administrative support (Bartha and Gubik, 2018; Souto-Otero et al., 2013; Teichler, 2004a). Therefore, universities should strengthen their actions in order to overcome such barriers and provide foreign and domestic students with adequate incentives to participate in exchanges (for the distinctions between financial, curricular and personal incentives, see Teichler, Ferencz and Wächter, 2011). For instance, since universities represent the public administration that is closest to the students, they must enhance their efforts in the fields of information and administrative support. They should adequately promote the Erasmus programme and its benefits, help to identify possible receiving institutions and assess their educational quality, simplify bureaucratic processes, suggest appropriate timing for the SA period and clearly identify the courses that will be recognized (Teichler, Ferencz and Wächter, 2011).

Universities are not the only public institutions in charge of realizing the Erasmus programme. We must also consider that while responsibility for the implementation of the programme at the Union level belongs to the Commission, at a state level, it falls under the competencies of specific national agencies,[24] as supervised by national authorities.[25] Specifically, national authorities designate a national agency or several national agencies to oversee the programme. The national authorities monitor and supervise the management of the programme at a national level, satisfy duties of information and consultation with the Commission, take responsibility for the proper management of the Union funds transferred by the Commission to the national agency and co-finance the operations of their national agency. For instance, in Italy, three ministries have been chosen as national authorities (the Ministry of Education, Universities and Research; the Ministry of Labour and Social Policy; and the Presidency of the Council of Ministers – Department of Youth and National Civil Service), one for each sector in which Erasmus+ is structured (school education, higher education and adult education; education and vocational training; and youth policies). In the UK, instead, there is a single national authority, the Department for Education. In any case, the political nature of these authorities clearly highlights their role of supervision, guidance and dialogue with the European institutions.

On the other hand, national agencies should have a legal personality or be part of an entity having legal personality. They should also have adequate operational and legal means, management capacity, staff and infrastructure to satisfactorily fulfil their tasks. These tasks consist of managing specific actions of the programme, such as that relating to the educational mobility of individuals. Typical assignments are funding and providing advice and assistance to universities and other institutions applying for the Erasmus programme. Looking at specific cases, in Italy, three national agencies have been created to carry out these tasks: *Agenzia nazionale Erasmus+ INDIRE*; *Agenzia nazionale Erasmus+ ISFOL*; and *Agenzia nazionale per i Giovani* – three public entities, one for each sector in which Erasmus+ is structured. In the UK, the National Agency is a partnership between the British Council (a public corporation) and Ecorys UK (a private consulting company) where each partner manages specific parts of the programme, with the British Council responsible for schools and higher education, and Ecorys UK responsible for adult education and vocational education and training.

In conclusion, the roles of different public entities for the execution of the Erasmus programme can be schematized as follows. As mentioned, the core function belongs to the universities. They have to stipulate partnership agreements with other higher education institutions in order to create their own mobility network, organize foreign students' reception and stimulate domestic students' participation. They must apply to the European Commission for the release of the Erasmus Charter for Higher Education, which is essential to participation in the programme. Upon fulfilling these requirements, universities can apply to their national agencies for funding, since these agencies are responsible for managing the resources granted by the European Commission and the national authorities. Finally, the national authorities are responsible for supervising the implementation of the programme at a state level and for coordinating national action within the European action.

Integration and public law: Public interventions through the lens of court decisions

In the previous section, we summarized the administrative structure built over the last thirty years as a concrete basis for the Erasmus programme. But, as mentioned, studying abroad cannot be seen as just an educational phenomenon – it is a moment of intercultural exchange creating contact between two societies (the host society and the foreign student's society). Therefore, the Erasmus programme can be considered a significant test as a benchmark for the integration dynamics of a Member State, where integration is a two-way process requiring adaptation on the part of the participant and also on the part of the host society.

Indeed, on the one hand, there is the foreign student whose decision to participate in the Erasmus programme is an expression of his/her willingness to experience a new reality (Teichler, 2004a),[26] and, on the other hand, there is the host community. A key component of this community is the public administration that is generally the first entity with which foreign student has contact. From this perspective, it is interesting to consider the appropriate measures that must be taken by the Member States to remove the legal and administrative obstacles which might negatively affect the SA experience and also to implement measures to support the student, thereby fostering integration.

The literature clearly hints at these barriers, such as complex administrative requirements, lack of suitable accommodation for the SA period and additional costs (for instance, additional insurance coverage or higher health care fees) (Desoff, 2006; Klahr and Ratti, 2000; Langley and Breese, 2005). Case law also gives explicit indications of the interventions and benefits that have to be granted by the Member States to the foreign students, especially if they are already conferred to national students, according to the non-discrimination principle that must characterize all fields of application of European law.[27] Indeed, the following exposition does not aim to depict the case law directly involving the right to study abroad (for a synthetic review of this kind of case law, see Barraggia, 2017); instead, it aims to offer some examples of concrete measures, provided by public administrations, that are helpful in supporting the students during their exchange experience and useful for their integration into the host community. A crucial point concerns the benefits that public institutions make available to students that are able to improve their daily life beyond a strictly educational perspective. For instance, they can offer discounts on books and textbooks, reduced prices for tickets to cultural events, reduced fares for public transportation and rent incentives.

Starting with the ECJ case law, some recent decisions deal with this matter directly – specifically, the 'reduced fares on public transport' that are ensured for domestic students but denied to foreign students, including participants in the Erasmus programme. In a 2011 decision, the ECJ[28] recognized that national supports granted to students to cover their maintenance costs fall within the scope of EU law, considering the above-mentioned inclusion of education in the EU Treaties.[29] Consequently, a Member State's compliance with EU law in its decision to only offer reduced fares to domestic students (or even to impose conditions for the concession of the reduction that are more easily achieved by domestic students than foreign ones) must be evaluated by taking into account the notion of European citizenship[30] and recalling the non-discrimination principle. Looking at the specifications of this principle given by art. 24(1) of Directive 2004/38,[31] 'all Union citizens residing, on the basis of this Directive, in the territory of the host Member State shall enjoy equal treatment with the nationals of that Member State within the scope of the Treaty'. Hence, according to the Court, the inequality of treatment arising from the denial of reduced fares is contrary to the principles which underpin the status of Union citizens.

On the other hand, a different principle expressed by Directive 2004/38 seems to contradict this interpretation. Recital 10 of the Directive recognizes that persons exercising their right of residence – students included – should not become an unreasonable burden on the social assistance system of the host Member State during their initial period of residence. This principle finds a first and direct expression in art. 7 of the Directive, which fixes specific conditions on obtaining the right of residence for Union citizens for periods in excess of three months, such as being 'enrolled at a private or public establishment, accredited or financed by the host Member State on the basis of its legislation or administrative practice, for the principal purpose of following a course of study, including vocational training' and having 'a comprehensive sickness insurance cover in the host Member State and assure the relevant national authority, by means of a declaration or by such equivalent means as they may choose, (to have) sufficient resources [...] not to become a burden on the social assistance system of the host Member State during their period of residence'.

A second, more specific expression is given in art. 24(2) of Directive 2004/38, which affirms that 'the host Member State [...] nor shall it be obliged, prior to acquisition of the right of permanent residence, to grant maintenance aid for studies, including vocational training, consisting in student grants or student loans to persons other than workers, self-employed persons, persons who retain such status and members of their families', where permanent residence, according to art. 16(1) of the same Directive, is recognized for 'Union citizens who have resided legally for a continuous period of five years in the host Member State' (for an analysis of student loan significance, see Skovgaard-Petersen, 2013). To overcome this obstacle, the Court explains the narrow interpretation that must be given to exceptions to the non-discrimination principle: even if reduced transport fares granted to students constitute a maintenance aid for them, only maintenance aid for studies 'consisting in student grants or student loans' falls within the derogation.

If the difference between reduced fees and student grants or loans is sufficient to decide this case, giving rise to the failure of the Member State to fulfil its obligations under EU law, nevertheless, the Court has formulated another interesting principle. Indeed, recalling the above-mentioned recital 10 – and its application in art. 7 and art.

24(2) – the European judges admit that a national scheme requiring a foreign student to provide proof of a genuine link with the host Member State to obtain a maintenance aid could represent, in principle, a legitimate difference of treatment.[32] However, 'the proof required to demonstrate the genuine link must not be too exclusive', and 'the genuine link required between the student claiming a benefit and the host Member State need not be fixed in a uniform manner for all benefits, but should be established according to the constitutive elements of the benefit in question, including its nature and purposes'. In this sense,

> the existence of a genuine link between the student pursuing his studies in the host Member State could actually be ascertained for the purposes of the reduced transport fares, inter alia, by checking whether the person in question is enrolled at a private or public establishment, accredited or financed by the host Member State on the basis of its legislation or administrative practice, for the principal purpose of following a course of study.[33]

With this statement, the Court seems to be rationally proposing a criterion for access to a maintenance aid for students, which is applicable to any kind of aid and different from the rigid 'acquisition of the right of permanent residence' indicated by art. 24, paragraph 2. The judges suggest a flexible parameter that could be proportional to the nature and the intensity of the requested aid: the enrolment in a national university may be sufficient to legitimate access to certain benefits. Thus, any form of reduction of public transportation costs, discounts on book prices, rent incentives and similar benefits may be more easily granted to the Erasmus student as well, for the duration of the exchange.

The rationale behind this interpretation could be understood, *a contrario*, by reading a more recent decision of the Court in the same field.[34] This time, the judges upheld the position of the Member State, affirming that a benefit on transport fares granted to domestic students was offered as a student grant, and thus it was an exception to the non-discrimination principle established by art. 24(2) of Directive 2004/38. Beyond the correct categorization of the aid as a grant or not, what is revealed by this decision (in comparison to the previous one) seems to be the validation of differences in treatment not only between domestic and foreign students within the same Member State but also between foreign students in two different Member States. In fact, the possibility of obtaining the same kind of benefit – in these cases, a reduction on transportation fares – depends only on the qualification (as a student grant/loan or not) that a Member State decides to attribute to the aid. This contradictory and hardly tolerable result is in stark contrast with the right to equality that must follow from holding EU citizenship (Kadelbach, 2003).[35]

Apart from the supranational dimension, national case law could also point to other public interventions that can lead to an enhanced integration of foreign students in the national context, thus indirectly supporting the Erasmus action. In this sense, two different decisions of the Italian Constitutional Court can be briefly mentioned, even if they do not directly take into account the position of Erasmus students. The first[36] deals with the constitutionality – and thus, compliance with EU law indirectly – of a provincial regulation that restricted access to several social benefits granted by a local administration not only on the basis of residence within the province's territory but also on the duration of the sojourn (from one to five years, depending on the kind of benefit). Among these benefits, one that could apply to Erasmus students concerns the possibility for EU citizens to obtain incentives to learn foreign languages, which in this case was restricted to individuals who had been living in the provincial territory for at least one year without interruption.

Considering the duration of the Erasmus exchange period,[37] this regulation would have automatically excluded foreign students from the possibility of accessing this kind of benefit, which would be useful for their integration not only in the Erasmus student community (considering the variety of languages and countries of origin that characterize it) but also in the local community, since the desire to learn a new language is a possible common interest shared by both Italians and foreigners. Indeed, language courses could provide locations where foreigners and local citizens could meet and establish relationships on a more equal footing: both would be learning a new language. Consequently, the effects of some intercultural communication barriers (the anxiety of not being understood, linguistic and non-verbal communication differences, etc.) that generally affect the daily life of a foreigner could be mitigated (Keles, 2013).

Therefore, the decision in which the Constitutional Court recognized the unconstitutionality of this rule, causing an illegitimate and irrational discrimination between Italian and European citizens (in clear contrast with the equality principle that is safeguarded by art. 3 of the Italian Constitution and by art. 18 TFEU and art. 24 of Directive 2004/38) should be welcomed. Also in this case, a more flexible criterion for access to the benefit is considered preferable, and enrolment in a local university may be considered sufficient evidence of a stable connection with the territory.

The second decision concerns the constitutionality of a law that authorizes universities to provide courses and teaching in a foreign language in order to sustain the internationalization of higher education institutions (art. 2, comma 2, lett. l of law no. 240 of 30 December 2010).[38] The judges recognized the legitimacy of this rule as long as it is not interpreted as capable of allowing the provision of entire university courses only in a foreign language.[39] For the Constitutional Court, this solution would be in contrast not only with the constitutional recognition of the Italian language as the official language of the country but also with the academic freedom of professors, who must be able to choose the language in which they teach, and the right of the students to study, since they must be able to access university studies even if they do not know a foreign language.

As a consequence, the Constitutional Court affirmed the possibility for a university, by expressing its autonomy, to introduce an entire course in a foreign language, but only if the same course is provided in Italian too. However, this duplication is not needed for single modules, which can be freely provided in a foreign language only, if this is reasonable in respect of the nature and characteristics of the subject.

Beyond the rationality and the cost-effectiveness of course duplication, the provision of some teaching in a foreign language seems a logical tool of internationalization for the universities (as recognized by the Constitutional Court's judges), and the literature has also proven that it could be a useful incentive for Erasmus students.[40]

Considering that the English language is presently a common global language and also dominates academia (Altbach, 2013), this solution would facilitate foreign students' comprehension of the subjects they are being taught and their integration in the local community, allowing them to connect with domestic students who are more inclined to speak a foreign language and probably to forge relationships in an international context. However, only the classes characterized by features compatible with the foreign language should not be offered in the local one as well. Allowing Erasmus students to attend lectures in the local language of instruction is a means of stimulating their study of that language, which is conceived not only as a tool of communication but also as an instrument of transmitting specific cultural values.[41]

Conclusions: The Erasmus programme and public law – An unbreakable bond

Concluding this chapter, it is clear that the path to realizing Jean Monnet's original dream is also a path of laws and regulations that have been essential to transforming the SA concept from an idea into a right and then into a concrete reality. The constant evolution and updating of the relevant legislation also highlight the political will, flowing from the European level, to extend the scope of the Erasmus programme, thereby making circulation between European countries not just a right but an ordinary aspect of the lives of European citizens from adolescence. Naturally, the recognition of the right to international studies on a legislative level is not enough. The implementation of a supportive administrative system is fundamental in order to create a network of educational institutions, to distribute funds and to support students and generally allow them to exercise this right to free movement.

But the role of the public law does not end with the actions directly connected to the Erasmus programme, since the Erasmus experience does not end with the right to study abroad; rather, it connects to the right to experience the hosting community. A thirty-year-long legislative path and the efforts of universities and the activities of the other administrative institutions involved in the programme's actualization may be thwarted by the presence of unjust discrimination affecting the lives of foreign students abroad. From this perspective, any kind of integration (permanent or temporary, as in the case of the Erasmus programme) in a host community must be based on concrete equality between foreigners and nationals, beginning with their relationship to public authorities. Therefore, as highlighted by the above-mentioned case law, other public interventions collateral to the Erasmus programme seem to be fundamental in order for foreigners to feel equal to nationals and not subject to less favourable treatment.

While the aim of this chapter was not to evaluate the capacity of the Erasmus programme to achieve its goals through the promotion of a European identity (Bruter, 2005; Fligstein, 2008; Green, 2007; Mitchell, 2012, 2015; Papatsiba, 2006; Sigalas, 2010; Wilson, 2011), it was to highlight the supporting, rather than hindering, role played by public law in the creation and the growth of the Erasmus programme. Participating in the Erasmus programme must be an experience through which the diversity of foreign students is embraced as offering the potential for cultural enrichment, rather than used as the basis for discrimination. International students have to feel like they are citizens of everywhere they go, not citizens of nowhere. However, creating an international community through mobility programmes and teaching internationalism is not enough; equality of rights is the undeniable starting point if we want to support the transformation of the concept of the international student from a fantasy into a concrete reality.

Notes

1. According to Corbett, 'He (Monnet) probably never did, but it is an aphorism which makes sense, wherever it comes from,' p. XI.
2. It was touched upon only marginally by art. 118 and art. 128, which considered professional training, and by art. 57, where the mutual recognition of qualifications was instrumental to encouraging professionals working in different Member States.
3. ECJ, Case 294/83, *Gravier v City of Liège*, Judgment of 13 February 1985.
4. It is useful to recall also the ECJ, Case 9/74, *Casagrande v Landeshauptstadt München*, Judgment of 3 July 1974. In this decision, previous to the *Gravier* case, the Court recognized to the child of a foreign worker the right to take advantage of benefits provided by the laws of the host country relating to educational grants under the same conditions as nationals who are in a similar position. For this reason, a child of an Italian worker in the Federal Republic of Germany has the right to access to an educational grant provided for by the Bavarian law on educational grants, even if this law only takes into account German citizens. Nevertheless, it must be underlined that the Court satisfied this need for equal treatment in so far as the individual is a family member of a foreign worker and not directly as a foreign student; the issue in focus was still worker mobility and not student internationalization. The *Casagrande* case took place in 1974 and so before any official recognition that education fell within the remit of the European Community.
5. Art. 2 of the Council decision of 15 June 1987.
6. ECJ, Case 242/87, *Commission v Council*, Judgment of 30 May 1989.
7. For a different and critical perspective on the Erasmus programme as being reserved for students of a higher socio-economic status, see Ballatore and Ferede (2013).
8. For more Erasmus numbers, see http://ec.europa.eu/education/resources/statistics_en. See also http://ec.europa.eu/education/tools/erasmus-3-million_en, which is dedicated to the achievement of the goal of three million students.
9. For a synthetic overview of how ECTS functions, see the *ECTS Users' Guide*, available at http://ec.europa.eu/dgs/education_culture/repository/education/ects/users-guide/docs/year-2009/ects-users-guide-2009_en.pdf.
10. Established by Decision no. 819/1995/EC of the European Parliament and of the Council of 14 March 1995.
11. Established by Decision no. 1720/2006/EC of the European Parliament and of the Council of 15 November 2006.
12. *Communiqué of the Conference of European Ministers Responsible for Higher Education*, Leuven and Louvain-la-Neuve, 28–29 April 2009.
13. Established by Regulation EU no. 1288/2013 of the European Parliament and of the Council of 11 December 2013.

14 Recital (1) of Regulation EU no. 1288/2013: 'A single programme in the field of education, training, youth and sport, including the international aspects of higher education, bringing together the action programme in the field of lifelong learning ("Lifelong Learning") established by Decision No. 1720/2006/EC of the European Parliament and of the Council, the Youth in Action programme ("Youth in Action") established by Decision No. 1719/2006/EC of the European Parliament and of the Council, the Erasmus Mundus action programme ("Erasmus Mundus") established by Decision No. 1298/2008/EC of the European Parliament and of the Council, the ALFA III programme established by Regulation (EC) No. 1905/2006 of the European Parliament and of the Council, and the Tempus and Edulink programmes, in order to ensure greater efficiency, a stronger strategic focus and synergies to be exploited between the various aspects of the single programme. In addition, sport is proposed as part of that single programme.'
15 See Recitals (8) and (17) and art. 4 of the Regulation.
16 Recital (7) of the Regulation.
17 Learning mobility is defined by art. 2, pt. 7, of the Regulation as 'moving physically to a country other than the country of residence, in order to undertake study, training or non-formal or informal learning; it may take the form of traineeships, apprenticeships, youth exchanges, volunteering, teaching or participation in a professional development activity, and may include preparatory activities, such as training in the host language, as well as sending, hosting and follow-up activities'.
18 Art. 2, pt. 10, of the Regulation.
19 The current Erasmus+ programme, with a budget of €14.7 billion, runs from 2014 to 2020. The last proposal is to double the budget (€30 billion) for the next seven years (2021–27). See the Proposal for a Regulation COM (2018) 367, available at https://eur-lex.europa.eu/legal-content/EN/TXT/?uri=COM%3A2018%3A367%3AFIN.
20 Art. 24 of the Regulation states: 'Country participation 1. The Programme shall be open to the participation of the following countries (the "Programme countries"): (a) the Member States; (b) the acceding countries, candidate countries and potential candidates benefiting from a pre-accession strategy, in accordance with the general principles and general terms and conditions for the participation of those countries in Union programmes established in the respective framework agreements, Association Council decisions or similar agreements; (c) those EFTA countries that are party to the EEA Agreement, in accordance with the provisions of that agreement; (d) the Swiss Confederation, on the basis of a bilateral agreement to be concluded with that country; (e) those countries covered by the European neighborhood policy which have concluded agreements with the Union providing for the possibility of their participation in the Union's programmes, subject to the conclusion of a bilateral agreement with the Union on the conditions of their participation in the Programme.'
21 See the Council Recommendation of 28 June 2011, *Youth on the Move – Promoting the Learning Mobility of Young People*, 2011/C 199/01, according to which 'Learning mobility, meaning transnational mobility for the purpose of acquiring new knowledge, skills and competences, is one of the fundamental ways in which young people can strengthen their future employability, as well as their intercultural awareness, personal development, creativity and active citizenship. Europeans who are mobile as young learners are more likely to be mobile as workers later in life. Learning mobility can make education and training systems and institutions more open, more European and international, more accessible and more efficient. It can

also strengthen Europe's competitiveness by helping to build a knowledge-intensive society.' For broader thoughts on the internationalization of higher education, see Teichler (2004b). On the concept of global citizenship, see Killick (2012), Bourn (2010), Langran (2009), Streitwieser and Light (2009).
22 This point of view has been clear since the Geneva Conference, 3–6 September 1969, General Assembly of the European Rectors.
23 This document can be found at https://ec.europa.eu/programmes/erasmus-plus/sites/erasmusplus/files/files/resources/he-charter_en.pdf. See also the *Erasmus Charter for Higher Education: Annotated Guidelines* for a more specific idea of the specific requirements for entering the Erasmus circuit: https://ec.europa.eu/programmes/erasmus-plus/sites/erasmusplus/files/files/resources/charter-annotated-guidelines_en.pdf.
24 Art. 28 of the Regulation EU no. 1288/2013.
25 Art. 27 of the Regulation EU no. 1288/2013.
26 Teichler (2004a, p. 397) indicates that the 'wish to improve understanding of the host country' has a strong influence on students making the decision to study abroad.
27 See, in this sense, art. 18 TFEU: 'Within the scope of application of the Treaties, and without prejudice to any special provisions contained therein, any discrimination on grounds of nationality shall be prohibited.'
28 ECJ, Case 75/11, *European Commission v Republic of Austria*, Judgment of 4 October 2012.
29 See section 'The Erasmus programme: Legal framework and evolution'.
30 Art. 20 TUFE.
31 Directive 2004/38/EC of the European Parliament and of the Council of 29 April 2004 on the right of citizens of the Union and their family members to move and reside freely within the territory of the Member States.
32 In this sense, *ex pluribus*, see also ECJ, Case 209/03, *Bidar v London Borough of Ealing*, Judgment of 15 March 2005.
33 ECJ, Case 75/11, *European Commission v Republic of Austria*, Judgment of 4 October 2012.
34 ECJ, Case 233/14, *European Commission v Kingdom of the Netherlands*, Judgment of 2 June 2016.
35 In this sense, Kadelbach (2003, p. 33) highlights that 'nationality could lose its significance as a criterion of social welfare law and gradually give way to the residence principle in relation to Union citizens' (on nationality, Union citizenship and the non-discrimination principle, see, *ex pluribus*, Van der Mei, 2011).
36 Italian Constitutional Court, 18 January 2013, no. 2.
37 A maximum of twelve months for every course of study.
38 Italian Constitutional Court, 24 February 2017, no. 42.
39 The trial relates to a university's decision to provide all of its postgraduate courses in English only, to the exclusion of any teaching in Italian. This university's decision was originally contested before the administrative judges, who, in the first instance, abolished it on the basis of its violation of the same constitutional rules and principles recalled by the Constitutional Court. In the second instance, however, the administrative judges decided to submit the interpretation of the above-mentioned art. 2 l. no. 240/2010 to the constitutional judges. This affair and the connection between the internationalization of higher education institutions and teaching in English more generally have been the subject of several Italian studies and commentaries (*ex pluribus*, Caretti, 2013; Giovannini, 2015; Gnes, 2017).

40 See section 'Internationalization and public law: The role of universities and other public administrations'.
41 This is the reasoning adopted by the administrative judges in Italy to support the annulment of the university decision that introduced the teaching of master and doctoral courses only in English. See Regional Administrative Tribunal of Lombardy, Milan, 3rd section, 23 May 2013, no. 1348.

References

Altbach, P. G. (2013), *The International Imperative in Higher Education*, Rotterdam: Sense Publisher.

Ballatore, M., and Ferede, M. K. (2013), 'The Erasmus Programme in France, Italy and the United Kingdom: Student Mobility as a Signal of Distinction and Privilege', *European Educational Research Journal*, 12 (4), 525–33.

Barraggia, A. (2017), 'Overstepping the Boundaries of National Higher Education System: The Role of the CJEU Case Law', in A. Barragia, M. Delsignore, L. Galli, and B. Rabai (eds.), Building Bridges: Towards Cohesion through the European University System, *Ius Publicum*, February 2017, 1–46, available online at www.ius-publicum.com.

Bartha, Z., and Gubik, A. S. (2018), 'Institutional Determinants of Higher Education Students' International Mobility within the Erasmus Programme Countries', *Club of Economics in Miskolc TMP*, 14 (2), 3–13.

Bourn, D. (2010), 'Students as Global Citizens', in E. Jones (ed.), *Internationalisation and the Student Voice*, 18–29, London: Routledge.

Bruter, M. (2005), *Citizen of Europe? The Emergence of a Mass European Identity*, New York: Palgrave Macmillan.

Caretti, P. (2013), 'Ufficialità della Lingua Italiana e Insegnamento Universitario: le Ragioni del Diritto Costituzionale contro gli Eccessi dell'Esterofilia Linguistica', *Giurisprudenza costituzionale*, 2, 1223–30.

Corbett, A. (2005), *Universities and the Europe of Knowledge: Ideas, Institutions and Policy Entrepreneurship in European Union Higher Education Policy*, London: Palgrave Macmillan.

Corbett, A. (2006), 'Higher Education as a Form of European Integration: How Novel Is the Bologna Process?', *ARENA Centre for European Studies Working Paper 15*, Oslo.

Corradi, S. (2015), 'Erasmus e Erasmus Plus. La Mobilità Internazionale degli Studenti Universitari', Rome, available online at https://www.unistrapg.it/sites/default/files/docs/mobilita/libro_corradi_2015.pdf.

Dahrendorf, R. (1974), 'Education in the European Community', *Bulletin of the European Communities*, supplement 3/74.

Desoff, A. (2006), 'Who Is Not Going Abroad?', *International Educator*, 15, 20–7.

Fenner, M., and Lanzilotta, S. (2012), 'Project Report. 20 Years of the Erasmus Programme', *Erasmus Student Network*, 50 (6), 994–1010.

Feyen, B., and Krzaklewska, E. (2013), *The Erasmus Phenomenon – Symbol of a New European Generation?*, Frankfurt: Peter Lang.

Field, J. (1998), *European Dimensions, Education, Training and the European Union*, London: Jessica Kingsley.

Fligstein, N. (2008), *Euroclash: The EU, European Identity, and the Future of Europe*, Oxford: Oxford University Press.

Giovannini, M. (2015), 'Internazionalizzazione e Lingua degli Insegnamenti Universitari: la Desiderabile Autonomia delle Università Italiane', *Rivista Trimestrale di Diritto Pubblico*, 1, 139–76.

Gnes, P. (2017), 'Una d'Arme, di Lingua …: l'Ufficialità della Lingua Italiana nelle Università', *Giornale di Diritto Amministrativo*, 3, 324–38.

Green, D. (2007), *The Europeans: Political Identity in an Emerging Polity*, Boulder, CO: Lynne Rienner.

Grimonprez, K. (2014), 'The European Dimension in Citizenship Education: Unused Potential of Article 165 TFEU', *European Law Review*, 39 (1), 3–26.

Jacobone, V., and Moro, G. (2015), 'Evaluating the Impact of the Erasmus Programme: Skills and European Identity', *Assessment & Evaluation in Higher Education*, 40 (2), 309–28.

Jones, H. C. (2017), 'Celebrating 30 Years of the Erasmus Programme', *European Journal of Education*, 52, 558–62.

Kadelbach, S. (2003), 'Union Citizenship', *Jean Monnet Working Paper*, 9/03.

Keles, Y. (2013), 'What Intercultural Communication Barriers Do Exchange Students of Erasmus Program Have during Their Stay in Turkey, Mugla?', *Procedia – Social and Behavioural Sciences*, 70, 1513–24.

Killick, D. (2012), 'Seeing Ourselves in the World: Developing Global Citizenship through International Mobility and Campus Community', *Journal of Studies in International Education*, 16 (4), 372–89.

Klahr, S., and Ratti, U. (2000), 'Increasing Engineering Student Participation in Study Abroad: A Study of U.S. and European Programs', *Journal of Studies in International Education*, 4 (1), 79–102.

Kuhn, T. (2012), 'Why Educational Exchange Programs Miss Their Marks: Cross-border Mobility, Education and European Identity', *Journal of Common Market Studies*, 50 (6), 94–101.

Langley, C. S., and Breese, J. R. (2005), 'Interacting Sojourners: A Study of Students Studying Abroad', *Social Science Journal*, 42 (2), 313–21.

Langran, E. (2009), 'Transforming Today's Students into Tomorrow's Global Citizens: Challenges for U.S. Educators', *New Global Studies*, 3 (1), 1–20.

Lonbay, J. (1989), 'Education and Law: The Community Context', *European Law Review*, 14, 363–74.

Martínez-Usarraldea, M. J., Murillo Pausáb, J., and García-López, R. (2017), 'The ERASMUS Experience and Its Capacitating Potential: Analysis of Adaptive Capabilities', *International Journal of Educational Development*, 53, 101–9.

Masclet, J. C. (1975), *The Intra-European Mobility of Students*, Paris: Institute of Education of the European Cultural Foundation.

Mitchell, K. (2012), 'Student Mobility and European Identity: Erasmus Study as a Civic Experience', *Journal of Contemporary European Research*, 8 (4), 490–518.

Mitchell, K. (2015), 'Rethinking the "Erasmus Effect" on European Identity', *Journal of Common Market Studies*, 53 (2), 330–48.

Murphy, M. (2003), 'Covert Action? Education, Social Policy and Law in the European Union', *Journal of Education Policy*, 18, 551–62.

Papatsiba, V. (2006), 'Making Higher Education More European through Student Mobility? Revising EU Initiatives in the Context of the Bologna Process', *Comparative Education*, 42 (1), 93–111.

Pappa, P., Sflomos, K., and Panagiaris, G. (2013), 'Internationalization and Quality Control of Education in TEI of Athens. Evaluation of the Erasmus Programme', *Procedia – Social and Behavioral Sciences*, 106, 1567–75.

Sigalas, E. (2010), 'Cross-border Mobility and European Identity: The Effectiveness of Intergroup Contact during the ERASMUS Year Abroad', *European Union Politics*, 11 (2), 241–65.

Skovgaard-Petersen, H. (2013), 'There and Back Again: Portability of Student Loans, Grants and Fee Support in a Free Movement Perspective', *European Law Review*, 38 (6), 783–804.

Souto-Otero, M., Huisman, J., Beerkens, M., deWit, H., and Vujic, S. (2013), 'Barriers to International Student Mobility: Evidence from the Erasmus Programme', *Educational Researcher*, 42 (2), 70–7.

Streitwieser, B., and Light, G. (2009), 'Study Abroad and the Easy Promise of Global Citizenship: Student Conceptions of a Contested Notion', *Comparative and International Education Society (CIES) Annual Meeting*, Charleston, retrieved from https://www.northwestern.edu/searle/research/docs/study-abroad-global-citizenship.pdf.

Teichler, U. (2004a), 'Temporary Study Abroad: The Life of ERASMUS Students', *European Journal of Education*, 39 (4), 395–408.

Teichler, U. (2004b), 'The Changing Debate on Internationalisation of Higher Education', *Higher Education*, 48, 5–26.

Teichler, U., and Jhar, V. (2001), 'Mobility during the Course of Study and after Graduation', *European Journal of Education*, 36 (4), 443–58.

Teichler, U., Ferencz, I., and Wächter, B. (2011), *Mapping Mobility in European Higher Education, Volume I: Overview and Trends*, Brussels: Directorate General for Education and Culture of the European Commission.

Van der Mei, A. P. (2011), 'The Outer Limits of the Prohibition of Discrimination on Grounds of Nationality: A Look through the Lens of Union Citizenship', *Maastricht Journal of European and Comparative Law*, 18, 62–85.

Vossensteyn, H., Beerkens, M., Cremonini, L., Huisman, J., Souto-Otero, M., Bresancon, B., Focken, N., Leurs, B., McCoshan, A., Mozuraityte, N., Pimentel Bótas, P. C., and de Wit, H. (2010), 'Improving Participation in the Erasmus Programme', *Final Report to the European Parliament*, European Parliament.

Wilson, I. (2011), 'What Should We Expect of "Erasmus Generations"?', *Journal of Common Market Studies*, 49, 1113–40.

2

Should I stay or should I go? Factors that influence one's decision to participate in a student mobility programme

Katarzyna Ożańska-Ponikwia and Angélica Carlet
University of Bielsko-Biala, Poland/Universitat Internacional de Catalunya, Spain

Introduction

International student mobility programmes expand learning mobility, making an important contribution to the personal, educational and professional development of many participants. Zimmermann and Neyer (2013) noted that international sojourns have become increasingly important as both higher education boards and employers have strong expectations regarding young graduates' international experiences and their subsequent readiness for global job mobility. Since student mobility is a global phenomenon, it is of crucial importance to understand not only how, why and to what degree the immersive experience is beneficial for learners' language, cultural and personal growth but also what influences students' decision to take part in the programme. So far, it has been agreed that international mobility is a relevant life event for the personality development of young adults (Basow and Gaugler, 2017; Zimmermann and Neyer, 2013) as 'international exchange, like sailing uncharted waters, provides manifold challenges and opportunities for young adults' (Greischel, Noack and Neyer, 2016, p. 2307). Basow and Gaugler (2017, p. 39) note that the potential benefits of study abroad (SA) experiences are significant: the broadening of one's world view, greater cultural sensitivity, increased creativity and complex thinking, the development of new neural networks and better career outcomes. Moreover, long-lasting effects have been found on the social and personal development of sojourners (Hutteman et al., 2015; Zimmermann and Neyer, 2013). At the same time, there are still many questions yet to be answered, which may contribute to our understanding of the mechanisms underlying not only successful foreign language learning while abroad but also variables influencing participation in such programmes. Hence, the main aim of the present chapter is to investigate psychological factors (emotional intelligence (EI), personality) and linguistic factors (L2 proficiency) in relation to self-selection processes in the mobility context.

Personality and EI as potential factors influencing linguistic development in an SA context

The set of the Big Five personality factors is claimed to be the most dominant model of personality structure in contemporary personality psychology. It measures such higher-order personality traits as neuroticism (the tendency to experience negative emotions such as sadness or anxiety, as well as mood swings), extraversion (the tendency to be talkative, sociable and to enjoy other people), openness to experience (the tendency to appreciate new ideas, values, feelings and behaviours), agreeableness (the tendency to agree and go along with others) and conscientiousness (the tendency to be hardworking, well-organized and to follow rules) that represent the five fundamental ways by which people's personalities vary (Matthews, Deary and Whiteman, 2003). However, it needs to be remembered that personality traits are hierarchically organized with more specific or lower-order traits combining to form more generalized higher-order traits. Consequently, EI, which itself concerns a constellation of emotion-related self-perceptions and dispositions, was reported to be a compound personality construct located at the lower levels of the higher-order taxonomies. Therefore, it was termed a lower-order personality trait (Petrides, Furnham and Mavraveli, 2007). At the same time, there are good reasons to consider that both higher- and lower-order levels of the hierarchy are important for understanding personality that shapes various aspects of our life including second language acquisition (SLA) or affective socialization processes (Ożańska-Ponikwia and Dewaele, 2012).

Study abroad research has shown that the linguistic gains made by participants are often subtle and subject to substantial individual differences (Hessel, 2017; Kinginger, 2015; Sanz, 2014). As a consequence, there has been considerable research interest in identifying factors that can account for differential linguistic progress while abroad. It has also been observed that second language (L2) gains during study abroad are related to several variables including length of stay (Llanes, 2011), language use (Martinsen et al., 2010) and social network development (Isabelli-García, 2006; Ożańska-Ponikwia, Carlet and Pujol Valls, 2019), among others. However, not many studies have focused on the possible role of personality traits in sojourners' linguistic development. One of the few studies that took personality into account as a potential predictor of L2 gains while abroad is that by Arvidsson et al. (2018), showing that personality could be linked to the amount of target language (TL) use and self-perceived speaking proficiency among SA students. An increase in cultural empathy correlated with both self-perceived progress in speaking and the amount of TL use, while an increase in open-mindedness correlated with the amount of TL use. These results suggest that the more open and culturally emphatic one becomes, the more frequently one tends to use the TL while abroad. Consequently, self-perceived progress in speaking a foreign language also increases. Dewey, Belnap and Hillstrom (2013) also observed that a learner's openness to new experiences was a predictor of L2 use. However, they also noted that programme requirements could push even less extrovert and less open students to use the TL as frequently as those students who scored higher on these personality traits. These studies show that even though high scores on openness and extraversion are not a prerequisite for TL use while abroad, they might, in fact, facilitate frequent L2 use in the SA context. Regarding the potential role of personality and EI in linguistic development while abroad, Ożańska-Ponikwia, Carlet and Pujol Valls (2019) in their small-scale qualitative study examined two groups of students (at-home students ($n = 5$) and stay abroad students ($n = 6$)), prior to and after their three-month practicum experience. Their findings demonstrated that four out of six students who took part in the Erasmus+ mobility programme showed greater linguistic gains in grammar and speaking abilities in comparison to at-home students. Interestingly, a detailed analysis and follow-up interviews revealed that the two cases that failed to progress after the stay abroad experience could be explained by factors such as attitude, language engagement, social network development and satisfaction with the student mobility experience. Thus, it was suggested that these factors might influence and shape TL learning while abroad. Consequently, the investigators speculated that the progress of the informants in grammar and speaking could be related mostly to the quantity and quality of the language input outside of the classroom setting. With regard to the personality profiles of the high- and low gainers, it was noticed that their scores differed minimally in cultural empathy and open-mindedness, but there were large discrepancies in their scores on EI. At the same time, scores on the personality traits mentioned in the case of the low gainers in the at-home group were much lower than those of the low-gainer sojourners abroad. Therefore, the investigators postulated that personality might be a mediating variable influencing intercultural adjustment, social network development and intensity of L2 use while abroad.

Personality and EI as potential factors influencing intercultural adjustment in an SA context

It has been noted in a number of studies (Baker-Smemoe et al., 2014; Martinsen, 2010; Martinsen and Alvord, 2012; Vande Berg, Connor-Linton and Paige, 2009) that informants' intercultural development and adjustment could, in fact, predict the development of L2 skills while abroad. Along the same lines, Basow and Gaugler (2017) reported that intercultural adjustment at the end of a study abroad semester was related not only to the frequency of L2 use but also to positive attitudes towards the whole experience. In their sample, those who had less difficulty with cultural adjustment had stronger language skills, as well as higher levels of social interaction with locals during their sojourn. Interestingly, a higher level of social interaction, in turn, mediated the effects of higher levels of open-mindedness and more positive homestay experiences, which shows that personality can also influence this aspect of the SA experience. A range of factors can impact intercultural adjustment. Savicki et al. (2004) found that clusters of personality traits (e.g. anxiety, extraversion, openness and agreeableness) and coping strategies (e.g. active, planning, denial and behavioural disengagement) were significantly related to intercultural adjustment. Similarly, Harrison and Voelker (2008) investigated the cross-cultural adjustment of study abroad students and reported that three sub-dimensions of EI were significantly related to general adjustment to a host culture. Individuals with higher self-emotional appraisal, higher emotional appraisal of others and higher use of emotion exhibited stronger general adjustment than those who scored lower in these dimensions. In a similar way, a number of studies in an immigrant setting have also found personality and EI to play an important role in explaining cross-cultural adjustment and expatriate employee success (Gabel, Dolan and Cerdin, 2005; Huang, Chi and Lawler, 2005; Jassawalla, Truglia and Garvey, 2004), but also L2 proficiency and frequency of L2 use (Ożańska-Ponikwia and Dewaele, 2012). Taken together, based on the studies presented, it could be noted that although personality was not always directly linked to the SA students' L2 gains, it might, in fact, shape the process of TL development while abroad by influencing sojourners' intercultural adjustment, development of social networks as well as frequency of L2 use in an immersive context.

Personality and EI as potential factors influencing mobility and participation in SA programmes

A number of studies (Jokela, 2009; Jokela et al., 2008; Silventoinen et al., 2008) have suggested that personality differences may be a relevant factor in understanding mobility patterns. Silventoinen et al. (2008) found that high extraversion and high neuroticism indicated higher likelihood of migration. Another interesting finding was that high emotionality tended to increase migration propensity and predicted shorter migration distances (Jokela et al., 2008). Similarly, a study examining the role of personality in predicting the propensity to migrate within and between US states by Jokela (2009) showed that extraversion and openness to experience predicted increased migration propensity. It was therefore suggested that outgoing and open-minded individuals who prefer novel stimuli are most likely to change their locations. Another interesting association reported in the study was that between high agreeableness and decreased migration propensity. The author hypothesized that since agreeableness reflects trustful, warm and caring attitudes towards other people, it could be hypothesized that individuals with high agreeableness tend to form strong bonds to their community, friends and relatives (e.g. Lounsbury, Loveland and Gibson, 2003) and are therefore less willing to change location than people with low agreeableness. Since it was suggested that 'temperament predicts the self-selection of environments on a demographic scale and may be relevant in understanding population dynamics' (Jokela et al., 2008, p. 831), it might be hypothesized to also influence the self-selection process in an SA context.

Zimmermann and Neyer (2013) demonstrated that pre-departure levels of extraversion and conscientiousness among their residence abroad (RA) participants ($n = 527$) predicted their choice of a short-term exchange, whereas extraversion and openness to experience predicted long-term residence. Also, the RA participants were found to have increased their openness to experience and agreeableness, along with a decrease in neuroticism. A study by Niehoff, Petersdotter and Freund (2017) also attempted to answer similar research questions relating to who chooses to study abroad and how study abroad possibly impacts personality. A total of 221 students from a German university completed the Big Five personality test. Those students ($n = 93$) who studied abroad were found to rate higher on agreeableness and openness to experience prior to the international experience than their fellow students who did not sojourn abroad. In turn, sojourning abroad evoked increases in both extraversion and agreeableness and a decrease in neuroticism. Similarly, another study by Greischel, Noack and Neyer (2016) showed that sojourners ($n = 457$) demonstrated higher pre-departure levels of extraversion and agreeableness as well as lower levels of neuroticism.

Longitudinal results indicated a steeper increase in openness and agreeableness trajectories, as well as a buffered increase in neuroticism for exchange students. Thus, it could be concluded that personality is implicated in mobility patterns and might influence not only the very decision to take part in the exchange programme but also the length of such stay abroad.

Method

The overview of the literature presented earlier shows that certain personality traits and EI traits might influence not only the adjustment to the host culture, intensity of L2 use and social network development but also the decision of whether to sojourn abroad or not. Therefore, the current study was designed to further investigate the possible role of different psychological variables as well as the initial levels of the L2 proficiency in the self-selection process concerning participation in SA programmes.

Research questions

The study aims to address the following research questions:

1. Do students who choose to go abroad have higher L2 proficiency levels than those who do not enrol in an international student mobility programme?
2. Is there any difference in the personality profiles of the pre-departure SA students and at-home students?

Participants

The participants were thirty Spanish and forty-seven Polish university students, aged 20–21 years ($n = 77$, mean = 20.43; SD = 0.43); fifty were females and twenty-seven were males. The informants were specialist language learners at different levels of L2 proficiency starting with the A2 level (5.2 per cent); 10.4 per cent of the informants were at the B1 level, 63.6 per cent were at the B2 level and the remaining 20.8 per cent of participants were at the C1 level according to the Common European Framework of Reference (CEFR) scale. In the case of the Spanish sample, there were thirty specialist language learners whose L1 was Spanish and Catalan with L2 English. Their L2 proficiency varied from the A2 level (13.3 per cent) to the C1 level (33.3 per cent), with 23.4 per cent being at the B1 level and 30 per cent at the B2 level. The Polish sample consisted of forty-seven specialist language learners whose L1 was Polish with L2 English. The Polish informants were mostly at the B2 level of L2 proficiency (85.1 per cent). The remaining seven participants were either at the B1 level (2.1 per cent) or C1 level (12.8 per cent). The informants self-selected themselves to either take part in the European Erasmus+ mobility programme or continue their education at their home universities in Spain or Poland. Thus, the study involves two groups, namely pre-departure SA students ($n = 37$), among whom there were sixteen Spanish students who were going to the UK ($n = 11$) and Finland ($n = 5$) to complete a three-month teaching practicum; and twenty-one Polish students who were going to study abroad at a university for one semester, mostly in Spain ($n = 10$), Slovakia ($n = 7$) and the Czech Republic ($n = 4$). The second group comprised at-home students ($n = 40$), among whom there were fourteen Spanish students and twenty-six Polish students who decided to continue their studies or teaching practicum at their local universities or in local schools.

Instruments

For the purpose of the present study, a battery of tests was applied to both groups of students. Data collection took place at their local universities in Poland and Spain before the departure of those who were enrolled in the exchange programmes. The research instruments consisted of two questionnaires that measured personality traits (Big Five Personality Questionnaire; Multicultural Personality Questionnaire), one questionnaire that measured EI (Trait Emotional Intelligence Questionnaire) and three other tests that measured English (L2) proficiency (Oxford Placement Test; Self-reported Proficiency Questionnaire; speaking test based on the Cambridge Advanced Exam). A detailed description of all instruments, as well as the internal consistency of the measures of scales (Cronbach's alpha), is provided below.

The Big Five Personality Questionnaire

The Big Five broad domains personality test (Goldberg, 1992), obtained from the International Personality Item Pool (IPIP), measured the personality traits of extraversion, agreeableness, conscientiousness, emotional stability/neuroticism and intellect. Subjects responded to each item on a five-point Likert scale, indicating 'never or almost never true of me', 'usually not true of me', 'somewhat true of me', 'usually true of me', 'always or almost always true of me'. These categories were assigned values of 1, 2, 3, 4 and 5, respectively. The correlation of the IPIP Big Five broad domains personality test with Costa and McCrae's (1992) Big Five factor structure ranged from .66 to .90, with an overall correlation reported of .81 (Goldberg, 1992). The Cronbach's alpha for the Big Five broad domains personality test was .84.

Multicultural Personality Questionnaire (MPQ)

The Multicultural Personality Questionnaire developed by Van Der Zee and Van Oudenhoven (2000) is a personality assessment questionnaire that was constructed specifically to describe behaviour when one is interacting with people from different cultures. The MPQ consisted of forty Likert-type items measuring such factors as cultural empathy, flexibility, social initiative, emotional sociability and open-mindedness. The Cronbach's alpha for the MPQ was .86.

Trait Emotional Intelligence Questionnaire (TEIQue)

Petrides and Furnham's (2003) TEIQue used in the present study comprised thirty items rated on a seven-point Likert scale providing scores on four factors of broad relevance: well-being, self-control, emotionality and sociability. TEIQue required participants to use the rating scale from 'completely disagree' to 'completely agree' with a mid-point of 'neither agree nor disagree'. The TEIQue Cronbach's alpha for the whole questionnaire was .88.

Oxford Placement Test

The Oxford Placement Test was administered to the participants. The test was completed online and contained 100 questions addressing English grammar and vocabulary. Each correct answer was attributed two points. Immediately after the test, participants were given their score, feedback and an explanation of their approximate level according to the CEFR.

Self-reported Proficiency Questionnaire

The Self-reported Proficiency Questionnaire (Ożańska-Ponikwia, 2016) was used in order to gather data concerning the participants' opinions of their overall L2 proficiency as well as L2 proficiency in the four skills of speaking, writing, listening and reading. It comprised five Likert-type items: How would you rate your overall proficiency in English? How would you rate your L2 speaking proficiency? How would you rate your L2 writing proficiency? How would you rate your L2 listening proficiency? How would you rate your L2 reading proficiency? The Cronbach's alpha for the whole questionnaire was .85.

Speaking test based on the Cambridge Advanced Exam (CAE)

The speaking test followed the guidelines of part two of the Cambridge Advanced Exam. Participants were given a set of three pictures and were instructed to select and talk about two of the three pictures individually for one minute. Testing took place in a quiet room and participants' individual output was recorded. Three Cambridge-trained evaluators rated learners' speaking abilities on the basis of five different skills: pronunciation, vocabulary, accuracy, communication and fluency. A four-point-scale rubric was used for evaluation, and a reliability analysis using an intra-class correlation coefficient (ICC) with a level of 'absolute agreement' was conducted on the rating scores. The Cronbach's alpha reliability coefficient for each speaking skill ranged from .84 to .87, indicating strong inter-rater reliability.

Results

The first research question concerned a possible difference in the pre-departure L2 proficiency scores between the SA students and the at-home students. In order to answer this question, the mean scores for self-perceived L2 proficiency (overall L2 proficiency and self-perceived L2 proficiency in all measured language skills) and the mean scores for speaking and grammar tests were compared. Detailed results are presented in Tables 2.1 and 2.2.

Table 2.1 Self-perceived L2 Proficiency – At-home vs. Stay Abroad Group

Variable		Mean	SD	t	df	p-Value
Overall L2 proficiency	At-home students	3.50	.64	-1.75	75	.083
	Pre-SA students	3.75	.64			
L2 speaking proficiency	At-home students	3.50	.78	-2.62	75	.011
	Pre-SA students	3.97	.79			
L2 reading proficiency	At-home students	3.65	.76	-.321	75	.749
	Pre-SA students	3.70	.66			
L2 writing proficiency	At-home students	3.55	.78	.198	75	.844
	Pre-SA students	3.51	.83			
L2 listening proficiency	At-home students	3.90	.67	1.22	75	.224
	Pre-SA students	3.70	.74			

Table 2.2 L2 Proficiency Test Scores – At-home vs. Stay Abroad Group

Variable		M	SD	t	df	p-Value
L2 proficiency test	At-home students	136.52	13.23	-1.82	75	.070
	Pre-SA students	141.64	11.17			
L2 speaking proficiency test	At-home students	35.47	5.25	-1.89	75	.062
	Pre-SA students	38.01	6.98			

The results presented show that both groups perceived their overall L2 proficiency very similarly, between intermediate and upper-intermediate levels. However, a more detailed analysis of the separate L2 skills (e.g. speaking, reading, writing and listening) revealed some discrepancies. First of all, it is important to notice that both pre-SA students and at-home students scored almost identically on self-perceived L2 reading and writing proficiency. However, their scores on self-perceived L2 speaking and listening proficiency were slightly different, with the at-home students rating their L2 listening proficiency higher and L2 speaking proficiency lower than the pre-SA students. At the same time, self-perceived L2 speaking proficiency was the only variable that significantly differentiated both groups, with the pre-SA students rating their L2 speaking proficiency significantly higher than the at-home students ($t = -2.62$, $p = .011$). The effect size was medium with Cohen's $d = .59$. Therefore, we decided to compare these results with the objective scores for both L2 grammar and speaking, which are presented in Table 2.2.

As can be observed in Table 2.2, both groups did not differ significantly when it came to the L2 proficiency test and L2 speaking test results. It is important to note that in both cases the pre-SA students scored somewhat higher than the at-home students, but in each case, these differences in scores were not statistically significant. The next step of the analysis was to compare the mean scores for speaking abilities on the basis of five different skills: pronunciation, vocabulary, accuracy, communication and fluency. Detailed results of the *t*-test analysis are presented in Table 2.3.

Table 2.3 L2 Speaking Abilities – At-home vs. Stay Abroad Group

Variable		M	SD	t	df	p-Value
Accuracy	At-home students	7.93	1.68	2.46	75	.016
	Pre-SA students	7.02	1.54			
Vocabulary	At-home students	7.68	1.82	1.81	75	.073
	Pre-SA students	6.95	1.68			
Fluency	At-home students	5.28	1.11	−5.37	75	.001
	Pre-SA students	7.43	2.24			
Pronunciation	At-home students	7.81	1.80	−.130	75	.897
	Pre-SA students	7.86	1.71			
Communication	At-home students	6.76	1.52	−5.62	75	.001
	Pre-SA students	8.71	1.51			

With regard to L2 speaking abilities, the results presented in Table 2.3 clearly show some differences between the scores of the pre-SA students and at-home students. The at-home students had higher scores in L2 speaking accuracy and vocabulary but their scores were statistically significantly higher only for accuracy ($t = 2.46, p = .016$), showing medium effect size. On the other hand, pre-SA students scored significantly higher on L2 fluency ($t = -5.37, p = .001$) and communication ($t = -5.62, p = .001$), skills that in both cases showed large effect sizes. At the same time, both groups received almost identical scores on L2 pronunciation. Based on the results presented, it could be concluded that although there were no statistically significant differences in the overall scores on L2 proficiency tests among the pre-SA and at-home students, there were some differences in speaking ability scores in both groups under investigation. Consequently, the aforementioned discrepancies may have influenced the informants' scores on self-perceived L2 speaking proficiency, which was the only reported variable that statistically differentiated both groups in self-perceived L2 proficiency.

The second research question concerned possible differences in the personality profiles of the pre-SA students and the at-home students. In order to answer this question, the participants' scores on the Big Five Personality Questionnaire, MPQ and TEIQue were analysed. Detailed results of the *t*-test analyses for each personality questionnaire are presented in Table 2.4.

The results of the Big Five personality test show that the participants significantly differed only in two personality traits: extraversion ($t = -4.63, p = .001$) and agreeableness ($t = -2.63, p = .010$). The effect size was large for extraversion and medium for agreeableness. In both cases, the pre-SA students obtained statistically higher scores than the at-home students. Therefore, it could be concluded that the participants of the present study who are outgoing, sociable and optimistic (extraversion) as well as kind, cooperative, warm and considerate (agreeableness) tend to self-select themselves to take part in the Erasmus+ mobility programme more often than informants who scored lower on these personality traits. Regarding the remaining results, at-home participants scored slightly higher on the personality traits of conscientiousness and

Table 2.4 The Big Five Personality Questionnaire – At-home vs. Stay Abroad Group

Variable		M	SD	t	df	p-Value
Extraversion	At-home students	31.22	6.22	−4.63	75	.001
	Pre-SA students	38.16	6.98			
Agreeableness	At-home students	43.60	4.98	−2.63	75	.010
	Pre-SA students	46.18	3.42			
Conscientiousness	At-home students	38.00	5.66	.436	75	.664
	Pre-SA students	37.45	6.30			
Emotional stability	At-home students	31.07	10.03	1.167	75	.247
	Pre-SA students	28.56	8.07			
Intellect	At-home students	38.02	5.38	−.507	75	.614
	Pre-SA students	38.64	5.69			

emotional stability and almost identically when it comes to the personality trait of intellect. However, these results were not statistically significant.

In the case of the results of the MPQ, as presented in Table 2.5, it can be noted that scores on cultural empathy ($t = -3.74$, $p = .001$) and open-mindedness ($t = -2.84$, $p = .006$) were significantly different among informants in the pre-SA group and the at-home group. In both cases, pre-SA participants scored statistically higher than the at-home students. However, in the first case, the reported effect size was large and in the second one, it was medium. Consequently, it could be hypothesized that those participants who are able to identify with the feelings, thoughts and behaviours of people who are members of other different cultures (cultural empathy) as well as those who are open and unprejudiced when encountering people outside of their own cultural group (open-mindedness) decide to take part in the SA programme to a greater extent than those who scored lower on these personality traits. Concerning other MPQ traits, both groups scored almost identically on flexibility and social initiative traits, and the at-home students received slightly higher scores on emotional stability in comparison to the SA students. Nevertheless, these differences did not reach statistic significance.

The results of the statistic analysis concerning trait emotional intelligence, which are presented in Table 2.6, showed that the informants scored significantly differently on only one EI trait, namely a global trait EI ($t = -2.41$, $p = .018$), where the pre-SA students obtained statistically higher scores than the at-home students, showing medium effect size. Therefore, it could be speculated that those informants who are able to recognize their own and others' emotions, as well as to manage and adjust emotions to adapt to environments or achieve one's goals, tend to enrol in the Erasmus+ mobility programme more often than the informants who lack these abilities. When it comes to students' scores on the remaining four factors of sociability, emotionality, self-control and well-being, the pre-SA students obtained slightly higher results on all of the factors mentioned apart from self-control, where the at-home group scored slightly higher. At the same time, it needs to be considered that the differences reported were not statistically significant.

Table 2.5 Multicultural Personality Questionnaire – At-home vs. Stay Abroad Group

Variable		M	SD	t	df	p-Value
Cultural empathy	At-home students	32.52	3.09	−3.74	75	.001
	Pre-SA students	35.21	3.21			
Flexibility	At-home students	30.15	5.62	−.405	75	.678
	Pre-SA students	30.64	5.13			
Social initiative	At-home students	24.60	4.65	−.049	75	.961
	Pre-SA students	24.64	4.0			
Emotional stability	At-home students	28.10	3.40	−1.86	75	.067
	Pre-SA students	26.55	3.89			
Open-mindedness	At-home students	29.42	3.68	−2.84	75	.006
	Pre-SA students	31.78	3.58			

Table 2.6 Trait Emotional Intelligence Questionnaire – At-home vs. Stay Abroad Group

Variable		M	SD	t	df	p-Value
Global trait EI	At-home students	132.5	10.40	−2.41	75	.018
	Pre-SA students	137.6	8.23			
Sociability	At-home students	27.07	5.15	−.539	75	.591
	Pre-SA students	28.64	5.80			
Emotionality	At-home students	39.81	8.62	−1.06	75	.292
	Pre-SA students	41.07	7.91			
Self-control	At-home students	30.42	6.99	.710	75	.480
	Pre-SA students	29.43	5.02			
Well-being	At-home students	34.32	6.23	.539	75	.591
	Pre-SA students	38.53	5.84			

Discussion

The current study was designed to assess group-related differences concerning psychological variables as well as initial levels of L2 proficiency in the self-selection process underpinning participation in SA programmes. The first research question concerned possible differences in the pre-departure L2 proficiency levels among sojourners and non-sojourners. The results of our study showed that there were no statistically significant differences between both groups under investigation when it comes to their written and oral L2 proficiency test scores as well as self-perceived L2 proficiency. However, after more detailed analyses, the pre-SA students scored significantly higher on such L2 speaking skills as fluency and communication, whereas the at-home students significantly outperformed the pre-SA students on accuracy. Additionally, the pre-SA students also scored significantly higher on self-perceived L2 speaking proficiency. These results could be explained by the fact that pre-SA students also scored significantly higher on the personality trait of extraversion, which is directly related to speaking in a foreign language. Previous studies reported positive correlations between extraversion and fluency (Dewaele, 1996, 2007; Hassan, 2001; Ockey, 2011; Ożańska-Ponikwia, 2016, 2017; van Deale et al., 2006) but not accuracy (Dewaele and Furnham, 2000). Indeed, it has been suggested that 'extraverts' better stress-resistance and better short-term memory allow them to maintain automaticity of speech production when they are under some sort of arousal/stress while introverts slide back to controlled processing which overloads their working memory. This short-term memory advantage does not make the extraverts "better" learners in terms of errors but better "performers" in terms of fluency' (Dewaele and Furnham, 2000, cited in Ożańska-Ponikwia and Dewaele, 2012, p. 120).

Therefore, it could be speculated that the personality profiles of our informants influenced both their self-perceptions concerning global L2 speaking proficiency and specific L2 speaking abilities concerning fluency and communication (for the pre-SA students), along with accuracy (for the at-home students).

Addressing the second research question which concerned possible differences in the personality profiles of the pre-sojourners and non-sojourners, data analysis showed that there were indeed some significant differences in the test scores among informants of our study. The pre-SA students scored significantly higher on personality traits such as extraversion, agreeableness, cultural empathy, open-mindedness and the global trait of EI. Consequently, when it comes to the personality profiles of the informants of the present study who self-selected to take part in the Erasmus+ mobility programme, they could be characterized as being sociable, outgoing, friendly (extraversion); cooperative, helpful, good-natured and considerate (agreeableness); able to identify with the feelings, thoughts and behaviour of individuals from different cultural backgrounds (cultural empathy); having an open and unprejudiced attitude towards other groups, cultural values and norms and being open to new ideas (open-mindedness); having the capability to recognize their own emotions and those of others as well as to use emotional information to guide thinking and behaviour, and manage and adjust emotions to adapt to environments or achieve one's goal (EI). The findings reported are in line with some previous studies which show that the personality traits of extraversion, openness and agreeableness as well as EI traits are significantly related not only to intercultural adjustment (Harrison and Voelker, 2008; Savicki et al., 2004) but also to mobility patterns (Jokela, 2009; Jokela et al., 2008; Silventoinen et al., 2008). In the case of the self-selection process in an SA context, some previous studies have also shown that higher pre-departure levels of such personality traits as extraversion, agreeableness and openness (Greischel, Noack and Neyer, 2016; Niehoff, Petersdotter and Freund, 2017; Zimmermann and Neyer, 2013) are observed among self-selected SA students. However, this study is innovative in incorporating EI as a possible factor influencing the self-selection process in an SA context. The results reported showed that EI might, in fact, influence the decision to take part in the Erasmus+ mobility programme. Recall that the pre-SA students in our study were shown to score significantly higher on this personality trait.

Conclusions

The literature overview we presented at the outset, as well as the results of the present study, showed that personality and EI underpin the self-selection process in SA mobility (Greischel, Noack and Neyer, 2016; Zimmermann and Neyer, 2013). At the same time, it has been noted in a number of studies that they might also play a role when it comes to adaptation in the host culture as well as frequency of L2 use (Arvidsson et al., 2018; Basow and Gaugler, 2017; Harrison and Voelker, 2008; Ożańska-Ponikwia and Dewaele, 2012; Savicki et al., 2004). It was even argued that EI might impact frequency of L2 use while abroad, which leads to establishing larger social networks, better cultural adaptation, greater satisfaction with the SA experience as well as greater L2 gains (Ożańska-Ponikwia, Carlet and Pujol Valls, 2019).

The results of the present study clearly show that learner personality profiles should be taken into account when planning and encouraging participation in SA programmes. The outcomes presented contribute to the already existing body of knowledge, allowing stakeholders to understand the self-selection process better and to implement certain actions in order to encourage more students to participate in SA programmes, as well as to maximize understanding of study abroad by taking into account various student profiles and their needs and expectations.

The present study is not devoid of some limitations. The first one concerns the sample size which is relatively small and consists of students who were language specialists, thus representing a narrow age range and academic background. Another important issue concerns their countries of origin as well as some discrepancies in their L2 proficiency scores. In future, a replication study should be conducted with a larger, more balanced sample so that more robust claims can be made.

Acknowledgements

The data collection and analyses were possible thanks to a Short-term Scientific Mission (STSM) grant awarded by COST Action CA15130 'Study Abroad Research in European Perspective'.

References

Arvidsson, K., Eyckmans, J., Rosier, A., and Forsberg Lundell, F. (2018), 'Self-perceived Linguistic Progress, Target Language Use and Personality Development during Study Abroad', *Study Abroad Research in Second Language Acquisition and International Education*, 3 (1), 144–66.
Baker-Smemoe, W., Dewey, D. P., Bown, J., and Martinsen, R. A. (2014), 'Variables Affecting L2 Gains during Study Abroad', *Foreign Language Annals*, 47, 464–86.
Basow, S. A., and Gaugler, T. (2017), 'Predicting Adjustment of U.S. College Students Studying Abroad: Beyond the Multicultural Personality', *International Journal of Intercultural Relations*, 56, 39–51.
Costa, P. T., and McCrae, R. R. (1992), *Revised NEO Personality Inventory (NEO-PI-R) and NEO Five-Factor Inventory (NEO-FFI) Professional Manual*, Odessa, FL: Psychological Assessment Resources.
Dewaele, J.-M. (1996), 'How to Measure Formality of Speech? A Model of Synchronic Variation', in K. Sajavaara, and C. Fairweather (eds.), *Approaches to Second Language Acquisition, Jyväskylä Cross-Language Studies* Vol. 17, 119–33, Jyväskylä: University of Jyväskylä.

Dewaele, J.-M. (2007), 'The Effect of Multilingualism, Sociobiographical and Situational Factors on Communicative Anxiety and Foreign Language Anxiety of Mature Language Learners', *The International Journal of Bilingualism*, 11 (4), 391–410.

Dewaele, J.-M., and Furnham, A. (2000), 'Personality and Speech Production: A Pilot Study of Second Language Learners', *Personality and Individual Differences*, 28, 355–65.

Dewey, D., Belnap, R., and Hillstrom, R. (2013), 'Social Network Development, Language Use, and Language Acquisition during Study Abroad: Arabic Language Learners' Perspectives', *Frontiers: The Interdisciplinary Journal of Study Abroad*, 22, 84–110.

Gabel, R. S., Dolan, S. L., and Cerdin, J. L. (2005), 'Emotional Intelligence as Predictor of Cultural Adjustment for Success in Global Assignments', *Career Development International*, 10 (5), 375–95.

Goldberg, L. R. (1992), 'The Development of Markers for the Big-Five Factor Structure', *Psychological Assessment*, 4 (1), 26–42.

Greischel, H., Noack, P., and Neyer, F. (2016), 'Sailing Uncharted Waters: Adolescent Personality Development and Social Relationship Experiences during a Year Abroad', *Journal of Youth and Adolescence*, 45, 2307–20.

Harrison, J. K., and Voelker, E. (2008), 'Two Personality Variables and the Cross-cultural Adjustment of Study Abroad Students', *Frontiers: The Interdisciplinary Journal of Study Abroad*, 17, 69–87.

Hassan, B. A. (2001), *Extraversion/Introversion and Gender in Relation to the English Pronunciation Accuracy of Arabic-speaking College Students*, Mansoura, Egypt: College of Education, Mansoura University.

Hessel, G. (2017), 'A New Take on Individual Differences in L2 Proficiency Gain during Study Abroad', *System*, 66, 39–55.

Huang, T.-J., Chi, S.-C., and Lawler, J. J. (2005), 'The Relationship between Expatriates' Personality Traits and Their Adjustment to International Assignments', *International Journal of Human Research Management*, 16, 1656–70.

Hutteman, R., Nestler, S., Wagner, J., Egloff, B., and Back, M. D. (2015), 'Wherever I May Roam: Processes of Self-esteem Development from Adolescence to Emerging Adulthood in the Context of International Student Exchange', *Journal of Personality and Social Psychology*, 108 (5), 767–83.

Isabelli-García, C. (2006), 'Study Abroad Social Networks, Motivation, and Attitudes: Implications for Second Language Acquisition', in M. DuFon, and E. Churchill (eds.), *Language Learners in Study Abroad Contexts*, 231–58, Clevedon: Multilingual Matters.

Jassawalla, A., Truglia, C., and Garvey, J. (2004), 'Cross-cultural Conflict and Expatriate Manager Adjustment: An Exploratory Study', *Management Decision*, 42 (7), 837–49.

Jokela, M. (2009), 'Personality Predicts Migration within and between U.S. States', *Journal of Research in Personality*, 43, 79–83.

Jokela, M., Elovainio, M., Kivimäki, M., and Keltikangas-Järvinen, L. (2008), 'Temperament and Migration Patterns in Finland', *Psychological Science*, 19, 831–7.

Kinginger, C. (2015), 'Language Socialization in the Homestay: American High School Students in China', in R. Mitchell, N. Tracy-Ventura, and K. McManus (eds.), *Social Interaction, Identity and Language Learning during Residence Abroad*, EUROSLA Monographs 4, 53–74, Amsterdam: European Second Language Association.

Llanes, À. (2011), 'The Many Faces of Study Abroad: An Update on the Research on L2 Gains Emerged during a Study Abroad Experience', *International Journal of Multilingualism*, 8, 189–215.

Lounsbury, J. W., Loveland, J. L., and Gibson, L. W. (2003), 'An Investigation of Big Five Personality Traits in Relation to the Psychological Sense of Community', *Journal of Community Psychology*, 31 (5), 531–41.

Martinsen, R. A. (2010), 'Predicting Changes in Cultural Sensitivity among Students of Spanish during Short-term Study Abroad', *Hispania*, 94, 121–42.

Martinsen, R. A., and Alvord, S. M. (2012), 'On the Relationship between L2 Pronunciation and Culture', *Spanish in Context*, 9, 443–65.

Martinsen, R. A., Baker, W., Dewey, D., Bown, J., and Johnson, C. (2010), 'Exploring Diverse Settings for Language Acquisition and Use: Comparing Study Abroad, Service Learning Abroad, and Foreign Language Housing', *Applied Language Learning*, 20, 45–69.

Matthews, G., Deary, I. J., and Whiteman, M. C. (2003), *Personality Traits*, Cambridge: Cambridge University Press.

Niehoff, E., Petersdotter, L., and Freund, P. (2017), 'International Sojourn Experience and Personality Development: Selection and Socialization Effects of Studying Abroad and the Big Five', *Personality and Individual Differences*, 112, 55–61.

Ockey, G. (2011), 'Self-consciousness and Assertiveness as Explanatory Variables of L2 Oral Ability: A Latent Variable Approach', *Language Learning*, 61, 968–89.

Ożańska-Ponikwia, K. (2016), 'Personality, Emotional Intelligence and L2 Use in an Immigrant and Non-immigrant Context', in D. Gabryś-Barker, and D. Gałajda (eds.), *Positive Psychology Perspectives on Foreign Language Learning and Teaching, Second Language Learning and Teaching*, 175–92, Berlin: Springer.

Ożańska-Ponikwia, K. (2017), 'Extraverts and Introverts in the EFL Classroom Setting', in E. Piechurska-Kuciel, E. Szymańska Czaplak, and M. Szyszka (eds.), *At the Crossroads: Challenges of Foreign Language Learning*, 93–106, Berlin: Springer.

Ożańska-Ponikwia, K., Carlet, A., and Pujol Valls, M. (2019), 'L2 Gain or L2 Pain? A Comparative Case Study of the Target Language Development among the Erasmus+ Mobility Students and at Home Students', *Theory and Practice of Second Language Acquisition*, 5 (1), 73–92.

Ożańska-Ponikwia, K., and Dewaele, J.-M. (2012), 'Personality and L2 Use: The Advantage of Being Openminded and Self-confident in an Immigrant Context', *EUROSLA Yearbook*, 12, 112–34.

Petrides, K. V., and Furnham, A. (2003), 'Trait Emotional Intelligence: Behavioural Validation in Two Studies of Emotion Recognition and Reactivity to Mood Induction', *European Journal of Personality*, 17, 39–57.

Petrides, K. V., Furnham, A., and Mavraveli, S. (2007), 'Trait Emotional Intelligence: Moving Forward in the Field of EI', in G. Matthews, M. Zeidner, and R. Roberts (eds.), *Emotional Intelligence: Knowns and Unknowns*, 151–66, Oxford: Oxford University Press.

Sanz, C. (2014), 'Contributions of Study Abroad Research to Our Understanding of SLA Processes and Outcomes: The SALA Project, an Appraisal', in C. Pérez-Vidal (ed.), *Language Acquisition in Study Abroad and Formal Instruction Contexts*, 1–13, Philadelphia, PA/Amsterdam: John Benjamins.

Savicki, V., Downing-Burnette, R., Heller, L., Binder, F., and Suntinger, W. (2004), 'Contrasts, Changes, and Correlates in Actual and Potential Intercultural Adjustment', *International Journal of Intercultural Relations*, 28, 311–29.

Silventoinen, K., Hammar, N., Hedlund, E., Koskenvuo, M., Rönnemaa, T., and Kaprio, J. (2008), 'Selective International Migration by Social Position, Health Behaviour and Personality', *European Journal of Public Health*, 18, 150–5.

van Deale, S., Housen, A., Pierrard, M., and Debruyn, L. (2006), 'The Effect of Extraversion on Oral L2 Proficiency', *EUROSLA Yearbook*, 6, 213–36.

Van Der Zee, K. I., and Van Oudenhoven, J. P. (2000), 'The Multicultural Personality Questionnaire: A Multidimensional Instrument of Multicultural Effectiveness', *European Journal of Personality*, 14 (4), 291–309.

Vande Berg, M., Connor-Linton, J., and Paige, R. M. (2009), 'The Georgetown Consortium Project: Interventions for Student Learning Abroad', *Frontiers: The Interdisciplinary Journal of Study Abroad*, 18, 1–75.

Zimmermann, J., and Neyer, F. J. (2013), 'Do We Become a Different Person When Hitting the Road? Personality Development of Sojourners', *Journal of Personality and Social Psychology*, 105 (3), 515–30.

3

Study abroad marketing and L2 self-efficacy beliefs

Emre Güvendir, Meltem Acar-Güvendir and Sinem Dündar
Trakya University

Introduction

Marketing is commonly used by study abroad (SA) institutions to encourage students to participate in their language programmes. As Zemach-Bersin (2009) noted, once university students step onto their home campuses, they are exposed to SA advertisements that urge them to spend a spring break, summer, semester or year encountering new people, places and languages in a destination of their choice. Hence, students both unconsciously and consciously absorb the images and rhetoric of SA advertisements which influence how they approach SA programmes. These advertisements direct students to their websites where several means and marketing content that promote study abroad include the use of images of students and travel options; interactive items such as maps; testimonials of student success; and descriptive instances of SA involvement (Apperson, 2015; Michelson and Alvarez Valencia, 2016). A website is a key Internet marketing resource because 'no matter how you choose to deploy web content to reach your buyers, the place that brings everything together in a unified place is a content rich website' (Scott, 2009, p. 101). A number of studies have shown that students also seek information about SA programmes through sources such as 'newspaper advertising' and 'television advertising' (Güvendir, 2017; Michelson and Alvarez Valencia, 2016). Güvendir's (2017) research revealed that SA marketing provides persuasive information for learners as the majority of his participants reported that their decision to participate in an SA programme was influenced by SA websites and student testimonials that depicted learning English abroad as a simple and enjoyable process. SA websites function as semiotic spaces that create and mobilize various discourses and ideologies through multimodal semiotic resources such as language, visual elements and layouts (Michelson and Alvarez Valencia, 2016). Although pre-sojourn exposure to SA marketing is widespread among SA candidates, the potential of the marketing content to influence learner beliefs and shape their expectations has not attracted the attention of SA researchers. In her comprehensive review on beliefs about language learning in study abroad, Surtees (2016) aimed to draw the attention of SA researchers to learners' pre-sojourn beliefs. She stressed that research on learners' pre-sojourn beliefs has in the main presented such beliefs as learner-internal and consequences of individuals' actions, knowledge and desires. Surtees calls for re-conceptualizing these beliefs as socially and historically created and to study programmatic, institutional and interactional roles in their formation.

A potential belief construct that marketing influences is self-efficacy. According to the social cognitive framework for marketing, self-efficacy is one of the most central individual elements that marketing can affect. Supporting this argument, studies on marketing have found that the persuasiveness of marketing tools such as advertisements stems from their emphasis on increasing consumer self-efficacy beliefs and creating projected self-efficacy images through the process of vicarious learning and social persuasions (Bandura, 2001; Ben-Ami et al., 2014; Combs, 2016; Mukhopadhyay and Johar, 2005; Pajares, 2002). Marketers aim to increase individuals' self-efficacy beliefs by using advertising messages that underline users' capacity to challenge problems and deal with their apprehensions and, accordingly, encourage consumers to buy the product (Ben-Ami et al., 2014).

Self-efficacy is a key concept in L2 learning and teaching as self-efficacy beliefs impact task choice, determination, persistence and success (Bandura, 1997; Usher and Pajares, 2008). Furthermore, studies on L2 learners' beliefs argue that understanding language learners' beliefs is vital as these beliefs shape their conceptualizations of language learning, influence their L2 learning attitudes, govern how they see the host culture and community, and the language learning process, and influence their use of learning strategies and emotional states (Ellis, 1994; Horwitz, 1999; Zaykovskaya, Rawal and De Costa, 2017). It is also stressed that understanding language learners' beliefs is significant in order to implement effective language teaching strategies and procedures and provide consistent language instruction (Horwitz, 1999).

Despite the common use of SA marketing tools to promote SA enrolment, no study of marketing's potential to influence learners' perceived self-efficacy beliefs has been reported in the SA literature. SA research has primarily focused on how SA programmes influence students' self-efficacy beliefs (Cubillos and Ilvento, 2012; Milstein, 2005) and how learners' beliefs in general change during the course of study abroad (Amuzie and Winke, 2009; Kaypak and Ortaçtepe, 2014; Tanaka and Ellis, 2003; Yang and Kim, 2011). Considering the common use of marketing tools by SA programmes and their potential to influence learners' pre-sojourn self-efficacy beliefs, this study addresses the research question of how the marketing content on SA websites influences L2 learners' projected self-efficacy beliefs.

Literature review

Self-efficacy

Self-efficacy is one of the main principles of social cognitive theory and has been investigated comprehensively in different research fields. Bandura (1986) defined it as 'people's judgments of their capabilities to organize and execute courses of action required to attain designated types of performances' (p. 391). According to Bandura

(1997), self-efficacy beliefs are principal elements of human functioning. People will commonly only attempt activities they believe they can achieve and will not attempt to try tasks they believe they will fail. 'People's level of motivation, affective states, and actions are based more on what they believe than on what is objectively true' (Bandura, 1997, p. 2).

Self-efficacy beliefs depend on four experiences. These are mastery experiences, vicarious experiences, social persuasions (verbal persuasions) and emotional and physiological states (Bandura, 1994). Mastery experiences are considered as the first and primary source of perceived self-efficacy as they include having direct experiences. According to Bandura (1994), experiencing an achievement, for example in mastering a task, will enhance self-efficacy in that task, while a failure will weaken that efficacy belief especially if it occurs before a sense of efficacy is strongly achieved. The second source of self-efficacy is vicarious experiences. Observation of successful individuals (especially role models) increases perceived self-efficacy. The individual can draw deductions by observing the activities done by other people, this observation being mostly effective in circumstances in which the person has no prior personal involvement. If individuals see the role models as very distinct from themselves, their self-efficacy belief is not much affected by the models' behaviour and the consequences it leads to (Bandura, 1994). The third source of self-efficacy, social persuasions, is commonly used to make individuals believe they possess the skills necessary for accomplishing certain tasks (Bandura, 1994). Such social persuasion is broadly applied in education to encourage learners to believe that they can in fact cope with challenging circumstances. However, overly positive persuasive comments are typically of little use, especially if the person being influenced eventually fails (Bandura, 1997). The fourth source of self-efficacy, emotional and physiological states, comes from one's own physiological and emotional self-reflections during task performance. Stress, anxiety and fear all negatively influence self-efficacy and can lead to a self-fulfilling prediction of failure or incompetence to complete the featured tasks (Pajares, 2002). According to Bandura (1994), individuals are inclined to anticipate achievement, to a larger degree, when they are not overwhelmed by anxiety responses than if they are nervous.

Studies have shown that self-efficacy beliefs impact task selection, determination and success (Schunk and Pajares, 2002; Schunk and Zimmerman, 1994; Usher and Pajares, 2008). Compared with learners who distrusted their learning abilities, those who had high self-efficacy beliefs studied harder, persisted longer when they faced problems and succeeded at a higher level (Schunk and Pajares, 2002). Schunk and Zimmerman (1994) found that training students to have higher self-efficacy beliefs resulted in considerable academic improvement. Similarly, other studies have shown that self-efficacy has a positive relationship with learner achievement and task accomplishment (Usher and Pajares, 2008).

Despite these positive findings, other studies have stressed that learners' self-efficacy beliefs should be realistic. For example, Lerner (1986) suggests that an unrealistically high self-concept may be more of a handicap than an advantage. According to Baumeister, Smart and Boden (1996), students with high but unrealistic self-efficacy beliefs responded negatively to experiences where their real level of competence failed to match their personal judgement. In particular, when students judged their capabilities unrealistically, they adopted maladaptive learning behaviours which resulted in unexpected learning outcomes (Pajares and Graham, 1999). Vancouver, Thomson and Williams (2001) found that high self-efficacy beliefs resulted in overconfidence, relaxation and performance reduction for learners. Self-efficacy is about perceived competence and does not necessarily mean that the individual with high self-efficacy beliefs is a capable person in a particular field. Studies have proposed that most learners overvalue their academic skills (Bandura, 1997). Bandura (1986) claimed, however, that the most beneficial efficacy beliefs are those that slightly surpass one's real skills. To sum up, although self-efficacy beliefs are important for learner achievement, unrealistic high self-efficacy beliefs may result in overconfidence and have the potential to impact the learning process negatively.

Marketing and self-efficacy

Self-efficacy has drawn the attention of researchers in marketing with the purpose of examining whether increasing customers' self-efficacy elevates their propensity to buy products (Mukhopadhyay and Johar, 2005). Marketing research on self-efficacy has been based on the proposition that by increasing potential buyers' self-efficacy, marketers may be able to encourage them to overcome their conflicts about the product and have higher inclination to buy it (Ben-Ami et al., 2014). How something is presented to the audience aims to shape their perceptions on different issues and affects the choices individuals make about how to process that information (Goffman, 1974). According to the social cognitive framework, marketing tools function within the often vast and intricate network of personal, environmental and behavioural elements that impact individuals. They, then, are but one component in the group of variables that make up the numerous underlying networks which direct thought, affect and emotion (Combs, 2016). The social cognitive framework for marketing stresses that individuals form mental connections by attending to the messages displayed in marketing tools through vicarious learning, and 'in terms of subsequently affecting cognition, affect, and behaviour, self-efficacy is one of the most important personal determinants that marketing can influence' (Combs, 2016, p. 31).

One of the common marketing strategies used by SA organizations is the use of models. As in the case of student testimonials, SA websites refer to student narratives that reflect how valuable the SA process was for the learner who has already participated in the related programme. Spillinger and Parush (2012) found that the existence of testimonials on shopping websites had a positive influence on consumers and was associated with increased trust. According to Bandura (2001), 'the actions of models acquire the power to activate and channel behaviour when they are good predictors for observers that positive results can be gained by similar conduct' (p. 282). He further stressed that the strength of vicarious influences can be heightened by presenting modelled acts resulting in rewarding outcomes. Drawing on data that resemble the model creates a positive attitude towards the product, with some marketing content depicting individuals significantly benefiting from the products marketed. 'Modelling influences serve diverse functions – as tutors, motivators, inhibitors, disinhibitors, social prompters, emotion arousers, and shapers of values and conceptions of reality' (Bandura, 2001, p. 283). Referring to Bandura's (2001) dual paths of media influence, Pajares (2002) stated that sources of self-efficacy can be both vicarious experience and verbal persuasions. Accordingly, the modelling that the viewers are exposed to offers vicarious experiences and any data based on advertisement messages transmitted among individuals provide verbal persuasions.

Study abroad and learner beliefs

Learner beliefs are defined as 'student opinions on a variety of issues and controversies related to language learning' (Horwitz, 1988, p. 284). They are an essential constituent of language learning as they govern how learners approach the target language (TL), the community where it is used and the process of language learning itself (Zaykovskaya, Rawal and De Costa, 2017). Learner beliefs affect learners' actions, in particular, choice of learning strategies and their emotional states such as confidence and anxiety (Ellis, 1994). While the earlier studies on learner beliefs proposed that beliefs be considered as fixed perceptual considerations of learners, further studies increasingly started to approach learner beliefs as complex and multidimensional, and dynamic (Amuzie and Winke, 2009; Tanaka and Ellis, 2003; Wesely, 2012) due to their dynamic contextual representations (Zaykovskaya, Rawal and De Costa, 2017). Despite these contrasting opinions on the nature of learner beliefs, learner beliefs contribute to the SA experience process, as learner beliefs about language learning are related to learners' SA expectations, attachment, achievement and satisfaction (Kaypak and Ortaçtepe, 2014).

Research on learner beliefs and study abroad has primarily focused on how SA experiences have influenced learner beliefs (Amuzie and Winke; Kaypak and Ortaçtepe, 2014; Tanaka and Ellis, 2003; Yang and Kim, 2011). Using interviews, Amuzie and Winke's (2009) comparative study examined learners' pre- and post-sojourn beliefs. Their study revealed that learner beliefs on learner autonomy underwent changes, which were more significant as the duration of stay abroad increased. On the other hand, participants' pre-sojourn self-efficacy beliefs were significantly higher than their mid-sojourn efficacy beliefs, demonstrating a noticeable decline in confidence. These authors conclude that belief systems are dynamic, socially constructed and influenced by learning context. Kaypak and Ortaçtepe's (2014) research on fifty-three Turkish exchange students found no statistically significant changes in their beliefs about English language learning after spending approximately five months abroad. However, the authors reported that SA experiences caused decreased self-confidence and self-efficacy for their participants. Tanaka and Ellis (2003) compared Japanese learners' pre- and post-sojourn beliefs and found statistically significant changes for the learners' beliefs in terms of self-efficacy and confidence. They reported significant increases in self-efficacy ratings for their participants. Similarly, Pyper and Slagter (2015) also found significant increases in self-efficacy beliefs for 135 American students at the end of their SA experience. In a case study of two Korean ESL learners, Yang and Kim (2011) found that their two learners' beliefs evolved continuously in line with their experiences abroad and their L2 goals.

Zaykovskaya, Rawal and De Costa (2017) stressed that although several earlier studies examined the transformation of learner beliefs with regard to the SA experience, notably absent is an examination of the influence of the pre-existing system of learner beliefs on an SA experience. On the basis of this absence in the field, they explored the beliefs of an American college learner of Russian and how these beliefs shaped his SA experience. Their findings show that the learner's pre-sojourn views about the TL and the community had positive influences during his stay in Russia. For example, his optimistic beliefs regarding Russia and the Russian culture kept him interested and supported him in handling culture shock. Another topic that has not drawn enough attention is how learners' pre-sojourn beliefs regarding study abroad are constructed. Surtees (2016) proposed to identify where learners' beliefs come from and how institutions and other stakeholders co-construct these beliefs which are so central to participants' subjective impressions of their SA experience. Following Surtees's proposal, Güvendir (2017) found that L2 learners' pre-sojourn beliefs regarding SA participation are influenced by the individuals and social circles with which L2 learners interact, their educational experiences, local discourses about second language proficiency, employment opportunities, recruitment literature and SA marketing. However, more research is needed to identify how much and in what direction these factors influence L2 learners' pre-sojourn beliefs and the influence of the pre-existing system of learner beliefs on study abroad.

Method

Research design

The study adopts a quantitative approach, where quantitative research aims to 'establish relationships between variables and look for and sometimes explain the causes of such relationships' (Frankel and Wallen, 2009, p. 15). It enables the scientist to use a pre-constructed standardized instrument into which the participants' varying viewpoints and practices are predicted to fit (Kumar, 2011). In particular, the study used a one-group pre-test and post-test design which included the measurement of a single group not only after being exposed to an intervention but also before (Frankel and Wallen, 2009). 'A before-and-after design can be described as two sets of cross-sectional data collection points on the same population to find the change in the phenomenon or variable(s) between two points in time. The change is measured by comparing the difference in the phenomenon or variable(s) before and after the intervention' (Kumar, 2011, p. 107). The disadvantage of this design is that it lacks a control group and random assignment (Frankel and Wallen, 2009). In the current research, the study group was selected by considering L2 proficiency, educational status, plans to study abroad, previous use of SA websites and previous travel abroad. During the design of the study, attempts to create a control group resulted in non-equivalent groups as the number of volunteers who displayed similar criteria was limited. Thus, the research proceeded with a one-group pre-test and post-test design which was the only available option to examine the influence of the intervention.

Participants

The participants of the study included forty (twenty-seven females and thirteen males) university students in Turkey during the 2018–19 academic year. As noted, the participants were selected by considering their educational status, L2 levels, plans to study abroad, previous use of SA websites and previous travel abroad. All the participants were university students attending the same university. Their English proficiency level was B1 on the Common European Framework of Reference (CEFR). All the participants reported that they were planning to study English abroad through a short-term SA programme. Although they all had the intention of attending a short-term summer study programme in an English-speaking country in the future, none of them had examined the websites of SA programmes prior to the study. The average age of the participants was twenty-two years. At the time the study was conducted, the participants had never travelled or studied abroad before. Learners volunteered to participate in the current research.

Data collection and intervention procedure

The study used Güvendir, Acar Güvendir and Dündar's (in press) 'Study Abroad and L2 Self-Efficacy Beliefs Scale' (see Appendix) to measure the participants' projected self-efficacy beliefs. The scale has twenty-four items and four factors that focus on projected self-efficacy beliefs in relation to the four skills in English (7 listening, 4 reading, 4 speaking and 9 writing). The Cronbach alpha coefficient score of the whole scale is .94, with a Cronbach alpha coefficient score of .87 for the listening factor, .82 for the reading factor, .84 for the speaking factor and .91 for the writing factor. 'An Alpha score above 0.75 is generally taken to indicate a scale of high reliability. 0.5 to 0.75 is generally accepted as indicating a moderately reliable scale, while a figure below this generally indicates a scale of low reliability' (Hinton et al., 2004, p. 363). Hence, the scores for the whole scale and each factor indicate high reliability.

Additionally, a Cronbach alpha coefficient was calculated to find the reliability of the obtained data from the participants of the current research. While the reliability of the pre-test data was .843, the reliability of the data gathered for the post-test scores was .817. Hence, the reliability of the pre-test and post-test data collected from the scale was high. Additionally, the Cronbach alpha coefficient was calculated for each factor in the scale. Accordingly, the reliability value for listening pre-test scores was .713 and .641 for post-test listening scores; .549 for reading pre-test scores, .646 for post-test reading scores; .737 for pre-test speaking scores, .734 for post-test speaking scores; .616 for pre-test writing scores and .722 for post-test writing scores. Consequently, the reliability of the pre-test and post-test data obtained from both scales was moderately reliable as the values were between .5 and .75.

The instrument calls for the participants to imagine attending a short-term (maximum six months) SA programme and answer questions that aim to measure their L2 self-efficacy beliefs at the end of that programme. The instrument was administered at the beginning and at the end of the intervention which was spread over twenty days (five days per week, spread over four weeks). The intervention included the participants' exposure to the marketing material provided on the websites of twenty popular international SA schools that had representatives in Turkey.

The participants consulted only one website individually for one hour each day under the researcher's supervision. The researcher chose the website each day and reminded the participants to pay particular attention to student testimonials, information about the format and content of the language courses and the opening pages of the websites that included the majority of the marketing material. Following the scanning process, they were given tasks that required them to write overviews of the language schools advertised on the SA websites. The researcher requested the participants not to share their ideas with each other. At the end of the intervention process, they were asked to compare the programmes and convey their personal preferences and ideas about the programmes to the researcher in the format of a written report.

In addition to information about their language courses, the language programme websites presented colourful images of people and travel destinations; entertainment options; brochures, housing information; interactive content such as maps, calendars and news; student testimonials reporting success stories; and descriptive examples of SA experiences. None of these websites mentioned any problems that students might face during their stay abroad. The opening pages of the websites that were examined by the participants used messages such as 'unique experience', 'learn English fast', 'guaranteed progress', 'learn real English', 'unforgettable English courses', 'boost your English skills', to frame the programmes and the experiences of the SA alumni positively. Some of the information related to the courses offered claimed that the courses will help learners:

- boost their English skills dramatically in a short space of time,
- quickly achieve English fluency, learn grammar and vocabulary that will be useful in everyday situations,
- pass specific exams such as TOEFL or IELTS,
- make the fastest possible progress with their English abilities,
- improve their English-language skills, whatever their current language levels are,
- achieve a detailed understanding of the English language,
- gain a deeper immersion in English,
- master difficult grammatical structures and fine-tune their pronunciation,
- read complex texts and build a large working vocabulary,
- explore current events and different cultures,
- go beyond the classroom into the community by introducing them to social activities and local events,
- practice and test their English skills.

Correspondingly, student testimonials that were presented on the websites included achievement stories and did not provide any details about individual differences, creating the impression that anyone enrolled in one of the programmes will inevitably succeed. The following points were highlighted in the student testimonials:

- considerable L2 improvement in all skills in a short time,
- feeling self-confident and more international,

- achievement in tests such as TOEFL,
- social interaction opportunities with the locals,
- praise for the SA programme in comparison with former learning experiences.

The SA programmes included in this study are located in the United States (7), England (6), Australia (3), Canada (2), New Zealand (1) and Malta (1). According to the Global English Language Market Report (Global Info Research, 2018), these countries are the most popular SA destinations for students who study English. These programmes have Turkish partners who organize the marketing and administration operations and offer information in Turkish for students who are not proficient enough in English to understand the information on the original websites.

Data analysis

As the first step in the data analysis, the study examined the significance of the difference between the pre-test and the post-test scores. In order to determine whether there were any extreme values in the pre-test and post-test scores, all the scores were converted to z scores and these z scores were scaled between +3 and −3 with an average of 0. Values other than these are described as multivariable extreme values and removing these values from the data set is suggested (Walsh and Betz, 1990). 'An extreme value is defined as a data point that deviates so far from the other observations, that it becomes suspicious to be generated by a totally different mechanism or simply by error' (Daroczi, 2015, p. 185). In this study there was no extreme value in the data as all values in the data set were between −3 and +3.

In order to test whether the pre-test and post-test scores were normally distributed, the study examined the skewness and kurtosis values of the scores. The results of the pre-test and post-test scores were found to be normally distributed since the skewness (.355; −.393) and kurtosis (−.557; .209) values were between −1 and +1. Accordingly, the study used a paired samples t-test to analyse the significance of the difference between the pre-test and the post-test scores, taking a .05 significance level.

As the second step of the data analysis, the study focused on the factors of the scale (reading, writing, speaking and listening) independently. It examined the significance of the difference between the factors of the pre-test and the post-test scores of the scale. Similar to the first step in the data analysis, the second step also included identifying the extreme values of the data and examining the normality of distribution. The skewness and kurtosis values of the pre-test and post-test scores according to the factors of the scale are given in Table 3.1.

Table 3.1 shows that the scores other than the post-test scores of the listening and speaking skills are normally distributed since the values are between −1 and +1. Hence, a Wilcoxon test, a non-parametric method, was used to test the significance of the difference between pre-test and post-test scores for listening and speaking. A paired samples t-test was used for the significance of the difference between the pre-test and post-test scores of reading and writing skills.

Table 3.1 Skewness and Kurtosis Values of the Pre-test and Post-test Scores according to the Factors

	Skewness	Kurtosis
Pre-listening	−.263	−.590
Pre-reading	−.247	−.585
Pre-speaking	−.442	−.930
Pre-writing	.383	−.207
Post-listening	−1.240	2.501
Post-reading	−.738	−.558
Post-speaking	−1.180	.509
Post-writing	−.409	−.195

Findings

Table 3.2 displays the results of the *t*-test for the significance of the difference between the pre-test and the post-test scores.

The findings in Table 3.2 show that the difference between the pre-test and post-test scores is statistically significant ($t39 = 6.628; p < .05$) with the post-test score mean ($\bar{X} = 70.350$) being higher than the pre-test score mean ($\bar{X} = 56.525$). This result shows that the participants had higher projected self-efficacy beliefs at the end of the intervention. Additionally, the magnitude of the significant difference between the two means was calculated by the effect size. Accordingly, the obtained value was found to be 1.095. If the effect size is 0, it indicates that the mean is equal to the fixed value to which it is compared. An effect size greater than 1 is considered too large, .8 large, .5 medium and .2 small (Green and Salkind, 2005). According to the effect size obtained here, the difference between pre-test and post-test mean scores is very large.

Table 3.3 shows the results of the Wilcoxon signed rankings test for the significance of the difference between the pre-test and the post-test listening scores.

The results in Table 3.3 show that there is a significant difference between the pre-test and post-test listening factor scores of the students participating in the study ($z = 4.251; p < .01$). The mean and sum of rank scores for the post-test listening factor are higher than the pre-test. This result shows that the participants had higher projected listening self-efficacy beliefs at the end of the intervention. Furthermore, the magnitude of the significant difference between the two means compared was calculated with the effect size. Accordingly, the value obtained was found to be .672. According to the effect size value obtained here, the difference between the average of the pre-test and post-test scores is medium.

Table 3.4 displays the results of the *t*-test for the significance of the difference between the pre-test and the post-test reading scores.

Table 3.4 shows that the difference between the pre-test and post-test scores of the reading factor is statistically significant ($t39 = 5.421; p < .01$). The mean post-test score ($\bar{X} = 11.70$) is higher than the pre-test mean score ($\bar{X} = 8.58$). This finding shows that

Table 3.2 *t*-Test Results for the Pre-test and Post-test Scores

Test	N	M	S	SD	t	p	Effect Size
Pre-test	40	56.525	14.361	39	6.628	.001	1.095
Post-test	40	70.350	13.319				

Table 3.3 Listening Factor: Pre-test and Post-test Wilcoxon Signed Rankings Test Scores

Post-test–Pre-test	N	Mean Rank	Sum of Rank	z	p	Effect Size
Negative ranks	5	11.20	56.00	4.251	.001	.672
Positive ranks	30	19.13	574.00			
Ties	5					
Total	25					

Table 3.4 Reading Factor: Pre-test and Post-test *t*-Test Results

Test	N	M	Std. Dev.	df	t	p	Effect Size
Pre-test	40	8.58	3.622	39	5.421	.001	.857
Post-test	40	11.70	3.708				

Table 3.5 Speaking Factor: Pre-test and Post-test Wilcoxon Signed Rankings Test Scores

Post-test–Pre-test	N	Mean Rank	Sum of Rank	z	p	Effect Size
Negative ranks	8	14.63	117.00	3.260	.001	.515
Positive ranks	27	19.00	513.00			
Ties	5					
Total	25					

the participants had higher projected reading self-efficacy beliefs at the end of the study. The magnitude of the significant difference between the two means was found to be .857. Hence, the difference between pre-test and post-test mean reading factor scores is very large.

Table 3.5 displays the results of the Wilcoxon signed rankings test for the significance of the difference between the pre-test and the post-test speaking factor scores.

The results of the analysis show that there is a significant difference between the pre-test and post-test speaking scores of the students participating in the study ($z = 3.260$; $p < .01$). The mean and sum of rank scores for the post-test speaking factor are higher than the pre-test. The magnitude of the significant difference between the two means is .515 which signals a moderate difference between the average of the pre-test and post-test scores.

Table 3.6 shows the results of the *t*-test for the significance of the difference between the pre-test and the post-test writing factor scores.

Table 3.6 Writing Factor: Pre-test and Post-test *t*-Test Results

Test	N	M	Std. Dev.	df	t	p	Effect Size
Pre-test	40	19.68	5.627	39	4.799	.001	.759
Post-test	40	24.62	6.651				

Table 3.7 Pre-test and Post-test Mean Values

Factors	Pre-test Mean	Post-test Mean
Listening	2.49	3.03
Reading	2.19	2.93
Speaking	2.71	3.21
Writing	2.14	2.74

Note: As different statistical procedures are applied for different purposes, the mean values obtained here from descriptive statistics are different from the mean values obtained from parametric and non-parametric calculations.

The findings in Table 3.6 show that the difference between the pre-test and post-test scores of the writing factor is statistically significant ($t39 = 4.799$; $p < .01$). The mean post-test score ($\bar{X} = 24.62$) is higher than the pre-test mean ($\bar{X} = 19.68$). According to this finding, the participants had higher projected writing self-efficacy beliefs at the end of the intervention procedure. The magnitude of the significant difference between the two means is .759. Hence, the difference between pre-test and post-test mean writing factor scores is large.

Table 3.7 demonstrates the descriptive statistics results in relation to the mean values of the factor scores.

In order to make a comparison between the factors, the total scores obtained from each factor were divided by the number of items in that factor. As a result, the mean comparisons display students' projected self-efficacy beliefs for each factor. The results presented in Table 3.7 show that participants had the highest pre-test and post post-test projected self-efficacy beliefs for the speaking factor (pre-test $\bar{X} = 2.71$; post-test $\bar{X} = 3.21$) followed sequentially by listening (pre-test $\bar{X} = 2.49$; post-test $\bar{X} = 3.03$), reading (pre-test $\bar{X} = 2.19$; post-test $\bar{X} = 2.93$) and writing (pre-test $\bar{X} = 2.14$; post-test $\bar{X} = 2.74$).

Discussion

This study examined how pre-sojourn exposure to SA marketing influenced students' projected L2 self-efficacy beliefs. The findings show that pre-sojourn exposure to the marketed material on SA websites resulted in higher projected L2 self-efficacy beliefs for the participants which support previous research findings that underscore the role of marketing on consumers' self-efficacy beliefs (Ben-Ami et al., 2014; Combs, 2016; Mukhopadhyay and Johar, 2005). Researchers propose that marketing tools increase consumer self-efficacy by demonstrating behaviour models, instruction, encouragement and the reduction of adverse emotions connected with behaviours (Bandura, 1994; Flora and Maibach, 1989). According to Bandura's (1986) sources of self-efficacy, the observation of successful models that display similarities to the learner increases perceived self-efficacy. On the other hand, these observations are more effective in situations in which the individual has no preceding personal involvement. In the present study, the participants had no previous study or travel abroad experiences which made them more open to be influenced by vicarious experiences, as the lack of previous personal involvement increased the potential to be impacted by observing models.

When the study findings are considered within the social cognitive framework for marketing, marketing tools operate within the web of personal, environmental and behavioural structures that impact individuals. As Combs (2016) put it, advertisements, then, are but one constituent in the group of variables that form the numerous underlying networks which direct and regulate thought, affect and emotion. According to Bandura's (1986) social cognitive theory, people do not learn novel behaviours only by trying them and either succeeding or failing but rather by the reproduction of the practices of models. Depending on the outcome of the models' behaviour, the observer may decide to copy the behaviour modelled. Hence, during observational learning, models can also increase or decrease the observer's belief in his/her self-efficacy to enact observed behaviours and bring about desired outcomes from those behaviours. When people recognize similarities between the model and themselves, they believe they can be capable of succeeding. Hence, when SA candidates read student testimonials that mention success stories of other students who struggled with learning an L2 in their home institutions but achieved in the SA programme, they are exposed to persuasive content that matches their current situation.

The study results presented here suggest that exposure to the marketing content on the websites not only influenced the participants' overall self-efficacy beliefs but also developed the participants' higher projected self-efficacy beliefs for each L2 skill. As the websites included promises with regard to proficiency gains across all L2 skills, there was no skill in the current study that was negatively influenced by the marketed content. In relation to projected L2 self-efficacies, the highest scores were obtained for speaking and listening and somewhat lower scores were shown for reading and writing in both the pre- and post-tests. Similarly, participants in Badstübner and Ecke's (2009) research reported higher pre-sojourn projected gains for listening and speaking than reading and writing. According to these authors, students might have been influenced by the widely held belief that one becomes more fluent in the L2 during study abroad. This is based on the general assumption regarding study abroad that naturalistic settings involving informal learning through out-of-class contact with the L2 leads to higher levels of oral proficiency than educational settings where instruction is provided (Tanaka and Ellis, 2003). Our participants' initial projected self-efficacies for speaking and listening might have been influenced by such general SA assumptions. However, higher projected self-efficacies for speaking and listening at the end of the intervention might be an outcome of exposure to the marketing content as the SA websites made promises to help learners quickly achieve English fluency by introducing them to activities and local events that will provide them interactional opportunities to use the L2.

Although high self-efficacy contributes to learning and is desirable for learner achievement (Schunk and Pajares, 2002; Schunk and Zimmerman, 1994; Usher and Pajares, 2008), individuals cannot undertake tasks beyond their capabilities only by believing they can; efficacy will not produce a competent performance in the absence of necessary skills (Pajares et al., 2009). In several studies, students with unrealistic self-efficacy beliefs struggled and reacted adversely to practices where their actual skills and competence failed to match their personal self-efficacy judgements (Baumeister, Smart and Boden, 1996; Lerner, 1986; Pajares and Graham, 1999; Vancouver, Thompson and Williams, 2001). Hence, vicarious experiences and social persuasions used by SA marketing tools which only present positive aspects of study abroad bear the risk of creating unrealistic projected self-efficacy beliefs and SA expectations for L2 learners. Although study abroad has some advantages in terms of L2 improvement (Dewey, 2008; Llanes and Muñoz, 2009; Pérez-Vidal and Juan-Garau, 2009), there are numerous studies that dispute the common belief that study abroad is wholly beneficial for L2 learning and present cases where learners failed to benefit from the SA experience (e.g. Amuzie and Winke, 2009; DeKeyser, 1990; Güvendir, 2017; Wilkinson, 1998). As Marijuan and Sanz (2018) put it, 'the inconclusive findings generated by SA research to date, along with an explosion of new SA programs that differ considerably in terms of length, goals, and features, leave many questions unanswered about the efficacy of SA in terms of L2 gains' (p. 186). Correspondingly, studies examining the influence of SA experiences on self-efficacy beliefs have also found contrasting findings in terms of self-efficacy gains. While Amuzie and Winke (2009) and Kaypak and Ortaçtepe (2014) found that study abroad resulted in decreases in self-efficacy, studies by Tanaka and Ellis (2003) and Pyper and Slagter (2015) found that SA experience increased learners' self-efficacy beliefs. These contrasting findings show that the actual SA experiences do not always increase learners' self-efficacies and may contradict with their pre-sojourn expectations.

By not mentioning the problems that students might face during their stay abroad and not referring to the role of individual differences in SA achievement, SA websites select certain aspects of reality and make them more salient, while leaving other negative aspects out of the package (Michelson and Alvarez Valencia, 2016). These marketing strategies may cause learners to expect miraculous gains from study abroad and ignore their concerns about it. Anticipation of what to experience during study abroad is central in the decision-making process of all students. How accurate such expectations and pre-departure beliefs turn out to be in reality depends on a combination of the kind of information students can access, the reliability of their sources and their ability to interpret this information.

The findings of the current research suggest that there is a need for further inquiry into how learners construct their perceptions of language learning before going abroad and how realistic these perceptions are. This is relevant because studies have shown that the discrepancy between pre-sojourn beliefs and real SA experiences had negative consequences for students who had solely positive pre-sojourn beliefs and thus were not psychologically ready for negative experiences (Jackson, 2019; Mendelson, 2004). In Jackson's (2019) study, the unmet expectations of the participants caused them to spend most of their free time with co-nationals which minimized their social interaction with native speakers and limited their opportunities to use the TL in communicative encounters. Mendelson (2004) underscores the feeling of missed opportunities that some SA students had during the post-sojourn period. She notes that when real SA experiences do not overlap with an established ideal, learners can feel as if their actions were inadequate and that their experience was somehow flawed. According to Mendelson, these feelings of inadequacy may be a result of overestimation of one's language skills before going abroad.

Badstübner and Ecke (2009) recommended helping students to create more realistic expectations and beliefs before embarking on study abroad. Several researchers (e.g. Bell, 2016; Shao and Crook, 2015) have used group blogs that revealed the real SA experiences and problems of SA students to assist prospective SA participants before their departure. As these blogs did not have any marketing purposes, prospective SA students had access to both positive and negative aspects of study abroad which made the participants construct realistic pre-sojourn beliefs and expectations. Ciftci and Cendel Karaman (2018) recommended organizing a network that would allow for exchanges between SA alumni and SA candidates and assist learners during the pre-sojourn phase. Bretag et al. (2016) stressed the importance of constructing realistic SA expectations by providing beneficial and nuanced information about the target country and the types of experiences and situations the learners are likely to encounter. Michelson and Alvarez Valencia (2016) note that SA websites should stop approaching learners as consumers and tourists, and instead, shift their focus to creating more realistic information for learners and providing opportunities for intercultural and linguistic development. According to Twombly et al. (2012), the use of heroic motives as marketing slogans should be avoided and SA programmes should shift from a focus on perceptually increased participation to purposefully designed educational impact. Pre-sojourn preparations must be carefully structured so that educators and sojourners have mutual expectations and objectives and that the students who are travelling take advantage of the sojourn experience as much as possible.

Conclusion

This study has considered how pre-sojourn exposure to SA marketing can cause changes in students' projected L2 self-efficacy beliefs. Considering that this topic was not investigated by SA researchers before, the study aims to draw the attention of SA researchers to a potential factor that shapes learners' beliefs before they embark on SA experience. Future research that examines other factors in the co-construction of SA beliefs will be useful in terms of understanding the historical constitution of students' beliefs and how students come to have these expectations and SA beliefs in the first place.

One of the limitations of this study was the lack of a control group. Replication studies, which have two identical groups, might close this gap and provide solid findings in terms of identifying the role of SA marketing on L2 learners' pre-sojourn beliefs. Additionally, the current research solely focused on students' projected self-efficacy beliefs and did not examine whether these beliefs would differ at the end of the SA experience. Further research that includes a post-test and longitudinally examines how students' pre-sojourn self-efficacy beliefs evolve in the SA context will be useful.

References

Amuzie, G. L., and Winke, P. (2009), 'Changes in Language Learning Beliefs as a Result of Study Abroad', *System*, 37 (3), 366–79.

Apperson, G. (2015), 'How University Websites Portray Study Abroad', *Elon Journal of Undergraduate Research in Communications*, 6 (2), 5–13.

Badstubner, T., and Ecke, P. (2009), 'Students' Expectations, Target Language Use, and Perceived Learning Progress in a Summer Study Abroad Program in Germany', *Die Unterrichtspraxis: Teaching German*, 42, 41–9.

Bandura, A. (1986), *Social Foundations of Thought and Action: A Social Cognitive Theory*, Englewood Cliffs, NJ: Prentice Hall.

Bandura, A. (1994), 'Self-efficacy', in V. S. Ramachaudran (ed.), *Encyclopedia of Human Behavior*, 71–81, New York: Academic Press.

Bandura, A. (1997), *Self-efficacy: The Exercise of Control*, New York: Freeman.

Bandura, A. (2001), 'Social Cognitive Theory of Mass Communication', *Media Psychology*, 3, 265–99.

Baumeister, R. F., Smart, L., and Boden, J. M. (1996), 'Relation of Threatened Egotism to Violence and Aggression: The Dark Side of High Self-Esteem', *Psychological Review*, 103, 5–33.

Bell, R. (2016), 'Concerns and Expectations of Students Participating in Study Abroad Programmes: Blogging to Reveal the Dynamic Student Voice', *Journal of Research in International Education*, 15, 196–207.

Ben-Ami, M., Hornik, J., Eden, D., and Kaplan, O. (2014), 'Boosting Consumers' Self-efficacy by Repositioning the Self', *European Journal of Marketing*, 48, 1914–38.

Bretag, T., van der Veen, R., Saddiqui, S., and Zhu, Y. (2016), 'Critical Components in Preparing Students for Short-term Study Tours to Asia', in D. M. Velliaris, and D. Coleman-George (eds.), *Handbook of Research on Study Abroad Programs and Outbound Mobility*, 188–214, Hershey, PA: IGI Global.

Ciftci, E. Y., and Cendel Karaman, A. (2018), 'I Do Not Have to Love Them, I'm Just Interested in Their Language: Preparation for a Study Abroad Period and the Negotiation(s) of Intercultural Competence', *Language and Intercultural Communication*, 18 (6), 595–612.

Combs, J. (2016), 'Social Cognitive Framework for Advertising', doctoral dissertation, Retrieved from http://acumen.lib.ua.edu/content/u0015/0000001/0002327/u0015_0000001_0002327.pdf

Cubillos, J. H., and Ilvento, T. (2012), 'The Impact of Study Abroad on Students' Self-efficacy Perceptions', *Foreign Language Annals*, 45, 449–511.

Daroczi, G. (2015), *Mastering Data Analysis with R*, Birmingham, UK: Packt Publishing.

DeKeyser, R. (1990), 'From Learning to Acquisition? Monitoring in the Classroom and Abroad', *Hispania*, 73, 238–47.

Dewey, D. (2008), 'Japanese Vocabulary Acquisition by Learners in Three Contexts', *Frontiers: The Interdisciplinary Journal of Study Abroad*, 15, 127–48.

Ellis, R. (1994), *The Study of Second Language Acquisition*, Oxford, UK: Oxford University Press.

Flora, J. A., and Maibach, E. W. (1989), 'The Role of Media across Four Levels of Health Promotion Intervention', *Annual Review of Public Health*, 10, 181–201.

Frankel, J. R., and Wallen, N. E. (2009), *How to Design and Evaluate Research in Education*, Boston, MA: McGraw-Hill.

Global Info Research. (2018), 'Global English Language Learning Market 2018 by Manufacturers, Countries, Type and Application, Forecast to 2023', Retrieved from https://www.decisiondatabases.com/ip/32756-language-training-market-analysis-report

Goffman, E. (1974), *Frame Analysis: An Essay on the Organization of Experience*, Boston, MA: Harvard University Press.

Green, S. B., and Salkind, N. J. (2005), *Using SPSS for Windows and Macintosh: Analyzing and Understanding Data*, New Jersey: Pearson.

Güvendir, E. (2017), 'Turkish Students and Their Experiences during a Short-term Summer Visit to the US', *Study Abroad Research in Second Language Acquisition and International Education*, 2 (1), 21–52.

Güvendir, E., Acar Güvendir, M., and Dündar, S. (in press), 'Study Abroad and L2 Self-efficacy Beliefs Scale', *Journal of Theory and Practice in Education*.

Hinton, P. R., Brownlow, C., McMurray, I., and Cozens, C. (2004), *SPSS Explained*, Hove: Routledge.

Horwitz, E. K. (1988), 'The Beliefs about Language Learning of Beginning University Foreign Language Students', *Modern Language Journal*, 72, 283–94.

Horwitz, E. K. (1999), 'Cultural and Situational Influences on Foreign Language Learners' Beliefs about Language Learning: A Review of BALLI Studies', *System*, 27, 557–76.

Jackson, J. (2019), '"Cantonese Is My Own Eyes and English Is Just My Glasses": The Evolving Language and Intercultural Attitudes of a Chinese Study Abroad Student', in M. Howard (ed.), *Study Abroad, Second Language Acquisition and Interculturality: Contemporary Perspectives*, 15–45, Bristol: Multilingual Matters.

Kaypak, E., and Ortaçtepe, D. (2014), 'Language Learner Beliefs and Study Abroad: A Study on English as a Lingua Franca (ELF)', *System*, 42, 355–67.

Kern, R. G. (1995), 'Students' and Teachers' Beliefs about Language Learning', *Foreign Language Annals*, 28, 71–91.

Kumar, R. (2011), *Research Methodology: A Step-by-Step Guide for Beginners*, New Delhi: Sage.

Lerner, R. M. (1986), *Concepts and Theories of Human Development*, New York: Random House.

Llanes, À., and Muñoz, C. (2009), 'A Short Stay Abroad: Does It Make a Difference?', *System*, 37, 353–65.

Marijuan, S., and Sanz, C. (2018), 'Expanding Boundaries: Current and New Directions in Study Abroad Research and Practice', *Foreign Language Annals*, 51 (1), 185–204.

Mendelson, V. G. (2004), 'Hindsight Is 20/20: Student Perceptions of Language Learning and the Study Abroad Experience', *Frontiers: The Interdisciplinary Journal of Study Abroad*, 10, 43–63.

Michelson, K., and Alvarez Valencia, J. A. (2016), 'Study Abroad: Tourism or Education? A Multimodal Social Semiotic Analysis of Institutional Discourses of a Promotional Website', *Discourse and Communication*, 10 (3), 235–56.

Milstein, T. (2005), 'Transformation Abroad: Sojourning and the Perceived Enhancement of Self-efficacy', *International Journal of Intercultural Relations*, 29 (2), 217–38.

Mukhopadhyay, A., and Johar, G. V. (2005), 'Where There Is a Will, Is There a Way? The Effects of Consumers' Lay Theories of Self-control on Setting and Keeping Resolutions', *Journal of Consumer Research*, 31, 779–86.

Pajares, F. (2002), 'Overview of Social Cognitive Theory and of Self-efficacy', retrieved from http://www.emory.edu/EDUCATION/mfp/eff.html

Pajares, F., and Graham, L. (1999), 'Self Efficacy, Motivation Constructs and Mathematics Performance of Entering Middle School Students', *Contemporary Educational Psychology*, 42, 190–8.

Pajares, F., Prestin, A., Chen, J., and Nabi, R. L. (2009), 'Social Cognitive Theory and Media Effects', in R. L. Nabi, and M. B. Oliver (eds.), *The Sage Handbook of Media Processes and Effects*, 283–97, Los Angeles, CA: Sage.

Pérez-Vidal, C., and Juan-Garau, M. (2009), 'The Effect of Study Abroad on Written Performance', *Eurosla Yearbook*, 9, 269–95.

Pyper, M. J., and Slagter, C. (2015), 'Competing Priorities: Student Perceptions of Helps and Hindrances to Language Acquisition during Study Abroad', *Frontiers: The Interdisciplinary Journal of Study Abroad*, 26, 83–106.

Schunk, D. H., and Pajares, F. (2002), 'The Development of Academic Self-Efficacy', in A. Wigfield, and J. S. Eccles (eds.), *Development of Achievement Motivation*, 15–31, San Diego, CA: Academic Press.

Schunk, D. H., and Zimmerman, B. J. (1994), *Self-regulation of Learning and Performance: Issues and Educational Applications*, Hillsdale, NJ: Lawrence Erlbaum Associates.

Scott, D. M. (2009), *The New Rules of Marketing and PR: How to Use News Releases, Blogs, Podcasting, Viral Marketing and Online Media to Reach Buyers Directly*, New Jersey: John Wiley & Sons.

Shao, Y., and Crook, C. (2015), 'The Potential of a Mobile Group Blog to Support Cultural Learning among Overseas Students', *Journal of Studies in International Education*, 19 (5), 399–422.

Spillinger, A., and Parush, A. (2012), 'The Impact of Testimonials on Purchase Intentions in a Mock e-Commerce Website', *Journal of Theoretical and Applied Electronic Commerce Research*, 7 (1), 51–63.

Surtees, V. (2016), 'Beliefs about Language Learning in Study Abroad: Advocating for a Language Ideology Approach', *Frontiers: The Interdisciplinary Journal of Study Abroad*, 17, 85–103.

Tanaka, K., and Ellis, R. (2003), 'Study-abroad, Language Proficiency, and Learner Beliefs about Language Learning', *JALT Journal*, 25, 63–85.

Twombly, S. B., Salisbury, M. H., Tumanut, S. D., and Klute, P. (2012), *Study Abroad in a New Global Century: Renewing the Promise, Refining the Purpose*, London: John Wiley & Sons.

Usher, E. L., and Pajares, F. (2008), 'Self-efficacy for Self-regulated Learning: A Validation Study', *Educational and Psychological Measurement*, 68, 443–63.

Vancouver, J. B., Thompson, C. M., and Williams, A. A. (2001), 'The Changing Signs in the Relationships among Self-efficacy, Personal Goals, and Performance', *Journal of Applied Psychology*, 86, 605–20.

Walsh, W. B., and Betz, N. E. (1990), *Tests and Assessment*, Englewood Cliffs, NJ: Prentice Hall.

Wesely, P. M. (2012), 'Learner Attitudes, Perceptions, and Beliefs in Language Learning', *Foreign Language Annals*, 45, 98–117.

Wilkinson, S. (1998), 'On the Nature of Immersion during Study Abroad: Some Participant Perspectives', *Frontiers: The Interdisciplinary Journal of Study Abroad*, 4, 121–38.
Yang, J. S., and Kim, T. Y. (2011), 'Sociocultural Analysis of Second Language Learner Beliefs: A Qualitative Case Study of Two Study-abroad ESL Learners', *System*, 39, 325–34.
Zaykovskaya, I., Rawal, H., and De Costa, P. I. (2017), 'Learner Beliefs for Successful Study Abroad Experience: A Case Study', *System*, 71, 113–21.
Zemach-Bersin, T. (2009), 'Selling the World', in R. Lewin (ed.), *The Handbook of Practice and Research in Study Abroad*, 303–20, New York: Routledge.

Appendix. Study Abroad and L2 Self-Efficacy Beliefs Scale

If I study English abroad in a language teaching programme for a maximum duration of six months, at the end of the SA experience ...

Items	No Idea	Strongly Disagree	Disagree	Agree	Disagree
1. I can easily understand English idioms when I hear them.	0 ( )	1 ( )	2 ( )	3 ( )	4 ( )
2. I can understand English movies without difficulty when I watch them without subtitles.	0 ( )	1 ( )	2 ( )	3 ( )	4 ( )
3. I can easily understand long conversations in English.	0 ( )	1 ( )	2 ( )	3 ( )	4 ( )
4. When English is spoken with different accents (e.g. British, Irish, Canadian, American, Australian), I can easily understand what is spoken.	0 ( )	1 ( )	2 ( )	3 ( )	4 ( )
5. I can easily understand the different uses of English in different social situations (in hospital, bank, between a teacher and a student, among close friends, etc.).	0 ( )	1 ( )	2 ( )	3 ( )	4 ( )
6. I can easily understand what is spoken in group discussions in English.	0 ( )	1 ( )	2 ( )	3 ( )	4 ( )
7. I can easily understand lectures/presentations in my study field involving an academic language of English.	0 ( )	1 ( )	2 ( )	3 ( )	4 ( )
8. I can easily understand English texts containing abstract expressions.	0 ( )	1 ( )	2 ( )	3 ( )	4 ( )

Items	No Idea	Strongly Disagree	Disagree	Agree	Disagree
9. I can easily understand implicit expressions in English texts.	0 ( )	1 ( )	2 ( )	3 ( )	4 ( )
10. I can easily understand the details of news texts written in English.	0 ( )	1 ( )	2 ( )	3 ( )	4 ( )
11. I can easily understand the attitude of the author of a text written in English.	0 ( )	1 ( )	2 ( )	3 ( )	4 ( )
12. I can speak English effectively for social purposes (establishing relations, being part of a different group, etc.).	0 ( )	1 ( )	2 ( )	3 ( )	4 ( )
13. I can easily express my thoughts orally in English.	0 ( )	1 ( )	2 ( )	3 ( )	4 ( )
14. I can speak English appropriately in different environments (school, friends, bank, etc.).	0 ( )	1 ( )	2 ( )	3 ( )	4 ( )
15. I can offer oral advice in English to others on issues related to my profession/field of study.	0 ( )	1 ( )	2 ( )	3 ( )	4 ( )
16. I can create English texts on complex topics.	0 ( )	1 ( )	2 ( )	3 ( )	4 ( )
17. My English writing skill advances to the level of someone whose native language is English.	0 ( )	1 ( )	2 ( )	3 ( )	4 ( )
18. I can write long reports about my profession/field in English.	0 ( )	1 ( )	2 ( )	3 ( )	4 ( )
19. I can get a high score in the writing section of a high-level English exam.	0 ( )	1 ( )	2 ( )	3 ( )	4 ( )
20. I can write English texts without making grammatical errors.	0 ( )	1 ( )	2 ( )	3 ( )	4 ( )
21. I can choose a style appropriate for the reader when writing English texts.	0 ( )	1 ( )	2 ( )	3 ( )	4 ( )
22. I can get a high score in the grammar section of a high-level English exam.	0 ( )	1 ( )	2 ( )	3 ( )	4 ( )
23. I can easily write English texts using complex structures.	0 ( )	1 ( )	2 ( )	3 ( )	4 ( )
24. I can use English idioms while writing texts in English.	0 ( )	1 ( )	2 ( )	3 ( )	4 ( )

4

Close encounters of the third kind: Quantity, type and quality of language contact during study abroad

Jessica Briggs Baffoe-Djan and Siyang Zhou
University of Oxford

Introduction

There is a long-held belief among second language (L2) learners and educators that a period of residence in the target language (TL) community is the sine qua non of mastery of a second language. This belief is predicated on the further conviction that residing in the TL community will engender a greater quantity and variety of types of contact with the L2 than are afforded in a foreign language learning context. L2 learners expect – and indeed are sometimes promised (Briggs, 2015b) – to be able to use the L2 in almost every aspect of their daily lives during study abroad (SA) and for this enhanced level of input and interaction to beget better language learning outcomes than could be achieved in their home country. Much research into study abroad has concerned itself with determining whether and to what extent these beliefs hold true, indicating that improved outcomes as a result of study abroad are by no means a given (e.g. Cubillos, Chieffo and Fan, 2008; Godfrey, Treacy and Tarone, 2014) and that the L2 contact that SA learners actually experience varies hugely and is subject to a host of learner-internal and learner-external factors (e.g. Isabelli-García, 2006; McManus, Mitchell and Tracy-Ventura, 2014; Zhou, 2018).

A myriad of approaches to studying language contact during study abroad has been utilized over the years. These include language contact questionnaires; social network analysis; learner journals, diaries and logs and interviews inter alia. For the most part, these approaches aim to capture one or both of two facets of language contact: (1) quantity (e.g. regularity of interaction, number of interlocutors); and (2) type (e.g. reading versus speaking, L1 versus L2 interlocutor). In this chapter we will critically review studies which probe the relationship between L2 contact and linguistic gain during study abroad to argue that evidence derived from the full gamut of approaches to measuring L2 contact suggests that another third factor – quality of L2 contact – is a key mediator in the relationship between L2 contact and linguistic gain during study abroad.

We first draw on the literature to demonstrate that language contact is most commonly measured in terms of amount and type, and illustrate the plethora of measurements and operationalizations of these two facets of the construct. We then present an overview of empirical works investigating the relationship between language contact and linguistic outcomes during study abroad. Drawing from this literature we show that the evidence suggests that amount and type of language contact are not in and of themselves clearly related to linguistic gain. We will argue that the evidence in fact points to an effect of specific features of specific types of language contact, and that these features taken together are indicators of what we will term quality of language contact. Having formulated from this discussion a working definition of quality of language contact, we elaborate on our conceptualization and refer back to our discussion of measurement approaches to proffer suggestions as to how quality might usefully be captured in future SA research.

Defining, operationalizing and measuring language contact

Language contact in the SA literature refers to individual and group contact with and use of the L2 during a sojourn in the TL community. Variously termed 'L2 contact' (e.g. Briggs, 2015a; Hernández, 2010), 'L2 exposure' (e.g. Devlin, 2018; Montero, 2019; Reynolds-Case, 2013), 'L2 use' (e.g. Baker-Smemoe et al., 2014), 'language use' (e.g. Muñoz and Llanes, 2014), 'linguistic experience' (e.g. Mora and Valls-Ferrer, 2012), 'language engagement' (McManus, Mitchell and Tracy-Ventura, 2014) and 'extramural activity' (e.g. Tragant, 2012), while some scholars include both in-class and out-of-class contact in their operationalization of the term (e.g. Dewey et al., 2014), others specify that out-of-class (or 'informal') contact is their focus of interest (e.g. Briggs, 2016), given that it is this feature of language contact which (should) differentiate between the at-home and SA settings. Likewise, some studies have focused only on L2 contact (e.g. Dewey et al., 2014; Martinsen et al., 2010), whereas others aim to capture L1 contact in addition, as a means of determining a relative ratio of language contact by linguistic code (e.g. Gautier and Chevrot, 2015; Tanaka, 2007) or in recognition of study abroad as a multilingual, rather than L2-only, experience (e.g. McManus, Mitchell and Tracy-Ventura, 2014).

Measuring language contact is a key pursuit in SA research because the extent to which a learner has contact with the L2 determines the extent to which the sojourn has in fact been an 'immersion experience' (Marijuan and Sanz, 2018) in linguistic terms. That is to say, common research designs and learner-external variables in the SA literature – such as between-groups comparisons of at-home and SA learners and measures of length of stay – are predicated on the belief that a greater amount of (naturalistic) language contact is experienced by those resident in the TL community. Language contact in study abroad is most commonly measured via a language contact questionnaire, the most prevalent of which is (adaptations of) the Language Contact Profile (LCP), developed by Freed et al. (2004). The original LCP was developed for use with L1 English learners of L2 Spanish and comprises two sections: one for use before the study abroad and the other to be administered after the study abroad has ended.

The pre-SA section collects demographic data (e.g. gender, age) and information about the respondent's proficiency in the L2, including the number of years of formal L2 instruction and previous experience of living in the TL community. There then follow thirteen items that describe contact with the L2 in the home country, e.g., 'Reading Spanish language newspapers' (2004, p. 352), to which the respondent chooses the most appropriate answer from a five-point frequency scale (from 'Almost Never' to 'Daily'). The post-SA section of the LCP collects data about the respondents' living arrangements during the study abroad, including whether they lived with L1 and/or L2 speakers, and then presents forty-one items that describe contact with the L2 and the L1. The respondent must state on average how many days per week (from zero to seven) during the study abroad they engaged in each listed type of contact and then on average how many hours per day (from zero to more than five). The items are listed in order of skill; in other words, all of the types of contact that involve speaking in the L2 are listed together, followed by reading, listening and writing, and then the same structure is repeated for contact scenarios that involve the L1 (see Fernández and Gates Tapia, 2016, for a critical appraisal of the LCP).

Another approach to measuring language contact during study abroad that has been gaining traction in recent years is social network analysis. In an early study of social networks in study abroad, Isabelli-García (2006) employed informal interviews, learner diaries and 'network contact logs' to probe the experiences and attitudes of four L1-English SA learners of Spanish in Argentina. Respondents were prompted in the diaries and interviews to comment on their attitudes towards Argentina, Argentines and Argentine culture, including a prompt to describe their feelings about specific events and situations they had reported. The network contact log – completed daily for one week at three different timepoints during the sojourn – prompted respondents to 'recognise their personal networks' (p. 241). These data were analysed according to 'network zone', whereby contacts directly linked to the respondent are classified as belonging to the first-order zone, and anyone introduced to the respondent by one of the first-order contacts and who then becomes a contact of the respondent belongs to the second-order zone. The premise of this approach is that in open (i.e. to L2 interlocutors), multiplex networks (i.e. once a second-order zone has been established) there is greater variety – of interlocutors, input, interactions, topics, etc. – and thus a greater level of acculturation and, concordantly, of linguistic development.

Dewey and colleagues (Baker-Smemoe et al., 2014; Dewey, Belnap and Hillstrom, 2013; Dewey, Bown and Eggett, 2012; Dewey et al., 2013) have arguably led the charge as regards quantitative measurement of social network during study abroad to date, via their development and use of the Study Abroad Social Interaction Questionnaire (SASIQ), an adaptation of the Montréal Index of Linguistic Integration (Segalowitz and Ryder, 2006). The SASIQ operationalizes social network in terms of size (i.e. number of contacts); durability (average time spent with each contact); intensity (how close to each contact the respondent feels, on a scale from 'acquaintance' to 'close friend/confidant'); density (the extent to which the contacts are connected, yielding the average social group size and the size of the largest social group); dispersion (the number of social groups to which the respondent belongs); and proficiency (the reported L2 proficiency of the respondent's contacts). McManus, Mitchell and Tracy-Ventura's (2014) Social

Network Questionnaire (SNQ) operates similarly, yielding measures of total network size at different time points, number of contacts by social context (home; work/university; online; organized free time; general free time), frequency and length of language use by social context and the most frequent interlocutors per time point.

Gautier and Chevrot (2015) employed a language contact diary and a questionnaire to elicit social network data from their sample of seven L1-English SA learners in France. Participants were tasked with completing the diary daily for one week, recording for each conversation they had: the name of the interlocutor, length of the conversation and the language (code) used. The interlocutor names were then added to a questionnaire designed to elicit interlocutor characteristics (e.g. age; sex; nationality; language usually spoken); characteristics of the relationship between the participant and interlocutor (e.g. host family member; co-worker); the frequency of contact with the interlocutor; and the types of activities the participant and interlocutor share. The authors classified the data elicited in terms of structural information (regarding links between network members) and compositional information (regarding network member attributes), from which they selected for focus one structural criterion (density) and three compositional criteria (number of L1 native-speaker contacts; number of L2 native-speaker contacts; time spent speaking L2 daily). Density was operationalized as the ratio of total possible links between individuals in the network against the total actual links, based on the premise that the greater the density, the more cohesive the social network and thus the more socially integrated the SA learner. Kennedy Terry's (2017) Social Network Strength Scale (SNSS) similarly relies on measures of density via quantification of (1) the number of native-speaker contacts; (2) the links between the respondent and his/her contacts; and (3) the links between the respondent's contacts (i.e. independently of the respondent). In addition, her instrument captures multiplexity via estimation of (1) the range of activities carried out with each native-speaker contact; (2) the time spent interacting with native-speaker interlocutors who are not part of the social network (i.e. strangers; service personnel); and (3) the complexity and range of topics of conversation held with networked contacts.

In the paradigm of narrative enquiry, Kinginger (2008) combined case histories of six American SA learners in France, generated from interviews and observations, with language learning documentation in the form of self-assessments and objective tests. These mixed-methods data were used to draw links between linguistic development, language contact in the form of social integration and identity development. In another mixed-methods study, Martinsen et al. (2010) used email-based language logs – completed daily for a period of one week by forty-three American SA learners in Spain – to gather qualitative data on language contact. The instrument lists a series of situations (e.g. 'Preparing meals' or 'Talking on the phone') and tasks the respondent with recording the number of minutes per day spent in receptive and/or productive contact with Spanish while engaged in each situation. Amaya-García's (2017) Daily Linguistic Questionnaire also elicits a minutes-per-day measurement and tasks respondents with categorizing activities based on the time of day in which they were experienced (e.g. morning, dinnertime). Mitchell (2015) used semi-structured interviews to gather data from twenty-eight SA participants – who were teaching assistants, work interns or exchange students for one year in France – about their social network opportunities and relationship development. Three interviews were conducted with each participant, roughly at the beginning, middle and end of the sojourn, and data were cross-checked across timepoints and triangulated with supplementary questionnaire data as a means of establishing their trustworthiness. In a purely qualitative approach to capturing the language contact of Japanese SA learners in New Zealand, Tanaka (2007) employed both learner diaries and open-ended, semi-structured interviews, completed during and after the sojourn respectively. Data were analysed via thematic content analysis, and reports of out-of-class language contact were further classified as either interactive or non-interactive. Conroy (2018) used learner diaries and journals to probe the language contact of L1-Chinese learners from Hong Kong in Australia, similarly using thematic analysis to determine the factors to which the learners attributed perceived development.

In appraising the strengths and limitations of the myriad approaches to measuring language contact it is clear that, by their very nature, measures of social network capture only interactive language contact and are thus limited in their capacity to represent the full range of activity an SA learner may experience, whereas language contact questionnaires (and diaries, logs and interviews) can capture both interactive and non-interactive contact types. Language contact questionnaires are therefore arguably a more valid measure of amount of language contact as regards range, yet they lack specificity: a clear advantage of social network measures and qualitative approaches is that respondents comment on specific relationships and/or specific contact situations rather than on generalized activity type such as 'Reading magazines in the L2'. Generalized activity as per language contact questionnaires may be more or less meaningful to or engaging for the learner depending on, for example, the specific magazine (whether it appeals to their interests or not); the language of the text (the extent to which it is within their level of comprehension); the reading context (e.g. alone in one's room with ample time versus in a crowded dentist's waiting room with five minutes before the appointment time); the significance of the contact to social relations (e.g. if the magazine was recommended by a friend) and so on. Thus, even in quantitative studies which combine the use of language contact questionnaires and social network analysis (e.g. Baker-Smemoe et al., 2014; George, 2014; McManus, Mitchell and Tracy-Ventura, 2014), there is no measure of the intensity, density, etc., of non-interactive language contact. The trade-off with more in-depth, specific measures, however, is an evitable impact on sample size of eliciting a greater level of detail from respondents. In addition, the field lacks a unifying conceptual framework for language contact such that reconciling qualitative findings across studies can be challenging.

It should also be noted that studies which comprehensively measure both face-to-face and virtual language contact are few and far between, despite a wealth of evidence to show that SA learners' online activity is frequent, widespread and meaningful (e.g. Coleman and Chafer, 2010; Hetz, Dawson and Cullen, 2015; Kelly, 2010). Notable exceptions in this regard are McManus, Mitchell and Tracy-Ventura (2014), Taguchi (2015), Seibert Hanson and Dracos (2016) and Martínez-Arbelaiz, Areizaga and Camps (2017). The evidence to date as regards virtual language contact suggests an imbalance between L1 and L2 use in online activities, with more L1 usage. For example, Martínez-Arbelaiz, Areizaga and Camps (2017) found that learners use Facebook and Skype in the L1 more than the L2, whereas they use WhatsApp with a balanced L1/L2 ratio. McManus, Mitchell and Tracy-Ventura (2014) noted that among four different social contexts, the largest proportion of L1 contact took place online, whereas the virtual setting yielded the smallest proportion of L2 contact. Studies suggest that frequent Internet use is usually associated with homesickness and a stronger need for support from home, which negatively correlates with L2 learning motivation and L2 gains (e.g. Seibert Hanson and Dracos, 2016). It is also found that learners with higher L2 proficiency tend to use technology in the L2 more (Durbidge, 2018).

Amount of language contact and L2 gains

Amount of L2 contact – as measured predominantly by language contact questionnaires – is operationalized in the SA literature in a variety of ways. These include number, regularity, frequency, extent and length. For example, the total number of hours of contact (or average hours per day/week/month) in a given period (e.g. Hardison, 2014); the number of (native L2-speaking) interlocutors a learner has (e.g. Milton and Meara, 1995); the extent of contact with a particular linguistic form (e.g. Reynolds-Case, 2013); the frequency with which the L2 is used (e.g. Apple and Aliponga, 2018); the length of time spent in L2 contact overall (e.g. Devlin, 2018); or the total length of stay in the target discourse community (e.g. Baró and Serrano, 2011; Briggs, 2015b).

Findings yielded by studies that have probed the relationship between quantity of L2 contact and L2 gains are mixed, with many studies failing to observe a link between the two. While it is possible that no relationship exists, it may be the case that extant approaches to measuring quantity of language contact have obscured any link between these variables, and/or that the populations studied to date did not experience an amount of contact sufficient to engender measurable linguistic gain. In the realm of vocabulary studies, for example, Milton and Meara (1995) examined the receptive vocabulary knowledge of fifty-three European Erasmus exchange students in the UK. Pre- and post-tests were administered to participants at the beginning and the end of the six-month exchange programme, and vocabulary knowledge was measured via the Eurocentres Vocabulary Size Tests (EVST), which contains straightforward yes/no questions on target words selected in light of corpus frequency. The L2 contact of participants was measured by a retrospective questionnaire. Results suggest that study abroad greatly facilitated vocabulary development among the sample. However, the size of native-speaker networks made little contribution to the vocabulary growth in study abroad: the number of English-speaking neighbours and the number of native-speaker friends did not significantly correlate with the absolute development of EVST scores or the percentage improvement scores. Likewise, Hardison (2014) tracked the L2 development of twenty-four American participants who studied abroad in Germany for six weeks. Language contact data were gathered through a modified LCP and post-study interviews, and online speaking tasks were completed before and after the SA programme. German vocabulary saw the largest improvement among all language skills, but linguistic gains were not significantly correlated with amount of L2 contact. Similar findings as regards a lack of relationship between amount of language contact and vocabulary gain were yielded by Briggs (2015b).

There is also evidence to suggest that quantity of L2 contact is in and of itself not related to oral proficiency gains. For example, Segalowitz and Freed (2004) and Segalowitz et al. (2004) found that significant gains on pre- and post-test Oral Proficiency Interviews (OPIs) did not correlate with the amount of out-of-class language contact their SA participants experienced. Likewise, in Martinsen et al. (2010), there was no clear relationship between the amount of language contact and oral proficiency gain: the researchers investigated three learning contexts – a traditional SA programme, a service-learning SA programme and a domestic immersion programme – in which SA learners of L2 Spanish were asked to complete a language log detailing the frequency of L2 activity and to complete pre- and post-immersion oral tasks. Although participants in two of the programme types made significant linguistic gains, correlation analysis and comparing the high-achievers with low-achievers revealed no clear relationship between amount of TL use and oral proficiency development. Baker-Smemoe et al. (2014) compared the SA outcomes of 102 English native-speaking students enrolled in SA programmes in six countries to learn an L2. Various internal and external factors were measured and an OPI was administered at pre- and post-test. Results showed a significant improvement in speaking proficiency across all six SA programmes, yet in a comparison of the characteristics of gainers and non-gainers, it is striking that there was no significant difference in the average hours of L2 use between the two groups.

Phonological studies is another area of SA research where findings are mixed in showing a link between amount of language contact and linguistic gain. For example, Díaz-Campos (2004) compared the acquisition of Spanish phonology among twenty-five L1-English learners in Spain and twenty L1-English learners in the United States. Data were gathered via the LCP and a read-aloud task administered before and after the SA group's sojourn. Regression analysis indicated that amount of out-of-class language contact 'slightly favored the production of more nativelike variants' (p. 268). However, the US-based learners made greater phonological gains than their SA counterparts, a finding the author explains as a possible lack of match between the groups' participants in terms of linguistic experience (i.e. number of years of formal instruction and age of onset of L2 learning). In another study with somewhat opaque findings as regards contact and phonological gain, George (2014) studied the acquisition of the interdental fricative [θ] and uvular fricative [χ] among twenty-five L1-English SA learners of Spanish in Spain. Three speaking tasks were administered at three timepoints across the sojourn, in tandem with a language contact questionnaire and a social networking questionnaire. Correlation analysis revealed that more Spanish and less English contact correlated with production of [θ], yet there was no significant improvement in the production of [θ] across the semester-long SA period. While improvements were seen in the production of [χ], no language contact or social networking variables were correlated with this gain.

Where a significant relationship has been detected between overall amount of language contact and linguistic gain during study abroad, it is generally the case that a multiplicity of types of contact have been conflated into one or more generic language contact variable. This is an unhelpful practice because it implies that all types of contact are equally beneficial (or not) and are comparable in terms of the time they take, and it precludes fine-grained analysis of language contact data. For example, in a study of the effects of motivation and L2 contact on oral proficiency among twenty L1-English learners of Spanish in Madrid, Hernández (2010) administered an OPI, a motivation index and a modified version of the LCP. Results showed a significant gain in oral proficiency from pre- to post-test, with hours of L2 contact a significant predictor ($\beta = .693$, $t = 4.080$, $p = .001$), explaining nearly 50 per cent of the variance in the gain scores. The language contact variable was the sum of responses to ten LCP items that covered reading, writing, speaking and listening, yet the sample reported spending almost twice as much time on speaking (to native speakers) than on any other type of contact. As such, it is likely that speaking to native speakers accounted for the lion's share of the predictive power of the language contact variable, and it may be the case that features of this type of contact (such as its interactive nature or the characteristics of the interlocutors), rather than the amount of time spent on it, are what made the difference.

Type of language contact and L2 gains

As per amount of language contact, type of language contact is operationalized in the SA literature in a variety of ways. These include dividing language contact by the skill being used (i.e. reading, writing, listening, speaking) (e.g. Dewey, 2008; Segalowitz et al., 2004); into interactive versus non-interactive contact (e.g. Tanaka, 2007); by the nature of the contact (e.g. service encounter, general free time activity) (e.g. McManus, Mitchell and Tracy-Ventura, 2014); the location of the contact (e.g. in-class vs out-of-class) (e.g. Lennon, 1989; Pellegrino, 1996); the relationship of the interlocutor to the respondent (e.g. stranger vs known individual) (e.g. Briggs, 2015a); the linguistic and/or national background of the interlocutor (e.g. international vs local contact) (e.g. Wright and Schartner, 2013; c.f. Coleman, 2013); the proficiency of the interlocutor in the respondent's TL (e.g. Baker-Smemoe et al., 2014); and the activity through which the contact is experienced (e.g. while making dinner, while commuting/travelling) (e.g. Briggs, 2016; Kennedy Terry, 2017; Martinsen et al., 2010).

There is more robust evidence that linguistic gain during study abroad is related to type of language contact than to amount of contact. For the most part, interactive contact is associated with gain: for example, Yager (1998) studied the development of $n = 30$ learners of Spanish on a summer abroad in Mexico. An oral proficiency test and an early version of the LCP were administered pre and post the experimental period. Interactive L2 contact was positively correlated ($r = .39$, $p < .05$) with native-like speaking overall, whereas solitary L2 contact was negatively correlated with gains in native-like pronunciation ($r = -.41$, $p < .05$). Similarly, Martinsen (2011) investigated the effects of pre-SA motivational intensity, pre-SA oral skills, relationship with host family and language contact on the development of intercultural competence among forty-five L1-English L2-Spanish learners in Argentina. Oral interaction with L2 speakers was the only variable significant to predict gains in cultural sensitivity.

Closer inspection of the literature, however, points to an effect of certain qualities of types of language contact as opposed to types themselves. That is to say, within broad categorizations of language type (such as interactive vs non-interactive) there appear to be sub-features of types of language contact that are making a difference. For example, Dewey (2008) compared the L2 Japanese vocabulary acquisition of fifty-six students in study abroad, domestic immersion and an academic year formal classroom setting. Data were collected via three vocabulary knowledge tests, the LCP, weekly diaries and informal interviews. The SA group outperformed the academic year group on all of the tests, yet performed similarly to the domestic immersion group. Estimates of amount of contact did not consistently correlate with vocabulary test scores: only two estimates – total time speaking Japanese to others and total time writing in Japanese – were related to gain in the SA context, and each only to the scores of one of the three tests. The only language contact variable to correlate with more than one of the vocabulary measures was speaking Japanese with friends, which showed a relationship to depth of vocabulary knowledge ($r = .610$, $p < .01$) and to situational Japanese vocabulary knowledge ($r = .459$, $p = < .05$). Other than speaking Japanese with friends, the only variable with a large-sized relationship to gain was listening to songs in Japanese, which correlated positively with vocabulary depth ($r = .602$, $p = < .01$). Thus, Dewey's (2008) study indicates that where types of L2 contact are used for the development/maintenance of social relationships and for the pursuit of personal interests and enjoyment, they show a strong positive relationship to vocabulary gain.

Research into SA learners' social networks indicates that the pursuit of personal interest for enjoyment during study abroad is a key factor in developing meaningful social relationships. For example, McManus, Mitchell and Tracy-Ventura (2014, p. 35) note that 'the participants who most successfully developed local contacts (other than with boyfriends) [...] had a skill of some kind to attract local interest. For this minority group, organized leisure activity (music, sport, a fashion show) opened doors to friendships and to other types of leisure spent in company with locals'. Briggs (2015b) also alludes to the significance of personal interest in language contact in a longitudinal investigation of the vocabulary acquisition of 241 SA learners of English in the UK: the findings revealed that the types of language contact that the sample most identified with were not facilitative of varied input or opportunities for use of newly encountered lexis (e.g. short exchanges with service personnel) and did not hold any significance for the learners beyond the context in which the contact took place. It is this factor, Briggs postulates, that explains why language contact did not predict vocabulary gain in her study.

Over and above the pursuit of personal interests, living arrangements have been seen to have an effect on relationship development, and thus linguistic gain, during study abroad. Serrano, Tragant and Llanes (2012) examined the effects of an academic year abroad in the UK among fourteen L1 speakers of Spanish in terms of oral and written fluency, complexity, accuracy and lexical richness. Oral and written tasks and a language contact questionnaire were administered at roughly the beginning, middle and end of the year abroad. Type of language contact was operationalized as living arrangement (apartment/house vs hall of residence), number of Spanish-speaking roommates and number of English-speaking roommates. Results revealed that participants living in an apartment/house showed statistically greater gains in oral lexical richness and that participants who interacted more with English speakers than Spanish speakers experienced medium-to-large gains in written lexical richness and oral accuracy. These findings indicate that sharing accommodation with speakers of the L2 – such as in a homestay or flat share setting – can be beneficial to linguistic gain, an assertion supported by the findings of Mancheño (2008), Vande Berg, Connor-Linton and Paige (2009), Serrano, Tragant and Llanes (2012) and Di Silvio, Donovan and Malone (2014). Conversely, Magnan and Back (2007) found no difference in oral proficiency gain by living arrangement during study abroad. However, their group sizes in this regard ($n = 11$ and $n = 9$) were arguably too small for reliable detection of significance. As with the findings of Dewey (2008), it is likely that positive effects of living in a shared setting with L2 speakers are predicated first and foremost on the development of social relationships, and that through these relationships more, and more meaningful, contact with the L2 is engendered. Concordantly, where living arrangements beget negative experiences for SA learners, they may preclude the formation of close relationships and cause the learner to disengage from the TL and culture (e.g. Di Silvio, Donovan and Malone, 2014; Kinginger, 2008; Magnan and Back, 2007).

The positive influence of meaningful social relationships on linguistic development during study abroad is supported by the findings of Kinginger and Blattner (2008), who carried out a case study of three American learners of French studying abroad in France. Colloquial French phrase knowledge was tested and participants participated in interviews and completed journal entries. Findings revealed that knowledge of colloquial forms and awareness of their social meaning were closely related to strong social relationships with locals. For example, 'Benjamin' demonstrated the largest improvement of all the participants, with a post-test score quadruple that of his pre-test. He did not feel positively towards his American classmates during study abroad and instead formed strong relationships with his host family members and spent most of his free time at home or on weekend trips with the family. Likewise, 'Camille' had a French boyfriend 'Gabriel' while studying in France. She doubled her score in the colloquial phrases tasks and increased her usage of colloquial lexis in her journal, attributing this gain to the intimate nature of her relationship with Gabriel and the friendships she formed within his social circle. On the contrary, 'Ailis' did not enjoy the homestay experience and mostly socialized with other American students. Not surprisingly, she showed no improvement in the colloquial phrase task. Kinginger and Blattner conclude that an advantage accrues for learners who form close relationships with a variety of interlocutors: an assertion corroborated by Bardovi-Harlig and Bastos (2011) in the realm of L2 pragmatic development, whose high-gaining participants were those who had formed the greatest number of friendships with native speakers of the TL. Further evidence in this regard is found in Dewey et al. (2013) and Baker-Smemoe et al. (2014).

The literature suggests that meaningful social relationships developed during study abroad are beneficial to linguistic gain even where those relationships are likely to be carried out partially or wholly in the participant's L1. For example, Baker-Smemoe et al.'s (2014) study of L1-English participants in a range of SA contexts employed the SASIQ to measure the nature of their sample's social network, administering the instrument two weeks after the SA programmes had commenced and again two weeks prior to their conclusion. Social network was operationalized in terms of network size, durability (average time spent with each contact); intensity (how close to each contact the respondent feels); density (the extent to which the social groups reported are closely connected); dispersion (the number of social groups to which the respondent belongs); and proficiency (the reported L2-English proficiency of the respondent's contacts). Results revealed that higher proficiency and a decrease in size predicted linguistic gain, and that intensity and dispersion differentiated between the gainers and non-gainers.

Baker-Smemoe et al. (2014) argue that while socializing with an interlocutor who has high proficiency in one's L1 may encourage a lower level of L2 usage, in fact this type of language contact may be beneficial to gain because a local interlocutor with whom the SA learner can easily communicate in the L1 is likely to share common experience with the SA learner (i.e. likely having studied abroad themselves to develop their L2-English proficiency), thus providing a basis for forming a meaningful relationship based on common ground. In addition, a local contact with whom the learner has a meaningful connection is a potential broker in terms of access to local social groups. The finding that a decrease in network size predicted gain is another indication of the effect of close social relationships, with other research (e.g. Hillstrom, 2011) supporting the observation that SA learners' social networks tend to move from an initially larger network of less close relationships to a smaller number of contacts with whom they have a genuine emotional connection.

Baker-Smemoe et al.'s (2014) finding that dispersion differentiates between gainers and non-gainers supports the further notion that engaging in a variety of contexts of L2 use is beneficial to linguistic development. This is a feature of language contact type that has been explored beyond the confines of the SA literature. For example, in a discussion of the research evidence as regards 'exceptional L2 learners' (i.e. individuals who attain native-like phonological control despite an onset of L2 learning after age 9-10), Moyer (2014) states that the one facet of L2 experience which all exceptional learners report is 'L2 use in multiple domains': in other words, a permeation of the L2 into every aspect of their lives, and particularly as regards relaxation/enjoyment (allied to Dewey's 2008 finding regarding listening to L2 music) and socialization (allied to Baker-Smemoe et al.'s 2014 finding regarding dispersion). Moyer's assertion is supported by a wealth of evidence showing that a multiplicity of interactive L2 contact in a variety of contexts is linked to greater phonological control (Derwing, Munro and Thomson, 2008; Díaz-Campos, 2004; Flege and Liu, 2001; Jia et al., 2006; MacKay, Flege and Imai, 2006; Moyer, 2011; Thompson, 1991).

Another study which uncovered a benefit of contextual dispersion in study abroad was that of Pérez-Vidal and Juan-Garau (2009), who investigated the written L2 development of Spanish students studying for three months in Anglophone countries. All participants were allocated thirty minutes to write an argumentative essay, and the social dimension of their SA experience was measured via a study abroad conditions questionnaire, which included measures of language contact. It was found that successful learners made use of social opportunities, such as developing a wide social network, and that having a job and travelling in groups also correlated with gain. Likewise, Fraser (2002) and Whitworth (2006) found that contextual dispersion during study abroad (such as playing on football teams or in orchestras and working as an intern) predicted linguistic gain. Similarly, Kennedy Terry (2017) examined the relationship between sociostylistic variation in French and the social networks of seventeen learners of French in France to find that social networks in which SA learners could participate in an array of activities and discuss a variety of topics were crucial to the acquisition of sociolinguistic competence.

Diversity in language contact has been shown to be important not only to types of contexts but also as regards interlocutors. For example, in an investigation of the pragmatic development of 122 ESL learners in the United States, Bardovi-Harlig and Bastos (2011) administered two computer-based tasks: an aural recognition task and an oral production task, both targeting conventional expressions. A self-developed questionnaire captured amount and type of second language contact (length of stay; time spent speaking with native speakers of English outside of class; time spent speaking with other international students outside of class; regularity of American TV watching; and type of contact, e.g. landlord, teacher, friend). Regression analysis revealed that intensity of interaction (i.e. the time in type of contact variables) significantly predicted recognition and production of conventional expressions, whereas length of stay had no effect. Interestingly, those who gained the most were those who had the highest number of native-speaker friends and reported interacting with a greater range of types of contacts. In a similar vein, Dörnyei, Durow and Zahran (2004) found that international students in the UK who exhibited strong gains in formulaic sequence acquisition made a high quantity and variety of contacts, including locals, co-national students and other international students. One indicative example from these data is 'Daniel', whose quest for dispersion in his social network led him to strike up conversation with strangers on the street, in one case leading to an invitation for coffee in the home of a British native.

Towards a working definition of quality of language contact

What we have seen thus far indicates that quantity and type of language contact in and of themselves do not consistently show a clear relationship with linguistic development during study abroad. Where relationships have been found, studies have tended either to conflate a myriad of types of contact into one amount variable, or there is evidence that the observed relationships arise from specific elements of certain types of contact – elements that may be markers of quality of language contact. There have been attempts to define quality of language contact in the extant SA literature, yet these arguably lack specificity. For example, Fernández and Gates Tapia (2016, p. 248) consider it 'students' level of involvement in the quotidian language practices of the local community while abroad'. Other scholars have not explicitly tried to define quality of language contact yet have summarized some characteristics of language contact that they deem favourable to linguistic gain. For example, Kinginger and Blattner (2008) conclude that language contact in which learners are more engaged in interaction with interlocutors of more varied ages and backgrounds is the most advantageous. Churchill and DuFon (2006) argue that linguistic gains might be related to diverse language contact (i.e. a combination of modified and unmodified L2 input, either with individual interlocutors or in groups). Martinsen et al. (2010, p. 59) highlight the importance of spoken L2 contact between L2 learners themselves, which 'cover[s] a wider range of topics in great depth due to their similarity in age, culture, and the amount of time they spend with one another'. From our critical appraisal of the literature, and in line with the statements above, a number of features of language contact emerge that are consistently evident where gains are found and which we propose are the key features of what we term quality of language contact. We posit that the pillars of quality of language contact in an SA setting are *diversity*, *significance* and *activation*. That is to say, quality of language contact is contact which is:

- diverse in terms of individuals, groups, contexts and activities;
- significant – socially and/or emotionally – to the learner; and
- active, in that nodes in the social network (i.e. individuals, groups, contexts) see consistent activation.

Diversity relates to the importance of a variety of contacts, social groups and language use contexts during study abroad and derives from the wealth of studies whose findings indicate that interacting with an array of interlocutors in multiple different domains is beneficial. In effect, the diversity criterion is a combination of measures of size and of dispersion as per social network measurement: it presupposes a sufficient number of contacts to allow for a range of difference between them and denotes that the learner is engaging in contexts and groups that vary (e.g. by typical activity, by topic). The literature clearly points to an effect of diversity over and above the classification and quantification of individual interlocutors by, for example, their linguistic proficiency in the TL, their 'native-speaker' status or whether they are locals, co-nationals or internationals. In other words, no one type of interlocutor or context clearly emerges from the studies' findings as being more beneficial to the SA learner, but rather where a range of different types are reported or observed – in tandem with the significance and activation criteria discussed below – an advantage to the learner is accrued.

The significance criterion is included in recognition of the evidence that where language contact during study abroad is serving genuine human social or emotional need – as opposed to limited, perfunctory, basic transactional purposes – there is evidence of linguistic gain. Significance embraces the concept of 'intensity' in social network analysis (i.e. how close a respondent feels to each of their contacts) but extends this construct to postulate an influence of 'closeness' (i.e. personal interest and emotional investment) to non-interactive contact (e.g. listening to music), to contexts of language use that hold personal importance (e.g. participating in an amateur dramatics society), to the significance of a specific task (e.g. a public theatre performance vs a closed rehearsal) and even as far as the topic of the input or interaction (e.g. the director explaining the significance of a particular scene). Thus, significance is dynamic, subject to both individual and contextual factors, and can be actuated at many levels. Ostensibly, where multiple levels of significance are activated simultaneously, the quality of the contact is enhanced.

Activation refers to the consistent triggering of significant and diverse nodes (e.g. individual contacts, groups of contacts) in a learner's social network. Activation does not necessarily denote that a social network will grow in size over a SA period (i.e. referring to the adding of new individuals, contexts or groups) – indeed, as we have seen, a learner is likely to narrow down his/her social network to a smaller number of more significant contacts and groups over time. Neither does it signify that the same nodes will be activated consistently over time, because through activating different nodes the significance of those nodes is likely to change (e.g. the learner will feel closer to or more distant from an individual; more or less invested in a group or activity). Rather, activation describes a longitudinal maintenance, if not increase, of the regularity and consistency of opportunities for meaningful TL use. Where activation occurs across a diversity of significant people, contexts and groups, the quality of the language contact experienced stands to benefit.

Measuring quality of language contact

We concur with Moyer (2014, p. 17) that 'measures of L2 experience must signify active, meaningful, and consistent language use, and [L2 experience] must be appreciated for what it says about the role of that language in the learner's life', and that 'traditional measures like length of residence and time on task (e.g. hours of use per week) provide too little detail on how the learner uses L2, with whom, and under what circumstances' (p. 16). In a similar vein, Kinginger (2009, p. 145) argues that 'few studies expressly investigate the qualities of informal contact [...] that study abroad students enjoy'. Study abroad researchers are aware of the legion of variables that come into play in SA experience that might ultimately affect learning (Gass, 2017), yet study abroad is often described as a 'black box' in which the social contact and cultural experiences of learners are difficult to measure and record (Taguchi, 2018). In line with our tripartite conceptualization, therefore, we hereby posit some specific recommendations for eliciting data that speak to the quality of language contact during study abroad.

In terms of diversity, measures of language contact need to be capable of encompassing both the interactive and non-interactive contact that SA learners experience: the full extent of diversity cannot be revealed by social network mapping alone. Therefore, where self-report methodologies such as questionnaires, journals and interviews are employed, prompts regarding both social and individual activities, online and in face-to-face settings, are vital. Direct measures of diversity of contact, such as ethnographic shadowing or GPS tracking, would serve to triangulate self-reported diversity data and provide stimuli for recall interviews in which the specifics of the diversity of language contact situations (e.g. links between individuals across social groups) are accounted for.

Data on the significance to the learner of the language contact she/he experiences would usefully extend beyond solely the intensity of relationships with individuals (as per traditional social network mapping) to further refer to investment and engagement in groups, contexts, tasks and activities, including activities that are non-interactive in nature (e.g. surfing the web, listening to music). Given our argument that significance is dynamic and influenced by both individual and contextual factors, its natural methodological bedfellows are direct observations, event-contingent self-reports and stimulated recall protocols. For example, data on a learner's activation of contact nodes in their social network could be analysed to determine the more and less typical situations she/he experiences, and, with consent from other (if any) individuals typically present, these situations recorded and used as stimuli in interviews to elicit the extent to which the learner feels invested in the relationships, tasks and activities at play; whether and how significance fluctuates within the situation; and the learner's perceptions as to the reason(s) for fluctuation and change.

The current moves in the second language acquisition literature towards focusing on learner engagement at the task level, such as Dörnyei's (2019) work on task motivation and Arndt's (2019) application of an engagement framework to informal second language learning, could feasibly be applied to the coding of qualitative language contact data to gain a better understanding of whether, how and to what extent different contact situations are significant to the individual and whether these attributions bear a relationship to behaviour and to language learning outcomes. For example, Dörnyei (2019, p. 60) characterizes task engagement as active participation in meaningful activity, linking the construct to linguistic outcomes via the tenet of 'learning-through-doing'. He posits six characteristics of an engaging task, which are all applicable to coding qualitative data for the significance of informal language contact during study abroad:

1. presentation: referring to the extent to which an individual 'can see clearly how [the task] contributes to reaching their overall [...] goals/vision' (2019, p. 62). In the case of pedagogical tasks, the goals/vision referred to are language learning-specific. In informal contexts during study abroad, these may instead/additionally be social goals or other goals related to learning beyond the linguistic realm;
2. goals: whereby the aim of the task 'concerns issues that are in some way meaningful and of value to the students' (2019, p. 62);
3. content: meaning the content area is relevant, enjoyable, attractive or entertaining to the learner in some manner and allows them to respond to it authentically;
4. ownership: in which the individual feels they have control/influence over aspects of the task and has the skills (linguistic and/or otherwise) requisite to do so;
5. structure: referring to the extent an individual's expectations are met as regards the phases and order of the particular activity or situation, the role(s) she/he is to adopt and the criteria for (successfully) achieving the goal; and
6. positive tenor: meaning that the individual experiences positive affect due to enhanced social acceptance and well-being by virtue of participating in the activity.

Our arguments as regards activation of language contact denote that the construct is most meaningfully measured longitudinally, ideally at multiple time points to reflect its dynamic, multiplex nature. Data on activation therefore need to pinpoint the frequency and regularity with which each node in the social network is triggered over time. This aim could be achieved via social network mapping technologies: recent software such as the Graphical Ego-centered Network Survey Interface (GENSI: Stark and Krosnick, 2017) and Network Canvas (Hogan et al., 2019) create graphical representation of social network data at the point at which it is reported by the participant and have the capacity to allow the respondent to interact with their network map via touchscreen interface. Ostensibly, then, if a learner has online access to their map and were prompted via push message to access it daily, they could use the interactive capability to indicate which nodes had been activated that day and how many times, in tandem with adding any new nodes, thus providing detailed data on both activation and diversity.

Finally, while our conceptualization of quality of language contact extends as far as the opportunity it proffers for meaningful TL use, it does not speak to the quality, or lack thereof, of the TL input or discourse that SA learners experience. Therefore, and in line with Fernández and Gates Tapia (2016), we suggest that gathering and analysing naturally occurring linguistic data that is representative in some way of a learner's language contact during study abroad is an important complement to the methodologies hereby proposed. One approach in this regard would be to identify, via prior or concurrent measure(s) of diversity and significance, specific nodes in the learner's social network that are typical, extreme or critical in some way, and to create a corpus of language used in these situations (seeking prior consent from other individuals involved) to determine whether and how the input and interaction in these settings are subject to change based on diversity, significance and activation.

Conclusion

In this chapter we have argued, based on our critical reading of the research, that diversity, significance and activation are three features of language contact during study abroad that speak to the quality of the opportunity for linguistic gain. Our tripartite conceptualization of quality of language contact implicates future SA research that utilizes and coordinates a wide repertoire of methodological approaches such that diversity, significance and activation can be captured at the macro and micro levels and over time. Broadly speaking, we have endorsed a mixed methods, longitudinal approach with multiple data points, in which the strengths of quantitative methodologies such as language contact questionnaires and social network mapping are combined and used in tandem with detailed, event-specific qualitative data, the coding of which is focused at a task-level unit of analysis. In addition, we have argued for greater use of direct observation and recording of language contact during study abroad: while naturalistic data collection brings with it greater ethical and analytical complexity, it would also confer insight into language contact beyond that which the SA literature currently encapsulates.

References

Amaya-García, L. (2017), 'Detailing L1 and L2 Use in Study-abroad Research: Data from the Daily Linguistic Questionnaire', *System*, 71, 60–72.

Apple, M. T., and Aliponga, J. (2018), 'Intercultural Communication Competence and Possible L2 Selves in a Short Term Study Abroad Program', in I. Walker, D. K. G. Chan,

M. Nagami, and C. Bourguignon (eds.), *New Perspectives on the Development of Communicative and Related Competence in Foreign Language Education*, 289–308, Berlin: Walter de Gruyter.

Arndt, H. (2019), 'Informal Second Language Learning: The Role of Engagement, Proficiency, Attitudes, and Motivation', unpublished doctoral thesis, University of Oxford.

Baker-Smemoe, W., Dewey, D. P., Bown, J., and Martinsen, R. A. (2014), 'Variables Affecting L2 Gains during Study Abroad', *Foreign Language Annals*, 47 (3), 464–86.

Bardovi-Harlig, K., and Bastos, M. T. (2011), 'Proficiency, Length of Stay, and Intensity of Interaction and the Acquisition of Conventional Expressions in L2 Pragmatics', *Intercultural Pragmatics*, 8 (3), 347–84.

Baró, A. L., and Serrano, R. (2011), 'Length of Stay and Study Abroad: Language Gains in Two versus Three Months Abroad', *Revista Espanola de Linguistica Aplicada*, 24, 95–110.

Briggs, J. G. (2015a), 'A Context-specific Research Tool to Probe the Out-of-class Vocabulary-related Strategies of Study-abroad Learners', *International Journal of Applied Linguistics*, 25 (3), 291–314.

Briggs, J. G. (2015b), 'Out-of-class Language Contact and Vocabulary Gain in a Study Abroad Context', *System*, 53, 129–40.

Briggs, J. G. (2016), 'A Mixed-methods Study of Vocabulary-related Strategic Behaviour in Informal Second Language Contact', *Study Abroad Research in Second Language Acquisition and International Education*, 1 (1), 61–87.

Coleman, J. A. (2013), 'Researching Whole People and Whole Lives', in C. Kinginger (ed.), *Social and Cultural Aspects of Language Learning in Study Abroad*, 17–44, Amsterdam: John Benjamins.

Coleman, J. A., and Chafer, T. (2010), 'Study Abroad and the Internet: Physical and Virtual Context in an Era of Expanding Telecommunications', *Frontiers: The Interdisciplinary Journal of Study Abroad*, 19, 151–67.

Conroy, M. A. (2018), 'Contextual Factors in Second Language Learning in a Short-term Study Abroad Programme in Australia', *The Language Learning Journal*, 46 (3), 311–28.

Cubillos, J. H., Chieffo, L., and Fan, C. (2008), 'The Impact of Short-term Study Abroad Programs on L2 Listening Comprehension Skills', *Foreign Language Annals*, 41, 157–85.

Derwing, T. M., Munro, M. J., and Thomson, R. I. (2008), 'A Longitudinal Study of ESL Learners' Fluency and Comprehensibility Development', *Applied Linguistics*, 29, 359–80.

Devlin, A. M. (2018), 'The Interaction between Duration of Study Abroad, Diversity of Loci of Learning and Sociopragmatic Variation Patterns: A Comparative Study', *Journal of Pragmatics*, 146, 121–36.

Dewey, D. P. (2008), 'Japanese Vocabulary Acquisition by Learners in Three Contexts', *Frontiers: The Interdisciplinary Journal of Study Abroad*, 15, 127–48.

Dewey, D. P., Belnap, R. K., and Hillstrom, R. (2013), 'Social Network Development, Language Use, and Language Acquisition during Study Abroad: Arabic Language Learners' Perspectives', *Frontiers: The Interdisciplinary Journal of Study Abroad*, 22, 84–110.

Dewey, D. P., Bown, J., and Eggett, D. (2012), 'Japanese Language Proficiency, Social Networking, and Language Use during Study Abroad: Learners' Perspectives', *Canadian Modern Language Review*, 68 (2), 111–37.

Dewey, D. P., Ring, S., Gardner, D., and Belnap, R. K. (2013), 'Social Network Formation and Development during Study Abroad in the Middle East', *System*, 41 (2), 269–82.

Dewey, D. P., Bown, J., Baker, W., Martinsen, R. A., Gold, C., and Eggett, D. (2014), 'Language Use in Six Study Abroad Programs: An Exploratory Analysis of Possible Predictors', *Language Learning*, 64 (1), 36–71.

Di Silvio, F., Donovan, A., and Malone, M. E. (2014), 'The Effect of Study Abroad Homestay Placements: Participant Perspectives and Oral Proficiency Gains', *Foreign Language Annals*, 47 (1), 168–88.

Díaz-Campos, M. (2004), 'Context of Learning in the Acquisition of Spanish Second Language Phonology', *Studies in Second Language Acquisition*, 26 (2), 249–73.

Dörnyei, Z. (2019), 'Task Motivation: What Makes an L2 Task Engaging?', in Z. Wen, and M. J. Ahmadian (eds.), *Researching L2 Task Performance and Pedagogy: In Honour of Peter Skehan*, 53–66, Amsterdam: John Benjamins.

Dörnyei, Z., Durow, V., and Zahran, K. (2004), 'Individual Differences and Their Effects on Formulaic Sequence Acquisition', in N. Schmitt (ed.), *Formulaic Sequences: Acquisition, Processing and Use*, 87–106, Amsterdam: John Benjamins.

DuFon, M., and Churchill, E. (2006), 'Evolving Threads in Study Abroad Research', in M. DuFon, and E. Churchill (eds.), *Language Learners in Study Abroad Contexts*, 1–30, Clevedon: Multilingual Matters.

Durbidge, L. (2018), 'Technology and L2 Engagement in Study Abroad: Enabler or Immersion Breaker?', *System*, 80, 224–34.

Fernández, J., and Gates Tapia, A. N. (2016), 'An Appraisal of the Language Contact Profile as a Tool to Research Local Engagement in Study Abroad', *Study Abroad Research in Second Language Acquisition and International Education*, 1 (2), 248–76.

Flege, J., and Liu, S. (2001), 'The Effect of Experience on Adults' Acquisition of a Second Language', *Studies in Second Language Acquisition*, 23, 527–52.

Fraser, C. C. (2002), 'Study Abroad: An Attempt to Measure the Gains', *German as a Foreign Language Journal*, 1, 45–65.

Freed, B. F., Dewey, D. P., Segalowitz, N., and Halter, R. (2004), 'The Language Contact Profile', *Studies in Second Language Acquisition*, 26 (2), 349–56.

Gass, S. (2017), 'Commentary 1: SLA and Study Abroad: A Focus on Methodology', *System*, 71, 46–8.

Gautier, R., and Chevrot, J. (2015), 'Social Networks and Acquisition of Sociolinguistic Variation in a Study Abroad Context: A Preliminary Study', in R. Mitchell, N. Tracy-Ventura, and K. McManus (eds.), *Social Interaction, Identity and Language Learning during Residence Abroad*, 169–84, Eurosla Monographs Series, 4. Amsterdam: John Benjamins.

George, A. (2014), 'Study Abroad in Central Spain: The Development of Regional Phonological Features', *Foreign Language Annals*, 47 (1), 97–114.

Godfrey, L., Treacy, C., and Tarone, E. (2014), 'Change in French L2 Writing in Study Abroad and Domestic Contexts', *Foreign Language Annals*, 47 (1), 48–65.

Hardison, D. M. (2014), 'Changes in Second-language Learners' Oral Skills and Socio-affective Profiles following Study Abroad: A Mixed-methods Approach', *Canadian Modern Language Review*, 70 (4), 415–44.

Hernández, T. A. (2010), 'The Relationship among Motivation, Interaction, and the Development of Second Language Oral Proficiency in a Study-abroad Context', *The Modern Language Journal*, 94 (4), 600–17.

Hetz, P. R., Dawson, C. L., and Cullen, T. A. (2015), 'Social Media Use and the Fear of Missing Out (fomo) While Studying Abroad', *Journal of Research on Technology in Education*, 47 (4), 259–72.

Hillstrom, R. A. (2011), 'Social Networks, Language Acquisition, and Time on Task While Studying Abroad', unpublished master's dissertation, Provo, UT: Brigham Young University.

Hogan, B., Janulis, P., Phillips II, G. L., Melville, J., Mustanski, B., Contractor, N., and Birkett, M. (2019), 'Assessing the Stability of Ego-centered Networks over Time Using the Digital Participant-aided Sociogram Tool Network Canvas', *Network Science*.

Isabelli-García, C. (2006), 'Study Abroad Social Networks, Motivation and Attitudes: Implications for Second Language Acquisition', M. DuFon, and E. Churchill (eds.), *Language Learners in Study Abroad Contexts*, 231–58, Bristol: Multilingual Matters.

Jia, G., Strange, W., Wu, Y., Collado, J., and Guan, Q. (2006), 'Perception and Production of English Vowels by Mandarin Speakers: Age-related Differences Vary with Amount of L2 Exposure', *Journal of the Acoustical Society of America*, 119 (2), 1118–30.

Kelly, D. (2010), 'Student Learning in an International Setting', *New Directions for Higher Education*, 150, 97–108.

Kennedy Terry, K. M. (2017), 'Contact, Context, and Collocation. The Emergence of Sociostylistic Variation in L2 French Learners during Study Abroad', *Studies in Second Language Acquisition*, 39 (3), 553–78.

Kinginger, C. (2008), 'Language Learning in Study Abroad: Case Studies of Americans in France', *The Modern Language Journal*, 92 (s1), 1–124.

Kinginger, C. (2009), *Language Learning and Study Abroad: A Critical Reading of Research*, Houndsmills, Basingstoke, UK: Palgrave Macmillan.

Kinginger, C., and Blattner, G. (2008), 'Histories of Engagement and Sociolinguistic Awareness in Study Abroad: Colloquial French', in L. Ortega, and H. Byrnes (eds.), *The Longitudinal Study of Advanced L2 Capacities*, 223–46, New York: Routledge.

Lennon, P. (1989), 'Introspection and Intentionality in Advanced Second-language Acquisition', *Language Learning*, 39, 375–96.

MacKay, I. R. A., Flege, J. E., and Imai, S. (2006), 'Evaluating the Effects of Chronological Age and Sentence Duration on Degree of Perceived Foreign Accent', *Applied Psycholinguistics*, 27, 157–83.

Magnan, S., and Back, M. (2007), 'Social Interaction and Linguistic Gain during Study Abroad', *Foreign Language Annals*, 40 (1), 43–61.

Mancheño, A. A. (2008), 'A Study of the Effect of Study Abroad and the Homestay on the Development of Linguistic and Interactional Practices by Spanish L2 Learners', unpublished doctoral thesis, University of Texas at Austin.

Marijuan, S., and Sanz, C. (2018), 'Expanding Boundaries: Current and New Directions in Study Abroad Research and Practice', *Foreign Language Annals*, 51 (1), 185–204.

Martínez-Arbelaiz, A., Areizaga, E., and Camps, C. (2017), 'An Update on the Study Abroad Experience: Language Choices and Social Media Abroad', *International Journal of Multilingualism*, 14 (4), 350–65.

Martinsen, R. (2011), 'Predicting Changes in Cultural Sensitivity among Students of Spanish during Short-term Study Abroad', *Hispania*, 94 (1), 121–41.

Martinsen, R. A., Baker, W., Dewey, D. P., Bown, J., and Johnson, C. (2010), 'Exploring Diverse Settings for Language Acquisition and Use: Comparing Study Abroad, Service Learning Abroad, and Foreign Language Housing', *Applied Language Learning*, 20 (1–2), 45–69.

McManus, K., Mitchell, R., and Tracy-Ventura, N. (2014), 'Understanding Insertion and Integration in a Study Abroad Context: The Case of English-speaking Sojourners in France', *Revue Française de Linguistique Appliquée*, XIX (2), 97–116.

Milton, J., and Meara, P. (1995), 'How Periods Abroad Affect Vocabulary Growth in a Foreign Language', *ITL International Journal of Applied Linguistics*, 107–8, 17–34.

Mitchell, R. (2015), 'The Development of Social Relations during Residence Abroad', *Innovation in Language Learning and Teaching*, 9 (1), 22–33.

Montero, L. (2019), 'Developing Effective L2 Communication Strategies Abroad and at Home', *The Language Learning Journal*, 47 (5), 642-52.

Mora, J. C., and Valls-Ferrer, M. (2012), 'Oral Fluency, Accuracy, and Complexity in Formal Instruction and Study Abroad Learning Contexts', *TESOL Quarterly*, 46 (4), 610-41.

Moyer, A. (2011), 'An Investigation of Experience in L2 Phonology: Does Quality Matter More than Quantity?', *The Canadian Modern Language Review*, 67 (2), 191-216.

Moyer, A. (2014), 'Exceptional Outcomes in L2 Phonology: The Critical Factors of Learner Engagement and Self-regulation', *Applied Linguistics*, 35 (4), 418-40.

Muñoz, C., and Llanes, À. (2014), 'Study Abroad and Changes in Degree of Foreign Accent in Children and Adults', *The Modern Language Journal*, 98, 432-49.

Pellegrino, V. (1996), 'Factors Affecting Risk-management Behavior among Students during Study-abroad', Presentation at AATSEEL Convention, Washington, DC, December 1996.

Pérez Vidal, C., and Juan-Garau, M. (2009), 'The Effect of Study Abroad (SA) on Written Performance', *EUROSLA Yearbook*, 9, 269-95.

Reynolds-Case, A. (2013), 'The Value of Short-term Study Abroad: An Increase in Students' Cultural and Pragmatic Competency', *Foreign Language Annals*, 46, 311-22.

Segalowitz, N., and Freed, B. F. (2004), 'Context, Contact, and Cognition in Oral Fluency Acquisition: Learning Spanish in at Home and Study Abroad Contexts', *Studies in Second Language Acquisition*, 26 (2), 173-99.

Segalowitz, N., and Ryder, A. (2006), 'Montreal Index of Linguistic Integration (MILI)', unpublished questionnaire, Concordia University, Montreal.

Segalowitz, N., Freed, B. F., Collentine, J., Lafford, B. A., Lazar, N., and Díaz-Campos, M. (2004), 'A Comparison of Spanish Second Language Acquisition in Two Different Learning Contexts: Study Abroad and the Domestic Classroom', *Frontiers: The Interdisciplinary Journal of Study Abroad*, 10, 1-18.

Seibert Hanson, A. E., and Dracos, M. J. (2016), 'Motivation and Technology Use during Second-language Study Abroad in the Digital Age', *Canadian Journal of Applied Linguistics*, 19, 64-84.

Serrano, R., Tragant, E., and Llanes, À. (2012), 'A Longitudinal Analysis of the Effects of One Year Abroad', *Canadian Modern Language Review*, 68 (2), 138-63.

Stark, T. H., and Krosnick, J. A. (2017), 'GENSI: A New Graphical Tool to Collect Ego-centered Network Data', *Social Networks*, 48, 36-45.

Taguchi, N. (2015), 'Contextually Speaking: A Survey of Pragmatics Learning Abroad, in Class and Online', *System*, 48, 3-20.

Taguchi, N. (2018), 'Contexts and Pragmatics Learning: Problems and Opportunities of the Study Abroad Research', *Language Teaching*, 51 (1), 124-37.

Tanaka, K. (2007), 'Japanese Students' Contact with English Outside the Classroom during Study Abroad', *New Zealand Studies in Applied Linguistics*, 13, 36-54.

Thompson, I. (1991), 'Foreign Accents Revisited: The English Pronunciation of Russian Immigrants', *Language Learning*, 41, 177-204.

Tragant, E. (2012), 'Change or Stability in Learners' Perceptions as a Result of a Study Abroad', in C. Muñoz (ed.), *Intensive Exposure Experiences in Second Language Learning*, 161-92, Bristol, UK: Multilingual Matters.

Vande Berg, M., Connor-Linton, J., and Paige, R. M. (2009), 'The Georgetown Consortium Project: Interventions for Student Learning Abroad', *Frontiers: The Interdisciplinary Journal of Study Abroad*, XVIII, 1-75.

Whitworth, K. F. (2006), 'Access to Language Learning during Study Abroad: The Roles of Identity and Subject Positioning', unpublished doctoral thesis, Pennsylvania State University.

Wright, C., and Schartner, A. (2013), '"I Can't ... I Won't?" International Students at the Threshold of Social Interaction', *Journal of Research in International Education*, 12 (2), 113–28.

Yager, K. (1998), 'Learning Spanish in Mexico: The Effect of Informal Contact and Student Attitudes on Language Gain', *Hispania*, 81 (4), 898–913.

Zhou, S. (2018), '"You Just Picked It Up." The Influence of Informal Language Contact on the Phrasal Verb Knowledge of International Students in the UK', unpublished master's dissertation, University of Cambridge.

5

Study abroad for secondary and higher education students: Differences and similarities in their interaction with the learning environment

Sofía Moratinos-Johnston, Maria Juan-Garau and Joana Salazar Noguera
University of the Balearic Islands

Introduction

There have been a number of studies (Evans and Fisher, 2005; Llanes and Muñoz, 2009; Serrano, Llanes and Tragant, 2016) that suggest that even short summer stays abroad (SA) (less than three weeks) during secondary education (SE) are beneficial for language learning. Besides developing language skills, Tan and Kinginger (2013) also highlight the opportunities that summer intensive courses (four to six weeks) provide for teenage exchange students to immerse themselves in the local culture and enhance intercultural competence. Various researchers (see Churchill, 2006; Crealock, Derwing and Gibson, 1999; Hashimoto, 1993; Spenader, 2011) have also described the mixed experiences of SA among students placed in foreign secondary schools on long-term exchanges. However, studies on SA during SE only represent a very small percentage of the considerable number of studies of higher education (HE) students (e.g. Amuzie and Winke, 2009; Cubillos and Ilvento, 2018; Jackson, 2008a; Pellegrino Aveni, 2005; Willis Allen, 2010), despite the fact that research indicates that the former might be quite different from the latter. For instance, Perrefort (2008) compared an SA programme in a European secondary school with the Erasmus experience of university students. She revealed that secondary students were more likely to refer to language-related experiences than university students, because of their daily interactions with native speakers in very diverse social circles. Moreover, the adolescents under study were more likely to experience identity problems rather than 'cultural shock' when confronting an unknown environment. Their interaction with locals helped them to develop social skills, such as personal autonomy and self-confidence. By contrast, university students seemed disappointed at their lack of easy access to local social networks and tended to interact mainly with other Erasmus students, very often in their mother tongue. This dearth of cultural exchanges and the lack of insight into the local customs and traditions often resulted in students falling back on negative stereotypes.

Due to a disparity in findings, more research into the differences and similarities that exist between the language and culture learning experiences that secondary and university students undergo when abroad is needed. These experiences are often determined by living arrangements and the degree to which both groups of students interact and build relationships with native or fluent speakers of the target language (TL), which in turn define how they negotiate cultural differences or achieve language learning goals. This study intends to explore these uncharted waters by capturing the narratives of Spanish students who went through either short- or long-term SA at different stages in their lives (secondary or higher education) and who sojourned either in an English- or a non-English-speaking country. All students, except for one, whose TL was German and sojourned in Switzerland, narrated their experiences learning English, which was used to communicate with native or non-native speakers while abroad, since in most cases students possessed insufficient knowledge of the local language in the non-English-speaking countries. Thus, many of the participants in the study to be presented here experienced SA in contexts where English is used as a lingua franca, which is considered as '*any use of English among speakers of different first languages, for whom English is the communicative medium of choice and often the only option.* Due to the number of speakers involved worldwide, this means that ENL [English as a Native Language] speakers will often be in a minority' (Seidlhofer, 2011, p. 7, original italics). The concept of *lingua franca* reflects that English is very often used in contexts where it is 'far removed from its native speakers' linguacultural norms and identities' (Seidlhofer, 2001, p. 133) and that people will use a variety of Englishes in transcultural communication among multilingual English speakers (Jenkins, 2017).

This study focuses on the retrospective representations that university students provide of their previous SA during SE and the lasting influence it had in their lives compared to the more recent experience of university students on an Erasmus exchange and how it affected personal and language-related initiatives.

The next section will present in more detail a review of previous research on study abroad at different educational stages focusing on the choice of accommodation, the variation in interaction and relationships with native and non-native speakers of the TL, and how this affects language input and insights into the local culture.

Literature review

Study abroad during secondary or higher education: Differences and similarities

Living arrangements – homestay versus halls of residence – and how they affect TL learning and ELF communication

Although there are many features that distinguish the sojourn of secondary and higher education students, as mentioned above, there is one element that seems key in various studies (Kinginger, 2015; Perrefort, 2008; Tan and Kinginger, 2013) and relates to accommodation type. While HE students, particularly Erasmus students in a

European context, live primarily in halls of residence, in the case of secondary school students their choice of accommodation varies, but they often experience homestays and these have important effects on their social relations.

Kinginger (2015) points out that no clear correlation has been discovered between choice of accommodation and TL proficiency (Diao, Donovan and Malone, 2018; Freed et al., 2004; Magnan and Back, 2007; Rivers, 1998) and that homestay experiences do not automatically lead to linguistic gains, but this will depend enormously on the welcome extended by the host family and their desire to integrate the student into their routines. Vande Berg, Connor-Linton and Paige (2009) also highlight that it is a matter not only of the amount of language exposure that the homestay allows but of how the students respond to it. In fact, research carried out by Kinginger (2015) with secondary school students indicates that younger learners 'tend to develop more intimate relationships with their hosts than do their older counterparts' (p. 53).

The experiences of secondary students as reported in the literature are quite varied. For instance, Crealock, Derwing and Gibson (1999) studied nineteen Japanese adolescents learning English in rural Canada and several of them enjoyed the time they spent with the family and the leisure opportunities this brought including watching TV, camping and reading. However, one-third of the students missed out on these opportunities because they had to change families for different reasons, such as student behaviour problems or lack of commitment on the part of the host family. For the rest of the participants, pre-departure information was lacking, including advice on the personal adjustments necessary to fit into a rural community and advice on cultural differences. Although such cases are rare, the authors conclude that the host families and the exchange programmes should be closely monitored to avoid such events from happening.

Ní Chasaide and Regan (2010) analysed the acquisition of French by Irish adolescents during their SA and unveiled mixed results as regards the relationship with their host families and their degree of integration into francophone social networks. Some participants integrated easily into their host family and school, while others socialized in French mainly among the international community and, finally, one of the participants completely refused to engage with his host family. Similarly, in a study of twenty-six German teenagers, Grieve (2015) described the relationship of some of them with their Australian host families as sometimes tense due to personality clashes and differences in lifestyle; yet most of the students made an effort to improve relations with their host families.

Turning now to the research on university students, although their experiences are equally varied, these may be affected by their adult perspective, since they have a greater sense of independence, choose their own activities and have a different outlook on life. For example, in their study of forty-two American university students participating in an eight-week sojourn abroad in Luxembourg, Rodríguez and Chornet-Roses (2014) discovered that 'more than half of the participants indicated that their expectations about their homestay experience were not met' (p. 168). The main complaints were the lack of involvement in family activities or lack of interest on the part of the host family. Apart from this, some students also commented on insufficient privacy, an inconvenience that was also highlighted by Juveland's (2011) study of 116 undergraduate American language students, who reported lack of freedom or being treated as children rather than adults.

Regarding non-homestay accommodation, the research on the experience of secondary school students in halls of residence is quite limited. Serrano, Tragant and Llanes (2014) analysed a four-week SA intensive language course for Spaniards with teenage students living in halls of residence in the UK and reported that students did not fully profit from their SA experience because they ended up mixing with their co-nationals and spent most of their free time speaking their mother tongue outside the classroom. Likewise, feelings of frustration with their halls of residence were reported at university level by Kaplan (1989) since the American students under study craved opportunities to use the TL, but were placed in residences in Paris with speakers of their own language and this decreased opportunities for contact with fluent speakers of the TL.

Overall, the secondary school students are considered to be more adaptable, open-minded and willing to take risks, which benefits integration into the host family (Perrefort, 2008; Tan and Kinginger, 2013). Kinginger (2015) also highlights the fact that it is the younger students who have a tendency to establish closer relationships with their hosts than their older counterparts. However, both older and younger students agreed that living with a family promoted greater integration into the local community, because of the close bonds that are built in such circumstances leading to increased language ability and acculturation (Kinginger, 2015; Murphy-Lejeune, 2002). As regards halls of residence, the most common choice of accommodation for Erasmus students in Europe, various researchers (e.g. Klapper and Rees, 2012; Mitchell, Tracy-Ventura and McManus, 2015; Papatsiba, 2006) report that they did not facilitate communication in the TL mainly because of students being placed with other co-nationals or non-native speakers of the TL.

Local social networks: Building up relationships

An important factor that determines levels of satisfaction and language learning during the SA experience is the 'quantity and quality of the social relationships which students manage to generate' (Murphy-Lejeune, 2002, p. 184). In the case of adolescents, apart from the host family, friendships with local teenagers are important to accomplish a sense of belonging and these relationships may be facilitated by same-age siblings within the host family (Grieve, 2015). Unfortunately, sometimes the set-up of the SA programme allows for few opportunities for contact with the locals, as Serrano, Tragant and Llanes's (2014) study of Spanish adolescents on a summer SA programme demonstrates. The main problem was that the majority of the students' time was spent in the classroom and the free time they had was mainly spent interacting with their L1-speaking peers. By contrast, both Hashimoto (1993) and Marriott (1995), who researched the experience of Australian secondary school students spending a year at different schools in Japan, praised the individualized attention and special treatment afforded by their Japanese family hosts. These had intensive language exposure to the Japanese language both during the regular school programme and during the time spent with the host families, who took an active role in offering corrective language feedback and provided them with increased opportunities for interaction. As Marriott (1995) suggests, all this results in an immersion in the TL community in a way that is not always available to the university exchange student placed in a hall of residence.

Although students seem to be aware that social interaction with native speakers will enhance their language skills (Ife, 2000), in some cases the adolescent exchange students may be beginners and this might lead to feelings of disappointment and social isolation (Paige, 1993). However, if the relationship with the host nationals is successful, even beginners can make impressive improvements in their language skills, as Spenader (2011) discovered in her study of American adolescents in Sweden, who reached an intermediate-high or higher ACFTL level after five months in the host country.[1] Additionally, an important consideration with adolescents, as pointed out by Perrefort (2008), is 'risk taking', i.e. how they react to taking on the challenge of communication in the TL. For instance, some are worried about being laughed at and yet, when they succeed, their linguistic self-confidence increases and the advantages of speaking outweighs the potential embarrassment.

In the case of university students, there are a number of studies that have documented their attempts to establish social networks and the influence such networks have on language acquisition in different contexts: Russia (Pellegrino Aveni, 2005), England (Jackson, 2008a), German-speaking countries (Klapper and Rees, 2012), Jordan and Egypt (Dewey et al., 2013). In general terms, university exchange students build contacts mainly with their own co-nationals, who offer a support network because of the shared language and culture, other foreign students, who represent the majority of their new friends, and finally with locals, who normally represent a much smaller percentage of their acquaintances (Budke, 2008). The mix of members of these three groups within the social networks of each individual will depend on a series of circumstances, including their milieu and their willingness to invest in learning the TL and culture (Willis Allen, 2010). According to Papatsiba (2006), the danger is the 'ERASMUS cocoon' which appears 'when the grouping of "Erasmus" students isolates them from the reality of the host country and prevents them from engaging with the host culture and interacting with the natives' (p. 121). Budke (2008) blames this partly on the characteristics of the Erasmus programme, since, in most universities, exchange students tend to take small courses specifically designed for foreign students or they attend large courses, which does not help interaction with local students. Apart from this, university exchange students are often quite busy with academic work and may be put off by the indifference of the locals (Murphy-Lejeune, 2002). This indifference, according to Coleman (2015), may be caused not only by the fact that the native speakers are not particularly keen to make contact with newcomers, who come for a short stay and may not be particularly fluent in the local language, but also by the native speakers already having a network of close friends and family members. These difficulties contrast with the priorities identified in a comprehensive survey assessing the main concerns of American university students ($n = 16,529$) enrolled in modern language courses in the United States. This showed that the top priority for students was 'communication and communities', which were described 'as the desire to use the TL in social interaction as well as the pleasure they received, and anticipated receiving, from that use' (Magnan, Murphy and Sahakyan, 2014, p. 224).

To conclude, apart from the benefits for linguistic development, various studies (e.g. Dewey, 2017; Isabelli-García, 2006; Lapkin, Hart and Swain, 1995) have demonstrated that the amount of contact with native speakers is also a key aspect in determining the acquisition of sociocultural knowledge. This leads us to analyse the impact that these contacts have on the intercultural competence of adolescent and young adult learners during residence abroad.

Intercultural encounters: Building intercultural communicative competence and intercultural awareness

According to Byram (1997), intercultural communicative competence (ICC) focuses on 'the ability to interact with people from another country and culture in a foreign language' (p. 71). This skill relates to the ability of the learner to appreciate differences among cultures while functioning efficiently in a foreign environment (Anderson and Lawton, 2011). Cubillos and Ilvento (2018) claim that intercultural competence is increased by studying abroad even if it is only short term, although this will depend on the kind of SA programme, the students' previous intercultural training (Behrnd and Porzelt, 2012) and their social skills. Brislin (1993) found that students who became interculturally competent have frequent contact with foreigners, enjoy it and are good at achieving their goals in a foreign environment. Other factors that play a role for students abroad are their foreign language proficiency level (Churchill and DuFon, 2006), their interest in establishing friendships with native speakers (Budke, 2008) and the quality of their intercultural encounters (Bloom and Miranda, 2015). Furthermore, for those students who use ELF to communicate in SA settings, the concept of intercultural awareness (ICA) suggested by Baker (2011) and described as 'the knowledge, skills and attitudes needed to communicate through English in diverse global contexts' (p. 197) may become relevant. This concept, which builds on the definition of ICC, refers to the awareness of the similarities and disparities between cultures particularly in multilingual and multicultural contexts. Some researchers (Baker, 2009; Kaypak and Ortaçtepe, 2014) have shown that foreign students in ELF settings can communicate successfully in English irrespective of their knowledge of the culture of English-speaking countries. However, the importance of intercultural sensitivity in ELF contexts increases due to the lack of shared linguistic and cultural background among speakers (Cavalheiro, 2015).

Previous work points to differences in how adolescents and young adults become aware of the disparities between cultures and adapt to their new surroundings. For instance, when Tan and Kinginger (2013) analysed the recollections of US adolescents during their summer abroad in China, they noticed that their intercultural experiences had left an important impression on them. For example, one of the participants, 'William', described how he reacted to the biased opinions that the Chinese had about Americans and how these might be mirrored by his compatriots back home. These experiences led to intercultural knowledge, since they helped the learners become more considerate and understanding of the differences between the two ways of life. According to Perrefort (2008), when adolescents were confronted with 'otherness', they tended to reflect upon themselves and became more self-aware, while young adults who had more life experiences could draw from them to make sense of their SA experience, but might also be less open to the new learning environment. Duerden et al. (2018) analysed such issues in their study of thirty American adolescents between fifteen and seventeen years of age who went to Cambodia on a trip intending to awaken social conscience through organized cultural exchanges and homestays with local Cambodians. One student, upon seeing the living conditions, stated: 'I'm learning about the culture here, but I think I'm learning more about myself also [...] and about how I feel about people, and the way they are treated and the way they live' (p. 23). Personality factors may also come into play as Spenader's (2011) research into the integration of four American teenage students in Sweden indicated, where there were two traits that benefited cross-cultural adaptation: assertiveness and a sense of humour.

As regards studies focusing on university students and their intercultural encounters during SA, research carried out by Teichler (2004) indicated that the surveyed students valued their cultural experiences, the improvement in their language skills and their personal growth, which were in fact their priorities before departure, more than academic achievements. Moreover, Murphy-Lejeune (2002) described the cultural experiences of European exchange students not so much as a 'cultural shock' but as a series of small U-curves, which may involve initial euphoria followed by confusion, rejection of the foreign culture, but then end with a problem-solving stage. These U-curves may repeat themselves several times throughout the year abroad and therefore take the form of a gentle wave. Overcoming the feelings of unease, frustration and loneliness associated with the dip in the curve will depend on the learner's personal initiatives to become involved in student activities and access social networks. Besides, their intercultural competence is improved by certain character traits such as curiosity, linked to an interest in new cultures (Coleman, 2015) and other personality dispositions such as openness, flexibility, empathy and resilience to stress (Jackson, 2008b).

In conclusion, the differences reported in the literature regarding how students experience SA during SE and HE are determined partly by their living arrangements, the type of social networks they build up and their exposure to TL speakers, which in turn facilitate the acquisition of ICC and ICA. All these factors vary greatly according to the individual circumstances of each SA student. Hence, this study intends to identify differences and similarities that can be found between students, who engaged in either on a short- or a long-term basis at different stages in their lives (secondary or higher education).

Method

The study

This study is based on a series of interviews with undergraduate students at a Spanish university. These university students were asked to narrate their previous SA experiences which had taken place either during their secondary school years or while at university. The study aims at identifying differences and similarities that can be found between students who have experienced SA during SE and HE and thus intends to answer the following research questions:

RQ1: How do the students' living arrangements and social networks affect their TL learning and ELF communication depending on whether they are SE or HE students?

RQ2: How do university students portray their relationships and cultural exchanges with TL speakers during their SA experiences depending on whether they occurred during SE or HE?

Participants

The interviewees ($n = 11$) were Spanish undergraduate students, who exemplify the varied character of SA experiences. These include students in homestays ($n = 4$) and halls of residence ($n = 7$), sojourns during secondary ($n = 6$) and higher education ($n = 5$) in English- ($n = 5$) and non-English-speaking countries ($n = 6$). Table 5.1 presents the main personal characteristics of the participants, including their perceived level of English at the time of interview and the main features of their SA programme.

There were only two specialist language students, studying English in both cases. The remainder represented a wide range of degree areas: humanities, science, social sciences and law. There was only one student who stated that her main aim was to learn German. All the rest stated that their TL was English.

Instruments

Individual interviews with the participants elicited the students' accounts of their SA experiences, in terms of what they did and how they felt during their study abroad. The interviews allowed the participants to point to and develop those factors that they found the most relevant during their language learning histories. The semi-structured interviews with set questions aimed at exploring: (i) the participants' general and TL-related feelings at the time of their study abroad; (ii) their impressions on their living arrangements and social networks and how they affected their language learning; and (iii) their perception of the local culture and how they felt and learnt about it. The interviews were conducted in the participants' mother tongue and lasted between 60 and 90 minutes.

The interviews were fully transcribed following Richards's (2003) recommendations, which include aiming for 'maximum readability without sacrificing essential features' (p. 81) such as pauses, emphasis, fillers and non-verbal features. The participants verified the accuracy of the transcribed interviews. Excerpts presented in this study were translated from Catalan or Spanish into English by the interviewer (the first author). Cross-case comparisons were drawn among the narratives in order to analyse the impact of the different types of programmes, living arrangements and cultural exchanges on the participants. Participants' quotations are reported using an identification code, which includes the initials of their first and last name plus the acronyms SE/HE indicating whether they went on a SA during SE or HE.

Table 5.1 Characteristics of the Interviewees

Initials	Gender	Degree	Year	Perceived Level of English	SA Period	Length	Target Language	Country	Living Arrangements
MF	Male	ICT	2	B2	SE	3 wks	Eng.	UK	Homestay
IM	Male	History	1	A2	SE	2 wks	Eng.	Germany	Homestay
IR	Male	History	1	B2	SE	3 wks	Eng.	UK	Halls of res.
CS	Female	Law	2	B2	SE	3 wks	Eng.	UK	Halls of res.
AR	Female	Pedagogy	3	A2	SE	2 wks	German	Switzerland	Homestay
TV	Female	Primary Ed.	2	A1	SE	2 wks	Eng.	Germany	Homestay
JS	Male	Economics	3	C1	HE	6–12 mths	Eng.	Slovakia	Halls of res.
LLM	Female	English	4	C2	HE	1–6 mths	Eng.	Ireland	Halls of res.
LM	Female	English	4	C2	HE	6–12 mths	Eng.	Austria	Halls of res.
DC	Female	Primary Ed.	3	C1	HE	1–6 mths	Eng.	Germany	Halls of res.
VM	Female	Tourism	3	C1	HE	6–12 mths	Eng.	UK	Halls or res.

Data analysis

NVIVO 11 was the software chosen to sort and interrogate the database of transcribed interviews. When the research objectives were formulated, the important concepts and a set of theoretically driven codes were identified. These codes represented broad concepts, which were then followed by the detection of more refined codes arising from the data (Richards, 2003). The analysis of these latter codes, which refer to categories symbolized by a word or short phrase capturing content present in the data, leads to the emergence of each separate theme. A theme is defined as a 'relational statement derived from the data that identifies both content and meaning' (Bazeley, 2013, p. 190) and which indicates a possible trend or pattern (Saldaña, 2016). This process of thematic analysis, described as a 'method for identifying themes and patterns of meaning across a dataset in relation to a research question' (Clarke and Braun, 2013), has been used to analyse data in a wide range of qualitative SA studies (Barkhuizen, 2017; Campbell, 2015; Czerwionka, Artamonova and Barbosa, 2015; Kaypak and Ortaçtepe, 2014; Williams and Goikonomidoy, 2017).

After the most frequent significant codes and themes were identified, they were considered in terms of differences between students who had experienced SA either during SE or HE. Finally, the transcripts were considered in greater depth and cross-case comparisons were carried out between the two groups of students on the coded categories recorded. A summary of the main coded categories and themes used is provided in Table 5.2 and will be illustrated by data extracts in the section 'Results and Discussion'.[2]

Table 5.2 Main Codes and Themes Used in the Study

Overarching Main Codes	Description of the Codes	Emergent Themes
Experiences with host families	The participants portray positive and negative learning experiences related to their relationship with the host family	**TL learning experiences** 'Homestays involve immersion in the TL' 'Homestays mean successful integration into family and social structures' 'Feelings of language progress after a short time span' 'The importance of bonding with the host family' 'Complaints about frequent contact with co-nationals' 'Efforts to open up social networks to include TL speakers' 'Difficulty in establishing contact with local students in classes' 'Ease of communication while using ELF with non-native TL speakers'
Experiences in halls of residence	The participants portray positive and negative learning experiences related to their daily routine in the halls of residence	
Language progress	The participants refer to language learning episodes	
Contact with native TL speakers vs lack thereof	The participants describe instances of contact (or lack thereof) with native TL speakers and refer to language learning episodes	
Contact with non-native TL speakers vs lack thereof	The participants describe instances of contact with non-native TL speakers and their use of ELF	

Table 5.2 Main Codes and Themes Used in the Study *(Continue)*

Overarching Main Codes	Description of the Codes	Emergent Themes
Cultural interest in the host country	Signs of interest in the culture of the host country including steps taken to get to know it better	**Cultural exchanges** 'Access to the local communities and culture requires a strong resolve'
Acculturation	Positive cultural experiences indicating adaptation to the new culture	'ICC gains through interest and openness to the new culture' 'A conscious effort to access the local social circles leads to ICC'
Culture shock	Negative cultural experiences associated with feelings of frustration or disorientation	'Missing out on cultural experiences due to busy academic lives'
Cultural stereotypes	Instances when the participants turned to generalizations of positive or negative qualities attributed to the inhabitants of a certain country	'Opportunities to learn about one's own culture through the foreign culture' 'Problems integrating into the local culture due to negative stereotypes'

Results and discussion

Differences and similarities between SE and HE students according to their living arrangements and social networks

Within the group who had experienced SA as SE students, there were differences as regards their social networks depending on accommodation and participation in formal instruction abroad. For instance, 'MF' (SE) and 'AR' (SE) participated in homestay exchange schemes, which involved staying with a host sibling, who was subsequently placed within their own Spanish family. These summer exchanges were short (two to three weeks) and did not include formal instruction. However, from the students' narratives we gather that these homestays involved successful integration not only into the family but also into the circle of friends of the host sibling. The whole experience points to extensive immersion into the TL with no recourse to their mother tongue. For instance, 'MF' (SE) who went to the UK to learn English, described how he improved his language ability in London, thanks to the warm welcome he received, the intensive language exposure and the use of corrective feedback:

> I loved being there, since he [his host sibling] introduced me to all his friends and I was integrated. They didn't keep me at arm's length, they took me under their wing and I had a great time, because it involved mainly entertainment. Nevertheless, I spoke English all the time, I also constantly listened to English and it was fantastic! […]. They also corrected me. He [his host sibling] said 'I don't think you said it correctly' or 'I don't think you meant to say that' and he repeated it correctly.
>
> ('MF', SE)

In fact, 'MF' (SE) elaborates on how the homestay experience helped him vastly improve his language skills by describing his long conversations with his family about football in the park. In parallel to these conversations, he was very aware of his own learning process by mentally reflecting on what and how he could respond to his new friends. By contrast, 'MF' (SE) stated that 'with the parents [I spoke] the bare minimum. We talked during dinner, lunchtime and that was it, because they had to go to work, but with our friends we talked all the time, we didn't stop talking, it was different'. 'MF' (SE) seems to describe attitudes which are quite common among adolescents, who value particularly their young friends over their relationships with adults.

'AR' (SE), whose aim was to learn German and sojourned in Switzerland with a host family, had a similar experience in terms of language learning. In fact, she declared: 'When I arrived I didn't know how to say "I am hungry" but in only two days I had already learnt to make these quick sentences to communicate with them and in fourteen days I had already learnt a lot.' Furthermore, the family afforded her the possibility of meeting a whole range of host nationals including neighbours and distant relatives. Unlike 'MF' (SE), she treasured the time spent both with the host family and her host siblings. She described the many opportunities for interaction she enjoyed: 'We went on lots of excursions, because they were a very Swiss family and they took me to the border with Austria, to Liechtenstein, and we did a bit of tourism, but also stayed at home and played board games together.' The best learning experience involved a big family dinner gathering 'with the uncles and grandparents of my "Swiss [brother]" and there was a table with loads of people and I spoke German with everyone there. It was actually on the last day, but it was at that moment that I felt satisfied and I told myself "gosh, how much I've learnt!"'

The successful experiences related by 'MF' and 'AR' give rise to a number of considerations. Firstly, students with low initial proficiency may also build close bonds with the host family, depending on both the family and the student's positive disposition (see also Tan and Kinginger, 2013). Secondly, short stays abroad can give students the feeling that they have improved considerably although their initial level was low and this might restrict their ability to communicate. In fact, Evans and Fisher (2005) attribute the beginner learner's rapid progression in naturalistic immersion, which seems to have positive effects even after one or two weeks. They also point to the possible link between 'improved performance and perceived support from the host family, in terms of the amount of communication in the TL and degree of help and correction provided to the pupils' (p. 190). This perceived language improvement during short-term SA is corroborated by results from language tests collected in previous research (e.g. Serrano, Llanes and Tragant, 2016). Thirdly, our results are similar to Spenader's (2011) study on American adolescents in Sweden who ascribed their language progress not so much to their formal instruction but to the close relationships with and support of their host families. These results also raise a few questions including the importance of the initial language level and the role of formal instruction during stays abroad. Next, we look at secondary school students who lived in halls of residence and received formal instruction.

One of the common complaints about accommodation in halls of residence is the fact that students are sometimes placed with other co-nationals, which restricts TL use. In these cases, it is up to the individuals to make an effort to extricate themselves from their ethnic group, whose common language and culture may appeal to students who feel scared and miss their families and friends. This was the case of 'CS' (SE), who initially felt very lonely and overwhelmed when she first arrived in the UK to learn English. Her first encounter with the receptionist at the halls of residence made her painfully aware of the fact that she did not understand the accent nor the vocabulary used by some native speakers. However, having overcome her initial difficulties, she resolved to make a conscious effort to seek out international students in order to make the most of her short stay in the UK:

> We were a group of five Spaniards and a Czech and we spoke mostly Spanish, since all the Spaniards had only an A1 or A2 level [in English], but I told them to speak English because of the Czech student. [...] I also insisted: 'speak to me in English, I am paying to speak English, so if you talk to me in Spanish you waste my time and my money.' But it was very difficult. They had a very low level and they immediately switched [to Spanish] and you had to accept it. Most people spent a long time there. The Spaniards went for seven weeks, because they had an A1 and wanted to reach a B1. I was there for three weeks and had to make the most of it, so I befriended the Czech boy and talked to him.
>
> ('CS', SE)

'CS' (SE) efforts paid off and during the second week she started to feel more integrated. She made friends with some Japanese students and went out of her way to meet other foreign students in order to improve her language skills. All this helped her build up her self-confidence and develop as a person. Overall, she was happy with her experience, but was disappointed that it was too short, and she complained about the number of Spaniards in her course (ten out of fourteen). Again, in order to avoid her compatriots, 'CS' (SE) asked for a change of class and was placed in a business English course, which she found particularly relevant to her interests and a useful source of new vocabulary. Unfortunately, apart from the teachers, she had hardly any contact with the locals. Yet, she managed to communicate effectively in conversations with fluent non-native speakers, which she described as important learning moments. 'IR' (SE), who was also accommodated in halls of residence in the UK, reported very similar experiences to 'CS' (SE); he tried to avoid his compatriots and other international students became his main social resource abroad, which led to increased language learning. He was also impressed with the native teachers, smaller classes and innovative teaching methodologies, which included more spoken interaction. Generally, these two students seemed satisfied with their SA experiences, although they had only a limited number of options to meet host nationals (apart from the classroom interaction). The possibility to experience wide-ranging language interaction and risk-taking experiences was thus also limited. The success of these sheltered programmes depends enormously on the willingness of the participants to actively seek out learning opportunities and establish very clear language learning objectives. In the case of the two participants under study, although they were very young and found it hard to deal with the emotional challenges and initial language shock, they persevered in establishing close friendships with international students, which have in some cases been maintained over the years.

Likewise, some university students also find it difficult to establish contact with local native speakers. For instance, 'LLM' (HE) – an English-language student who went to Ireland to improve her English – describes her efforts to interact with Irish people as very complicated. Initially, she found the Irish accent very difficult to understand. The type of accommodation she chose determined her social contacts and she struck up a close friendship with a group of Americans, who happened to live in her halls of residence. Although she was not living with local students in rented accommodation, this fulfilled her SA expectations, since her aim was to learn English and avoid mixing with Spaniards. According to 'LLM' (HE), these American exchange students were 'marvellous […] they corrected and helped me, when I got stuck with a word, if I described it to them, they told me'. She made up for her lack of local contacts with the enriching experience that her American friends brought to her life and the fact that all her social life took place using English.

Another participant, 'LM' (HE), is an English-language student who went to Austria on an Erasmus university exchange. She used ELF to communicate with teachers, students and flatmates at the halls of residence, since she felt that her level of German was not good enough. She felt comfortable speaking to non-native speakers of English, because she felt she would not be judged harshly for her mistakes:

> When I spoke, if I knew that someone was a native-speaker, I felt a bit more insecure since I thought 'this person will know that I have not used the right preposition or that I have got the wrong verb tense' and if I spoke with a Serbian for example I said to myself 'he will not kill me' or 'he is not judging me so much,' so I felt comfortable, very comfortable.
>
> ('LM', SE)

Similarly, 'DC' (HE) – an Erasmus exchange student who took a teacher-training course in Germany – felt she was not at a disadvantage vis-à-vis the local students who were also taking courses in a foreign language – most often English. 'JS' (HE), who sojourned in Slovakia to study economics, reported that the foreign teachers who taught content subjects through English did not have a strong local native accent: 'In fact I have fewer problems understanding "neutral" English than understanding a Mancunian, if you like.' Both of these students intended to improve their English using ELF.

As regards the choice of friends of 'LM', in the first semester she used mainly English to communicate with her group of international friends, since there were no Spaniards. However, in the second semester she felt guilty since she interacted mainly with a group of Spaniards and did not get as much practice. At the university she continued to use English with her Austrian fellow students, but she ended up having less exposure to English than in the first semester since she did not build close friendships with these students. The difficulty not only lies in having access to local students, but there also needs to be reciprocal interest on the part of the locals to strike up successful friendships, as 'VM' (HE) – a tourism student on Erasmus in Ireland – reports:

My objective was meeting native students and making Northern Irish friends, but it was a lot more difficult than I expected, since at university they organised lots of activities so you got to meet the international students, but no (Northern) Irish students came to these meetings. So, you only meet them when you go to class. Some of them live in the halls of residence, but they might already have their own groups of friends, since they already know one another, and it is difficult. For example, I lived with a (Northern) Irish girl and at the beginning we got together a bit more, but she left at the weekends, so it was difficult. I tried and I am happy because I finally met people through the Christian Union, Irish dancing and the (Northern) Irish family thanks to the 'International families' scheme.

('VM', HE)

The differences in the experiences between the adolescents and young adults during their SA are in part related to their accommodation choices and the opportunities they had to practise the language. Both the younger and the older students placed in halls of residence found their opportunities for interaction with the locals restricted. They tended to develop their social networks among the international students, who were in a similar situation to them and were easily accessible. By contrast, the bonds built within the local family provided a useful introduction into local society and also offered access to the routine communicative situations within the host family. Their narratives revealed an open-minded and flexible attitude that aided this successful integration. Most research indicates that levels of satisfaction in the host country are related to the development of close relationships with the local inhabitants (Gareis, 2000).

Differences and similarities between SE and HE students according to their cultural exchanges

The SA cultural experience for some SE students is not always as positive as in the narratives portrayed above, with many facing adaptation problems when abroad. A case in point is the description that 'TV' (SE) makes of her two-week experience as an exchange student in Germany, where she used ELF: 'It was never-ending.' She described the people in the street as cold compared with those in Spain: '[…] here (in Spain) the people in the street go to the bars and they talk and there (in Germany) [….] there they don't do anything. There they go to bed early'. She did not seem to have a very positive predisposition towards the country, she found the weather too cold and grey, the same way she described the school. The fact that she had to change her host family, which was very unstable, and did not properly accommodate or look after her did not help matters. However, after the change there was an improvement and she reported opportunities for conversations during meals, which took place in English and brought her closer to her host mother and the local culture. They also increased her linguistic self-confidence. Unlike the other SE students portrayed above, who had very clear learning objectives, 'TV' (SE), who was 14 at the time, felt she was young and had no clear goals; she left home thinking 'I wonder what it will be like there' and 'will I manage?' By contrast, 'IM' (SE), who was in a similar exchange scheme in Germany also using ELF, described this experience as the best he had had in terms of intercultural knowledge: 'There was a before and after as regards language and culture. It opened my mind enormously, culturally, but also linguistically.' In the case of 'IM', it was his culinary experiences that brought him closer to the local culture and to the host mother in particular. He stated: 'I helped the mum in the kitchen, because I like cooking and that was when I started to speak.'

As regards university students, 'LLM' (HE) did a fair amount of travelling because she found it difficult to meet local students in Ireland. However, tourism might not always be a very successful way to meet local inhabitants, as Papatsiba (2006) highlights in her study of French Erasmus students, who mainly travelled with other foreigners or their compatriots. 'LLM' (HE) also followed a different route to learn about Irish culture by taking two subjects related to Irish culture at university:

> I sometimes tried to mix with Irish people to get to know them, because I was living in Ireland and wanted to get to know something about its culture. In fact, I decided to take two subjects, one each semester related to Irish culture so that I felt I had learnt something about Ireland, since that was where I had been living. I took a mythology and a religion course and, when people asked me why, I told them that I was interested in learning about the different religions in Ireland.
>
> (LLM, HE)

Another participant, 'LM' (HE), felt very comfortable with the local culture, thanks to her efforts to join an exchange scheme within the university. She described her experiences getting to know Austrian culture:

> In Austria there was a programme [...] at university that was called Tandem, which meant that each Austrian student that enrolled said 'I want to find an Italian person' and you enrol, and the ERASMUS who arrived enrolled too to speak German obviously, and they would distribute us [...] and I joined this programme and I looked for three Austrian tandems and the truth was that I was extremely lucky with all three. They were really nice and they were very helpful in introducing me into their culture, for example when we met up, we did not just meet up for a coffee. We met up to go and see something important in their country and once they took me to meet their family.
>
> ('LM', HE)

Similarly, 'VM' (HE) strove to learn about the culture of Northern Ireland, where she spent nine months on an Erasmus exchange learning English. Her efforts included joining the Christian Union club, Irish dancing, surfing and a university-led scheme called 'International Friends'. This scheme involved being invited for meals at a local family's house, but also going on excursions or joining the family for mass. Another valuable source of cultural knowledge originated from her teachers at university. Particularly useful was her English-language course teacher:

> During the first semester I took English lessons and the teacher told us a lot about the culture, the traditions and the local festivities. Besides, this teacher had lived through very traumatic experiences related to the IRA and he told us about them

first hand and it was a very delicate subject in this class with this teacher. All this was vital in order to start understanding Northern Irish culture, where the national identity issue was very important.

('VM', HE)

In fact, 'VM' (HE) admitted that she was particularly interested in national identity issues and queried her friends once she got to know them better regarding their own national identity. She displayed certain character traits which have been associated with ICC: curiosity, interest, openness and empathy (Coleman, 2015; Jackson, 2008b), particularly when tackling certain delicate matters in a divided society. In fact, she declared that her exposure to these national identity disputes helped her understand similar questions that are divisive and topical, affecting regional and national identities within the Spanish state: 'Now I see it from a different perspective and this has helped me understand what is happening here. Learning from that culture has helped me learn about my own culture.'

The only thing she regretted was that her competitive and hardworking nature led her to focus mainly on her academic work, even if that meant missing out on certain social events or activities, such as rowing or horse-riding that she wished she had done. These would have meant meeting more native speakers, which she defined as one of her priorities pre-departure.

From the SE students' narratives it emerges that it is not only the HE students who turn to certain cultural stereotypes, as the review of the literature unveiled (Budke, 2008), but that the SE students also resorted to familiar stereotypes to describe 'otherness', as in the case of 'TV'. Notwithstanding 'TV's' initial problems settling into the culture of the host country, the majority of the SE SA participants described successful and rewarding intercultural exchanges, displaying an open mind and interest in expanding their knowledge of different cultures. These findings are in line with previous research that indicates that even short-term SA programmes offer the necessary conditions to provide opportunities for cultural enrichment and development of ICC (Anderson, Lawton and Hubbard, 2015; Cubillos and Ilvento, 2018; Shiveley and Misco, 2015), if the students are motivated and the individual circumstances – including successful homestay arrangements – allow for it.

As regards HE students, unlike Perrefort (2008), who sees the cultural knowledge acquired by Erasmus students as being basically factual, the majority of Erasmus students in this study appear to have made an effort to acquire an in-depth knowledge of the local culture. This requires students to be determined to overcome the obstacles they face, such as lack of interest from local students in establishing friendships, the design of the SA programme, the type of accommodation and their busy academic lives. These results are in line with Deardorff (2006) and Haas (2018), who showed that students demonstrating intent and effort were more likely to increase their gains in ICC and ICA.

Conclusion

This study has aimed at unveiling the perceptions that university students have of their previous SA either during secondary or higher education. It analyses how the students who were adolescents at the time of their SA, and thus at a critical developmental stage in life, handled various challenges such as building relationships with native TL speakers in a new cultural and linguistic environment as compared with how the more mature university students faced these challenges. The research questions enquired about the students' choice of accommodation, their relationships with native and non-native speakers of the TL and how this influenced language input and insights into the local culture.

Regarding the type of SA programme and living arrangements, results indicate that the secondary students' homestay experience often automatically immersed the foreign student into the language and culture of the host community and allowed them to meet native speakers, while the Erasmus students who sojourned in halls of residence needed to make a conscious effort to access local social circles. Immersion into the host family's life meant SE students enjoyed access to the local social networks and had more intense language experiences. The participants' accounts suggest that the SE students, who were younger, were probably more flexible and adaptable, which in turn facilitated the benefits of the homestay experience. By contrast, the SE and HE students placed in halls of residence described limited opportunities for interaction with the locals and tended to build their social networks around international students.

As far as cultural knowledge is concerned, data from our study have shown that those university Erasmus students who sojourned in halls of residence, but who aspired to learn about the culture of their host country, needed to go out of their way to, inter alia, take extracurricular courses or join sports associations or religious groups. Access to the local communities required a strong resolve and this was sometimes accomplished through university schemes such as the 'Tandem' or the 'International families' initiatives, which bring Erasmus students into contact with either local students or families. Nevertheless, we did find examples of HE students who were very receptive and willing to learn about the local culture and whose intercultural exchanges also led to a better understanding and awareness of their own culture and even national identity problems. Similarly, the majority of SE participants described successful and rewarding intercultural exchanges, displaying an open mind and interest in expanding their knowledge of different cultures. Another similarity between HE and SE students is that they all describe the efforts they made to find opportunities to speak with native speakers. However, those SE and HE students who communicated mainly with non-native speakers felt less pressure because of their lack of self-consciousness when using ELF.

Overall, results indicate that both for SE and HE students SA is a life-changing experience (Zaykovskaya, Rawal and De Costa, 2017) and that, in the case of the SE students, even a short stay abroad can be sufficient to improve their motivation and self-confidence, while for HE students – although their stay may be longer – they might have to make greater efforts to more fully enjoy the benefits SA offers. Thus, investment by parents in sending their children on exchange schemes during adolescence appears to be worthwhile.

Limitations of this study include the fact that there were no participants who had experienced SA both during SE and HE and could therefore compare each of these experiences. Further, students who shared their SA experience during SE were interviewed a number of years after their experience, while the HE students were describing more recent events. Since the great majority of Erasmus students live in halls of residence, it was difficult to find HE students who had experienced a homestay. Another difference between the types of SA programmes portrayed in this study is that, unlike the longer stays of students in HE (up to a year), the school exchange visits or summer courses among SE participants are most commonly between two to three weeks long. Notwithstanding, the experiences recorded here have revealed that the SE students' experiences (particularly for homestay students) were very intense and enriching both linguistically and culturally.

Implications for SA programme organizers include the fact that not only should exchange university students be encouraged to learn about the local culture of the host country, but also the host university should offer programmes which allow for this to happen. According to the testimonies gathered in this study from SA students who were involved in programmes that encourage interaction between families and exchange students, they are beneficial for all parties involved. These schemes are more common in UK universities (Coleman, 2015; Murphy-Lejeune, 2002) but could be extended to other parts of the world. Apart from these schemes, another possibility would be to encourage and facilitate the accommodation of Erasmus students in shared flats with local students or families. Specific pedagogic interventions targeting the improvement of ICA and ICC both throughout the SA experience as well as before and on the students' return is also a measure that is strongly recommended by some researchers (Haas, 2018; Pedersen, 2010; Salisbury, An and Pascarella, 2013). In the same vein, in terms of language improvement, previous training in the use of language learning strategies, particularly when students face content language learning through the L2, together with the implementation of programmes designed to allow for structured learning activities with the host nationals – both during homestays and in halls of residence (see also Kinginger, 2011; Knight and Schmidt-Rinehart, 2010; Vande Berg, Conner-Linton and Paige, 2009) – are also possible suggestions to enhance language acquisition. Finally, the conclusion to be drawn from the study is that SA, whether during SE or HE, is linguistically and culturally rewarding, although the challenges involved are not necessarily the same in each case.

Notes

1   ACFTL: American Council on the Teaching of Foreign Languages.
2   The codes described in Table 5.2 are further divided into subcategories in a hierarchical manner. However, for the sake of concision, just the parent codes and not their subdivisions are presented.

References

Amuzie, G., and Winke, P. (2009), 'Changes in Language Learning Beliefs as a Result of Study Abroad', *System*, 37 (3), 366–79.

Anderson, P. H., and Lawton, L. (2011), 'Intercultural Development: Study Abroad vs. On-Campus Study', *Frontiers: The Interdisciplinary Journal of Study Abroad*, XXI, 86–108.

Anderson, P. H., Lawton, L., and Hubbard, A. (2015), 'Student Motivation to Study Abroad and Their Intercultural Development', *Frontiers: The Interdisciplinary Journal of Study Abroad*, XXVI, 39–52.

Baker, W. (2009), 'The Cultures of English as a Lingua Franca', *TESOL Quarterly*, 43 (4), 567–92.

Baker, W. (2011), 'Intercultural Awareness: Modelling an Understanding of Cultures in Intercultural Communication through English as a Lingua Franca', *Language and Intercultural Communication*, 11 (3), 197–214.

Barkhuizen, G. (2017), 'Investigating Multilingual Identity in Study Abroad Contexts: A Short Story Analysis Approach', *System*, 71, 102–12.

Bazeley, P. (2013), *Qualitative Data Analysis: Practical Strategies*, London: Sage.

Behrnd, V., and Porzelt, S. (2012), 'Intercultural Competence and Training Outcomes of Students with Experiences Abroad', *International Journal of Intercultural Relations*, 36 (2), 213–23.

Bloom, M., and Miranda, A. (2015), 'Intercultural Sensitivity through Short-Term Study Abroad', *Language and Intercultural Communication*, 15 (4), 567–80.

Brislin, R. (1993), *Understanding Culture's Influence on Behavior*, New York: Harcourt Brace College Publishers.

Budke, A. (2008), 'Contacts Culturels et Identités Ethniques des Etudiants ERASMUS en Allemagne', in F. Dervin, and M. Byram (eds.), *Echanges et Mobilités Académiques. Quel Bilan ?*, 17–43, Paris: L'Harmattan.

Byram, M. (1997), *Teaching and Assessing Intercultural Competence*, Clevedon: Multilingual Matters.

Campbell, R. (2015), 'Life Post-Study Abroad for the Japanese Language Learner: Social Networks, Interaction and Language Usage', in R. Mitchell, N. Tracy-Ventura, and K. McManus (eds.), *Social Interaction, Identity and Language Learning during Residence Abroad*, 241–62, Amsterdam: European Second Language Association.

Cavalheiro, L. (2015), 'Developing Intercultural Communicative Competence in ELF Communication', *ELOPE: English Language Overseas Perspectives and Enquiries*, 12 (1), 49–60.

Churchill, E. (2006), 'Variability in the Study Abroad Classroom and Learner Competence', in M. A. DuFon, and E. Churchill (eds.), *Language Learners in Study Abroad Contexts*, 203–27, Clevedon: Multilingual Matters.

Churchill, E., and DuFon, M. A. (2006), 'Evolving Threads in Study Abroad Research', in M. A. DuFon, and E. Churchill (eds.), *Language Learners in Study Abroad Contexts*, 1–27, Clevedon: Multilingual Matters.

Clarke, V., and Braun, V. (2013), *Successful Qualitative Research: A Practical Guide for Beginners*, London: Sage.

Coleman, J. A. (1998), 'Evolving Intercultural Perceptions among University Language Learners in Europe', in M. Byram, and M. Fleming (eds.), *Language Learning in Intercultural Perspective*, 45–75, Cambridge: Cambridge University Press.

Coleman, J. A. (2015), 'Social Circles during Residence Abroad: What Students Do, and Who With', in R. Mitchell, K. McManus, and N. Tracy-Ventura (eds.), *Social Interaction, Identity and Language Learning during Residence Abroad*, 33–51, Amsterdam: European Second Language Association.

Crealock, E., Derwing, T. M., and Gibson, M. (1999), 'To Homestay or to Stay Home: The Canadian-Japanese Experience', *TESL Canada Journal*, 16 (2), 53–61.

Cubillos, J., and Ilvento, T. (2018), 'Intercultural Contact in Short-Term Study Abroad Programs', *Hispania*, 101 (2), 249–66.

Czerwionka, L., Artamonova, T., and Barbosa, M. (2015), 'Intercultural Knowledge Development: Evidence from Student Interviews during Short-Term Study Abroad', *International Journal of Intercultural Relations*, 49, 80–99.

Deardorff, D. K. (2006), 'Identification and Assessment of Intercultural Competence as a Student Outcome of Internationalization', *Journal of Studies in International Education*, 10 (3), 241–66.

Dewey, D. P. (2017), 'Measuring Social Interaction during Study Abroad: Quantitative Methods and Challenges', *System*, 71, 49–59.

Dewey, D. P., Ring, S., Gardner, D., and Belnap, R. K. (2013), 'Social Network Formation and Development during Study Abroad in the Middle East', *System*, 41 (2), 269–82.

Diao, W., Donovan, A., and Malone, M. (2018), 'Oral Language Development among Mandarin Learners in Chinese Homestays', *Study Abroad Research in Second Language Acquisition and International Education*, 3 (1), 32–57.

Duerden, M. D., Layland, E., Petriello, M., Stronza, A., Dunn, M., and Shelby, A. (2018), 'Understanding the Unique Nature of the Adolescent Study Abroad Experience', *Journal of Hospitality, Leisure, Sport and Tourism Education*, 23, 18–28.

Evans, M., and Fisher, L. (2005), 'Measuring Gains in Pupils' Foreign Language Competence as a Result of Participation in a School Exchange Visit: The Case of Y9 Pupils at Three Comprehensive Schools in the UK', *Language Teaching Research*, 9 (2), 173–92.

Freed, B., Dewey, D. P., Segalowitz, N., and Halter, R. (2004), 'The Language Contact Profile', *Studies in Second Language Acquisition*, 26 (2), 349–56.

Gareis, E. (2000), 'Intercultural Friendship: Five Case Studies of German Students in the USA', *Journal of Intercultural Studies*, 21 (1), 67–91.

Grieve, A. M. (2015), 'The Impact of Host Family Relations and Length of Stay on Adolescent Identity Expression during Study Abroad', *Multilingua*, 34 (5), 623–57.

Haas, B. W. (2018), 'The Impact of Study Abroad on Improved Cultural Awareness: A Quantitative Review', *Intercultural Education*, 29 (5–6), 571–88.

Hashimoto, H. (1993), 'Language Acquisition of an Exchange Student within the Homestay Environment', *Journal of Asian Pacific Communication*, 4, 209–24.

Ife, A. (2000), 'Language Learning and Residence Abroad: How Self-Directed Are Students?', *The Language Learning Journal*, 22 (1), 30–7.

Isabelli-García, C. (2006), 'Study Abroad Social Networks, Motivation and Attitudes: Implications for Second Language Acquisition', in M. A. DuFon, and E. Churchill (eds.), *Language Learners in Study Abroad Contexts*, 231–58, Clevedon: Multilingual Matters.

Jackson, J. (2008a), 'Globalization, Internationalization, and Short-Term Stays Abroad', *International Journal of Intercultural Relations*, 32 (4), 349–58.

Jackson, J. (2008b), *Language, Identity and Study Abroad*, London: Equinox.

Jenkins, J. (2017), 'The Pragmatics of English as a Lingua Franca?', in J. Jenkins, W. Baker, and M. Dewey (eds.), *The Routledge Handbook of English as a Lingua Franca*, 1–12, New York: Routledge.

Juan-Garau, M., Salazar-Noguera, J., and Prieto-Arranz, J. I. (2014), 'English L2 Learners' Lexico-Grammatical and Motivational Development at Home and Abroad', in C. Pérez-Vidal (ed.), *Language Acquisition in Study Abroad and Formal Instruction Contexts*, 235–58, Amsterdam: John Benjamins.

Juveland, S. (2011), 'Foreign Language Students' Beliefs about Homestays', Master's thesis, Portland State University.

Kaplan, M. A. (1989), 'French in the Community : A Survey of Language Use Abroad', *The French Review*, 63 (2), 290–9.

Kaypak, E., and Ortaçtepe, D. (2014), 'Language Learner Beliefs and Study Abroad: A Study on English as a Lingua Franca (ELF)', *System*, 42 (4), 355–67.

Kinginger, C. (2011), 'Enhancing Language Learning in Study Abroad', *Annual Review of Applied Linguistics*, 31 (3), 58–73.

Kinginger, C. (2015), 'Language Socialization in the Homestay: American High School Students in China', in R. Mitchell, N. Tracy-Ventura, and K. McManus (eds.), *Social Interaction, Identity and Language Learning during Residence Abroad*, 53–74, Amsterdam: European Second Language Association.

Klapper, J., and Rees, J. (2012), 'University Residence Abroad for Foreign Language Students: Analysing the Linguistic Benefits', *The Language Learning Journal*, 40 (3), 335–58.

Knight, S. M., and Schmidt-Rinehart, B. C. (2010), 'Exploring Conditions to Enhance Student/Host Family Interaction Abroad', *Foreign Language Annals*, 43 (1), 64–71.

Lapkin, S., Hart, D., and Swain, M. (1995), 'A Canadian Interprovincial Exchange: Evaluating the Linguistic Impact of a Three-Month Stay in Quebec', in B. Freed (ed.), *Second Language Acquisition in a Study Abroad Context*, 67–94, Amsterdam: John Benjamins.

Llanes, À., and Muñoz, C. (2009), 'A Short Stay Abroad: Does It Make a Difference?', *System*, 37 (3), 353–65.

Magnan, S. S., and Back, M. (2007), 'Social Interaction and Linguistic Gain during Study Abroad', *Foreign Language Annals*, 40 (1), 43–61.

Magnan, S. S., Murphy, D., and Sahakyan, N. (2014), 'Goals of Collegiate Learners and the Standards for Foreign Language Learning', *The Modern Language Journal*, 98, 1–293.

Marriott, H. (1995), 'The Acquisition of Politeness Patterns', in B. Freed (ed.), *Second Language Acquisition in a Study Abroad Context*, 197–225, Amsterdam: John Benjamins.

Mitchell, R., Tracy-Ventura, N., and McManus, K. (2015), *Social Interaction, Identity and Language Learning during Residence Abroad*, Amsterdam: European Second Language Association.

Murphy-Lejeune, E. (2002), *Student Mobility and Narrative in Europe: The New Strangers*, New York: Routledge.

Ní Chasaide, C., and Regan, V. (2010), 'Irish Adolescents, Three Languages and Identity Construction: Finding a Voice in French', in C. Ní Chasaide, and V. Regan (eds.), *Language Practices and Identity Construction by Multilingual Speakers of French*, 51–79, Bern: Peter Lang.

Paige, M. R. (1993), *Education for the Intercultural Experience*, Yarmouth: Intercultural Press.

Papatsiba, V. (2006), 'Study Abroad and the Experiences of Cultural Distance and Proximity: French Erasmus Students', in M. Byram, and A. Feng (eds.), *Living and Studying Abroad: Research and Practice*, 108–33, Clevedon: Multilingual Matters.

Pedersen, P. J. (2010), 'Assessing Intercultural Effectiveness Outcomes in a Year-Long Study Abroad Program', *International Journal of Intercultural Relations*, 34 (1), 70–80.

Pellegrino Aveni, V. A. (2005), *Study Abroad and Second Language Use: Constructing the Self*, Cambridge: Cambridge University Press.

Perrefort, M. (2008), 'Changer en Echangeant? Mobilités et Expériences Langagières', in F. Dervin, and M. Byram (eds.), *Echanges et Mobilités Académiques: Quel Bilan?*, 65–91, Paris: L'Harmattan.

Richards, K. (2003), *Qualitative Inquiry in TESOL*, Basingstoke: Palgrave Macmillan.

Rivers, W. P. (1998), 'Is Being There Enough? The Effects of Homestay Placements on Language Gain during Study Abroad', *Foreign Language Annals*, 31 (4), 492–500.

Rodríguez, S. R., and Chornet-Roses, D. (2014), 'How "Family" Is Your Host Family?: An Examination of Student-Host Relationships during Study Abroad', *International Journal of Intercultural Relations*, 39, 164–74.

Saldaña, J. (2016), *The Coding Manual for Qualitative Researchers*, Los Angeles, CA: Sage.

Salisbury, M. H., An, B. P., and Pascarella, E. T. (2013), 'The Effect of Study Abroad on Intercultural Competence among Undergraduate College Students', *Journal of Student Affairs Research and Practice*, 50 (1), 1–20.

Seidlhofer, B. (2001), 'Closing a Conceptual Gap: The Case for a Description of English as a Lingua Franca', *International Journal of Applied Linguistics*, 11 (2), 133–58.

Seidlhofer, B. (2011), *Understanding English as a Lingua Franca*, Oxford: Oxford University Press.

Serrano, R., Llanes, À., and Tragant, E. (2016), 'Examining L2 Development in Two Short-Term Intensive Programs for Teenagers: Study Abroad vs. "at Home"', *System*, 57, 43–54.

Serrano, R., Tragant, E., and Llanes, À. (2014), 'Summer English Courses Abroad versus "at Home"', *ELT Journal*, 68 (4), 397–409.

Shiveley, J., and Misco, T. (2015), 'Long-Term Impacts of Short-Term Study Abroad: Teacher Perceptions of Preservice Study Abroad Experiences', *Frontiers: The Interdisciplinary Journal of Study Abroad*, 26, 107–20.

Spenader, A. J. (2011), 'Language Learning and Acculturation: Lessons from High School and Gap Year Students', *Foreign Language Annals*, 44, 381–98.

Tan, D., and Kinginger, C. (2013), 'Exploring the Potential of High School Homestays as a Context for Local Engagement and Negotiation of Difference', in C. Kinginger (ed.), *Social and Cultural Aspects of Language Learning in Study Abroad*, 155–79, Amsterdam: John Benjamins.

Teichler, U. (2004), 'Temporary Study Abroad: The Life of ERASMUS Students', *European Journal of Education*, 39 (4), 395–408.

Vande Berg, M., Conner-Linton, J., and Paige, M. R. (2009), 'The Georgetown Consortium Project: Interventions for Student Learning Abroad', *Frontiers: The Interdisciplinary Journal of Study Abroad*, XVIII, 1–75.

Williams, G. M., and Goikonomidoy, E. (2017), 'Exploring the L2 Motivational Self System of Japanese Study Abroad Students', *Asian EFL*, 19 (2), 141–59.

Willis Allen, H. (2010), 'Language-Learning Motivation during Short-Term Study Abroad: An Activity Theory Perspective', *Foreign Language Annals*, 43 (1), 27–49.

Zaykovskaya, I., Rawal, H., and De Costa, P. I. (2017), 'Learner Beliefs for Successful Study Abroad Experience: A Case Study', *System*, 71, 113–21.

6

Assessing the impact of educational support abroad on sojourners' interactional contacts, L2 acquisition and intercultural development

Ana Maria Moreno Bruna, July De Wilde,
June Eyckmans and Patrick Goethals
Ghent University

Introduction

In the context of international education and language learning, participation in international exchange programmes has become increasingly popular (Macready and Tucker, 2011; Vande Berg, Paige and Lou, 2012). It has often been argued that study abroad (SA) is the perfect opportunity for language learners to master a language successfully, not only at a linguistic level but also at an intercultural level. This belief is shared by ordinary citizens, but also by policy decision-makers, language-curriculum designers and teachers alike. For example, in the European context, the Erasmus+ programme has proven to be a strategic element that helps foster internationalization and language learning (European Commission, 2015).

The SA literature on learning gains abroad is extensive and continues to investigate possible effects of SA in several domains. Regarding intercultural and language learning, research, however, repeatedly shows that the mere fact of being abroad is not a fail-safe guarantee that the participants will automatically become fluent intercultural speakers (Coleman, 2013; Jackson, 2018; Kinginger, 2009). In fact, in some cases, students may even become more ethnocentric after going abroad and less willing to interact with members of the host community if they have had negative experiences (Lou, Andresen and Myers, 2011; Vande Berg, 2007; Vande Berg and Paige, 2009). These interactions in the host country have also been challenged by the effects of modern technology. According to Knight and Schmidt-Reinhart (2002), the so-called immersion experience no longer takes students away from their home environments, as technology gives them the possibility to remain closely connected to their first language (L1) and 'at-home' friends and family throughout their experience abroad. Coleman and Chafer (2010, p. 165) accurately point out that 'thanks to telecommunications technologies, abroad is less abroad than it once was'. Moreover, it has been observed in the literature that the increased availability of SA programmes has brought a change of attitude among the students, in that they are less committed to their learning process (Goldoni, 2013; Kinginger, 2013). This supports the fact that linguistic and intercultural benefits of SA programmes cannot be taken for granted.

Therefore, it is critical to look at how it is possible to maximize language use intensity and interactional contacts during SA through educational support. Goldoni (2013, p. 360) argues that the combination of SA programme features, student-specific factors and investment in social interactions with the host community can be decisive in terms of intercultural and language learning. Being aware of opportunities and being motivated to seize them with a view to becoming interculturally efficient do not come by themselves. As Jackson (2016, 2018) repeatedly maintains, participants may need guidance in order to turn first-hand experiences into potentially enriching intercultural experiences. These observations explain why scholars advocate more educational support at all stages of SA (Jackson, 2016; Lou and Bosley, 2008; Vande Berg, Paige and Lou, 2012). In this respect, technology can also be seen as a way to follow and guide the learning process of SA participants from their home institutions, as a means of enhancing opportunities to connect to the host community and allow them to maintain those connections when their SA experience ends. It may also serve to address issues in SA participants' commitment to their learning process abroad.

In this chapter, we report on the learning outcomes of an online pedagogical intervention specifically developed to enhance outgoing learners' interaction with the language and cultural reality of the host country while abroad. In the section 'Literature review', we will delve into previous efforts in SA research in terms of guidance abroad and detail the online intervention that is at the heart of this chapter. In the section 'Methodology', we will report on our research, which includes first a comparison of development of vocabulary size pre- and post-SA, along with pragmatic competence and cultural intelligence, defined by Earley and Ang (2003) as an individual's capability to detect, assimilate, reason and act on appropriate cultural cues in situations characterized by cultural diversity. The present research works with two groups of learners: the first participated in the online intervention while abroad and the second group did not. In order to assess the guidance efforts and explore its possible influence on students' interactional contacts, L2 acquisition and intercultural competence, we will explore in detail students' feedback regarding the 'popularity' and perceived 'usefulness' of the different activities that constituted the intervention. In conclusion, we describe how the data gathered served to improve the intervention for a next cohort of students and led to a practice-based reshuffle of tasks for an online application called 'Study Abroad Language Support App' (SALSA).

Literature review

Recent advances in SA research have gone beyond registering the effect of different variables on learning outcomes abroad. Rather, there is increased focus on 'shaping' the context for optimal language and intercultural learning abroad. Scholars argue that this can be achieved through research-based interventions that encourage intercultural contact beyond stereotypes with a view to cultivating meaningful intercultural relationships (Jackson, 2016; Lou and Bosley, 2008; Vande Berg, 2007; Vande Berg and Paige, 2012; Vande Berg, Paige and Lou, 2012). Indeed, a growing body of research supports the hypothesis that frequent and sustained intercultural interaction leads to language and intercultural development during SA (e.g. Dewey, Bown and Eggett, 2012; Isabelli-García, 2006). According to Dewey, Belnap and Hillstrom (2013), participants who seek out and befriend members of the host community use the L2 more and engage in more complex, extended discourse than those who do not. However, it is not realistic to expect that these meaningful intercultural relationships that would lead to better foreign language development simply naturally arise just because the students are abroad. Jackson (2010) argues that not all SA participants react to face-to-face intercultural contact in the same way. While some may limit their L2 use if they find the environment inhospitable, others may find their hosts welcoming and therefore make the most of the experience.

There are many examples of educational support abroad in terms of linguistic and intercultural learning. From the European perspective, the project 'Intercultural Education Resources for Erasmus Students and Their Teachers' (Van Maele, Vassilicos and Borghetti, 2016) developed a set of teaching modules on intercultural education for Erasmus students. The objective was to encourage learning mobility and to support students in terms of personal growth and intercultural awareness. Similar initiatives have been pursued in the North American ('Maximizing Study Abroad through Language and Culture Strategies', Paige et al., 2009) and Asian contexts (Jackson, 2016, 2018).

These projects have illustrated that students undergo a complex learning process that is affected by individual variables, the reality of the host country and surrounding cultural reality, participants' linguistic and intercultural interactions and the wide variety of individual and concrete experiences themselves. It has become clear that intercultural learning requires analysis of cultural facts (Beaven and Borghetti, 2018), reflection on participants' own language learning processes (Jackson, 2016), as well as awareness of identity and adjustment to the new situation (Vande Berg, Paige and Lou, 2012). Educational guidance should thus focus on this process of increasing awareness and critical reflection in order to allow SA participants to be more in charge of their own linguistic and intercultural learning process. As authors such as Dörnyei (2005) state, autonomous and self-regulated learners take a proactive role in the learning process rather than simply reacting to external stimuli.

This study evaluates the role played by an online pedagogical intervention carried out during the Erasmus SA experience. The overall focus of the intervention is to explore participants' linguistic and intercultural awareness development through a socialization approach. Within this framework, Kramsch (2002) and Lantolf (2000) conceptualize learning as a highly contextualized social practice, with a key role being assigned to communication with more expert speakers, thereby encouraging learners to leave their comfort zones (Dewey, Bown and Eggett, 2012, p. 113). Intercultural competence (henceforth IC) here follows Byram's definition (2000, p. 75) as 'the ability to interact successfully with others across cultural difference'. Intercultural learning is defined, at the same time, as the process which, through the affective, cognitive and behavioural dimensions of learning, allows individuals to grasp cultural affiliations with their interlocutors and make them act upon such awareness (Beaven and Borghetti, 2018). The concept of culture, implicit in the cultural affiliations mentioned by Beaven and Borghetti, is envisaged 'as membership in a discourse community that shares a common social space and history, and common imaginings' (Kramsch, 2002, p. 10). From an intercultural point of view, our main interest is not how the participants actually behave when they are abroad, but rather whether they are able to identify these social spaces and imaginings, and whether they are able to reflect on them. Within the context of the pedagogical intervention, the term host community used in the tasks refers to the members of the host city with whom they communicate in their target language (Spanish).

Didactically speaking, the intervention is inspired by authors such as Hammer (2012) and Jackson (2016, 2018), who recommend an experiential learning cycle (Kolb, 1984), with critical reflection as a central component (Passarelli and Kolb, 2012). This means that participants are encouraged to engage with the host community which, according to Zumbihl (2010), leads to rich but unpredictable learning experiences. The author claims that these experiences are then further developed by encouraging critical reflection.

Methodology

Research questions

With these notions in mind, the present study investigated the possible effects of an online intervention in the learning processes and outcomes of Erasmus SA students. Research questions addressed in this chapter are twofold:

> RQ1: Does the intervention designed to promote interaction with locals lead to higher learning gains in terms of linguistic and cultural competence?
> RQ2: How do students assess the intervention tasks in terms of popularity and usefulness for their learning processes?

Research sample and design

Participants

The participants ($n = 81$) were enrolled in their third year of Applied Language Studies at a Belgian university. They spent a four-month compulsory Erasmus sojourn in Spain, either during the academic year 2016–17 or 2017–18. All of them had to choose twenty-seven European Credit Transfer System (ECTS) credits from the host institution but some of them (the experimental group (EG), $n = 32$) enrolled in the pedagogical intervention at the beginning of their Erasmus stay, fulfilling three of those credits upon successful completion. The rest (comparison group (CG), $n = 49$) only followed courses from the host university during their Erasmus sojourn. Some EG students decided to enrol in the intervention, or 'Intercultural Project', because they were intrinsically interested in the project, as stated in the initial email motivating their choice sent to the instructor, while others needed extra credits to complete their learning agreement or found out late that some of their initial courses at the host university overlapped. The EG is, thus, rather heterogeneous in terms of motivation as well as place of stay (eight different universities). Upon departure, all EG and CG participants had a minimum CEFR level of B2 in Spanish, with at least a B2 level in another language (English, French or German). Participants had previously acquired knowledge about intercultural communication, intercultural pragmatics and cultural history during their first two years of study. Therefore, the intervention designed for this study focuses on a rather specific group of students who are already acquainted with abstract/conceptual terms and ideas regarding IC and foreign language knowledge.

Methodological design of the pedagogical intervention

The intervention consists of fourteen tasks, carried out through the eLearning platform of the university and divided into six thematic modules, each of which focuses on a more global topic (language, identity, social contacts, etc.), or moments we believe might be meaningful during an Erasmus experience such as trips, attending traditional festivities or meeting with locals. In terms of methodological design, the intervention is inspired by Paige's work (Paige et al., 2009) and the IEREST Project (Van Maele, Vassilicos and Borghetti, 2016). Hence, the intervention works on an experiential learning approach and focuses on critical reflection and mediation (Byram, 1997). The instructor serves as a moderator of the learning and socialization process. All activities followed Kolb's (1984) 'Model of Experiential Learning', which defines learning as 'the process whereby knowledge is created through the transformation of experience' (p. 41). Kolb defines two important dimensions of learning: perception and processing (see Figure 6.1). 'Perception' refers to how learners receive new information (how the instructor presents the content), either through 'abstract conceptualization' or 'concrete experience', while 'processing' refers to how learners transform this new information into knowledge, either through 'reflective observation' or 'active experimentation'.

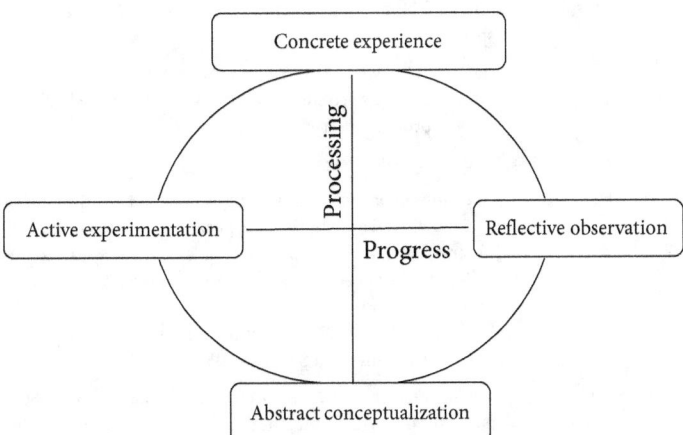

Figure 6.1 Kolb's (1984) Experiential Learning Cycle.

Given participants' academic profile (see section 'Participants'), tasks based on 'abstract conceptualization' were limited, giving more importance to those focused on 'concrete experience'. In fact, intercultural educators such as Bennett (2008) and Hammer (2012) recommend combining formal intercultural education with 'real-world' experience (Kolb, 1984; Passarelli and Kolb, 2012) in order to increase IC. For this reason, every module dealt with intercultural, social and linguistic aspects and form a continuum where both ways of 'processing' information (observation and experimentation) are present. After completing both tasks (outlined below) from a module, participants have to provide a critical reflection either in the written form in modules 2, 3, 5 and 6 or as part of an online conversation with the instructor in modules 1 and 4. The critical reflection phase is designed to enhance students' intercultural/social/linguistic awareness by means of critical thinking, on the one hand, and by actually getting in contact with the host community or facing specific intercultural situations, on the other.

Task descriptions

In this section, we provide an overview of the tasks within the intervention as well as the evaluation and completion requirements.

Task	Description
Module I: Warming up before the experience	
T1: Erasmus expectations	Reflection on their own Erasmus experience/expectations. Students post for their L1 peers in forum contributions.
T2: Activities with the host community	Students look for activities they could take part in in their city of destination in order to get to know locals, follow a specific one and post a photo and a written reflection.
Module II: Linguistic competence	
T3: Reflection on language used in social groups	Reflection on the language used by different social groups using a short film illustrating different cultural, sociological and linguistic aspects.
T4: Intercultural and linguistic references	Students work with comic strips on current trending topics with cultural and social connotations for which they need help from locals in order to interpret them.
Module III: Identities	
T5: European citizenship	Reflection on participants' identity as Erasmus students, Europeans, Belgians, shared among their L1 peers in a forum contribution. Students watch a video called 'Global citizenship', read some blog entries of other Erasmus students and answer lead questions for the purpose of a reflection such as 'Choose the definition of global citizen given in the video that most fits you and explain why' (adapted from the IEREST Project).
T6: Interview locals: economy	Students read about the socio-economic situation of the Spanish youth and interview a member of the host community willing to help them understand the situation.

Task	Description
	Module IV: Getting involved with locals
T7: Forum contribution: Home university	Task on 'reversed interculturality' – looking at their cultural perceptions through the eyes of local students. Students watch a video of Erasmus Spanish students at their home university and post about it for their L1 peers in forum contributions.
T8: Interview: Erasmus	Students interview four members of the host community eager to share their Erasmus experiences in the students' home city in Belgium.
	Module V: Interculturality
T9: IC situation: helping locals	Students reflect on intercultural aspects hindering or benefiting successful conversation and social interactions with L1 Spanish speakers (such as the understanding of personal space or ways of making a request) and ask members of the host community for help understanding those aspects.
T10: IC observation: reflection	Observation of intercultural situations where social interactions are challenged by local social or cultural norms. Students ask locals for help understanding these situations.
	Module VI: Life post-Erasmus
T11: PPT Erasmus experience	Students create a PowerPoint with pictures about their Erasmus experience in terms of intercultural/social or linguistic aspects.
T12: Blog advice Erasmus students	Students write a blog about the personal and professional experiences that they will bring back home after their Erasmus experience.
	Supplementary activities
T13: Online conversations instructor	The first conversation focuses on participants' expectations of the Erasmus experience, choice of destination, challenges of the experience, etc. The second conversation encourages reflections on participants' adaptation to the new intercultural and academic environment, interactional contacts, life experiences that might have influenced their Erasmus stay, etc.
T14: Intercultural diary	Weekly entries about real-life situations they have experienced. They reflect about them in terms of interculturality and social adaptation.

Regarding evaluation and task delivery, participants were required to complete each module every two/three weeks in order to receive gradual feedback from the instructor at their home institution. Students had all material at their disposal from the beginning of the semester. As such, they could organize their own workload and fit the tasks around their other Erasmus obligations. Participants were evaluated on task elaboration (if all questions were answered, if they had tried to see beyond generalizations and stereotypes and how personal their answers were), task presentation (formal aspects), respect for the deadlines and active participation on forums and online conversations with the instructor. Not completing some parts of the modules affected their final grades. Regarding task completion, those involving contact with the host community had to be written in Spanish. For the forum, interviews and blog tasks, participants could choose the language used, although the use of Spanish was highly encouraged and almost none of them used Dutch. The instructor gave participants feedback on their written and oral performance, but they were not penalized in terms of language accuracy.

Data collection and analysis

Quantitative measures of participants' learning outcomes

All participants ($n = 81$) completed three pre-/post-assessments online designed to measure their progress in Spanish vocabulary knowledge, perceived pragmatic competence and cultural intelligence. They completed this before leaving on Erasmus and upon their return. For assessing Spanish lexical proficiency, the Lexical Test for Advanced Learners of Spanish (LexTALE, Izura, Cuestos and Brysbaert, 2014) was adopted. The second measure implemented was the Modified Aural Vocabulary Knowledge Scale (VKS) for Pragmatic Purposes (Bardovi-Harlig, 2009). The scale measures recognition, production and meaning based on self-perception. We adapted it by including expressions to reflect the B2/C1 level in Spanish (*Curricular Plan Instituto Cervantes*, 2006) referring to request and refusal speech acts. Students were asked to rate their familiarity with the expressions on a five-point scale, where 1 stands for 'I have not seen this expression before, and I do not know what it means' and 5 corresponds to 'I know the meaning of this expression and I have used it outside class.'

In order to measure participants' IC, the 'Expanded Cultural Intelligence Scale' (E-CQS) was implemented and slightly adapted for SA purposes (Ng et al., 2012). IC can be measured in terms of intercultural traits, attitudes and world views, as well as intercultural capabilities. This scale was chosen because cultural intelligence is framed within the domain of intercultural capabilities, which emphasize what a person can do to be effective in intercultural interactions (Earley and Ang, 2003). The E-CQS was originally developed for expatriates and professionals living and working abroad, but it has also been used by Fehr and Kuo (2008) for analysing the development of social networks (SN) among international students. Moreover, the test comprises the four dimensions present in IC (metacognitive, cognitive, motivational and behavioural) and rates each dimension through single items on a seven-point Likert-type questionnaire. It is an aggregate multidimensional construct where the four dimensions reflect different capabilities that together form overall cultural intelligence. It allows a specific IC profile to be made for each participant and to define possible changes in this profile after the SA stay.

Learner assessment of the pedagogical intervention

Students completed an anonymous survey on the overall quality of the intervention after returning from their Erasmus stay and receiving final evaluation. The questions the students had to respond to were formulated as follows:

1. Which tasks did you like more? Grade the tasks from 1 to 10, 10 being the highest grade.

2. List the five most useful tasks in terms of language development in Spanish, 1 being the most useful. Mark if they were useful for written language development, oral development or both.
3. List the five most useful tasks in terms of IC development, 1 being the most useful.
4. List the five most useful tasks for getting in contact with locals from your host country, 1 being the most useful.

Questions regarding 'usefulness' covered only the five most useful tasks for methodological purposes. Otherwise, the survey would have been too time-consuming in combination with the other instruments used in this study. These rankings on 'popularity' and perceived 'usefulness' for every learning aspect were computed according to frequency and ranking order, as detailed in RQ2.

Results and discussion

RQ1: Does the intervention designed to promote interaction with locals lead to higher learning gains in terms of linguistic and cultural competence?

Results on standardized tests which the participants completed before and after the SA experience reveal that both groups of participants exhibit learning gains. Table 6.1 shows the descriptive statistics for both the CG and the EG of the test scores on L2 vocabulary size, L2 pragmatic competence and all four aspects of the Cultural Intelligence Scale (CQS): Motivational, Cognitive, Metacognitive and Behavioural Intelligence.

Table 6.1 Descriptive Statistics for Pre- and Post-SA Results of L2 Vocabulary Size (LexTALE), L2 Pragmatic Competence (VKS) and Cultural Intelligence Scale Variables (E-CQS)

	N	Range	Min	Max	Mean	SD
LexTALE pre	81	46	1	47	16.9	8.4
LexTALE post	81	46	3	49	21.0	8.3
VKS pre	81	2.6	1.7	4.3	2.7	.6
VKS post	81	3.1	1	47	2.9	.6
MOTIVATIONAL CQ pre	81	3.9	2.9	6.8	5.2	.9
MOTIVATIONAL CQ post	81	3.4	3.4	6.9	5.6	.8
COGNITIVE CQ pre	81	4.9	1.8	6.7	4.2	.9
COGNITIVE CQ post	81	3.8	2.6	6.4	4.9	.8
METACOGNITIVE CQ pre	81	4.4	2.1	6.6	4.6	.8
METACOGNITIVE CQ post	81	3.3	2.9	6.2	4.9	.7
BEHAVIOURAL CQ pre	81	4.0	2.6	6.6	4.4	.9
BEHAVIOURAL CQ pre	81	4.3	2.4	6.8	4.7	.9

Paired sample *t*-tests showed the learning gains to be statistically significant for all measures: L2 vocabulary size ($t = -4.905$; $df = 80$; $p = .000$); L2 pragmatic competence ($t = -4.156$; $df = 80$; $p = .000$); Motivational CQ ($t = -4.279$; $df = 80$; $p = .000$); Cognitive CQ ($t = -7.242$; $df = 80$; $p = .000$); Metacognitive CQ ($t = -4.048$; $df = 80$; $p = .000$) and Behavioural CQ ($t = -3.321$; $df = 80$; $p = .000$). These results demonstrate the learning potential of SA in the case of language learners who were already relatively advanced in terms of foreign language proficiency.

With respect to the impact of the pedagogical intervention on the participants' linguistic and intercultural learning, Table 6.2 reveals that the mean vocabulary size of students in the EG and the CG was virtually the same at the onset of the study, with the students in the EG showing a larger variation in scores. The vocabulary size measured after the SA experience points to a slightly higher increase in the EG than in the CG (EG: +4.5; CG: +3.9). However, this difference was not shown to be significant ($t = -.386$; $df = 79$; $p = .701$). Interestingly, the SD value decreases in the EG after the SA experience (SD pre = 10; SD post = 8.4), while it slightly increases in the CG (SD pre = 7.2; SD post = 8.3). One of the main reasons for implementing research-based interventions is the extensive individual variation reported in much of the literature on linguistic outcomes (for a review, see Kinginger, 2009). The decreased SD seems to indicate that the EG became more homogeneous in terms of vocabulary size, suggesting that the intervention may have played a role in enhancing vocabulary size across the participants during the SA experience.

Regarding pragmatic competence (VKS), results of independent *t*-tests in Table 6.3 show that learning gain differences between both groups after the SA experience are not significant ($t = -.343$; $df = 79$; $p = .732$). Table 6.3 reveals that students obtained similar scores before their departure and made small progress as a result of their SA experience (EG: +0.2; CG: +0.3). It is important to bear in mind that values ranged from 1 = 'I have not seen this expression before and I do not know what it means' to 5 = 'I know the meaning of this expression and I have used it outside class.' From 1–2, the survey measures 'noticing' of pragmatic expressions, while 3–5 refer to actual acquisition, with 5 relating to those expressions participants used outside the classroom (VKS = 5 in Table 6.3). Going from 'noticing' to actual 'acquisition' is a crucial step in the development of participants' L2 pragmatic competence.

Table 6.2 Participants' L2 Vocabulary Size (LexTALE), Pre- and Post-SA

	EG						CG					
	N	Range	Min	Max	Mean	SD	N	Range	Min	Max	Mean	SD
LEXT pre	32	44	3	47	16.8	10	49	29	1	30	16.9	7.2
LEXT post	32	37	3	40	**21.3**	8.4	49	43	6	49	**20.8**	8.3
LEXT gain					+4.5						+3.9	

Table 6.3 Participants' Pragmatic Knowledge (VKS), Pre- and Post-SA

	EG						CG					
	N	Range	Min	Max	Mean	SD	N	Range	Min	Max	Mean	SD
VKS pre	32	44	2.6	4.3	2.8	.6	49	2.4	1.7	4.1	2.6	.6
VKS post	32	37	2.4	4.5	**3.0**	.5	49	3	1.4	4.4	**2.9**	.7
VKS gains					+.2						+.3	

Although then-now self-assessment is often considered not to be objectively accurate, Dewey, Bown and Eggett (2012, p. 514) highlight two important benefits of this type of measures: its potential to promote self-efficacy and participants' ability to describe change as perceived by themselves. Moreover, research has shown that even when students are aware of what is pragmatically appropriate, they may choose not to use it for a variety of reasons. In the case of our participants, although they may have actually used these expressions out of class, there are a number of individual and contextual factors affecting the actual implementation of their knowledge in real-life situations, such as linguistic difficulty, identity and positioning in the host community (Taguchi, 2016). Hence, future analysis will need to cross-examine these results with other sets of data, such as actual use of the language during online conversations with the instructor or learner recordings of their interactions with the host community, in order to reveal 'how real-life constraints may or may not impact learners' use of the knowledge in the local community' (Taguchi, 2016, p. 87).

In relation to the results of the Cultural Intelligence Scale, Table 6.4 indicates that both groups of participants scored rather high on all dimensions of the scale before departing on their sojourn, with mean values exceeding 4 on a seven-point Likert-scale. These results show that this particular population has already developed their IC before departing on Erasmus. The highest scores in both groups are observed in Motivational Intelligence (EG: M = 5.6; CG: M = 5.5), which refers to an individual's capability to direct attention and energy towards learning about and functioning in situations characterized by cultural differences (Ang and van Dyne, 2008). Both groups of participants improved their scores on the different subdimensions to a similar degree, with gains ranging between 0.2 and 0.6. *t*-Tests did not reveal statistically significant differences between the two groups.

Summarizing the quantitative results, both groups of participants clearly benefited from the Erasmus experience in terms of linguistic and intercultural development, although significant differences between the groups' test scores as a result of the intervention were not attested. However, the scores show a tendency for the SD to decrease more in the EG than in the CG, which raises the question of how the intervention might have influenced the complex learning process of the participants in the EG by decreasing individual variation in their learning process abroad. Therefore, the second research question of this chapter is directed at participants' perceptions

Table 6.4 Participants' Cultural Intelligence Profile (E-CQS), Pre- and Post-SA

	EG						CG					
	N	Range	Min	Max	Mean	SD	N	Range	Min	Max	Mean	SD
MOT CQ pre	32	3.8	2.9	6.7	**5.2**	1	49	3.4	3.3	6.9	**5.1**	.9
MOT CQ post	32	3.2	3.7	6.9	**5.6**	.7	49	3.4	3.4	6.9	**5.5**	.8
MOT CQ gains					**+.4**	−.3					**+.4**	−1
COG CQ pre	32	4.0	2.7	6.7	4.3	.9	49	4.2	1.8	6.0	4.2	.8
COG CQ post	32	2.8	3.6	6.4	4.9	.7	49	3.7	2.6	6.3	4.8	.8
COG CQ gains					**+.6**	−.2					**+.6**	0
MET CQ pre	32	3.3	3.2	6.6	4.7	.8	49	3.8	2.1	5.9	4.5	.7
MET CQ post	32	2.3	3.8	6.1	4.9	.7	49	3.3	2.9	6.2	4.9	.7
MET CQ gains					**+.2**	−.1					**+.4**	0
BEH CQ pre	32	3.8	2.8	6.6	4.5	1	49	3.0	2.6	5.6	4.3	.8
BEH CQ post	32	3.4	3.3	6.8	4.8	.8	49	4.0	2.4	6.4	4.6	.9
BEH CQ gains					**+.3**	−.2					**+.3**	+.1

Motivational Intelligence (MOT CQ); Cognitive Intelligence (COG CQ); Metacognitive Intelligence (MET CQ); Behavioural Intelligence (BEH CQ)

of the impact of the intervention on their foreign language use, their social network formation and the development of their IC. This was done by analysing the students' feedback on their learning process with reference to the 'popularity' of the tasks and their perceived 'usefulness'.

RQ2: How do students assess the intervention tasks in terms of 'popularity' and 'usefulness' for their learning process?

We looked at students' rankings of task 'popularity' versus the perceived 'usefulness' of these tasks with reference to different dimensions of language and intercultural learning. The rankings in Table 6.5 show students' estimations for the fourteen tasks carried out during the intervention (with 1 referring to the most popular/useful task and 14 to the least popular/useful).

Table 6.5 Popularity and Perceived Usefulness of the Tasks

Task	Description	Popular	Useful L2 General	Useful L2 Written	Useful L2 Oral	Useful SNF	Useful IC
Task 13	Online conversations instructor	1	5	12	2	11	14
Task 12	Blog advice Erasmus students	2	6	3	10	13	10
Task 11	PPT Erasmus experience	3	9	11	5	9	11
Task 1	Forum contribution: Erasmus	4	11	9	10	13	13
Task 8	Interview locals: Erasmus	5	1	5	1	1	1
Task 4	L2/IC references: help locals	6	3	7	4	2	5
Task 9	IC situation: help locals	7	9	7	14	5	2
Task 3	Reflection on L2 social groups	8	7	4	5	7	9
Task 6	Interview locals: economy	9	2	1	3	3	3
Task 10	IC observation: reflection	10	8	9	10	4	8
Task 7	Forum contribution: Ghent	11	13	12	8	10	7
Task 5	Forum contribution: Europe	12	11	6	8	11	6
Task 2	Activities with L2 community	12	14	12	10	8	12
Task 14	Intercultural diary	14	4	2	7	6	4

N = 32 participants; grey = practical implementation tasks; black = guided reflection tasks.

L2 development (useful L2 general); L2 development on writing skills (useful L2 written); L2 development on oral skills (useful L2 oral); social network formation (useful SNF); intercultural competence (useful IC).

As detailed in the section 'Methodological design of the pedagogical intervention', all tasks in the proposed intervention used different types of authentic material as a starting point for the learning experience (perception phase) and focus on interculturality, contact with the host community and linguistic development. However, when it comes to processing the new information, all modules combine tasks on 'active implementation' with others based on observations and reflections that together lead to the critical reflection final phase of the module. Tasks 2, 4, 6, 8, 9 and 14 (marked in grey in Table 6.5) invite participants to put into practice what they have learned through 'practical implementation': they have to get involved with the host community, create a video about their host city, participate in an intercultural experience and so on. Tasks 1, 3, 5, 7, 10 and 11, 12 and 13 (marked in black in Table 6.5) are intended to make participants process concrete information through 'guided reflection' (blog entries or group discussions where they link what they have learned with their personal experiences/values, etc.).

Table 6.5 indicates that tasks 13, 12, 11 and 1 are respectively the most 'popular' tasks. However, their place in the ranking in terms of 'usefulness' is rather low. Task 13 (online conversations with the instructor about intercultural/social/linguistic aspects of the Erasmus experience) is in position 12 in terms of L2 written development, position 11 in terms of SN formation and position 14 in terms of IC development. In other words, although this task is the most popular, students do not think that it has helped them develop their IC, L2 written development or contact with the host community. The same pattern can be observed with task 11 (creating a PowerPoint with pictures of their own Erasmus experience). Students like the activity but their ranking of the task with reference to SN formation (9) and IC development (11) indicates that they do not find it useful for their intercultural development, nor for facilitating contact with the host community. Pictures included needed to be relevant in terms of intercultural/social or linguistic aspects. Guided reflection here aimed at going beyond stereotypes to think about how they managed to engage with the host community (this task was completed during their last weeks abroad). They only perceive this task to be useful in terms of L2 written development, which is surprising if we take into account that they had to add an audio explanation to every picture. However, it is possible that they wrote all their ideas down before making the presentation and it influenced their perception of the task.

Task 12 (blog entry with advice for future Erasmus students) is in position 10 in L2 oral development, position 13 in terms of SN formation and position 10 in terms of IC development. Students had to write about the intercultural or interactional importance of pictures following the guidelines given by the instructor. They had to reflect on linguistic, social and intercultural aspects they wished they had known before embarking on their experience in order to become involved with the host community. Participants seem to like the task but do not judge it very useful beyond their L2 writing skills. Task 1 (forum discussion on expectations, fears and objectives with reference to their Erasmus experience) is not considered useful for L2 development in general (position 11 of 14), nor for their L2 writing skills (position 9 of 14) or their oral skills (10 of 14). Although they had to introduce themselves and interact with each other in the L2, participants did not find the task useful in terms of SN formation and interculturality (position 13 of 14 in both cases). Again, the 'popularity' of a task does not relate to its estimated usefulness for intercultural and linguistic learning (in spite of the task's objectives).

If we look closely at the aforementioned tasks in terms of participants' learning processes and outcomes, we can conclude that all of them focus within their respective modules on 'guided reflection'. The analysis of students' feedback suggests that students did not conceive of these reflections as useful for intercultural or interactional purposes. While it goes beyond the scope of this chapter, it will be necessary to analyse in the future if students actually succeed in breaking stereotypes to delve into more profound intercultural reflections, as stated in the guidelines given by the instructor and intended to happen by the end of every module. To sum up, all four tasks are rather academic 'desktop' activities, in the sense that they are carefully delineated in terms of objectives and expected outcomes from the participants. The target audience is limited to the instructor and L1 peers following the intervention. It can be expected that the 'academic' aspect of the tasks makes participants feel confident with the expected outcome, which, it would appear, is an important reason for the overall 'popularity' of the activities.

When we look at the least popular tasks (ratings higher than 8), we see that several of these tasks score high in terms of 'usefulness'. The tasks in which the estimations of 'popularity' and 'usefulness' are most at odds are task 6 (place 9 in the 'popularity' ranking), where participants have to interview locals about the economic situation of the host country and task 14 (the intercultural diary, ranked 14 in the 'popularity' ranking). Task 6 is positioned high in the ranking on 'usefulness' for L2 development in general (2), L2 written (1) and oral (3) development. Moreover, task 6 is ranked at 3 for 'usefulness' in terms of both IC development and SN formation. Task 14 also scores high on the 'usefulness' dimension (position 4 for L2 in general, position 2 for L2 written development and position 4 and 6 for IC development and SN formation, respectively). When compared with the content of tasks 13, 12, 11 and 1 (considered as the most popular), both tasks 6 and 14 require a more direct involvement with the host environment. In task 6, participants have to confront members of the host community about a delicate topic and address them in Spanish. In task 14, participants have to be critical about social and cultural situations where values, traditions and perceptions of the local environment challenge their own. Both situations demand a high level of personal involvement while the audience in both tasks is not limited to L1 peers or the instructor. The students need to look for and engage with inhabitants from their city of destination, which is more challenging than the academic 'desktop' activities referred to before.

Finally, if we take into account that all tasks address at the same time diverse linguistic, intercultural and social aspects of the Erasmus experience, a further step in this research is to investigate if these perceptions of 'popularity' and 'usefulness' correlate significantly to each other. Table 6.6 presents the correlations between the participants' estimations of 'popularity' and 'usefulness' for L2 development in general, written development ('Useful L2 written'), oral development ('Useful L2 oral'), intercultural competence ('Useful IC') and social network formation ('Useful SNF'). As could be expected based on the analysis presented, Spearman's rank correlation coefficients do not reveal significant correlations between participants' perceptions

Table 6.6 Non-parametric Spearman's Rank-order Correlation (two-tailed) between Perceived Usefulness and Popularity of the Tasks

K = 14	1	2	3	4	5	6
1. Popularity		.288 (p <.318)	.243 (p <.402)	−.135 (p <.645)	−.363 (p <.202)	−.244 (p <.401)
2. Useful L2 general			.695 (p <.006)	.630 (p <.016)	.478 (p <.084)	.581 (p <.029)
3. Useful L2 oral				.188 (p <.519)	.185 (p <.527)	.378 (p <.182)
4. Useful L2 written					.586 (p <.028)	.316 (p <.217)
5. Useful IC						.736 (p <.003)
6. Useful SNF						

Spearman's rho (two-tailed correlations), n = 32 participants.

of the 'usefulness' of the fourteen tasks for the different aspects of learning and the 'popularity' of the tasks. This finding is significant with reference to the quality assurance of the pedagogical intervention. As instructors, we aim at developing didactic approaches where participants advance in their learning while also enjoying the learning process. Overall 'popularity' measures of the tasks do not correspond to the learners' perceptions of their 'usefulness' when it comes to intercultural development and language learning.

To conclude, we also observe that there are significant correlations between the perceptions of the 'usefulness' of tasks for different learning outcomes. Significant correlations between 'usefulness' for L2 development in general and 'usefulness' for L2 oral development as well as L2 written development are perhaps self-evident since both oral and written development are subsets of general L2 proficiency. Such a finding is important for further reiterations of the intervention since it shows that written and oral tasks are complementary and that both aspects need to be included in such training. More interesting is that perceived 'usefulness' in L2 development in general correlates significantly with perceived 'usefulness' for SN formation ($r = .581, p < .029$). This indicates that tasks considered useful for facilitating contact with locals are also considered useful for developing L2 proficiency. Table 6.6 also shows significant correlations between 'usefulness' for L2 written development and 'usefulness' for IC development ($r = .586, p < .028$). This correlation might be explained by the fact that all written reflections focused on intercultural aspects. Therefore, it would seem that participants perceived the written tasks as useful for fostering intercultural learning. At the same time, 'usefulness' in terms of IC development strongly correlates with 'usefulness' in terms of SN formation ($r = .736, p < .003$). In fact, this is the strongest correlation of all. Participants clearly consider that if the task is useful for interacting with the host community, it also helps them develop their IC. To sum up, the findings corroborate what we have seen in the qualitative analysis of the individual tasks, namely that the more popular tasks are not perceived as the most useful. However, tasks perceived as useful for SN formation and IC development are, at the same time, perceived as the most useful in terms of (different aspects of) L2 development. The high correlation between tasks that are perceived as useful for SN formation and tasks that are perceived as useful for IC development seems to point to the fact that students are conscious of the importance of interactions with the host community in order to become more interculturally competent.

Conclusions and implications for further studies

The data in this study served to answer two research questions, one concerning the learning gains of the proposed intervention and the other concerning the perceived 'popularity' and 'usefulness' of the tasks that make up the intervention.

With regard to the learning gains, all students have benefited from the SA experience in terms of linguistic and intercultural competence. However, we have not been able to establish a significant advantage of the online intervention based on the quantitative results. The fact that participants in our study had received extensive intercultural and linguistic training before departure makes it hard to pinpoint differences between both the EG and CG, particularly if we factor in that both groups were experiencing very similar SA conditions and followed similar academic programmes abroad. Given the multilingual profile of our students (detailed in the section 'Participants'), further studies should address, first of all, if the effect of this sort of intervention would be different if the students do not receive any pre-SA training, especially those not following specific language studies at their home institutions. Future studies should also focus on how the diverse socio-economic and intercultural reality of the host sites (where they may use their full linguistic repertoire, including their L1) may shape sojourners' access to the target language of the host country (Tullock and Ortega, 2017). Moreover, the fact that both groups of students showed a high level of 'Motivational Intelligence' reveals that they all departed for their sojourn with an explicit motivation to learn about the language and sociocultural reality of their host city. Further qualitative analysis of students' social and linguistic experiences based on their intercultural journals and interviews conducted during the sojourn may thus shed further light on this impact of the intervention.

With regard to the perceived 'popularity' and 'usefulness' of tasks, those dependent on interaction outside the L1 group were perceived as decidedly less popular, regardless of their perceived 'usefulness'. Students preferred guided activities in which their own reflections on intercultural and social aspects of living abroad or on what they perceive as specific habits or characteristics of the host community did not involve interactions. However, results clearly show that tasks perceived as useful for getting involved with the host community are also seen as the most useful in terms of developing IC. Hence, participants are certainly aware of the importance of social interactions abroad. However, it also became clear that it is very challenging to succeed in bringing the students out of their comfort zone to oblige them to seek contact outside their L1 peer group. Kinginger (2008) has remarked that SA participants are often unaware of the fact that developing advanced linguistic skills and IC requires considerable investment of time and effort, which may challenge their commitment to the learning experience. On the basis of our study, however, we cannot conclude that the participants were unaware of the effort that is required, but rather that they perceive this as a very challenging task, and that they prefer tasks where interaction outside their trusted L1 or Erasmus group of friends is avoided, even if it does not yield intercultural or language gains, as they expect.

As with every research report, there is a number of limitations. Regarding the standardized measurements on language proficiency and IC that were used, further replications of the online intervention will be necessary in order to draw more definitive conclusions about differences between the EG and CG and the adequacy of the measurements for comparing such closely related groups of (advanced) learners. Including qualitative data would also allow us to further understand the underlying detail of some of the results presented here, such as the linguistic features of the consecutive tasks (e.g. with measures of lexical richness and syntactic complexity of both written and oral production tasks) and the actual content of the intercultural reflections. This would allow for a dynamic triangulation of data that combine both product and process perspectives. The qualitative analysis of participants' perceived 'usefulness' of the tasks and their 'popularity' has proved most useful for the further refinement of the intervention's tasks, although the link between learner beliefs and their behaviour is of course indirect (Arvidsson et al., 2018; Barcelos, 2003; Ellis, 2008). Nevertheless, we acknowledge the reciprocal nature of the link between beliefs and experience since the role that beliefs play with regard to linguistic and cultural competence development may very well be proportional to the learner's will to self-reflect and to act on those beliefs.

This last argument together with the feedback provided on the proposed intercultural guidance has encouraged us to develop an online application to support students during their SA experience by focusing on those tasks they consider as more challenging and at the same time more useful. The application, called SALSA (Study Abroad Language Support App), was conceived to enrich students' sojourn abroad and consists of three types of tasks: tasks directed at developing L2 knowledge, tasks developed to enhance IC and tasks that serve to increase self-reflection and self-regulation (Eyckmans, 2017a, 2017b). Self-regulation has been brought to the fore in this application in order to enhance learners' responsibility for their own learning process while abroad. At the same time, the programme is focused on the development of self-efficacy because it is important for learners to experience the beneficial effects of their efforts during their time abroad. Although the participants in the present study displayed high levels of motivation before departure, we know that motivation is not a stable attribute (Grant and Shin, 2012). However, an individual's behaviour is contingent upon motivation and the experiences that result from behaviour in turn play an important role in maintaining or abandoning effort. With the affordances an online application offers in terms of learner autonomy, the hope is that SALSA will enhance learners' volition to engage with locals and to implement new linguistic and intercultural knowledge in real-life situations when abroad. Future research on the data that will be generated by the application may shed light on the constraints as well as the benefits of using online support systems in SA contexts.

References

Ang, S., and van Dyne, L. (2008), *Handbook of Cultural Intelligence Theory, Measurement, and Applications*, Armonk, NY: Sharpe.

Arvidsson, K., Eyckmans, J., Rosiers, A., and Forsberg Lundell, F. (2018), 'Self-perceived Linguistic Progress, Target Language Use and Its Link to Change in Personality Development during Study Abroad', *Study Abroad Research in Second Language Acquisition and International Education*, 3 (1), 143–65.

Barcelos, A. M. F. (2003), 'Researching Beliefs about SLA: A Critical Review', in P. Kalaja, and A. M. F. Barcelos (eds.), *Beliefs about SLA*, 7–33, Dordrecht: Springer.

Bardovi-Harlig, K. (2009), 'Conventional Expressions as a Pragmalinguistic Resource: Recognition and Production of Conventional Expressions in L2 Pragmatics', *Language Learning*, 59, 755–95.

Beaven, A., and Borghetti, C. (2018), 'Exploring Intercultural Learning and Second Language Identities in the ERASMUS Context', in J. Plews, and K. Misfeldt (eds.), *Second Language Study Abroad Programming, Pedagogy, and Participant Engagement*, 195–221, Basingstoke: Palgrave Macmillan.

Bennett, J. M. (2008), 'Transformative Training: Designing Programmes for Culture Learning', in M. Moodian (ed.), *Contemporary Leadership and Intercultural Competence: Understanding and Utilizing Cultural Diversity to Build Successful Organizations*, 95–110, London: Sage.

Byram, M. (1997), *Teaching and Assessing Intercultural Communicative Competence*, Clevedon: Multilingual Matters.

Byram, M. (2000), 'Assessing Intercultural Competence in Language Teaching', *Sprogforum*, 18 (6), 8–13.

Cervantes, I. (2006), *Plan Curricular del Instituto Cervantes. Niveles de Referencia para el Español. A1, A2*.

Coleman, J. A. (2013), 'Researching Whole People and Whole Lives', in C. Kinginger (ed.), *Social and Cultural Aspects of Language Learning in Study Abroad*, 17–44, Amsterdam: John Benjamins.

Coleman, J. A., and Chafer, T. (2010), 'Study Abroad and the Internet: Physical and Virtual Context in an Era of Expanding Telecommunications', *Frontiers: The Interdisciplinary Journal of Study Abroad*, 19, 151–67.

Dewey, D. P., Belnap, K. R., and Hillstrom, R. (2013), 'Social Network Development, Language Use, and Language Acquisition during Study Abroad: Arabic Language Learners' Perspectives', *Frontiers: The Interdisciplinary Journal of Study Abroad*, 22, 84–110.

Dewey, D. P., Bown, J., and Eggett, D. (2012), 'Japanese Language Proficiency, Social Networking, and Language Use during Study Abroad: Learners' Perspectives', *Canadian Modern Language Review*, 68 (2), 111–37.

Dörnyei, Z. (2005), *The Psychology of the Language Learner. Individual Differences in Second Language Acquisition*, Mahwah: Lawrence Erlbaum.

Earley, P. C., and Ang, S. (2003), *Cultural Intelligence: Individual Interactions across Cultures*, Stanford: University Press.

Ellis, R. (2008), 'Learner Beliefs and Language Learning', *Asian EFL Journal*, 10 (4), 7–25.

European Commission. (2015), *Erasmus+ Programme Annual Report 2014*, Luxembourg: Publications Office of the European Union.

Eyckmans, J. (2017a), 'Study Abroad Language Support (SALS)', Project funded by Ghent University's Educational Innovation Service. available online at https://www.ugent.be/nl/univgent/waarvoor-staat-ugent/kwaliteitszorg/oiprojecten/lw/lwprojecten2017.htm

Eyckmans, J. (2017b), 'SALSA: A Study Abroad Language Support App', Paper presented to COST Action CA15130 Study Abroad Research in European Perspective, Working Group 4 conference, Promoting success in study abroad: responding to individual differences. University of Split, Croatia, 21–22 September.

Fehr, R., and Kuo, E. (2008), 'The Impact of Cultural Intelligence in Multicultural Social Networks', Paper presented at the 23rd Annual Conference of the Society for Industrial and Organizational Psychology (SIOP), San Francisco, CA, 10–12 April.

Goldoni, F. (2013), 'Students' Immersion Experiences in Study Abroad', *Foreign Language Annals*, 46 (3), 359–76.

Grant, A. M., and Shin, J. (2012), 'Work Motivation: Directing, Energizing, and Maintaining Effort (and Research)', in R. M. Ryan (ed.), *The Oxford Handbook of Human Motivation*, New York: Oxford University Press.

Hammer, M. R. (2012), 'The Intercultural Development Inventory: A New Frontier in Assessment and Development of Intercultural Competence', in M. Vande Berg, R. M. Paige, and K. H. Lou (eds.), *Students Learning Abroad: What Our Students Are Learning, What They're Not, and What We Can Do about It*, 115–36, Sterling, VA: Stylus Publishing.

Isabelli-García, C. (2006), 'Study Abroad Social Networks, Motivation and Attitudes: Implications for Second Language Acquisition', in M. A. DuFon, and E. Churchill (eds.), *Language Learners in Study Abroad Contexts*, 231–58, Clevedon: Multilingual Matters.

Izura, C., Cuetos, F., and Brysbaert, M. (2014), 'Lextale-Esp: A Test to Rapidly and Efficiently Assess the Spanish Vocabulary Size', *Psicológica*, 35 (1), 49–66.

Jackson, J. (2010), *Intercultural Journeys: From Study to Residence Abroad*, London: Palgrave Macmillan.

Jackson, J. (2016), 'The Language Use, Attitudes, and Motivation of Chinese Students prior to a Semester-long Sojourn in an English-speaking Environment', *Study Abroad Research in Second Language Acquisition and International Education*, 1 (1), 4–33.

Jackson, J. (2018), 'Intervening in the Intercultural Learning of L2 Study Abroad Students: From Research to Practice', *Language Teaching*, 51 (3), 365–82.

Kinginger, C. (2008), 'Language Learning in Study Abroad: Case Studies of Americans in France', *The Modern Language Journal*, 92, 1–124.

Kinginger, C. (2009), *Language Learning and Study Abroad: A Critical Reading of Research*, London: Palgrave Macmillan.

Kinginger, C. (2013), 'Identity and Language Learning in Study Abroad', *Foreign Language Annals*, 46 (3), 339–58.

Knight, S. M., and Schmidt-Rinehart, B. C. (2002), 'Enhancing the Homestay: Study Abroad from the Host Family's Perspective', *Foreign Language Annals*, 35 (2), 190–201.

Kolb, D. (1984), *Experiential Learning as the Science of Learning and Development*, Englewood Cliffs, NJ: Prentice Hall.

Kramsch, C. (2002), 'Introduction: How Can We Tell the Dancer from the Dance', in C. Kramsch (ed.), *Language Acquisition and Language Socialization: Ecological Perspectives*, 1–30, London/New York: Continuum.

Lantolf, J. P. (2000), *Sociocultural Theory and Second Language Learning*, Oxford: Oxford University Press.

Lou, K., and Bosley, G. (2008), 'Dynamics of Cultural Contexts: Meta-level Intervention in the Study Abroad Experience', in V. Savicki (ed.), *Developing Intercultural Competence and Transformation: Theory, Research, and Application in International Education*, 276–96, Sterling, VA: Stylus Publishing.

Lou, K., Andresen, C., and Myers, C. (2011), 'Small Private Liberal Arts Colleges: Supporting International Students', Paper presented at the NAFSA 2011 conference, Vancouver, Canada.

Macready, C., and Tucker, C. (2011), 'Who Goes Where and Why: An Overview and Analysis of Global Educational Mobility'. Paper presented at the IIE and AIFS Foundation.

Ng, K.-Y., Van Dyne, L., Ang, S., and Ryan, A. (2012), 'Cultural Intelligence: A Review, Reflections, and Recommendations for Future Research', in A. M. Ryan, F. T. L. Leong, and F. L. Oswald (eds.), *Conducting Multinational Research Projects in Organizational Psychology*, 29–58, Washington, DC: American Psychological Association.

Paige, R. M., Fry, G. W., Stallman, E. M., Josić, J., and Jon, J. E. (2009), 'Study Abroad for Global Engagement: The Long-term Impact of Mobility Experiences', *Intercultural Education*, 20 (sup1), S29–S44.

Passarelli, A. M., and Kolb, D. A. (2012), 'Using Experiential Learning Theory to Promote Student Learning and Development in Programmes of Education Abroad', in M. Vande Berg, and K. Hemming Lou (eds.), *Student Learning Abroad: What Our Students Are Learning, What They're Not, and What We Can Do about It*, 137–61, Sterling, VA: Stylus Publishing.

Taguchi, N. (2016), 'Learning Speech Style in Japanese Study Abroad: Learners' Knowledge of Normative Use and Actual Use', in R. A. van Compernolle, and J. McGregor (eds.), *Authenticity, Language and Interaction in Second Language Contexts*, 82–108, Tonawanda, NY: Multilingual Matters.

Tullock, B., and Ortega, L. (2017), 'Fluency and Multilingualism in Study Abroad: Lessons from a Scoping Review', *System*, 71, 7–21.

Van Maele, J., Vassilicos, B., and Borghetti, C. (2016), 'Mobile Students' Appraisals of Keys to a Successful Stay Abroad Experience: Hints from the IEREST Project', *Language and Intercultural Communication*, 1–18.

Vande Berg, M. (2007), 'Intervening in the Learning of US Students Abroad', *Journal of Studies in International Education*, 11 (3–4), 392–9.

Vande Berg, M., and Paige, R. M. (2009), 'Applying Theory and Research: The Evolution of Intercultural Competence in US Study Abroad', in D. K. Deardorff (ed.), *The Sage Handbook of Intercultural Competence*, 419–37, Thousand Oakes, CA: Sage Publications, Inc.

Vande Berg, M., and Paige, R. M. (2012), 'Why Students Are and Are Not Learning Abroad', in M. Vande Berg, R. M. Paige, and K. H. Lou (eds.), *Student Learning Abroad: What Our Students Are Learning, What They're Not, and What We Can Do about It*, 29–60, Sterling, VA: Stylus Publishing.

Vande Berg, M., Paige, R. M., and Lou, K. H. (eds.) (2012), *Student Learning Abroad: What Our Students Are Learning, What They're Not, and What We Can Do about It*, Sterling, VA: Stylus Publishing.

Zumbihl, H. (2010), 'Preparing an Intercultural Program for University Studies Abroad. Paper presented at the Intercultural Competence Conference (ICC)', University of Arizona.

7

The complex challenges of delivering a university-wide intercultural mentoring programme for study abroad students

Susan Oguro and Annie Cottier
University of Technology Sydney/University of Bern

Introduction

Over the past decade, there has been an increasing focus across the higher education sector towards incorporating internationalization initiatives into strategic planning and institutional goals. One component of this attention to internationalization has been the significant increases in the number of students undertaking an international experience (including periods of study abroad, service-learning programmes or international internships) as part of their degree programmes. These international educational experiences are generally viewed positively and assumed to be transformative for students and leading to a range of outcomes including intercultural understandings and communicative competence, second language proficiency development or enhanced employability and global-mindedness.

As this trend of expanding international educational opportunities continues, it is imperative that universities are not complacent with simply dispatching students for a period of time abroad, but analyse the design and structures of study abroad (SA) programmes to determine the specific pedagogic practices which contribute best to learning outcomes being achieved (Gozik and Oguro, 2020). This chapter critically explores a comprehensive academic mentoring programme implemented to support students' development of intercultural awareness and skills through their participation in a semester-long SA sojourn. While the programme has been positively evaluated over consecutive semesters by students and external stakeholders and could be presented as a positive case study, this chapter focuses on the broader institutional-wide challenges of implementing such a comprehensive mentoring programme across multiple disciplinary areas and examines the ongoing challenges of the sustainability and scalability of such programmes.

Literature review

This review briefly outlines the research literature that explores assumptions about students' intercultural development in SA contexts and the calls for specific pedagogical interventions to ensure desired learning outcomes are achieved. It also explores the literature on mentoring as one approach for providing academic support to students before, during and after international experiences.

Intercultural development through study abroad

A period of study abroad is commonly assumed to contribute to the development of students' intercultural competence by providing the opportunity for them to engage with members of the host society, experience other cultural practices or traditions and develop the ability to interact effectively and appropriately with people with different cultural backgrounds (Byram, 2012; Fantini, 2019; Jackson, 2014). However, there is long-standing evidence in the research literature that the social networks of SA students are not extensively with local students (Coleman, 1997; Conacher, 2008; Milton and Meara, 1995; Willis et al., 1977) and indeed that SA students' engagement with the host society may not spread beyond university or retail staff in the host location (Dervin, 2009). Thus, while SA students might have some exposure to local culture(s) and practices, the potential for deeper understanding is limited, suggesting that many of the common aims of internationalization are not being realized by simply increasing participation rates in SA programmes (Brown, 2009; Leask, 2009; Montgomery, 2010).

In response to this situation, a growing body of scholarship has advocated for the inclusion of comprehensive academic support or mentoring to ensure learning outcomes are achieved (e.g. Gozik, 2014; Jackson, 2017; Jackson and Oguro, 2018a; Vande Berg, Paige and Lou, 2012). Specifically, SA scholars are advocating intercultural interventions in all phases of students' experiences (pre-sojourn, in-sojourn, post-sojourn) and seeking to track the intercultural learning of SA students over these phases to connect research to teaching practice (e.g. Beaven and Borghetti, 2015; Deardorff and Arasaratnam-Smith, 2017; Jackson, 2015; Jackson and Oguro, 2018b).

Intercultural mentoring in study abroad

To maximize the benefits of a period of study abroad and in particular to support students' intercultural development, one model undertaken by universities is to incorporate a purposeful intercultural mentoring programme for students. As Vande Berg, Paige and Lou (2012) have argued, most students learn to learn effectively while abroad 'only when an educator intervenes, strategically and intentionally' (p. 19). In such an intercultural mentoring programme 'the mentor provides ongoing support for and facilitation of intercultural learning and development' (Paige, 2013, p. 6). Depending on the specific intended learning outcomes, the programme could include the promotion of students' self-awareness and confidence in interacting in the language of the host society as well as encouragement to diversify their social networks (Jackson and Oguro, 2019).

Multiple possible models to deliver intercultural mentoring to students as part of their SA programme are examined in the research literature. These include models incorporating face-to-face workshops or seminars during pre- and post-sojourn periods (Borghetti and Beaven, 2018; Dervin and Härkönen, 2018; Hepple, 2018) or through academics from the home university accompanying or visiting students during the SA period (Giovanangeli, Oguro and Harbon, 2018; Hoult, 2018). Further models incorporate information and communication technologies to allow for remote mentoring using synchronous and/or asynchronous communication (Jackson, 2019; Lee, 2018). One common theme found in these studies from diverse learning contexts is the individualized nature of students' intercultural development and the value of programmes which scaffold students' cultural reflections (on both their own values and practices of those of the host society). These findings underline the benefits of an individual mentoring programme to maximize the value of an SA experience.

The research literature also demonstrates that irrespective of the mode of delivery, the scaffolding of complex intercultural learning outcomes for students requires the mentor to possess highly developed skills. Felten et al.'s (2013) research on various mentoring communities in the higher education sector highlights the importance of mentoring practices which go beyond simply imparting information and advice or proposing solutions to students. Instead, they argue that the mentor's role is to facilitate a space for discussion in which the mentee is able to seek guidance, problematize concerns and share ideas to subsequently form their own reflective responses. Jackson and Oguro (2019) have also argued that building a climate of respect and mutuality is crucial for a constructive mentoring relationship so that the mentor serves as a facilitator, motivator, resource and guide for the student. Such requirements demand a commensurate level of expertise for the educator/mentor.

Research context and methods

The research reported in this chapter is a qualitative case study focusing on the implementation and sustainability issues of providing an institution-wide mentoring programme for university students undertaking a semester-long period of study abroad as part of their degree programme. In outlining the steps undertaken to establish the programme and an analysis of complexities and challenges, the chapter aims to assist academic and administrative leaders in higher education working with similar organizational goals for their SA programmes. The programme in focus here is titled 'Mentoring Intercultural Learning through Study Abroad' (hereafter referred to by its acronym 'MILSA'), and has been in place at the University of Bern in Switzerland since 2016. The university is a large, comprehensive public university located in the nation's capital with a strong research and teaching reputation. The MILSA programme was initiated in response to the needs identified in the research literature as reviewed above, namely that if institutional strategies of internationalization include the goals of facilitating students' intercultural development and skills through SA programmes, then an intentional programme of mentoring for students is necessary. At the University of Bern, students' SA location is at one of the international partner universities under a bilateral exchange agreement. Students travel unaccompanied, enrol in a programme of study at the host university alongside local students and usually receive academic credit for their degree from the University of Bern. Before the MILSA programme commenced, students' SA programmes included little or no explicit mentoring of potential intercultural challenges students may need to face, nor support to maximize the opportunities afforded through studying abroad for students' futures.

Since its inception in 2016, the MILSA programme is offered to students from across the university undertaking an SA semester. To date, forty-seven students studying disciplines as diverse as Economics, Law, Biology, Psychology, Computer Science, Theatre Studies and Languages have participated. The programme comprises a series of face-to-face workshops with students during the pre-departure and post-sojourn phases of their study abroad and also supports and mentors the students throughout the SA period through interviews, emails, blogs and peer-group tasks. Each intervention is connected by the overarching and interconnected themes of expectations, cultural practices, language learning and intercultural experiences.

Students are mentored to reflect on and further develop these themes from the first face-to-face workshop before departing on their period of study abroad, throughout their sojourn and in follow-up workshops, reflections and evaluations at the end of the programme. A facilitator based at the home university in Bern mentors students while they are abroad. In addition, students are connected with their peers also on an SA programme (although usually in a different location globally) to complete a series of peer mentoring activities. Theoretically, the programme's various components and approach draw on the Experiential Learning Cycle (Kolb, 1984; Kolb and Kolb, 2017) comprising the interconnected phases of concrete experience, reflective observation, abstract conceptualization and active experimentation. Further details on the components of MILSA can be found at the programme's website (University of Bern, 2019).

As stated above, the MILSA programme has consistently received broadly positive feedback from participating students and key stakeholders since its inception, and this chapter could have presented it as a case study of successful practice and demonstrated the student learning outcomes. However, to offer more to SA researchers and administrators, particularly those reviewing or considering implementing a mentoring programme in their own institution, the chapter instead focuses on the challenges of implementing and sustaining a comprehensive university-wide mentoring programme for SA students. It is also a response to calls for the international higher education field to move beyond documentation of students' 'happy stories' (Clifford, 2018) and instead to make explicit the challenges of facilitating meaningful intercultural learning programmes around the SA experience.

In order to highlight for the SA field the broader programme design and institutional management issues of a mentoring programme, the chapter draws on data collected through online surveys of twenty-eight student participants who completed the MILSA programme in three different semesters (a two-year period). In addition, the perspectives of university staff involved in the delivery, administration or management of MILSA were collected from examination of programme evaluation documentation and individual interviews. While some quantitative data was collected from respondents, such as SA location, disciplinary area and demographic information, the survey items and interview questions were designed to allow for the collection of extensive experiences of students and staff to enable qualitative analysis of the data.

For the data collected from both groups of respondents (students and staff), items were first scanned to locate commentary on areas identified as problematic and suggestions for improvements. As described above, while there was significant positive responses about the MILSA programme in the surveys, documents and interviews, this chapter aims to draw attention to the challenges of implementation and maintenance of a mentoring programme for SA students and so focuses its analysis on data which highlight these aspects.

Following the initial scan of data to isolate responses relating to experienced challenges and suggested changes to the programme, this data subset was then re-scanned by both authors (first independently and then in collaboration) to further categorize the data and identify common themes and any outlying responses. This process drew on established data analysis practices for drawing meaning from qualitative information (Boyatzis, 1998) and is a method widely used in learning and teaching research and scholarship (Divan et al., 2017).

The methodological issue of response bias (Villar, 2011) is acknowledged; however, as survey participation and responses lacked a tangible reward (e.g. students were not receiving academic credit for their responses), the reliability of the data is considered acceptable. Furthermore, as the survey items specifically focused on collecting data on problems and challenges, there was not an issue with inflated positiveness in responses. The data reported in the sections below are presented as provided by the participants (students and staff), including any inconsistencies in English lexis or syntax.

Results and discussion

As described earlier, student and staff responses were collated and, through a process of categorization and thematic analysis (Boyatzis, 1998), seven broad areas of challenge emerged from the data: institutional structure of a mentoring programme; issues of academic credit; necessary staff expertise; funding; technology issues; scheduling issues and language of instruction. Each of these challenges is discussed in turn in the following sections and illuminated with the staff and student responses.

Institutional structures

The decision of where a university administratively locates a mentoring programme for students from across all faculties is particularly complex. In focus here is the MILSA programme, which is administrated from a central unit of the university. This has a positive effect as it enables the programme to be available to students across the university and contributes to the institution's broader strategic internationalization aims. As one staff member commented: 'Acceptance of the program within the university has been very good, presumably because the support of developing and deepening intercultural knowledge is part of the university's strategy.'

Location of the programme centrally within the university also enables interdisciplinary learning as students participate from across the institution. Centralizing also leads to efficiencies in the institution not needing to develop similar programme expertise across multiple faculties or departments, and the potential economies of scale can contribute to scalability and sustainability of the programme.

Academic credit

Despite the benefits of a programme run from a central unit rather than from within an academic teaching unit of the university, the responses of the university staff also identified the issues this structure creates for a mentoring programme, particularly in relation to students receiving some form of academic credit for completing the programme. As students were from disciplinary areas and faculties from across the university, there is not always consistency in how credit is assigned, nor how much additional credit can be accommodated within students' particular degree structure. In the data, staff described this as 'problematic' adding that while they make recommendations that the completion of the programme warranted the award of two 'ECTS' (the European Credit Transfer System) this was not always possible: 'We recommend that students clarify accreditation with their study counsellors – it seems that there are differences in all departments, needless to say between the faculties. It basically depends on whether study plans contain an option for extra-curricular activities. If they do not, then usually, students do not get any credits.'

This inconsistency can lead to tensions within the student cohort as not all are receiving the same credit for comparable effort. While all students received a certificate of completion, the inconsistencies in the award of ECTS points were concerning to staff who felt it could send a message to students that the programme is not valued and they feared it might result in only students with high levels of intrinsic motivation participating, thereby restricting access to the programme for all students.

Student responses also underscored the concerns reported by staff but related more to students feeling they did not need to invest as much effort into the programme, for example: 'The programme was not binding enough (maybe because we didn't get any ECTS, I don't know). Most of the participants didn't take the task seriously,' and even more specifically in this student's comment: 'It is a pity that there is no possibility to get ECTS points for the program ... Even if I think the participation is also very valuable without getting credits for it, one tends to limit the effort put into the project because it "doesn't count". As a result, some blog contributions and reports remained quite shallow in my opinion.'

Level of staff expertise

Related to the issue of where a university-wide mentoring programme could be institutionally located is the question of the personnel required for its successful delivery. Through this study, the need for extensive administrative support staff was identified. However, an even more challenging human resource issue emerged in relation to the level of expertise required by the staff member undertaking the mentor role. As outlined by Felten et al. (2013), mentors require specific skills, expertise and experience which go beyond simply imparting information and advice or proposing solutions to students. The MILSA staff, through their experience of successfully delivering the programme over several semesters, articulated the complex requirements of the mentor as 'responsible for teaching the workshops, giving feedback on student blogs, talking to students on Skype. This person encourages students' intercultural learning actively and consciously. Ideally, this person has a background in pedagogy or is an experienced teacher with a theoretical knowledge of intercultural studies'. This comment highlights the set of facilitation skills needed in the role of a mentor and specifically points to the need for the mentor to ideally have expertise in the field of intercultural pedagogy. In the case of the MILSA programme, the project included a scientific director and an advisory board of academic experts in the field of intercultural pedagogy and international education to provide research-driven ideas and support to the mentor.

The level of mentoring skills required by staff, as well as the administrative load of running such a programme, naturally also raises questions of how a comprehensive mentoring programme can be established and maintained to serve the needs across a university. While the costs of infrastructure are relatively low, the human resources required are fundamental to the success of the programme, as explained in the comment: 'Running a mentoring program is time-consuming and cannot be done on the side by staff who are already employed. The amount of time that is needed for this cannot be underestimated.'

Funding

In view of the complex workload that running a mentoring programme demands, procuring specific funding is a necessary requirement to employ the required staff. The MILSA programme received an initial external grant to assist with establishment and delivering of the programme to a preliminary cohort of students. This funding was supplemented by the university for the initial period and has been extended since the expiration of the external grant, as an ongoing investment towards achieving the university's internationalization strategy. Such commitment from central administration is vital. However, the challenge remains to ensure funding sustainably into the future.

Considering that the MILSA staff have engaged with colleagues across the university, and that the programme has been successful with students, makes for a strong case for continuing the programme. However, despite these positive factors, the programme's sustainability is ultimately linked financially to participant numbers. If students continue to take part in the programme, then funding will remain secure. However, should enrolments decline in the future, then funding is not necessarily guaranteed. Such a scenario is likely common across many higher education institutions.

Technology

The funding challenges discussed above related to human resourcing requirements. However, financing the set-up and ongoing delivery of a mentoring programme is also connected to challenges with technology, as reported by both students and staff. Some of these issues are beyond the control of the university, including service problems with communication software used in the during-sojourn mentoring or weak Internet connections in a student's particular SA location. However, other issues such as the infrastructural challenges staff reported in setting up the website and online support materials as integral components of the mentoring programme could be commonly expected in any large institution with complex systems such as a university. While these technical issues can also be found in more traditional teaching programmes delivered onsite at universities, their impacts were perhaps greater given the physical distance between mentors and students or students and their peers, and were perhaps more significant given that students were studying abroad and in interculturally more challenging environments.

Scheduling

An additional area of challenge identified in the data related to issues of scheduling and time. A programme designed to include communication between mentor and students and between student peers while on SA semesters is naturally going to include challenges of dealing in multiple time zones. However, staff reported that different global time zones proved less complicated than they had expected with problems being avoided by accurate scheduling of the interviews using Skype or other communication technologies. Beyond issues of global time zones, the greater challenge reported by staff was in implementing and managing the programme's complex annual schedule with two programme cycles over two semesters and students studying abroad in multiple locations simultaneously.

On a similar organizational level, students grappled with the coordination of the group task. This challenge was also a result of time zone differences but was attributed more to the variations in academic calendar in different SA locations. Semesters naturally do not commence and finish within the same week across the world. The following two students' comments in relation to the peer mentoring task highlight the time and scheduling challenges they experienced:

> For me, the timing was the worst aspect. As the end of my exchange almost overlapped with the start of the new semester here in MILSA, I was very busy and the same was true for my group members. As a consequence, we couldn't put in as much effort as we would have liked to.
>
> Depending on the diverse destinations and exchange lengths it can be even more difficult to get in touch with each other (as time change, some still have exams, etc.).

In addition, time challenges for students were also related to management of their study load in combination with their participation in the mentoring programme. As well as their academic subjects at the host university, as part of the MILSA programme students were asked to write blog posts, participate in calls with the mentor and complete peer mentoring tasks. Balancing this load sometimes led to less than optimum performance, as described by this student: 'Sometimes didn't have the time to write them carefully, because I had so much to do for my studies. So I didn't always meet the deadline, otherwise the blogs wouldn't have been written carefully.'

Accommodating a mentoring programme while also balancing the extra-curricular opportunities of an SA student was also a challenge reported: 'I liked least that it was a bit stressful to fulfil all the tasks while abroad. When you are abroad, there are so many new things to do and to experience. You have classes, you have to study for your exams, you want to enjoy your spare time. But it was worth it to participate in the MILSA program.'

Language of instruction

The final area of challenge identified in the data concerned the use of English as the language of the mentoring programme. This was evident in both staff and student comments, for example from a staff member: 'Some students found that writing [took] too much time – since most of them are not native speakers and not students of English, it is possible that their lack of practice in writing, firstly, and secondly writing in English was actually the problem.' While students' first language was German, they were studying abroad in English-medium universities in a range of global locations (in Anglophone and non-Anglophone societies). One of their primary goals was the development of their proficiency in English, and the research literature (e.g. Benson et al., 2012; Kinginger, 2013; Regan, Howard and Lemée, 2009) has established the value of study abroad for second language acquisition. Multilingual skills development is also an element of the university's internationalization strategy. It was a conscious choice in the programme design of the MILSA team to conduct the programme in English, even though it was acknowledged that the depth of reflection to be articulated and the complex intercultural topics to be explored would be linguistically challenging for students. This was evidenced in the comments of students, for example: 'It was difficult to experience in German and write them in English' and 'I was stressed because I have problems to express my thoughts/opinions accurately in English.'

Conclusion

This chapter has analysed the challenges posed for a university in implementing and sustaining a comprehensive mentoring programme to facilitate students' intercultural awareness and communication skills within the context of a learning abroad experience. The study was grounded in an extensive research evidence base supporting the need for universities to effectively scaffold students to maximize the opportunities afforded by an SA semester. As part of a larger evaluation of participants' experience of the effectiveness of the mentoring programme, this chapter focused on the institutional-wide challenges of implementation and sustainability of a mentoring programme.

Although this investigation was based on the experiences of a single university and mentoring programme, the challenges identified are presumed to be relevant across the higher education sector. The review of research studies (Borghetti and Beaven, 2018; Dervin and Härkönen, 2018; Giovanangeli, Oguro and Harbon, 2018; Hepple, 2018; Hoult, 2018; Jackson, 2019; Lee, 2018), which examined models for facilitating students' intercultural development through study abroad in the introductory section of this chapter, demonstrated how local contexts and diverse learning outcomes generated a wide variety of successful models of practice.

This chapter has gone beyond an analysis of successful programme elements to offer professionals in the field of study abroad insights into the less-often acknowledged complexities of implementing and maintaining an intensive mentoring programme to maximize the SA experiences of students. Through the analysis of the perspectives of key stakeholders of university students and staff, seven areas of challenge were identified under three broad categories:

1. issues of institutional structure, management and resourcing;
2. practical issues in implementation including technical issues and varied time zones;
3. pedagogical considerations, including the choice of the language of instruction and need to balance students' study loads and complex academic calendars.

This diverse range of challenges identified by both staff and students points to the need for institutions to extensively plan for and resource such programmes. The findings of the analysis of the experience of the MILSA programme also highlight the value of conducting ongoing evaluations with key stakeholders to ensure continuous improvement. Staff at universities with responsibilities for teaching and/or managing SA programmes may wish to use any or all of the three categories of challenge highlighted through this investigation to take into consideration if developing their own programme or to use in evaluation of existing programmes. It is hoped that through articulating the multiple challenges, this chapter will assist SA administrators and academics keen to maximize students' learning afforded by an SA experience, as well as university management keen to contribute to the realization of institutional strategic goals around internationalization.

References

Beaven, A., and Borghetti, C. (2015), 'Editorial: Interculturality in Study Abroad', *Intercultural Education*, 26 (1), 1–5.

Benson, P., Barkhuizen, G., Bodycott, P., and Brown, J. (2012), 'Study Abroad and the Development of Second Language Identities', *Applied Linguistics Review*, 3 (1), 173–93.

Borghetti, C., and Beaven, A. (2018), 'Monitoring Class Interaction to Maximise Intercultural Learning in Mobility Contexts', in J. Jackson, and S. Oguro (eds.), *Intercultural Interventions in Study Abroad*, 37–54, New York: Routledge.

Boyatzis, R. E. (1998), *Transforming Qualitative Information: Thematic Analysis and Code Development*, London: Sage.

Brown, L. (2009), 'A Failure to Communication on the Cross-cultural Campus', *Journal of Studies in International Education*, 13 (4), 439–54.

Byram, M. (2012), 'Culture in Foreign Language Teaching – the Implications for Teachers and Teacher Training', Paper presented at the conference 'Culture in Foreign Language Learning: Framing and Reframing the Issue', National University of Singapore.

Clifford, V. (2018), 'Revitalising and Growing the Agenda for Global Learning', Presented at the IEAA Internationalisation of the Curriculum Forum, International Education Association of Australia, Melbourne.

Coleman, J. A. (1997), 'Residence Abroad within Language Study', *Language Teaching*, 30 (1), 1–20.

Conacher, J. E. (2008), 'Home Thoughts on Abroad: Zur Identität und Integration irischer ERASMUS-Studentinnen in Deutschland', *GFL-Journal*, 2, 1–20.

Deardorff, D. K., and Arasaratnam-Smith, L. A. (2017), *Intercultural Competence in International Higher Education*, London: Routledge.

Dervin, F. (2009), 'Transcending the Culturalist Impasse in Stays Abroad: Helping Mobile Students to Appreciate Diverse Diversities', *Frontiers: The Interdisciplinary Journal of Study Abroad*, XVIII (Fall), 119–41.

Dervin, F., and Härkönen, A. (2018), '"I Want to Be Able to Understand Each and Every Person That I Come into Contact with": Critical Interculturality Training, Student Mobility, and Perceptions of the "Intercultural"', in J. Jackson, and S. Oguro (eds.), *Intercultural Interventions in Study Abroad*, 55–87, New York: Routledge.

Divan, A., Ludwig, L., Matthews, K., Motley, P., and Tomlienovic-Berube, A. (2017), 'Survey of Research Approaches Utilised in the Scholarship of Learning and Teaching Publications', *Teaching & Learning Inquiry*, 5 (2), 16–29.

Fantini, A. E. (2019), *Intercultural Communicative Competence in Educational Exchange: A Multinational Perspective*, New York/London: Routledge.

Felten, P., Bauman, H., Dirksen, L., Kheriaty, A., and Taylor, E. (2013), *Transformative Conversations: A Guide to Mentoring Communities among Colleagues in Higher Education*, Somerset: Jossey-Bass.

Giovanangeli, A., Oguro, S., and Harbon, L. (2018), 'Mentoring Students' Intercultural Learning during Study Abroad', in J. Jackson, and S. Oguro (eds.), *Intercultural Interventions in Study Abroad*, 88–102, New York: Routledge.

Gozik, N. (2014), 'The Theory and Practice of Outcomes Assessment in Education Abroad', in M. Hernandez, D. Wick, and M. Wiedenhoeft (eds.), *NAFSA's Guide to Education Abroad for Advisers and Administrators*, 407–21, Washington, DC: NAFSA.

Gozik, N., and Oguro, S. (2020), 'Program Components: (Re)considering the Role of Individual Areas of Programming in Education Abroad', in A. C. Ogden, B. Streitwieser, and C. Van Mol (eds.), *Education Abroad: Bridging Scholarship and Practice*, 59–72, London: Routledge.

Hepple, E. (2018), 'Designing and Implementing Pre-sojourn Intercultural Workshops in an Australian University', in J. Jackson, and S. Oguro (eds.), *Intercultural Interventions in Study Abroad*, 18–36, New York: Routledge.

Hoult, S. (2018), 'Aspiring to Postcolonial Engagement with the Other: Deepening Intercultural Learning through Reflection on a South India Sojourn', in J. Jackson, and S. Oguro (eds.), *Intercultural Interventions in Study Abroad*, 71–87, New York: Routledge.

Jackson, J. (2014), *Introducing Language and Intercultural Communication*, London/New York: Routledge.

Jackson, J. (2015), '"Unpacking" International Experience through Blended Intercultural Praxis', in R. D. Williams, and A. Lee (eds.), *Internationalizing Higher Education: Critical Collaborations across the Curriculum*, 231–52, Rotterdam: SENSE Publishers.

Jackson, J. (2017), 'Intercultural Communication and Engagement Abroad', in D. K. Deardorff, and L. A. Arasaratnam-Smith (eds.), *Intercultural Competence in Higher Education: International Approaches, Assessment and Application*, 197–201, London: Routledge.

Jackson, J. (2019), *Online Intercultural Education and Study Abroad: Theory into Practice*, London/New York: Routledge.

Jackson, J., and Oguro, S. (2018a), 'Introduction: Enhancing and Extending Study Abroad Learning through Intercultural Interventions', in J. Jackson, and S. Oguro (eds.), *Intercultural Interventions in Study Abroad*, 1–17, New York: Routledge.

Jackson, J., and Oguro, S. (eds.) (2018b), *Intercultural Interventions in Study Abroad*, New York: Routledge.

Jackson, J., and Oguro, S. (2019), 'Fostering Global-mindedness and Inclusivity through Intercultural Mentoring', Paper presented at the conference 'Internationalisation: Optimising Student Experience', Chinese University of Hong Kong.

Kinginger, C. (2013), 'Identity and Language Learning in Study Abroad', *Foreign Language Annals*, 46 (3), 339–58.

Kolb, A. Y., and Kolb, D. A. (2017), *The Experiential Educator: Principles and Practices of Experiential Learning*, Kaunakakai, Hawai'i: Experience Based Learning Systems.

Kolb, D. A. (1984), *Experiential Learning* (2nd ed.), Upper Saddle River: Pearson Education.

Leask, B. (2009), 'Using Formal and Informal Curricula to Improve Interactions between Home and International Students', *Journal of Studies in International Education*, 13 (2), 205–21.

Lee, L. (2018), 'Employing Telecollaborative Exchange to Extend Intercultural Learning after Study Abroad', in J. Jackson, and S. Oguro (eds.), *Intercultural Interventions in Study Abroad*, 137–54, Abingdon: Routledge.

Milton, J., and Meara, P. (1995), 'How Periods Abroad Affect Vocabulary Growth in a Foreign Language', *ITL Review of Applied Linguistics*, 107–108, 17–34.

Montgomery, C. (2010), *Understanding the International Student Experience*, Basingstoke, UK: Palgrave Macmillan.

Paige, R. M. (2013), 'Factors Impacting Intercultural Development in Study Abroad', Paper presented at Elon University, North Carolina, 16 August.

Regan, V., Howard, M., and Lemée, I. (2009), *The Acquisition of Sociolinguistic Competence in a Study Abroad Context*, Bristol: Multilingual Matters.

University of Bern (2019), 'Mentoring Intercultural Learning through Study Abroad', Retrieved from http://www.milsa.unibe.ch

Vande Berg, M., Paige, R. M., and Lou, K. H. (eds.) (2012), *Student Learning Abroad: What Our Students Are Learning, What They're Not, and What We Can Do about It*, Sterling, VA: Stylus.

Villar, A. (2011), 'Response Bias', in P. J. Lavrakas (ed.), *Encyclopedia of Survey Research Methods*, 752–3, Thousand Oaks, CA: Sage.

Willis, F. M., Doble, G., Sankarayya, U., and Smithers, A. (1977), *Residence Abroad and the Student of Modern Languages: A Preliminary Survey*, Bradford: University of Bradford, Modern Languages Centre.

8

Tapping into self-regulation in study abroad contexts: A pilot study

Kata Csizér,[1] Mirosław Pawlak,[2] Vanda Szatzker[1] and Kitti Erdő-Bonyár[1]
[1]*Eötvös University, Budapest*, [2]*Adam Mickiewicz University, Kalisz, Poland; State University of Applied Sciences, Konin, Poland*

Introduction

Mobility has become an integral part of education in the last three decades or so, mainly in response to the process of globalization, with learners at different educational levels spending a certain amount of time in a foreign land. This could involve a relatively short stay in Paris for American students learning French as a foreign language but also a much lengthier sojourn for students in European countries who complete part of their academic programme abroad within the Erasmus+ programme and spend at least a semester in a partner university. Whatever the nature of the study abroad (SA) programme, it is likely to confer both linguistic and non-linguistic benefits on participating learners on condition that they actively seek opportunities for growth in these areas or engage in the self-regulation of their learning process. While there are instruments that can be used to tap into self-regulation (e.g. Chirkov et al., 2007; Liu, 2009; Tseng, Dörnyei and Schmitt, 2006; Winne and Perry, 2000), some of them are not intended for examining self-regulatory capacity in second language learning, and when they are, the focus is limited either to one target language (TL) subsystem or a specific individual factor, even when study abroad is targeted.

For this reason, the study reported aimed to validate a questionnaire intended to investigate the degree of such self-regulation before, during and after study abroad with the purpose of investigating changes in this respect as a potential result of a sojourn abroad. In the first part of the chapter, an attempt will be made to highlight the role of autonomy and self-regulation in participating in SA programmes since the development of the new tool was based on the assumption that the two constructs are closely related. This will be followed by the presentation of the results of a validation study in which the tool for gauging self-regulation in SA situations will be put to the test. The chapter will close with the discussion of the advantages and disadvantages

This project was partly funded by the NKFI-6-K-129149 research grant.

of the instrument as well as consideration of the ways in which it could be improved upon to provide a more reliable picture of how students engage in self-regulation both in anticipation of and as a result of their participation in SA programmes.

Background to the study

Although the concepts of self-regulation and autonomy have quite different origins, coming from the fields of educational psychology and second language education, respectively, these two constructs have a lot in common, which is reflected in the tool we designed for the purpose of this study. With respect to the former, Zimmermann (2000) defines the concept as 'self-generated thoughts, feelings, and actions that are planned and cyclically adapted to the attainment of personal goals' (p. 14). As evident from this description and as Zimmermann and Schunk (2011) further elaborate, the process of self-regulation is characterized by both a cognitive, affective and behavioural dimension. These three facets come into play when the achievement of a personally important aim is at stake and the process is aided by motivational orientations. Understood in this way, self-regulation clearly ties in with the concept of motivation, because self-regulating the learning process inevitably calls for a certain degree of willingness and effort to engage in this process (Noels et al., 2000). Self-regulation also involves reliance on language learning strategies, for the simple reason that the process has to be aided by carefully chosen and orchestrated actions and thoughts (Oxford, 2011, 2017; Rose, 2012; Thomas and Rose, 2018). In addition, it is also closely related to the notion of agency, which Mercer (2015) defines as 'a combination of the learner's will, intent and capacity to act in order to achieve specific goals and outcomes within particular social settings and situations' (p. 2). She adds that agency comprises three elements, that is, a belief that goal attainment is possible and within reach, willingness to engage in the learning process and to take necessary steps to make it successful, and the requisite knowledge that enables managing learning. It is also clear that the achievement of self-regulation involves control over different aspects of learning (e.g. those related to management, cognitive functioning and the content to be learned), the process is gradual and involves successive stages, and it can be fostered in a variety of ways, being instigated by the learner himself/herself, supported by the teacher or enhanced by the use of state-of-the-art technology.

With regard to autonomy, Holec (1981) initially defined this as the 'ability to take charge of one's learning' (p. 3), but the construct has undergone considerable modifications over the years (cf. Benson, 2007, 2011). Since it is not possible to offer a detailed account of these here due to limitations of space, suffice it to say that the emphasis has been placed on the psychological aspects of autonomy, as it is clear that the extent to which learners can, in fact, assume responsibility for the learning process depends not only on the psychological make-up of the learner but also on his/her willingness to do so. In addition, autonomy can manifest itself in different ways, depending, for example, on the age of the learner or his/her specific goals or needs, and it constitutes an attribute of not only individuals but also groups (cf. Benson, 2007, 2011;

Little, 1991). It has also been suggested that autonomy is not an all-or-nothing attribute but rather a matter of degree, with the effect that several levels of being autonomous can be distinguished which do not have to mirror the level of linguistic proficiency (Benson, 2007; Littlewood, 1999; Nunan, 1997). Just like self-regulation, autonomy is closely tied to the use of learning strategies 'since it is by using strategies that learners are able to become autonomous' (Griffiths, 2013, p. 31). It is also related to motivation, particularly to such facets as instrumental goals, international posture and positive future self-guides, since these underlie the use of self-regulatory strategies (Kormos and Csizér, 2014). And also in this case, agency plays an important role because, as Benson (2007) argues, it constitutes 'a point of origin for the development of autonomy' (p. 30), whereas Gao and Zhang (2011) emphasize that agency and metacognition are closely linked to autonomy. As Benson (2007) has shown, autonomy can be related to control over the learning endeavour, the mental operations that underlie this process and the specific content that is to be learned.

As is the case with self-regulation, a variety of approaches can be adopted when it comes to fostering learner autonomy. Benson (2011) discusses six of them, namely the technology-based, learner-based, teacher-based, classroom-based, curriculum-based and resource-based approaches, which differently emphasize the importance of control over various aspects of the language learning process. As will be shown in the empirical part of this chapter, some of these approaches may be more important than others in different contexts and contribute to the development of self-regulation in different ways. At the same time, they may also mutually overlap, which warrants the decision to conflate them into fewer categories. For example, the use of modern technologies has become so ubiquitous and extensively integrated into the process of learning nowadays that it might no longer make sense to view it as a separate entity. By the same token, it could be argued that classroom-based, curriculum-based and resource-based approaches could be successfully subsumed under the rubrics of learner- and teacher-based approaches. This is because, depending on specific educational and local settings, both teachers and learners alike can influence the ways in which lessons are conducted, the manner in which instructional techniques are implemented, how the curriculum is constructed and how resources are taken advantage of with a view to fostering autonomy.

As can be seen from the earlier discussion, self-regulation and autonomy are closely related but the nature of this relationship can be further illuminated. Oxford (2017) argues that there is a major overlap between the two concepts (along with agency), emphasizing that the link is reciprocal in the sense that, as Ehrman (2002) noted, not only is self-regulation 'foundational of learner autonomy' (p. 256) but the reverse is the case as well. Ehrman also claims that while someone who exhibits a high degree of self-regulation is likely to be autonomous (and agentic), the opposite does not always have to be the case. It can also be argued, as Nakata (2014) does, that self-regulation constitutes just one component of autonomy, the former in itself being encompassed within learner agency. In light of this reasoning, neither self-regulation nor even agency by themselves are sufficient to ensure the exercise of autonomy in language learning. On the other hand, learners can hardly be expected to become autonomous if they cannot engage in self-regulation and are not able to display a sense of agency in their learning. One way or another, self-regulation and autonomy are closely intertwined, with the effect that the investigation of either of the two constructs is bound to shed light on the other, a rationale that drove the design and validation of the questionnaire described below.

Although the issues discussed so far are obviously relevant to the theme of the present chapter, the key question concerns the importance of self-regulation and autonomy in SA contexts. There are many envisaged benefits of SA programmes, irrespective of the form such programmes may take, ranging from gaining greater command of the TL in the case of language learners, be it in terms of different subsystems or communicative abilities, getting to know the language of the country where students reside, increasing intercultural awareness, as well as attaining educational goals that may subsequently be crucial in finding employment beyond the country of origin (cf. Pérez-Vidal, 2017). Diverse as these goals might seem at first, in most situations they are closely interrelated. This is because, for example, without achieving a threshold level of proficiency in the language in which instruction is provided during study abroad (Collentine, 2009), which could be an international language such as English as the global lingua franca, but also the native language of the host country in which mobility occurs (e.g. Italian for studying medicine in Bologna), it may be difficult, if not impossible, to accomplish non-linguistic goals, such as the familiarization with course content and engaging in practical activities based on this content. By the same token, if students lack the requisite communicative skills, the extent to which they can benefit interculturally from local peers or exchange students from other countries may also be limited.

Although there is evidence that SA programmes are effective in both linguistic and non-linguistic terms (Pérez-Vidal, 2015, 2017), there are instances when they fail to live up to the expectations of students, teachers and coordinators. This can be attributed to the fact that going to a foreign country to complete a part of the academic programme may be insufficient to ensure opportunities for TL use, ample levels of academic challenge and copious opportunities for intercultural encounters. In fact, much depends on the students themselves since, as Pérez-Vidal (2017) argues, 'it is ultimately for each learner to display the adequate strategies needed to establish contact with TL speakers while abroad […], in order to practice the language, to benefit from the linguistic landscape […] and the local culture (including the media, the arts, socio-political events, etc.)' (p. 342). This is precisely where self-regulation comes into play as it is logical that the expected advantages of study abroad are more likely to accrue when students strive to self-regulate their learning processes, adapting their thoughts, affective states and actions in such a way that a personally important goal is easier to attain, displaying autonomy and a considerable degree of agency. In effect, they will not passively wait for opportunities for input and interaction, intercultural contact and academic challenge to arise but, rather, endeavour to generate such opportunities. In effect, to quote Pérez-Vidal (2017) again, 'in order to prepare learners for SA, in at-home instruction we may need to concentrate on developing the "self-regulating" capacity learners are able to display, prior to their departure abroad, that is, the extent of their proactiveness in accessing such opportunities (Dörnyei and Ushioda, 2009)' (p. 344).

Given the importance of self-regulation (but also autonomy and agency) in SA programmes and the fact that scholars emphasize its positive contribution to the outcomes of these programmes, it is surprising how little has been done in this area empirically. Although there are studies which have focused on the self-regulation of students in SA contexts and have even proposed instruments to assess it, they have conceptualized the construct in different ways, typically with respect to strategy use (e.g. Allen, 2013), different aspects of motivation (e.g. Chirkov et al., 2007) or beliefs (Amuzie and Winke, 2009), and often doing so in a way that is far from straightforward. To the best of our knowledge, there has so far been no attempt to investigate self-regulation in SA programmes in a systematic manner, as a means of doing justice to its intricate links with autonomy and agency, and also tapping into the dynamic changes that it undergoes over time from before mobility and during mobility to after students' return to their home countries. In view of this, it is perhaps understandable that no studies have addressed the way in which the occurrence of self-regulation is mediated by individual and contextual factors which have been shown to impact the effects of study abroad, such as motivation, personality, willingness to communicate, aptitude (Pérez-Vidal, 2017), or the programme features as discussed by Pérez-Vidal (2014), such as overall objectives, length, housing arrangement, preparations prior to departure or debriefing upon return. While the study reported below cannot possibly shed light on the moderating influence of such variables, it brings us closer to this goal by initially validating a questionnaire that examined the self-regulatory processes of learners before, during and after study abroad, taking into account not only the experiences of students majoring in English but also those specializing in other fields of academic study.

Research questions

Building on the rationale presented in the literature review, we conducted a quantitative study in which we sought to initially validate an instrument to investigate self-regulation in study abroad. The tool was piloted in two different contexts, Hungary and Poland, in order to determine whether its utility is affected by a specific setting in which it is administered. Accordingly, we set out to answer the following research questions:

1. To what extent are the proposed constructs regarding self-regulation before, during and after study abroad (i.e. teacher-based, learner-based and technology-based with respect to social and academic domains) measured in a reliable way?
2. How do students manifest self-regulation before, during and after study abroad with respect to the constructs that are reliable?

Methods

Participants

The participants of the study were 136 university students in Hungary ($n = 48$) and Poland ($n = 88$) who had completed part of their programme in a foreign country or were currently studying abroad. In both cases, these were samples of convenience since the students were recruited based on the first two authors' networks of contacts in the respective countries. The learners' participation in the research project was voluntary. Among the participants, there were both incoming and outgoing students, currently or previously enrolled in either short- or long-term SA programmes. Seventy-six per cent ($n = 103$) of the participants were females and 24 per cent were males ($n = 33$). Their age varied between nineteen and twenty eight, with a mean of twenty-three years of age. The responses came from students from diverse cultural backgrounds, representing twenty-five different countries. The English language level of the participants was not specifically measured but, based on the authors' familiarity with the two respective contexts, it was hypothesized to fall between B2 and C1 according to the Common European Framework of Reference for Languages (CEFR).

Variation could also be observed in the students' subject major and the length of their stay in the target country. Although the majority of the participants were enrolled in English studies ($n = 74$), responses were also received from students in the field of social sciences, such as psychology and law. Fifty per cent of the students were still participating in the SA programme at the time of responding to the questionnaire, while the other half had already completed the programme. The time the participants spent studying in these programmes ranged from one semester to two years. The majority of the respondents, 63 per cent, indicated that the duration of their programme was one semester, but that differed depending on a given country.

Instrument

The constructs measured in the instrument were based on Benson's (2011) model of learner autonomy in learning a second or foreign language in accordance with the belief that these constructs underpinned self-regulatory processes in SA situations. As stated previously, the model differentiates between six approaches when it comes to promoting autonomy. These are technology-based, learner-based, teacher-based, classroom-based, curriculum-based and resource-based approaches. As elucidated in the literature review, in the instrument used for the purpose of the present study, the approaches relating to the classroom and the curriculum were measured together with learner- and teacher-based approaches. Furthermore, two further constructs proposed by Benson (2011), the resource-based and technology-based approaches, were intertwined due to the omnipresence of new technologies in both educational and non-educational contexts, and the fact that the use of these technologies has been integrated into the process of language learning as well. In effect, the approaches relating to learning resources were considered to be encompassed by the construct of technology-based approaches.

The instrument consisted of two sections. The first section included six questions which were related to biographical data about the participants (e.g. gender, nationality, length of study). The second section, which constituted the core of the tool, contained eighty-one five-point Likert-scale items (1 – totally disagree and 5 – totally agree) which aimed to measure the students' self-regulatory processes regarding their social and academic lives before (e.g. 'Before the study abroad …'), during (e.g. 'During the study abroad …') and after (e.g. 'After study abroad, I plan to …') a short- or long-term

SA programme. The eighty-one statements in this section were subsumed under three main constructs. The first was concerned with approaches relating to the teacher who constitutes an authority figure for most students, both in his/her capacity as a lecturer and possibly a mentor. This construct incorporated twenty-one items (e.g. 'During the study abroad, I think the success of my academic performance depends on my teachers', 'During the study abroad, I need a mentor who can help me with everyday affairs related to the university'). The second construct reflected technology-based approaches and comprised thirty-two items aimed at measuring independent use of learning materials, resources and educational technologies (e.g. 'Before the study abroad, I checked the courses offered by the university online'). The third construct, measured by twenty-eight items, was intended to tap into learner-based self-regulatory processes and, similar to Benson's (2011) study, to determine whether or not changes occur in the learner due to behavioural, psychological or social factors. The statements subsumed under this construct also aimed to investigate the degree to which learners take responsibility for their own academic and social lives inside and outside the classroom during the period of study abroad (e.g. 'Before travelling, I tried to look for opportunities to speak academic English as much as possible'). All the items were designed by the present authors and all of them were worded positively, with a higher value indicating a greater degree of self-regulation. The Likert-scale statements were formulated in simple English (not exceeding the A2 level according to the CEFR) so that participants would not experience any comprehension problems.

The novelty of the instrument lies in its structure and scope, as it goes beyond linking self-regulation to a specific individual factor as previous studies have typically done (e.g. Amuzie and Winke, 2009; Allen, 2013; Chirkov et al., 2007). As can be seen from Figure 8.1, the tool was intended to provide insights into autonomy and self-regulation in two domains on account of the fact that both the social (e.g. 'Before the

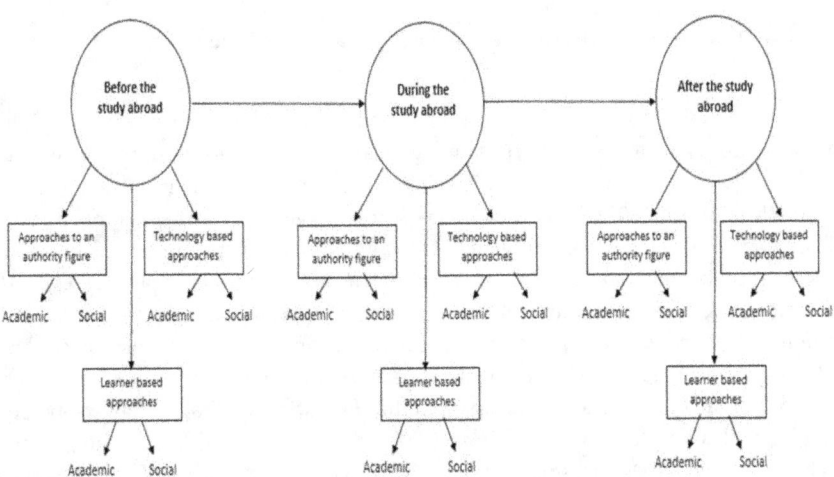

Figure 8.1 The Structure of the Questionnaire.

study abroad, I searched online for places in the target country where I can do my hobbies [sports, gym, theatre]') and academic (e.g. 'Before the study abroad, I checked the courses offered by the university online') aspect of every construct was measured.

Data collection and analysis

Since the participants were recruited from among SA students in two different countries (Hungary and Poland), the questionnaire was distributed online. The data were collected in the two contexts independently using the same Google form. The Hungarian data collection was finalized in the autumn of 2017 whereas the Polish data were collected in the spring term of 2018. Participation was voluntary and anonymous. Before analysing our data, the dataset was prepared for transfer to SPSS 22.0. Data analysis included calculating the Cronbach alpha values separately for the two contexts. Since the data were normally distributed, descriptive statistics (i.e. means and standard deviations) and paired-samples and independent samples t-tests were used to compare the various mean values within and between the two contexts for which the scales manifested an acceptable level of internal consistency reliability, namely the learner-based approaches in the academic domain. One-way ANOVAs were also computed to tap into the potential effect of age as a factor mediating self-regulation in the academic domain.

Results and discussion

The findings of the study are discussed in two sections. The first focuses on the internal reliability consistency of the scales included in the instrument and the other makes a comparison between the Polish and Hungarian context with respect to the construct that proved to be highly reliable, that is, learner-based approaches to self-regulation in the academic domain.

Research question 1: Internal consistency reliability of the constructs measured

In order to examine the internal consistency of the questionnaire, the Cronbach alpha values were calculated for each construct under investigation for both the Hungarian and the Polish sample. Even if we consider an admittedly lenient cut-off point of 0.60 (cf. Dörnyei, 2007), it can be observed from Table 8.1 that there is much room for improvement for the instrument. At this juncture, we can only speculate about the reasons for the apparent lack of reliability (i.e. low Cronbach alpha values) and, therefore, the ideas presented here should provide food for thought for subsequent studies intended to validate such a tool. The Cronbach alpha values exceeding .80 suggest that the most reliable constructs included questions concerning the learner-based approach in the academic domain in the Hungarian and Polish contexts before, during and after study abroad. These results could indicate that students' mental schemata of SA experiences relate especially to academic activities and that the social aspects of study abroad are not part of this conceptualization. The corresponding scales in the social domain come close to achieving reliability for before and after study abroad (Cronbach alpha values ranging from .63 to .81) but have unacceptably low reliability values for the during SA experience (Cronbach alpha values failing to exceed .50). One explanation for this could be possible problems with the conceptualization and wording of some of the items as well as the fact that there was perhaps some bias in the participants' profiles and the way in which the data were collected (e.g. unequal numbers of respondents in both contexts, lack of balance between males and females, voluntary nature of data collection). All of these factors are to some extent inevitable in an exploratory small-scale pilot study such as this one. Another possibility, however, is that such findings might be attributed again to how students conceptualize the social demands of the SA experience.

As far as the technology-based approaches are concerned, the results seem to be consistent across the two contexts in the case of social purposes. However, as the Cronbach alpha values in the range of .54 to .69 are not satisfactory, adding further items to those constructs could increase internal consistency reliability. With respect to the academic dimension of technology-based approaches, the Cronbach alpha values were below .60 for before study abroad in the case of the Polish participants (.45) and during study abroad for the Hungarian participants (.32). Interestingly, considerable differences were observed between the Cronbach alpha values in the Hungarian and Polish contexts, which might signal contextual differences concerning online university environments in the two countries. The fact that in the case of technology-based approaches the highest values were obtained for the after SA dimensions might again reflect contextual differences between home and host universities. The scales of teacher-based approaches show highly inconsistent results, which can be ascribed to a variety of possible reasons. First, it may have been a conceptual mistake to try to

Table 8.1 Cronbach Alpha Values for the Scales Included in the Tool

Constructs	Domain	Data Collected	Before Study Abroad	During Study Abroad	After Study Abroad
Technology-based approaches	Social	Hungary	.69	.55	.53
		Poland	.54	.65	.62
	Academic	Hungary	.60	.32	.66
		Poland	.45	.71	.82
Learner-based approaches	Social	Hungary	.70	.38	.69
		Poland	.63	.44	.81
	Academic	Hungary	.90	.85	.94
		Poland	.87	.88	.92
Teacher-based approaches	Social	Hungary	.26	.58	.10
		Poland	.47	.64	.10
	Academic	Hungary	.64	.27	.57
		Poland	.59	.49	.68

Table 8.2 Proposed Constructs for Further Studies with Sample Items

Constructs	Domain	Before Travelling, …	During Study Abroad, …	After Arriving Home, …
Learner-based approaches	Individual	Using the Internet to get to know the country/city of study abroad		
	Social	Getting in touch with people in the same context		
	Academic	Looking for opportunities to use academic English as much as possible		
Teacher-based approaches	Individual	Relying mainly on resources provided by the teacher to getting to know the target country		
	Social	Talking to teachers about issues related to the host university		
	Academic	Taking into account my teachers' opinions about the courses I should choose		

consider teacher-related approaches in the social domain for before and after study abroad as Cronbach alpha values are very low in those dimensions. These low values indicate that the constructs might be alien to participants' way of thinking or that there could be problems inherent in the items as such. Second, the somewhat higher results for the during SA dimension indicate that there are possible contextual differences related to teachers and tutors in various contexts. The data relating to the academic dimension of teacher-based approaches indicate that these items are especially unsuitable for the during SA dimensions.

Following the considerations outlined earlier, the instrument used in this pilot study is clearly in need of modifications to increase its effectiveness in future research projects. These modifications should first and foremost consist of including new dimensions of self-regulation and autonomy in SA contexts. As illustrated in Table 8.2, the main idea behind such a reconceptualization is that since the use of technology has become ubiquitous and permeates virtually all aspects of our lives, it might be more useful to see this dimension as an integral part of the learner- and teacher-based approaches with respect to both social and academic dimensions. Furthermore, introducing an additional, individual level of analysis would help to cover the full spectrum of the use of technology. It would also address the fact that self-regulation and autonomy can manifest themselves on the individual plane, which can be distinct from the social and academic planes. This individual plane would thus refer to self-regulatory processes involving students in doing things on their own, either of their own initiative (i.e. learner-based) or as a result of being instigated by the teacher in some way (i.e. teacher-based).

Research question 2: Learner-based approaches to self-regulation in the academic domain – Hungarian versus Polish context

This section offers further analysis of the scales tapping into learner-based approaches in academic domains. As previously demonstrated, these show the highest internal

Table 8.3 Differences between the Hungarian and Polish Students with Respect to the Academic Dimension of the Learner-based Approach before, during and after Study Abroad

Constructs	Domain	Context	Mean	Standard Deviation	p-Value
Learner-based approaches – before SA	Academic	Hungary	2.76	1.21	.003*
		Poland	3.36	1.05	
Learner-based approaches – during SA	Academic	Hungary	3.22	0.93	.029*
		Poland	3.60	0.98	
Learner-based approaches – after SA	Academic	Hungary	3.24	1.15	.004*
		Poland	3.81	1.01	

* Indicates a significant p value at .05

consistency reliability, with Cronbach alpha values exceeding .80. Table 8.3 contains the means and standard deviations for the scales in the Hungarian and Polish contexts, as well as the results of the independent samples t-tests' comparison between the two settings.

The results indicate significant differences between the Hungarian and Polish participants in relation to before, during and after the period of study abroad. The means for the latter are higher in all cases ($M = 2.76$ vs 3.36, $M = 3.22$ vs 3.60 and $M = 3.24$ vs 3.81), with corresponding p values being lower than .05 for each pair and thus the differences reaching significance. This suggests that the Polish participants were considerably more able to self-regulate their learning at different stages of their SA experience in the academic domain than their Hungarian counterparts. These results might stem from the fact that the contexts investigated in the two countries were very different: a medium-sized town (Konin) in Poland and the capital city of Hungary (Budapest). It could be argued, for example, that the latter, thanks to its status and beauty, is more likely to attract students who are more touristically than academically oriented. On the other hand, however, many of the participants were also Hungarian and Polish students who had visited other countries.

The disparate interpretations indicate that, at this point, only tentative explanations for the differences can be provided. Nevertheless, it is clear from these results that there are marked contextual differences that are likely to impinge on how students self-regulate their learning in SA contexts, at least with respect to the academic domain. This fact has at least two research implications. First, future studies focusing on self-regulation in study abroad need to take into account contextual differences between host countries, cities and universities. Second, more data should be collected about students' self-regulatory capacities before study abroad as this might impact their choice of future host university. This is because students with less self-confidence in their ability to self-regulate their academic and social lives might choose different locations for their sojourn abroad compared to those characterized by higher levels of self-regulation.

With regard to within-context differences, a paired-samples comparison of the Hungarian data showed a significant increase in students' self-regulation between before and during study abroad ($M = 2.76$ vs $M = 3.22$, $t = -4.023$; $p < .05$). This increase was carried over to after study abroad as a significant difference was observed between the levels of self-regulation before and after the sojourn in the target country ($M = 2.76$ vs $M = 3.24$, $t = -3.981$; $p < .05$). However, no statistically significant increase was detected between during and after study abroad ($M = 3.22$ vs $M = 3.24$, $t = -0.42$; $p < .05$). A slightly different pattern was revealed for the Polish participants, as in this case the mean values for learner-based self-regulatory approaches in the academic domain increased significantly not only from before study abroad to during study abroad ($M = 3.36$ vs 3.60, $t = -3.135$; $p < .05$) but also from during study abroad to after study abroad ($M = 3.60$ vs $M = 3.81$, $t = -2.732$; $p < .05$). In effect, the difference between the data pertaining to the before and after the SA experience was also significant ($M = 3.36$ vs $M = 3.81$, $t = -5.234$; $p < .05$). The results from both contexts indicate a link between SA experience and the capacity to engage in self-regulation in the academic domain, as long as students are the agents of such processes. Given the fact that data were only collected in two countries, it is difficult to determine whether these distinct patterns could be generalized to other contexts.

Obviously, a number of background variables could have had an effect on the self-regulatory processes revealed in the present study. However, due to the absence of requisite data, only gender and age can be considered at this juncture. In terms of gender, although more females than males participated in our study in both contexts, the comparison of relevant mean values did not yield any gender-based differences for learner-based approaches in the academic domain. In terms of student age, intuitively, one might think that older students are more able to self-regulate their own learning. Nevertheless, no age-related differences were detected in the Polish sub-sample when ANOVA was run with three distinct age groups: 18–21-year-old students, who are at an early stage of their tertiary education; 22–24-year-old students, who are about to finish their bachelor's or master's degrees, and mature learners, older than twenty-four years. In the Hungarian dataset, for one scale, learner-based approaches before the SA experience, significantly higher mean values were detected for students over 25 years old as opposed to the two younger groups (18–21 years old and 22–24 years old) (ANOVA analysis: $F = 3.344$; $p = .044$). Although the questionnaire provided data on other background variables, such as nationality, subject major or length of stay, the number of participants in some of the subgroups was too low for further analysis. This indicates that future studies must include a larger number of students in order to analyse differences according to background variables. In addition, it should be kept in mind that the degree of self-regulation may be mediated by an array of individual difference factors, such as motivation, willingness to communicate, beliefs or strategies, to name but a few. Future research should strive to shed light on the impact of such factors as well.

Conclusion

This chapter reported on a small-scale study which aimed to pilot a tool examining self-regulatory processes in SA situations and to investigate these processes for two different national contexts, the Hungarian and Polish one. The tool focused on both the social and academic domains with respect to teacher-based, learner-based and technology-based approaches to self-regulation before, during and after study abroad. In the first instance, the analysis of internal consistency reliability of the constructs demonstrated that the instrument is in need of further elaboration and refinement, which may involve reconsidering some of the scales and specific items. Second, the analysis of the differences between the Hungarian and Polish participants in the academic domain pointed to contextual differences that might play an essential role in shaping students' capacity to self-regulate their learning in SA contexts and how they think about their social and academic lives abroad. Thus, we see a clear need to restructure the initial instrument to provide a better representation of how students might approach their SA experiences. In particular, inclusion of the individual domain is proposed to complement the social and academic domains. This is motivated by the evidence suggesting that students undertake activities which cannot be captured by the two existing dimensions. Another proposed change involves the integration of technology-based approaches into learner- and teacher-based approaches. This reflects the fact that technology permeates our everyday lives and that it has become inherent in the self-regulatory processes in which students may engage in different domains.

The study has also determined some limitations of the research instrument and the ways to address them in future research. First, some constructs need modification to improve the instrument reliability. Second, the investigation was limited to two contexts and the inclusion of participants from other countries will allow more insights into the usefulness of the proposed research tool. Third, a more in-depth analysis will require more data on background variables relating to the participants as well as their home and host universities and countries. Fourth, as this study has only looked into students' self-regulation, there was no attempt to explore individual difference factors that may mediate self-regulatory capacities, such as motivated behaviour, self-efficacy, willingness to communicate or beliefs, to name but a few. Finally, no attempt was made to examine the relationship between the capacity to engage in self-regulation in study abroad and the effects of such sojourns in terms of linguistic, academic or intercultural gains. These issues should be addressed in future empirical investigations, whether such research projects aim to validate another version of the tool or shed light on self-regulation in SA contexts by means of such an instrument.

References

Allen, H. W. (2013), 'Self-regulatory Strategies of Foreign Language Learners: From the Classroom to Study Abroad and Beyond', in C. Kinginger (ed.), *Social and Cultural Aspects of Language Learning in Study Abroad*, 47–74, Amsterdam/Philadelphia: John Benjamins.

Amuzie, G. L., and Winke, P. (2009), 'Changes in Language Learning Beliefs as a Result of Study Abroad', *System*, 37, 366–79.

Benson, P. (2007), 'Autonomy in Language Teaching and Learning: State of the Art', *Language Teaching*, 40, 21–40.

Benson, P. (2011), *Teaching and Researching Autonomy in Language Learning*, Harlow, UK: Pearson Longman.

Chirkov, V., Vansteenkiste, M., Tao, R., and Lynch, M. (2007), 'The Role of Self-determined Motivation and Goals for Study Abroad in the Adaptation of International Students', *International Journal of Intercultural Relations*, 31, 199–222.

Collentine, J. (2009), 'Study Abroad Research: Findings, Implications, and Future Directions', in M. H. Long, and C. J. Doughty (eds.), *The Handbook of Second Language Teaching*, 218–33, Malden, MA: Blackwell.

Dörnyei, Z. (2007), *Research Methods in Applied Linguistics*, Oxford: Oxford University Press.

Dörnyei, Z., and Ushioda, E. (2009), *Motivational. Language Identity and the L2 Self*, Clevedon: Multilingual Matters.

Ehrman, M. E. (2002), 'Understanding the Learner at the Superior-Distinguished Threshold', in B. L. Leaver, and B. Shektman (eds.), *Developing Professional-level Language Proficiency*, 245–59, Cambridge: Cambridge University Press.

Gao, X., and Zhang, L. J. (2011), 'Joining Forces for Synergy: Agency and Metacognition as Interrelated Theoretical Perspectives on Learner Autonomy', in G. Murray, X. Gao, and T. Lamb (eds.), *Identity, Motivation, and Autonomy in Language Learning*, 25–41, Bristol: Multilingual Matters.

Griffiths, C. (2013), *The Strategy Factor in Successful Language Learning*, Bristol, UK: Multilingual Matters.

Holec, H. (1981), *Autonomy in Foreign Language Learning*, Strasbourg: Council of Europe.

Kormos, J., and Csizér, K. (2014), 'The Interaction of Motivation, Self-regulatory Strategies, and Autonomous Learning Behavior in Different Learner Groups', *TESOL Quarterly*, 48, 275–99.

Little, D. (1991), *Learner Autonomy 1: Definitions, Issues and Problems*, Dublin: Authentik.

Littlewood, W. (1999), 'Defining and Developing Autonomy in East Asian Contexts', *Applied Linguistics*, 20, 71–94.

Liu, H. H. T. (2009), 'Scale Development and Causal-effect Studies of Self-regulation in English Language Learning', Unpublished master's thesis, National Taiwan Normal University, Taipei, Taiwan.

Mercer, S. (2015), 'Learner Agency and Engagement: Believing You Can, Wanting to, and Knowing How to', *Humanizing Language Teaching*, 17 (4). Retrieved from www.http://old.hltmag.co.uk/aug15/mart01.htm.

Nakata, Y. (2014), 'Self-regulation: Why Is It Important for Promoting Learner Autonomy in the School Context?', *Studies in Self-Access Learning Journal*, 5, 342–56.

Noels, K. A., Pelletier, L., Clément, R., and Vallerand, R. J. (2000), 'Why Are You Learning a Second Language? Orientations and Self-Determination Theory', *Language Learning*, 50, 57–85.

Nunan, D. (1997), 'Designing and Adapting Materials to Encourage Learner Autonomy', in P. Benson, and P. Voller (eds.), *Autonomy and Independence in Language Learning*, 192–203, London: Longman.

Oxford, R. L. (2011), *Teaching and Researching Language Learning Strategies*, Harlow: Pearson Education.

Oxford, R. L. (2017), *Teaching and Researching Language Learning Strategies. Self-regulation in Context*, New York/London: Routledge.

Pérez-Vidal, C. (2014), 'Study Abroad and Formal Instruction Contrasted: The SALA Project', in C. Pérez-Vidal (ed.), *Language Acquisition in Study Abroad and Formal Instruction Contexts*, 17–59, Amsterdam/Philadelphia: John Benjamins.

Pérez-Vidal, C. (2015), 'Practice Makes Best: Contrasting Learning Contexts, Comparing Learner Progress', *International Journal of Multilingualism*, 12, 453–70.

Pérez-Vidal, C. (2017), 'Study Abroad in ISLA', in S. Loewen, and M. Sato (eds.), *The Routledge Handbook of Instructed Second Language Acquisition*, 339–60, London/New York: Routledge.

Rose, H. (2012), 'Reconceptualizing Strategic Learning in the Face of Self-regulation: Throwing Language Learning Strategies Out with the Bathwater', *Applied Linguistics*, 33, 92–8.

Thomas, N., and Rose, H. (2018), 'Do Language Learning Strategies Need to Be Self-directed? Disentangling Strategies from Self-regulated Learning', *TESOL Quarterly*, 53 (1), 248–57.

Tseng, W. T., Dörnyei, Z., and Schmitt, N. (2006), 'A New Approach to Assessing Strategic Learning: The Case of Self-regulation in Vocabulary Acquisition', *Applied Linguistics*, 27, 78–102.

Winne, P. H., and Perry, N. E. (2000), 'Measuring Self-regulated Learning', in M. Boekaerts, P. R. Pintrich, and M. Zeidner (eds.), *Handbook of Self-regulation*, 531–66, San Diego, CA: Academic Press.

Zimmerman, B. J. (2000), 'Attaining Self-regulation: A Social Cognitive Perspective', in M. Boekaerts, P. R. Pintrich, and M. Zeidner (eds.), *Handbook of Self-regulation*, 13–39, San Diego, CA: Academic Press.

Zimmerman, B. J., and Schunk, D. H. (2011), 'Self-regulated Learning and Performance: An Introduction and an Overview', in B. J. Zimmerman, and D. H. Schunk (eds.), *Handbook of Self-regulation of Learning and Performance*, 1–12, New York: Routledge.

9

Structure and agency in the development of plurilingual identities in study abroad

Josep M. Cots, Rosamond Mitchell and Ana Beaven
Universitat de Lleida/University of Southampton/Università di Bologna

Introduction

In this chapter we discuss a central aspect of students' educational experience of study abroad (SA), but which has been less studied so far by applied linguists in comparison with linguistic development: 'language identity'. Here we adopt the alternative concept of 'plurilingual identity', in our opinion a more useful conceptual tool to deal with an individual's experiences of communication in an intensely globalized and mobile world. Specifically, we are interested in how the development of plurilingual identities might be affected by the so-far undertheorized notion of the 'context' of study abroad, which we approach through the conceptual dichotomy of structure versus agency.

Students' interaction with their specific SA environment, through their participation in particular social practices, can be looked at, on the one hand, as constrained or enabled by different types of structures, ranging from the physical environment to individual social institutions and larger socio-economic configurations. On the other hand, students' participation can also be approached as resulting from their exercise of agency in terms of their efforts at self-regulation and their choice of goals. In turn, students' specific goals, and their willingness to exercise agency in pursuit of these, are related to their evolving sense of self, including their language identity. Our critical discussion is based on the premise that the subjective experience of plurilinguals is likely to transcend the identities associated with a particular language. We therefore explore how far the notion of plurilingual identity and the links between identity/agency/language practices have been addressed in SA research.

In this chapter, we place centre stage the notion of plurilingual identity as the result of a dialectical relationship between agency and structure. In the light of these three notions, we critically discuss existing European SA research, thus suggesting a new research avenue around two relatively recent interests in applied linguistics: identity and multilingualism. The chapter can be seen as the initial stage in the elaboration of a principled platform for future research on the constitution and evolution of plurilingual identities by taking into account the individuals' interactions with their contexts and how these interactions can be affected by and affect their linguistic repertoires. The chapter can also be considered as a useful preliminary step to reassess learners' experiences of SA programmes, showing the need to take into account (i) students' communicative repertoire as a whole, including both the development of their plurilingual skills and attitudes, and (ii) the structural opportunities and constraints with which students are confronted in the process of deploying their agency.

The agency–structure dichotomy

Identity in context

Identity work has been a focus of researchers of SLA for some time, at least since Norton's call for 'a comprehensive theory of identity that integrates the language learner and the language learning context' (Norton, 1995, p. 12), reflecting similar attention in other fields, including psychology, anthropology, sociology and sociolinguistics. At the same time, the move, on the part of many social scientists, including applied linguists, towards a post-structuralist approach to identity has resulted in a shift whereby identity is no longer seen as something solid and permanent but rather as 'socially constructed, self-conscious, ongoing narratives that individuals perform, interpret and project in dress, bodily movements, actions and language' (Block, 2007, p. 27). In other words, identities are sensitive to context and are constructed in interaction. From this perspective, it is clear that language and communication play a crucial role in identity work.

The first decade of this century saw the publication of a number of studies that focused on different aspects of identity that impact SLA, including race, gender, social class, nationality, ethnicity and language (Benson and Nunan, 2004; Norton, 2000; Omoniyi, 2004; Pavlenko and Blackledge, 2004; Pavlenko et al., 2001). Language identity is, of course, intrinsically intertwined with other aspects of identity. Thus, for example, in Polanyi's (1995), Twombly's (1995) and Talburt and Stewart's (1999) studies, gender identity is central to women participants' subject positioning through an L2. However, the focus of this review is studies in which language identity is salient for the individual.

Within the field of study abroad, the notion of 'identity' occupies a central position in three recent works: Jackson (2008), Benson et al. (2013) and Mitchell, Tracy-Ventura and McManus (2017). The three studies focus on the relationship between language learning and identity from a 'social-constructivist' or 'poststructuralist' perspective, according to which identities are 'socially conditioned and constrained' (Benson et al., 2013, p. 18) but also 'co-constructed, negotiated and transformed on an ongoing basis by means of language' (Jackson, 2008, p. 35). Despite their important contribution to the SA field, these three works can also be considered as representative of a general tendency in identity research described by Block (2009, p. 223): 'While most researchers adopt versions of Bourdieu's theory of practice and/or Giddens' structuration theory, they then proceed to present narratives of their informants, which position them as active shapers of their realities while leaving behind more explicit mention of how social constraints are at work at every juncture of their activity.'

Block sees this as a consequence of the fact that much research on identity takes the form of case studies and relies excessively on the individual's capacity for self-disclosure. This criticism can also be recognized in Kinginger's (2013, p. 3) introduction to her edited volume *Social and Cultural Aspects of Language Learning in Study Abroad*, when she refers to the abundance of, on the one hand, research focusing on outcomes and, on the other, research centred on 'the qualities of the study abroad experience from the perspective of the students'. The author also points out the scarcity of research on 'less commonly studied encounters of students and *local* communities abroad'. Block and Kinginger seem to be pointing at a lack of balance between a clearly dominant focus on the individual's subjectivity as the main (or sometimes the only) agent responsible for the success or failure of SA experiences and a relative scarcity of detailed descriptions of the social context as another equally responsible 'agent'. We realize that a considerable number of SA researchers have recently set out to document the 'social networks' and 'communities of practice' in which SA participants engage (Baker-Smemoe et al., 2014; Mitchell, Tracy-Ventura and McManus, 2017; Zappa-Hollman and Duff, 2015). However, in practice, SA researchers generally rely on SA participants as the sole informants about such networks, so that contextual information is still gathered through a lens of SA subjectivity (for an exception to this, see Surtees's (2019) recent study in which peers of SA students were also interviewed).

With the appearance of sociocultural theory in language learning and, in general, the 'social turn' in applied linguistics in the last decade of the twentieth century, as evidenced by works such as those by Lantolf (2000) and Block (2003), it has become clear that an individual's acquisition of the necessary competencies to form part of a sociocultural group depends not only on their cognitive capacities but also on the multiple contexts that the individuals interact with as part of their everyday life.

Mitchell, Tracy-Ventura and McManus (2017, p. 171), in their study of Anglophone students abroad, express a similar view when they consider that the clear differences in connection with levels of L2 engagement in Mexico (highest engagement), Spain (intermediate) and France (lowest) are attributable to 'underlying sociocultural/structural differences between the sojourner experience in these three locations, partly to do with immediate living conditions and partly to do with broader sociolinguistic factors'. However, while acknowledging the relevance of contextual factors, the authors suggest that, within each of these national contexts, the students also opted for different levels of agency, ranging between very proactive engagement at one end and avoiding engagement opportunities at the other.

According to Blommaert (2005, p. 40), context ranges from 'the infinitely small', that is the immediate verbal (and we could also include non-verbal) communicative tokens (a sentence, a sound, a gesture, etc.) surrounding a particular form or moment in communication, to the 'the infinitely big', which includes universal principles of human communication involving social categories (e.g. age, gender). Between these 'lies a world of different phenomena, operating at all levels of society and across societies, from the level of the individual all the way up to the level of the world system'. Another definition of context, perhaps somewhat more instrumental than Blommaert's, is provided by Goodwin and Duranti (1992, p. 6), who define context as 'a socially constituted, interactively sustained and time-bound phenomenon' and suggest four dimensions:

setting (i.e. the social and physical space), behavioural environment (i.e. body motion as a communicative resource), language (both as an object preceding a particular communicative act and as a tool to conjure up a particular 'world' or mental frame as relevant) and extra-situational context (participants' background knowledge, frames of relevance for the specific communicative situation, social/cultural discursive rules, etc.).

In the field of study abroad, Taguchi (2018, p. 128), in her review of research on the development of pragmatic competence, distinguishes 'three broad treatments of context', the first two adopting a quantitative and the third one a qualitative approach. She defines the first treatment as the one in which the researcher is not interested in what actually happens during study abroad and uses context as a categorical label to compare it with other contexts (e.g. SA vs at-home). The second treatment considers context as the accumulation of affordances for the learners to come into contact with the target language (TL) (either as input or output). Finally, the third treatment considers context as a site for different social practices, in which learners must adopt a specific social/institutional role involving particular discursive and non-discursive rules of behaviour. In closing her review, Taguchi (2018, p. 134) makes a clear appeal to incorporate context in future research through 'more context-oriented explanations' and 'the explicit application of social network analysis […] to allow us to examine social structures among individuals'.

Identity as agency

While Taguchi's appeal is undoubtedly important, it is also necessary to incorporate a balanced perspective on the interaction between individuals and their contexts, according to which both can be seen as *agents*, with their *own stances*, whose actions influence each other. Indeed, much research on the impact of study abroad has an egocentric bias, focusing exclusively on the subjective experience of the students, as felt and narrated by themselves, with very little presence of the experience of their individual or institutional interlocutors. An example of this bias is exemplified in the following quotation, taken from the recapitulating section that Jackson (2008, pp. 99–100) includes for one of her participants:

> Prior to her sojourn, **Ada** *preferred* to be identified as a Hong Konger, emphasizing that her core values were Chinese. […] **She** *felt* 'inferior' when speaking English with a native speaker […]. **Ada** *was* very anxious about her ability to cope in England. While **she** *experienced* a brief honeymoon period on arrival, **she** soon *succumbed* to the strains of living in an L2 in an alien environment. […] **Ada** *experienced* communication and identity misalignments […]. **Ada** *found* it difficult to build relationships with her hosts […] **she** *retained* an ethnocentric mindset throughout her stay […]. **Ada** returned home with a deeper appreciation of Hong Kong and Chinese culture.

Jackson's description consists of a total of fourteen sentences and Ada is the explicit subject in eleven of them (emphasized in bold characters), the other three having as subjects particular features of Ada's personality: 'Her language choices', 'This "lack of congruence," feelings of insecurity, and perceptions of discrimination', 'Her self-efficacy in the language'. In the same example, we can also find the dominance of predicates (emphasized in italics) reflecting mental processes involving perception, cognition, affect and desire. This final sketch of Ada, in which she is basically presented in the role of Experiencer of a series of mental processes, seems to reflect a notion of identity for which 'the self [is] seen not only as possessing an essential and unchanging core but also as independent and rational' (Vitanova et al., 2015, p. 2) and, one could add, fully conscious and responsible for their decisions and acts. The sketch can also reflect one of the problems that Miller (2012, p. 444), citing Ortner (2006), finds in the study of agency: 'Too much focus on the agency of individuals or groups threatens to oversimplify the processes of history and the complex social relations in which identities and agency develop.'

The view of identity as essentially involving an inner conscious and reflective self that creates a stable image of who we are has been questioned by interactionist and sociocultural views, according to which identities are dynamic and complex, constructed in interaction with others and socially, culturally and historically mediated (Vitanova et al., 2015). However, in the field of applied linguistics, Block (2009, p. 228) calls for a reconciliation between what he defines as psychological and social views of identity, respectively: 'Researchers [should] attempt to reconcile underlying and deep emotions and passion with semiotically-mediated surface-level behaviour.'

Complexity and variability in the definition of agency need not be a problem in itself as long as researchers clarify how they employ it (Block, 2009). More specifically, Block refers to the need to clearly distinguish between 'identity' and 'subjectivity', work out a clear and coherent model of the relations between structure and agency and articulate how a psychological and a sociological perspective of identity complement each other.

Identity as structure

Block's (2009) discussion reflects a long-established 'problem' or 'dichotomy' in social sciences to explain human behaviour: the opposition between individual freedom and social determinacy or, in other words, between *agency* and *structure* (Bakewell, 2010; Gidden and Sutton, 2014). According to Block (2012), the dilemma between prioritizing agency, as the individual's capacity to act upon society, and structure, as society's capacity to constrain the individual, has often been resolved in applied linguistics research by prioritizing the former over the latter. Block's critique, expressed in a paper on the role of agency in sociolinguistic research with migrants, may also be applied to research on the impact of study abroad on identity, since the experience of SA students, like that of migrants, often 'focuses on individual case studies and the struggles and conflicts engaged in by individuals as they become American, become French, gain a voice as an English speaker or obtain cultural and social capital' (Block, 2012, p. 58).

This marginalization of structure from identity research may be the consequence of what Bakewell (2010, p. 1695) considers as a 'tendency to reification in which social structures – such as states or cultural norms – come to be seen as rigid and beyond the reach of human agency', leading to the belief that the study of social structures falls outside the boundaries of the analysis of the individual. This, together with the tendency in identity research to consider identity as the sum of different temporary subject positions that individuals discursively adopt in their interaction with others (researchers included), may lead analysts to concentrate on assembling and making sense of the different narratives of self produced by the individuals, leaving very little space to supplement these narratives with analysis of the social structures through which their ordinary lives develop.

One example can be found in the work of Benson et al. (2013), which focuses on the L2 identity narratives of six Hong Kong students that the researchers themselves produced, based on pre- and post-SA interviews and correspondence during study abroad. If we take, for instance, Joey's story, we find five main social structures that are referred to as contributing (or not) to the student's welfare and happiness during study abroad: school (in Hong Kong), Australia (as a national community), Hong Kong (as a national community), host family and host university. What is relevant from our point of view is that most of the comments about Joey's relationship with these social structures reflect exclusively her personal perceptions. Examples like this may have led Block (2015, p. 25) to find 'the telling of life stories with only a passing reference to possible constraints and issues of power highly problematic'. In an attempt to address this problem, Block (2015, p. 21) proposes a model of structure consisting of five 'realms', of which realms 1–4 exist before the actual act of agency we are aiming to explain or justify: (1) economic structure, (2) physical structure, (3) social structure, (4) psychological embodied structure and (5) emergent sociocultural configurations in interaction.

In later sections of this chapter, after discussing the notion of language identity, we explore the extent to which empirical research on study abroad has paid attention more generally to these structural aspects and their formative role for SA participants' language identity.

Language identity

Leung, Harris and Rampton (1997) have defined language identity as the combination between what they call 'language expertise' (the level of proficiency necessary for a speaker to be accepted by other users of the language), 'language affiliation' (the language(s) that a speaker identifies with and feels emotionally attached to) and 'language inheritance' (the language(s) a speaker was born into, although this does not imply expertise in or affiliation to the given language(s)). More recently, Block has defined language identity as 'the assumed and/or attributed relationship between one's sense of self and a means of communication which might be known as a language (e.g. English), a dialect (e.g. Geordie) or a sociolect (e.g. football-speak)' (Block, 2007, p. 40). Other scholars (Baker, 2001; Vogel and García, 2017; Wei, 2011) have questioned the validity of differentiating between distinct named languages (and thereby between first and second languages) and suggest the concept of translanguaging as a more useful one when investigating plurilingualism. According to these scholars, translanguaging describes both the practice of using all the linguistic resources – seen as a single linguistic repertoire and not as a collection of discrete languages, dialects or sociolects – available to an individual and a meaning-making process, as it focuses on the negotiation of communicative contexts (Wei, 2017). In this chapter, we retain the traditional view that languages are most helpfully interpreted as distinct countable entities, from both psycholinguistic and sociocultural perspectives. That is to say, we accept both that the mind can accommodate multiple grammars (MacSwan, 2017; Sharwood Smith and Truscott, 2014) and that individual languages are historically and culturally grounded symbolic meaning systems which continue to attract robust societal allegiances. Of course, the linguistic repertoire of individuals is itself dynamic and constantly changing as a result of their lived experiences (including study abroad), and for the plurilingual individual, these changes will include mutual interactions among different known languages. In turn, these may facilitate multilingual language practices, i.e. translanguaging as we understand it. Such dynamism in the linguistic repertoire implies that language identity is also likely to evolve throughout the life of the individual.

L2 identity

In *Second Language Identities*, Block (2007) discusses L2 identity as one facet of language identity, in particular with reference to the notion of audibility, understood as

> a combination of the right accent as well as the right social and cultural capital to be an accepted member of a community of practice […] Adding a multimodal layer, and therefore stretching the construct substantially, audibility is about developing an identity in an additional language not only in terms of linguistic features, but also dress, expressions, movement, behaviour and other forms of semiotic behaviour. Audibility may thus be seen as corresponding to the extent to which the individual can 'do' the multimodal package required by a particular community of practice.
>
> (Block, 2007, pp. 41–2)

Benson et al. (2012, 2013) have also contributed to our understanding of L2-mediated identities, particularly in an SA context (though with an emphasis on the individual perspective, as discussed earlier). In their conceptual framework, they see L2-identity work as a continuum ranging from 'identity-related L2 proficiency' at one end to 'L2-mediated personal development' at the other, with 'linguistic self-concept' between them. Regarding the first dimension, the authors point out that although L2 proficiency itself is not necessarily related to identity, higher proficiency usually involves more developed pragmatic competence which may in turn affect what individuals can do with language and the kinds of identities they are able to express. In other words, 'language competence is a prerequisite for the projection of identities in a second language, but more importantly students' acquisition and use of pragmatic competence partly depends on the kinds of identities they want to project and the responses they receive to them' (2012, p. 183). Linguistic self-concept refers to 'the participants' sense of who they are as language learners and users, and their ability to negotiate personal identities through a second language' (2012, p. 184), while L2-mediated personal development refers to person development – which may happen in any case in a SA context that does not involve an additional language (e.g. the development of intercultural competence in a Spanish student studying in Argentina) – when such development is negotiated through an L2.

The work of Benson et al. (2012, 2013) is helpful in conceptualizing different facets of individual learner identity in the SA setting. Block (2007), however, reflects on the limitations of the concept of an L2-mediated identity, which implies a clear dichotomy with a single L1 (a 'mother tongue') to which a TL (L2 or TL) is added at a later stage, often through formal instruction. In any case, globally speaking, multilingualism/plurilingualism[1] is the norm, and not the exception, and many 'L2' learners are already users of other languages, dialects or sociolects. A relevant question would therefore be whether 'multilinguals, in any kind of patterned or generalizable sense, orient to TLs in a substantially different way from monolinguals and if the nature of their identity work is somewhat greater, lesser, richer or poorer' (Block, 2007, pp. 191–2). Other theorists of language identity have made positive proposals for a more integrated perspective, including the idea of the 'multilingual subject' (Kramsch, 2009). Similarly, in the field of language learning motivation, Henry (2017) has argued recently for expanding the concept of the L2 self system popularized by Dörnyei and associates (Dörnyei, 2009) to that of a 'multilingual self system', including an 'ideal multilingual self' (or in our terms, an ideal plurilingual self). In the SA literature, this issue is pursued further by McGregor (2016). She argues that SA research (like SLA more generally) has traditionally accepted an ideology of multiple monolingualism, in which study abroad contributes to mastery of a distinct TL, alongside a distinct L1. Following the 'multilingual turn' in SLA more generally (Douglas Fir Group, 2016), McGregor questions this 'pluralization of monolingualism' (Pennycook, 2010) as the most relevant/most appropriate goal for study abroad. Accordingly, we are investigating in this chapter the potential relevance for study abroad of a broader concept: not L2 identity but plurilingual identity.

Plurilingual identity

Although plurilingual identity as a concept is related to L2 identity, we can conceive it as identity negotiated through the entire linguistic repertoire available to a speaker regardless of their level of proficiency in each language, in opposition to the dichotomy L1/L2 or L1/other languages. Plurilingualism is, then, 'the complex but unique competence, in social communication, to use different languages for different purposes with different levels of command' (Beacco, 2005, p. 19). In fact, Beacco sees monolingualism as the first step in the lifelong process of becoming plurilingual. As for the link with identity: for Beacco, an individual's language repertoire 'provide[s] building blocks for affiliation to groups which see themselves as having shared cultural features and their own identifying languages' (Beacco, 2005). A plurilingual identity can also logically be associated with a greater awareness of linguistic and cultural diversity, and ability to understand the different values and behaviours of others (Language Policy Division, 2007, p. 36).

Discussions by other language identity theorists of the related constructs of 'multilinguality' (Aronin, 2016), the 'multilingual subject' (Kramsch, 2009) and the 'multilingual ideal self' (Henry, 2017) present a stronger, integrationist view of plurilingual identity and also make clearer the subjective nature of plurilingual identifications, independent of objective proficiency in relevant languages. Henry in particular makes it clear that someone proficient in more than one language has a range of choices regarding linguistic identity. They may see themselves as having distinct ideal selves in L1/L2/Ln, which may even be in conflict (so that, for example, a strong investment in an L2 English ideal self may have negative consequences for the ideal self in other additional languages). Or they may choose a more integrated multilingual ideal self, equivalent to 'a broader identity that encompasses but, in important ways, transcends a multilingual person's language-specific identities' (Henry, 2017, p. 548). Kramsch (2009) draws attention to multilingual speakers' emotional as well as instrumental needs for integrating their identity in such a way: 'To survive linguistically and emotionally the contradictions of everyday life, multilingual subjects draw on the formal semiotic and aesthetic resources afforded by various symbolic systems to reframe these contradictions and create alternative worlds of their own' (p. 22).

Empirical studies

In this section we review a selection of recent SA research on participant identity to explore how far attention has been paid to relations between structure, agency and identity and how far the field is beginning to demonstrate the emergence of a plurilingual identity among sojourners abroad. That is to say, we will explore to what extent SA-related research in particular has been influenced by the wider theoretical debates in the applied linguistics literature, discussed earlier. (There is a very large literature on study abroad, including consideration of identity development, which neglects the language dimension, which we will refer to only tangentially; see, for example, Lewin (2009) on the development of global citizenship among American sojourners or Feyen and Krzaklewska (2013), Llurda et al. (2016) on the development of European identity through the Erasmus programme.) Firstly, we consider briefly the group most studied in the SA field, i.e. monolingual Anglophone students enrolled for languages programmes in their home country (the United States, the UK: Kinginger, 2009, p. 213). Following this we examine in more detail research on the SA mobility of other groups, in particular European students with – in many cases – more multilingual home backgrounds and more complex histories of language education.

Structure, agency and the language identities of Anglophone SA participants

The SA experiences of Anglophone sojourners are commonly structured in distinctive ways, which can be related to the framework of Block introduced earlier and which have clear implications for identity development. They are likely to be female and middle class (material structuring: Hurst, 2019). They typically take part in study abroad within a home programme, such as a BA in languages or in business (institutional structuring); Anglophone language specialists spend time abroad in a country or region where the target L2 of their home programme is not only spoken but acknowledged as a dominant vehicle of education and public affairs (in de Swaan's (2001) terms, 'central' or 'supercentral' languages), reflecting geographical as well as ideological structuring. They may travel as a group and follow a specially devised programme, with implications for the social formations in which they take part. In different reviews, Kinginger (2009, 2015) acknowledges some of these structural forces. She discusses themes of conflict as well as personal growth, centring on cultural difference (e.g. on gendered relations between males and females), race and national identity (which may become heightened, e.g. by challenges to historical narratives or disputes around current affairs). A main focus of Kinginger's reviews is on such students' desire to 'craft a foreign language mediated identity' (2009, p. 202), through joining a defined L2 speech community, and their frustration at sometimes being positioned as outsiders and temporary sojourners by local community members (Brown, 2013; Cook, 2006; Iino, 2006; Wilkinson, 2002); she thus recognizes some of the structural constraints on SA participants' agency, in terms of the sociocultural configurations which are available to them.

Looking more closely at the language identity to which Anglophone SA participants aspire, we have seen earlier the view of Kramsch (2009) that they may be understood as 'multilingual subjects', at least potentially. However, empirical research has largely focused on Anglophone sojourners' language learning, socialization and identity development, with reference to one particular target L2, and has thus traditionally not questioned the prevailing ideology of multiple monolingualism (Pennycook, 2010), which structures many language-specialist SA programmes. Only a small amount of empirical research has so far explored explicitly Anglophone SA participants' interest and capacity for moving beyond an L2 identity/an L2 'ideal self' (or as Henry, 2017, puts it, a 'contentedly bilingual self') towards a plurilingual identity (e.g. McGregor, 2016).

Overall, the evidence suggests that the identity of Anglophone specialist language learners has largely been established pre-SA, through their previous educational history and agentive choices; in contrast to many of their Anglophone peers, they already identify as distinctive 'language people' (Evans, 1988). Their sense of personal success in navigating the SA sojourn reinforces this identification; the main contribution of SA is to transition from an 'L2 learner' identity to an 'L2 user' identity. This is generally promoted through key structural factors (including availability of predetermined roles as student, language assistant, etc., as well as in-principle access to a rich array of new language resources). A complication for Anglophone sojourners is the increasing possibility of communicating largely through English in most SA settings (universities, for example). The most successful sojourners, in terms of L2 gain, are generally those who show highest agency within such settings, e.g. making resilient efforts to live and/or socialize flexibly with non-peers, to undertake voluntary work in the community, to choose challenging academic courses, or to trade their English cultural capital for access to local networks (Mitchell, Tracy-Ventura and McManus, 2017).

As L2 users, such SA participants may also develop an enriched understanding of the actual sociolinguistic diversity attaching to host locations and to some extent embrace it (Geeslin and Schmidt, 2018; Ringer-Hilfinger, 2012; Shiri, 2013); in everyday language practices they are comfortable with codeswitching/translanguaging (McGregor, 2016). However, the desired vision of the plurilingual self in most cases remains that of 'multiple monolingualism', i.e. the ability to function effectively in two or more supercentral languages (Mitchell, Tracy-Ventura and McManus, 2017, Chapter 8). Aspirations to include more local languages within personal plurilingualism seem to depend on the development of strong local personal relationships.

Structure, agency and language identities of multilingual SA participants

Next we review in more detail selected research concerning SA sojourners with first languages other than English (Beaven and Spencer-Oatey, 2016; Dervin, 2013; Kalocsai, 2013; Kaypak and Ortaçtepe, 2014; Maeder-Qian, 2018; Martínez-Arbelaiz, Areizaga and Camps, 2017; Mas Alcolea, 2017; 2018; Virkkula and Nikula, 2010). We concentrate on participants in European higher education (HE) settings, mostly within the framework of the Erasmus programme. In a majority of these studies, the research is conducted by academic staff at the receiving university. Research instruments range from SA participant questionnaires to journals, interviews and participant observation, and in almost all the located studies (as in most SA research), the student experience is not triangulated with any evidence from the host community. Once again, we explore how far existing research explains the contributions of both structure and agency to linguistic identity development.

The Erasmus experience itself has been well researched, and there is a general consensus about its structural impact on participants' educational, social and personal development. It has been shown that participation in Erasmus is class-based (privileging middle-class participation); that sojourners from resource-poor countries and institutions gain lasting academic and economic benefit (but also that this is not necessarily the case for sojourners from resource-rich settings); that sojourners experience study abroad as a time of coming-of-age, reporting gains in self-confidence and intercultural capability; that their 'temporary' status leads primarily to bonding with other international sojourners and to more limited integration with local communities (Murphy-Lejeune, 2002; Teichler and Ferencz, 2011). These structural factors have implications for linguistic identity which we explore below.

Most of the language-related studies considered here involve students from one European Union country undertaking study abroad in another (e.g. Finns in Germany: Virkkula and Nikula, 2010; an Italian in Glasgow: Beaven and Spencer-Oatey, 2016; or Catalans in Wales, Italy and Denmark: Mas Alcolea, 2017, 2018); exceptions are studies of Turkish students undertaking study abroad in varied European destinations (Kaypak and Ortaçtepe, 2014) and of Chinese students in Germany (Maeder-Qian, 2018). The participants in these studies vary quite considerably in some ways, for example regarding their academic discipline and length of stay abroad. However, one institutional background factor they all have in common is a lengthy prior education in English at home, alongside socioculturally structured pre-sojourn expectations that they will be using English as a lingua franca during the sojourn, whether or not they are enrolled in English-medium academic programmes (Kalocsai, 2013; Maeder-Qian, 2018; Martínez-Arbelaiz, Areizaga and Camps, 2017). And indeed, there is emerging evidence that ELF usage in such settings is sufficient to have a positive impact on sojourners' English proficiency (Llanes, Arnó and Mancho-Barés, 2016).

The precise research focus of the selected studies is also variable. Some examine only sojourners' thoughts about English (e.g. Kaypak and Ortaçtepe, 2014), while others explore their thoughts about one or more other languages in addition (home languages, the dominant official language of the host country, other languages in play in the SA environment). Some explore language practices and/or attitudes, with no explicit reference to identity (Kaypak and Ortaçtepe, 2014; Martínez-Arbelaiz, Areizaga and Camps, 2017). When researchers focus explicitly on identity, a range of different theoretical frameworks is identified; thus Dervin (2013), for example, is concerned with sojourner 'identifications', while Virkkula and Nikula (2010), Mas Alcolea (2017) and Maeder-Qian (2018) are concerned with 'discursive identity construction' and 'cultural identity reconstruction'. Many studies focus primarily on cultural adaptation; here we consider only those studies which take some explicit account of language practices (Beaven and Spencer-Oatey, 2016; Maeder-Qian, 2018). Taken together, however, the research provides some insights into the structural factors promoting the increasingly multilingual nature of contemporary study abroad and the related evolution of sojourners' language identity.

Firstly, these studies provide ample evidence on the actuality of bi- or multilingual and translanguaging practices during contemporary study abroad and the structural factors promoting these. The questionnaire survey by Martínez-Arbelaiz, Areizaga and Camps (2017), conducted at two universities in the Basque region of Spain, explored incoming SA students' use of their home L1, Spanish and English, both in various types of face-to-face interaction and when online. (Remarkably, no questions were asked concerning Basque.) The influence of institutional and sociocultural structures was clear in sojourners' responses. Thus, the home L1 was most frequently used on line, to keep in touch with family and friends; English and Spanish featured roughly equally as languages of study. Regarding face-to-face interaction, it seemed some exercise of individual agency was possible: while Spanish was used predominantly in service encounters, both English and Spanish were used to conduct personal relations. About half the participants used translanguaging practices on a daily basis, arguably another symptom of increased agency.

However in other studies, sojourners in the sociolinguistic environment of the Nordic countries, where English is widely known outside the academy, are described as relying mainly on ELF for communication with locals as well as with international peers. These sojourners made only limited use of Danish or Finnish (Dervin, 2013; Mas Alcolea, 2017). The Chinese sojourners studied by Maeder-Qian (2018) were divided; those who had previously studied German reported making regular use of this in-sojourn, but those who arrived in the country with little German do not seem to have done so. Indeed, this group was very likely to associate primarily with fellow Chinese sojourners (who are the most numerous international student group in Germany) and thus to carry out much face-to-face social interaction in Chinese.

Regarding identity development, several studies suggest that European sojourners progress considerably from 'language learner' to 'language user'. However, the reference language is typically 'hypercentral' English, rather than a local national language. For example, Virkkula and Nikula (2010) tracked seven Finnish engineering students longitudinally through a work-experience sojourn in Germany. At work, the students were expected to use German, but in practice 'English was the principal lingua franca' (Räisänen, 2016, p. 160); the sojourners also lived in the sociocultural configuration of an ELF-using international student community. At the beginning of the sojourn, the participants voiced a 'learner' perspective regarding English, describing their English proficiency as inadequate, using school-learned formal categories (vocabulary, grammar, pronunciation). However, following study abroad, 'they embark on positioning themselves discursively as users of English rather than as incompetent learners. Their discursive choices also shift from concerns about coping with discrete language skills such as grammar, vocabulary, and speaking to descriptions of survival in English and using it in daily life' (Virkkula and Nikula, 2010, p. 263). In this structurally supportive setting, this group also ceased to compare themselves (negatively) with English native speakers. However, the researchers did not report on the participants' perceptions and accounts of themselves as speakers of any language other than English (in particular, of German). Thus, it is not possible to be certain whether this post-sojourn group has actually reached the position of 'contentedly bilingual self' (Henry, 2017) or rather that of a plurilingual self.

The study of Kaypak and Ortaçtepe (2014) with fifty-three students from Turkey undertaking a five-month Erasmus placement also focused on ELF. These participants came from different academic disciplines and sojourned in several countries, though the biggest group ($n = 19$) was in Poland. They completed a language attitudes questionnaire on departure and again on return, and some also maintained journals describing language practices in-sojourn. Before departure, the group were already very aware of the international standing and roles of English, and rather negative about their own L2 English abilities, which they attributed to the nature of their previous school education. By end sojourn, participants' perceptions of the high status of English were even further reinforced. Their social experience during study abroad meant they became less afraid of making mistakes in English and more positive about making international friends through English; they attached less importance to knowing British and American culture, in order to speak English well, though they remained anxious about interaction with native speakers. The qualitative data provided further evidence of a shift from learner to user perspective: 'While interacting with the Spanish, I feel like a native speaker of English. Moreover, I do not feel hindered anymore. I can ask anything in English without any hesitation' (p. 361). There were also some indications of an increase in sojourner agency, reflected in proactive steps to socialize within the ELF-using international community: 'I think attending social activities and meeting new people play a significant role in my development' (p. 362).

Turkish sojourners in the Netherlands and Germany commented on the usefulness of English outside the academy; others (e.g. in Poland) commented that locals did not generally speak English, but did not elaborate on how they communicated with them. Again, these authors do not pursue the issue, but it seems that a Turkish-English 'bilingual self', rather than a plurilingual self, may also be these sojourners' prime target.

Dervin (2013) reports on a questionnaire survey of Erasmus students studying in Finland as the host country ($n = 250$), concerning their use of ELF and also of Finnish. The questionnaire allowed for open-ended responses, which Dervin analyses in terms of participants' subjective self-identifications. Of the studies surveyed here, this investigation produced the most negative accounts of plurilingualism. The participants evaluated their own English proficiency negatively, and some considered that ELF use in Finland was leading to a deterioration: 'My English got a bit worse since most other people exchange students aren't native speakers and therefore make quite a lot of mistakes which you eventually get used to and adopt I used to speak good English until I landed in Finland I have to slow down and speak in a way that people understand that means no grammar, just broken words' (p. 108). Participants typically distinguished between 'formal'/'special'/'proper' English, which they associated with education settings and with native speakers, and 'informal'/'simple'/'slang' English, which they associated with (international) friendship. A very small number of participants wrote positively about versions of translanguaging: 'I speak multilanguage English ... why? Because of different accent that depends on who I am speaking to and also because we sometimes add some words in many other languages. It's not a strict English (esp. About the grammar) it is a kind of slang-global village-language' (p. 109). However, concerning Finnish, Dervin reports that none of the participants progressed beyond a survival level. Some participants were quite satisfied that they can 'go everywhere with my English' (p. 113), though a few expressed feelings of (mild) shame and guilt at having learned so little Finnish.

Mas Alcolea (2017) tracked nine case study participants from Catalonia who undertook study abroad in Wales (UK), Denmark and Italy; only one was a languages specialist. Mas Alcolea collected exceptionally rich data from her participants, including a pre-departure focus group, a pre-departure questionnaire, a sequence of written commentaries produced in-sojourn and a retrospective narrative interview. Unusually, she also visited and shadowed the participants for two to three days each at the SA location.

Mas Alcolea reports rather differently structured experiences, and evolution of linguistic identity, for her three host locations. In the UK and in Denmark, where instruction was English medium, participants began with feelings of inadequacy concerning their own level of English, but over time they progressed from learner to user identity, interacting socially with increasing confidence: 'now I am really not scared of speaking' (p. 295). Their self-evaluations changed from concerns with accuracy to communicative effectiveness. A similar evolution is reported by Beaven and Spencer-Oatey (2016) in their case study of an Italian Erasmus student in Glasgow, who found over time that she could increasingly 'be myself' in an international ELF-using network (though less so with locals) and also cope with academic study through English. However, it is clear that participants in these locations were concerned primarily with L2 English. Those sojourning in Wales noticed the formal presence of Welsh but dismissed it completely as redundant to their communicative needs. Those in Denmark viewed Danish as unnecessary for their current needs, because of the good level of English spoken in the community, though they recognized it would be necessary to learn it if migrating to the country long term for purposes of social integration with locals.

Mas Alcolea's sojourners in Italy had a somewhat different experience. They attended Italian-medium classes and socialized largely with fellow Catalans and Spaniards, the largest international group. Indeed there was some evidence of a reinforcement of a shared 'Spanish' identity, with acknowledgement by participants of greatest cultural compatibility between these groups. While other international students were using ELF, the case study students never broke into this group and maintained an unconfident, 'learner' identity with respect to English. It seemed they could follow Italian-medium instruction adequately without formal language study, though they believed that to integrate in the society, a good knowledge of Italian would be needed. Another outcome for this subgroup seemed to be the emergence of a 'Romance plurilingual' identity, exploiting commonalities between Spanish, Catalan and Italian, though this was never expressed very explicitly.

In conclusion, the Chinese student sojourners in Germany studied by Maeder-Qian (2018) can be considered briefly. Unlike Erasmus participants, they were enrolled for full-degree programmes at various German universities in different academic disciplines. Seven of these programmes were German medium, the rest were English medium or bilingual programmes. The participants ($n = 17$) were interviewed (in Chinese) three times over one academic year. Regardless of their proficiency in German, these sojourners generally reported difficulties in forming more-than-superficial relationships with local students. Many students in German-medium programmes perceived an 'interpersonal distance brought about by different cultures or their own insufficient multilingual competences [which] could not be reduced despite the friendly hosts they encountered' (p. 580). This is the case for physics major Jeremy: 'my feelings towards the Germans always stay like, we could gradually become friends, but I could never be that into them, like I could never regard them as the same sort of people as us. So I cannot blend into them, and I don't regard myself as a part of them' (p. 581).

Participants with limited German found that using ELF, they could easily network with other international students and that 'they could feel their English speaker status legitimised in the communication' (p. 581). However, while local students also spoke good English, for intimate and informal conversation, they used German, and the Chinese students felt excluded. Ultimately, many of the Chinese students developed a heightened sense that they had a distinctive, core Chinese identity, socialized increasingly with Chinese only and adopted a posture of 'observer' of German society.

Maeder-Qian identified a small number of exceptions: people such as chemistry major Boris, who 'realised that he could navigate his multilingual repertoire to position himself somewhat in between the two separated groups of Chinese and Germans in his laboratory' (p. 584) and negotiated a new subject position between cultures. And then there was language specialist Vera, a 'motivated and competent multilingual speaker', who sought German housemates and adapted to their food, drink and partying habits; she is finally described as 'the only participant that identified positively with Chinese, German and various [other] cultures that emerged in ELF' (p. 585).

To conclude this section: it seems that like monolingual Anglophone sojourners, multilingual sojourners in European contexts begin their stay abroad with an already-developed language identity formed through previous education, which is extended rather than transformed by the SA experience. They are well aware, pre-departure, of the global role of English, and the aspiration to become an English user is an important motivator for study abroad (for both language specialists and non-specialists). However, less academic students, non-language specialists and students from lower-resource contexts may have low self-confidence pre-departure and feelings of anxiety about English. Where study abroad offers structured opportunity for English-medium instruction and also for ELF interaction with international peers, these feelings are generally overcome, and sojourners can develop the identity of an L2 English user. (It seems that both these contextual components are required: see the studies of Mas Alcolea and Maeder-Qian.) Participants' increasing individual agency can help promote this identity, as seen in the study of Kaypak and Ortaçtepe and also in some case studies reported by Maeder-Qian. On the other hand, sojourners may still struggle to reconcile their actual ELF and translanguaging practices and ideologies of 'correct' English (see studies of Dervin and of Kaypak and Ortaçtepe).

A limitation of much European research to date is the general focus on hypercentral English. While some studies acknowledge ongoing home language use, its place in language identity and the structuring factors supporting this are treated in an atheoretical manner. The non-supercentral languages of some local hosts (e.g. Basque, Danish, Finnish, Welsh) are often invisible, and it seems that SA participants feel little sociocultural pressure to engage with these languages. The Catalan-speaking participants studied in Italy by Mas Alcolea do recognize some affinities across Romance languages; otherwise the main exception is the study of Maeder-Qian, who considers in some depth the evolving place of ELF, of L2 German and also of L1 Chinese in the sociocultural structuring of participant identity among Chinese sojourners in Germany. Overall, the evidence suggests that European sojourners are primarily seeking a 'stable bilingual' identity (in English plus L1) and that many structural factors combine to promote this. However, much more research is needed using the richer techniques of Mas Alcolea and Maeder-Qian, and including the perspectives of stakeholders in the local context, before a clear understanding can be developed of the meaning of 'plurilingual identity' for sojourners today.

Discussion

From a theoretical point of view, this chapter represents, in the first place, a call for SA research to go beyond a post-structural perspective by decentring the analysis from the individual, as the sole person responsible for his/her development through particular decisions to act, and acknowledging the role of social structure as a source of opportunities and constraints for the deployment of the individual's agency. In this sense, following the work of Block (2015), it would be important to think of the SA context as consisting of different levels (from the abstract economic structure to the particular interactional dynamics of a social practice) through which social structure adopts different forms and becomes an active participant with which the students need to negotiate in order to accomplish their goals. The second call for action that is made in this chapter is for the adoption of a holistic approach to the notion of language identity, which takes into account the speakers' skills as well as their beliefs and attitudes concerning their whole communicative repertoire. This could also require a more resolute adoption of the notion of 'plurilingual competence' when it comes to discussing the effects of study abroad on communicative competence.

Many of the studies reviewed, and particularly those that look at Anglophone students abroad, focus on the development of L2 identity by analysing almost exclusively how students move from seeing themselves as learners to being users of one TL. The focus shifts slightly when non-Anglophone students are investigated: these tend to either already have experiences of plurilingualism or develop their plurilingual identities during study abroad, although the languages concerned tend to be supercentral, with ELF often being the most frequently used language abroad.

Although the empirical studies reviewed do not generally address the issue of how structure may impact the development of the students' plurilingual identities, many do reveal that there is considerable structural support for the promotion of L2 (mostly English) user identity (rather than any broader plurilingual identity). Indeed, many HE institutions, particularly in countries of less-frequently spoken languages, promote this through EMI (English-medium instruction), thus marginalizing the local languages. In addition, this prevalence of English is reinforced by sociocultural configurations such as international student networks using ELF or SA programmes within local communities where English is widely spoken. Some HE institutions do attempt to promote local languages (e.g. through pre-sessional short intensive language courses), but often students do not see the point of learning a local language that offers little linguistic capital in a global context.

As for sojourner agency, several studies show participants actively pursuing opportunities to use and develop their English and to make the transition from 'English learner' to 'English user'. While many of these sojourners acknowledge that they are using ELF at least in informal situations, many have not at all abandoned an ideal 'native speaker' target either (on this, see Dervin, 2013). There is evidence that participants do engage in translanguaging practices, but very few of them celebrate this.

Perhaps understandably, the exceptions are principally the Anglophone language specialist students studied by Mitchell, Tracy-Ventura and McManus (2017), who are of course under no pressure to develop further their English-related identity, which is already that of the prestigious and desirable 'native speaker'. They can and do exercise agency to a greater or lesser extent to become users of other L2 (such as French or Spanish) especially through the sociocultural configurations they engage with during study abroad. Another striking feature is their continuing interest in additional languages (including after graduation). We have argued that for many of these students, a 'plurilingual identity', albeit one which favours supercentral languages, is their desired goal.

Another apparent exception to the general tendency to favour English as the main L2, and to move from L2 learner to L2 user during study abroad, is the Catalan/Spanish students studied by Mas Alcolea in Italy, who seem to discover they can function within institutions and also in the wider society without formally learning Italian, thus developing a broader 'Romance' identity while remaining at the level of 'L2 learner' as far as English is concerned.

The review of SA research we have presented in this chapter has allowed us to reflect on the range of language identities which are options for European sojourners: L2 learner, L2 user (or 'contented bilingual', in Henry's, 2017, terms), plurilingual speaker, translingual speaker and so on, showing which ones are actually the most likely under current structural conditions and to what extent individual agency can also affect identifications.

Conclusion

In this chapter we have discussed relevant SA research regarding two aspects of identity which we consider have been under-investigated as part of the SA experience: the relationship between agency and structure and the notion of plurilingual identity development. For each of these aspects, we suggest a possible reorientation of SA research. In the case of the agency–structure dichotomy, we claim that the role of structure needs to be emphasized, thereby compensating for what we consider as a present overemphasis on the individual. As for the second aspect, we think that the notion of 'plurilingual identity' can be a more flexible, and perhaps more realistic, theoretical construct than 'L2 identity' to explore more fully the individuals' development of their communicative repertoires, which often include more than just two languages.

The specific theoretical developments that we suggest in this chapter should have an impact not only on the research methodology employed but also in the management and analysis of SA programmes. From the point of view of research, we think, for instance, that it might not be easy to fully understand SA students' interaction with particular social structures if researchers do not attempt to learn about those social structures on their own. However, this would probably require (1) other methods of data collection beyond different forms of self-report and (2) the adoption of a wider, more sociologically/critically oriented theoretical approach to study abroad. Another issue regarding methodology is how we approach the notion of plurilingualism or plurilingual identity in our research. In this sense, it may be seen as paradoxical that despite the general acceptance of Beacco's (2005, p. 19) definition of plurilingualism as a 'complex but unique competence', in which languages are interrelated, in our research we still tend to keep languages clearly separate when we refer to them in interviews or questionnaires or when we try to measure 'language proficiency' in terms of monolingual tests. Instead, we might try to 'observe' (under natural or testing conditions) plurilinguals 'in action' and measure their communicative skills in terms of efficiency and effectiveness, for example by seeking evaluations from other plurilinguals. A greater understanding of plurilingualism as a more integrated concept could then underpin possible pedagogical interventions, in line with European policy goals (see, e.g., the new descriptors for plurilingual competence in the Common European Framework of Reference for Languages) (Council of Europe, 2018). Space does not allow further development of pedagogical discussion in this chapter, except to note that such interventions could helpfully be informed by existing pedagogical models in the fields of intercultural understanding and intercultural competence such as IEREST (see http://www.ierest-project.eu/).

The ideas presented in this chapter may also have an impact on the way SA programmes are managed and assessed. On the one hand, a greater focus on the interaction between agency and structure could provide a conceptual framework for programme managers to pay greater attention to the particular characteristics of different levels of social structure in different SA contexts. In doing this, they could consider the dynamics of the interaction of the students with these levels and the degree to which these dynamics act as constraints or opportunities in connection with the goals of the programme, including desired outcomes in terms of identity development. On the other hand, the notions of plurilingualism and plurilingual identity could also inform the design of tools to measure the impact of a particular programme on the students' communicative skills. These tools should reflect the individuals' ability to use flexibly their communicative resources and engage in typical actions of plurilinguals, which include switching between languages, expressing oneself in one language and listening in another, calling upon different languages to make sense of a text, mediating between individuals with no common language, experimenting with alternative forms of expressions or exploiting paralinguistics (Council of Europe, 2018, p. 28).

Note

1   In this chapter we have chosen to adopt the terminology used in European institutions, whereby 'plurilingualism should be understood in this dual sense: it constitutes a conception of the speaker as fundamentally plural and a value in that it is the basis of linguistic tolerance, an essential element of intercultural education. Multilingualism refers here exclusively to the presence of several languages in a given space, independently of those who use them: for example, the fact that two languages are present in the same geographical area does not indicate whether inhabitants know both languages, or only one' (Language Policy Division, 2007, p. 18).

References

Aronin, L. (2016), 'Multi-competence and Dominant Language Constellation', in V. Cook, and L. Wei (eds.), *The Cambridge Handbook of Linguistic Multicompetence*, 142–63, Cambridge: Cambridge University Press.

Baker, C. (2001), *Foundations of Bilingual Education and Bilingualism* (3rd ed.), Clevedon: Multilingual Matters.

Baker-Smemoe, W., Dewey, D. P., Bown, J., and Martinsen, R. A. (2014), 'Variables Affecting L2 Gains during Study Abroad', *Foreign Language Annals*, 47 (3), 464–86.

Bakewell, O. (2010), 'Some Reflection on Structure and Agency in Migration Theory', *Journal of Ethnic and Migration Studies*, 36 (10), 1689–708.

Beacco, J.-C. (2005), *Languages and Language Repertoires: Plurilingualism as a Way of Life in Europe. Guide for the Development of Language Education Policies in Europe: From Linguistic Diversity to Plurilingual Education. Reference Study*, Strasbourg, France: Council of Europe. Available online at https://rm.coe.int/languages-and-language-repertoires-plurilingualism-as-a-way-of-life-in/16802fc1ba.

Beaven, A., and Spencer-Oatey, H. (2016), 'Cultural Adaptation in Different Facets of Life and the Impact of Language: A Case Study of Personal Adjustment Patterns during Study Abroad', *Language and Intercultural Communication*, 16 (3), 349–67.

Benson, P., and Nunan, D. (eds.) (2004), *Learners' Stories: Difference and Diversity in Language Learning*, Cambridge: Cambridge University Press.

Benson, P., Barkhuizen, G., Bodycott, P., and Brown, J. (2012), 'Study Abroad and the Development of Second Language Identities', *Applied Linguistics Review*, 3 (1), 173–93.

Benson, P., Barkhuizen, G., Bodycott, P., and Brown, J. (2013), *Second Language Identity in Narratives of Study Abroad*, Basingstoke: Palgrave Macmillan.

Block, D. (2003), *The Social Turn in Second Language Acquisition*, Edinburgh: Edinburgh University Press.

Block, D. (2007), *Second Language Identities*, London: Continuum.

Block, D. (2009), 'Identity in Applied Linguistics: The Need for Conceptual Exploration', in L. Wei, and V. Cook (eds.), *Contemporary Applied Linguistics. Volume I*, 215–32, London: Continuum.

Block, D. (2012), 'Unpicking Agency in Sociolinguistic Research with Migrants', in S. Gardner, and M. Martin-Jones (eds.), *Multilingualism, Discourse and Ethnography*, 47–60, London: Routledge.

Block, D. (2013), 'The Structure and Agency Dilemma in Identity and Intercultural Communication Research', *Language and Intercultural Communication*, 13 (2), 126–47.

Block, D. (2015), 'Structure, Agency, Individualization and the Critical Realist Challenge', in P. Deters, X. Gao, E. R. Miller, and G. Vitanova (eds.), *Theorizing and Analyzing Agency in Second Language Learning: Interdisciplinary Approaches*, 17–36, Bristol: Multilingual Matters.

Blommaert, J. (2005), *Discourse*, Cambridge: Cambridge University Press.

Bourdieu, P. (1977), *Outline of a Theory of Practice*, Cambridge: Cambridge University Press.

Brown, L. (2013), 'Identity and Honorifics Use in Korean Study Abroad', in C. Kinginger (ed.), *Social and Cultural Dimensions of Language Learning in Study Abroad*, 269–98, Amsterdam: John Benjamins.

Cook, H. M. (2006), 'Joint Construction of Folk Beliefs by JFL Learners and Japanese Host Families', in M. A. DuFon, and E. Churchill (eds.), *Language Learners in Study Abroad Contexts*, 120–50, Clevedon: Multilingual Matters.

Council of Europe. (2018), *Common European Framework of Reference for Languages: Learning, Teaching and Assessment. Companion Volume with New Descriptors*, Strasbourg: Council of Europe. Available online at https://rm.coe.int/cefr-companion-volume-with-new-descriptors-2018/1680787989.

de Swaan, A. (2001), *Words of the World*, Cambridge: Polity Press.

Dervin, F. (2013), 'Politics of Identification in the Use of Lingua Francas in Student Mobility to Finland and France', in C. Kinginger (ed.), *Social and Cultural Aspects of Language Learning in Study Abroad*, 101–26, Amsterdam: John Benjamins.

Dewey, D. P., Bown, J., Baker, W., Martinsen, R. A., Gold, C., and Eggett, D. (2014), 'Language Use in Six Study Abroad Programs: An Exploratory Analysis of Possible Predictors', *Language Learning*, 64 (1), 36–71.

Dörnyei, Z. (2009), 'The L2 Motivational Self System', in Z. Dörnyei, and E. Ushioda (eds.), *Motivation, Language Identity and the L2 Self*, 9–42, Bristol: Multilingual Matters.

Douglas Fir Group. (2016), 'A Transdisciplinary Framework for SLA in a Multilingual World', *The Modern Language Journal*, 100 (S1), 19–47.

Evans, C. (1988), *Language People: The Experience of Teaching and Learning Modern Languages in British Universities*, Milton Keynes: Open University Press.

Feyen, B., and Krzaklewska, E. (eds.) (2013), *The ERASMUS Phenomenon: Symbol of a New European Generation?* Frankfurt am Main: Peter Lang.

Geeslin, K. L., and Schmidt, L. B. (2018), 'Study Abroad and L2 Learner Attitudes', in C. Sanz, and A. Morales-Front (eds.), *The Routledge Handbook of Study Abroad Research and Practice*, 387–405, Abingdon/New York: Routledge.

Gidden, A., and Sutton, P. W. (2014), *Essential Concepts in Sociology*, Cambridge: Polity Press.

Goodwin, C., and Duranti, A. (1992), 'Rethinking Context: An Introduction', in A. Duranti, and C. Goodwin (eds.), *Rethinking Context: Language as an Interactional Phenomenon*, 1–42, Cambridge: Cambridge University Press.

Henry, A. (2017), 'L2 Motivation and Multilingual Identities', *The Modern Language Journal*, 101 (3), 548–65.

Huensch, A., and Tracy-Ventura, N. (2017), 'L2 Utterance Fluency Development before, during, and after Residence Abroad: A Multidimensional Investigation', *The Modern Language Journal*, 101 (2), 275–93.

Hurst, A. L. (2019), 'Class and Gender as Predictors of Study Abroad Participation among US Liberal Arts College Students', *Studies in Higher Education*, 44 (7), 1241–55.

Iino, M. (2006), 'Norms of Interaction in a Japanese Homestay Setting: Toward a Two-way Flow of Linguistic and Cultural Resources', in M. A. DuFon, and E. Churchill (eds.), *Language Learners in Study Abroad Contexts*, 151–73, Clevedon: Multilingual Matters.

Jackson, J. (2008), *Language, Identity and Study Abroad: Sociocultural Perspectives*, London: Equinox.

Kalocsai, K. (2013), *Communities of Practice and English as a Lingua Franca: A Study of Students in a Central European Context*, Berlin: De Gruyter/Mouton.

Kaypak, E., and Ortaçtepe, D. (2014), 'Language Learner Beliefs and Study Abroad: A Study on English as a Lingua Franca (ELF)', *System*, 42, 355–67.

Kinginger, C. (2009), *Language Learning and Study Abroad: A Critical Reading of Research*, Basingstoke: Palgrave Macmillan.

Kinginger, C. (2013), 'Introduction. Social and Cultural Aspects of Language Learning in Study Abroad', in C. Kinginger (ed.), *Social and Cultural Aspects of Language Learning in Study Abroad*, 3–15, Amsterdam/Philadelphia: John Benjamins.

Kinginger, C. (2015), 'Student Mobility and Identity-related Language Learning', *Intercultural Education*, 26 (1), 6–15.

Kramsch, C. (2009), *The Multilingual Subject*, Oxford: Oxford University Press.

Language Policy Division. (2007), *From Linguistic Diversity to Plurilingual Education: Guide for the Development of Language Education Policies in Europe*, Strasbourg, Council of Europe. Available online at https://rm.coe.int/16802fc1c4.

Lantolf, J. (ed.) (2000), *Sociocultural Theory and Second Language Learning*, Oxford: Oxford University Press.

Leung, C., Harris, R., and Rampton, B. (1997), 'The Idealised Native Speaker, Reified Ethnicities, and Classroom Realities', *TESOL Quarterly*, 31, 543–60.

Lewin, R. (ed.) (2009), *The Handbook of Practice and Research in Study Abroad: Higher Education and the Quest for Global Citizenship*, Abingdon/New York: Routledge.

Llanes, À., Arnó, E., and Mancho-Barés, G. (2016), 'Erasmus Students Using English as a Lingua Franca: Does Study Abroad in a Non-English-speaking Country Improve L2 English?', *The Language Learning Journal*, 44 (3), 292–303.

Llurda, E., Gallego-Balsà, L., Barahona, C., and Martin-Rubió, X. (2016), 'Erasmus Student Mobility and the Construction of European Citizenship', *The Language Learning Journal*, 44 (3), 323–46.

MacSwan, J. (2017), 'A Multilingual Perspective on Translanguaging', *American Educational Research Journal*, 54 (1), 167–201.

Maeder-Qian, J. (2018), 'Intercultural Experiences and Cultural Identity Reconstruction of Multilingual Chinese International Students in Germany', *Journal of Multilingual and Multicultural Development*, 39 (7), 576–89.

Martínez-Arbelaiz, A., Areizaga, E., and Camps, C. (2017), 'An Update on the Study Abroad Experience: Language Choices and Social Media Abroad', *International Journal of Multilingualism*, 14 (4), 350–65.

Mas Alcolea, S. (2017), 'Discourses on Study Abroad: The Experience of Erasmus Students from a University in Catalonia', PhD thesis, University of Lleida, Lleida, Spain.

Mas Alcolea, S. (2018), '"I Thought I Was Prepared": Erasmus Students' Voices on Their Transition from L2 Learners to L2 Users', in J. Plews, and K. Misfeldt (eds.), *Second Language Study Abroad: Programming, Pedagogy, and Participant Engagement*, 223–55, Basingstoke: Palgrave Macmillan.

McGregor, J. (2016), '"I Thought that When I Was in Germany, I Would Speak Just German": Language Learning and Desire in Twenty-first Century Study Abroad', *L2 Journal*, 8 (2), 12–30.

Miller, E. R. (2012), 'Agency, Language Learning and Multilingual Spaces', *Multilingua*, 31, 441–68.

Mitchell, R., Tracy-Ventura, N., and McManus, K. (2017), *Anglophone Students Abroad: Identity, Social Relationships and Language Learning*, Abingdon/New York: Routledge.

Murphy-Lejeune, E. (2002), *Student Mobility and Narrative in Europe: The New Strangers*, New York: Routledge.

Norton, B. (1995), 'Social Identity, Investment, and Language Learning', *TESOL Quarterly*, 29 (1), 9–31.

Norton, B. (2000), *Identity and Language Learning. Extending the Conversation* (2nd ed.), Bristol: Multilingual Matters.

Omoniyi, T. (2004), *The Sociolinguistics of Borderlands: Two Nations, One Community*, Trenton, NJ: Africa World Press.

Ortner, S. B. (2006), *Anthropology and Social Theory: Culture, Power and the Acting Subject*, Durham, USA: Duke University Press.

Pavlenko, A., and Blackledge, A. (2004), 'Introduction: New Theoretical Approaches to the Study of Negotiation of Identities in Multilingual Contexts', in A. Pavlenko, and A. Blackledge (eds.), *Negotiation of Identities in Multilingual Contexts*, 1–33, Clevedon: Multilingual Matters.

Pavlenko, A., Blackledge, A., Piller, I., and Teutsch-Dwyer, M. (eds.) (2001), *Multilingualism, Second Language Learning, and Gender*, Berlin: Mouton de Gruyter.

Pennycook, A. (2010), *Language as a Local Practice*, London: Routledge.

Polanyi, L. (1995), 'Language Learning and Living Abroad: Stories from the Field', in B. F. Freed (ed.), *Second Language Acquisition in a Study Abroad Context*, 271–92, Amsterdam: John Benjamins.

Räisänen, T. (2016), 'Finnish Engineers' Trajectories of Socialisation into Global Working Life: From Language Learners to BELF Users and the Emergence of a Finnish Way of Speaking English', in P. Holmes, and F. Dervin (eds.), *The Cultural and Intercultural Dimensions of English as a Lingua Franca*, 157–79, Bristol: Multilingual Matters.

Ringer-Hilfinger, K. (2012), 'Learner Acquisition of Dialect Variation in a Study Abroad Context: The Case of the Spanish [θ]', *Foreign Language Annals*, 45 (3), 430–46.

Sharwood Smith, M., and Truscott, J. (2014), *The Multilingual Mind: A Modular Processing Perspective*, Cambridge: Cambridge University Press.

Shiri, S. (2013), 'Learners' Attitudes toward Regional Dialects and Destination Preferences in Study Abroad', *Foreign Language Annals*, 46 (4), 565–87.

Surtees, V. (2019), 'As a Friend, That's the One Thing I Always Am Very Conscious Not to Do: Categorization Practices in Interviews with Peers in the Host Community', *Study Abroad Research in Second Language Acquisition and International Education*, 4 (1), 45–69.

Taguchi, N. (2018), 'Contexts and Pragmatics Learning: Problems and Opportunities of the Study Abroad Research', *Language Teaching*, 51 (1), 124–37.

Talburt, S., and Stewart, M. A. (1999), 'What's the Subject of Study Abroad? Race, Gender and "Living Culture"', *Modern Language Journal*, 83 (2), 163–75.

Teichler, U. (2015), 'The Impact of Temporary Study Abroad', in R. Mitchell, N. Tracy-Ventura, and K. McManus (eds.), *Social Interaction, Identity and Language Learning during Residence Abroad. EUROSLA Monographs 4*, 15–32, Amsterdam: European Second Language Association.

Teichler, U., and Ferencz, I. (2011), 'Student Mobility Data: Recent Achievements, Current Issues and Future Prospects', in U. Teichler, I. Ferencz, and B. Wächter (eds.), *Mapping Mobility in Higher Education in Europe. Volume I: Overview and Trends*, 151–77, Bonn: Deutscher Akademischer Austauschdienst.

Twombly, S. (1995), 'Piropos and Friendships: Gender and Culture Clash in Study Abroad', *Frontiers: The Interdisciplinary Journal of Study Abroad*, 1, 1–27.

Virkkula, T., and Nikula, T. (2010), 'Identity Construction in ELF Contexts: A Case Study of Finnish Engineering Students Working in Germany', *International Journal of Applied Linguistics*, 20 (2), 251–73.

Vitanova, G., Miller, E. R., Gao, X., and Deters, P. (2015), 'Introduction to Theorizing and Analyzing Agency in Second Language Learning: Interdisciplinary Approaches', in P. Deters, X. Gao, E. R. Miller, and G. Vitanova (eds.), *Theorizing and Analyzing Agency in Second Language Learning: Interdisciplinary Approaches*, 1–13, Bristol: Multilingual Matters.

Vogel, S., and García, O. (2017), 'Translanguaging', in G. Noblit, and L. Moll (eds.), *Oxford Research Encyclopedia of Education*, 1–21, Oxford: Oxford University Press.

Wei, L. (2011), 'Multilinguality, Multimodality and Multicompetence: Code- and Mode-switching by Minority Ethnic Children in Complementary Schools', *The Modern Language Journal*, 95 (3), 370–84.

Wei, L. (2017), 'Translanguaging as a Practical Theory of Language', *Applied Linguistics*, 39 (1), 9–30.

Wilkinson, S. (2002), 'The Omnipresent Classroom during Summer Study Abroad: American Students in Conversation with Their French Hosts', *Modern Language Journal*, 86 (2), 157–73.

Zappa-Hollman, S., and Duff, P. A. (2015), 'Academic English Socialization through Individual Networks of Practice', *TESOL Quarterly*, 49 (2), 333–68.

10

Learning multiword expressions in a second language during study abroad: The role of individual differences

Klara Arvidsson
Stockholm University

Introduction

Multiword phenomena, or formulaic language, have become a featured research topic in applied linguistics (see Ellis, Römer and O'Donnell, 2016; Erman, Forsberg Lundell and Lewis, 2016). This study concerns the learning of multiword expressions (MWEs) in a second language (L2) and more specifically in L2 French. MWEs are conventionalized multiword form-meaning mappings, such as *tant mieux* ('all the better/good for you'), *au pire* ('at worst') and *c'est ça* ('that's right'). They fill a variety of communicative and social functions and are therefore useful to the L2 learner. Numerous studies, however, suggest that MWEs are a difficult aspect of L2 learning and that the learning of MWEs is a slow process. This has led to a surge of interest in what conditions and circumstances promote the development of MWE knowledge. Recent classroom-based studies report on the effects of different teaching methods for the learning of MWEs (for an overview, see Szudarski, 2017). However, there is a need for research on MWE learning in other learning contexts (Szudarski, 2017). For example, little is known about the learning of MWEs occurring in everyday informal speech in a naturalistic setting. This study contributes to filling this research gap. It presents the qualitative component of a mixed-methods project. The project investigates individual variation in the learning of conversational MWEs in a study abroad (SA) context. The aim of this study is to complement the findings from the quantitative part of the project (Arvidsson, 2019), where, contrary to expectations, we observed that amount of target language (TL) use outside of the classroom did not predict the development of MWE knowledge in L2 French among forty-one Swedish SA participants. With the purpose of further understanding what factors contribute to successful learning of MWEs, we conducted follow-up interviews with contrasting cases of learners who had also participated in the quantitative part of the study. These contrasting case studies are reported in this study. First, we provide a literature review including a detailed description of the preceding quantitative study before describing the methodology. We then present the findings, ending with a discussion of the results.

Background

Multiword expressions

It is increasingly acknowledged that a large proportion of language use is formulaic, that is we frequently use multiword expressions which express unitary meanings and functions (e.g. Ellis, Römer and O'Donnell, 2016; Wray, 2002). While such multiword phenomena are considered peripheral in generative views of linguistic competence, they occupy a central role in usage-based approaches (UBAs) to language knowledge and learning. UBAs include a number of theoretical approaches including cognitive linguistics (Langacker, 1987), construction grammar (Goldberg, 2003) and UBAs to L1 (Tomasello, 2000) and L2 acquisition (e.g. Ellis, 2002, 2003, 2015). UBAs hold that the language learning process involves the piecemeal commitment of concrete linguistic expressions to memory and the gradual building of knowledge of a more abstract kind, leading the learner to store a large number of constructions which are held to be the basic unit of linguistic representation. A construction is a conventionalized form-meaning mapping which can vary in size and abstraction. Expressions which are highly frequent in the linguistic input or which have formal or functional particularities are assumed to be entrenched as such in the learner's mind (Ellis, Römer and O'Donnell, 2016). This study concerns the learning of such lexically instantiated multiword form-meaning mappings, here termed 'multiword expressions'.

MWEs can be defined and identified in different ways. Frequency-distributional approaches typically define MWEs as frequently occurring word strings or as word strings with a statistically significant probability of occurring together. This is a form-first approach leading to the automatic corpus extraction of different kinds of MWEs, all of which do not necessarily correspond to symbolic units (such as 'was to', example taken from Martinez and Schmitt, 2012). This study takes a function-first approach and preliminarily defines MWEs as word combinations which together evoke unitary meaning or express unitary function in a conventionalized way (for a similar approach, see Smiskova-Gustafsson, 2013). This definition is learner-external rather than learner-internal, meaning that the MWEs of interest in this study are conceived as word sequences that are conventional in the TL rather than as word sequences that present a cognitive processing advantage for the learner (Myles and Cordier, 2017). A few examples from informal spoken language in French (the genre and TL in focus in this study) are *en fait* ('actually'), *du coup* ('and so') and *c'est ça* ('that's right').

MWE use facilitates both the speaker's production and the interlocutor's comprehension (Wray, 2002). Also, MWEs fill an important psychosocial function since the use of conventional linguistic forms signals group identity (Coulmas, 1981). All in all, they enhance idiomatic and fluent language use (e.g. Ellis, 2002; Erman, Forsberg Lundell and Lewis, 2016; Wray, 2002). It is therefore not surprising that scholars increasingly acknowledge that MWEs are highly useful to the L2 learner (e.g. Ellis, 2002; Erman, Forsberg Lundell and Lewis, 2016; Wray, 2002). In general, however, studies suggest that multiword phenomena are difficult in an L2, something which is often attributed to the adult learner's lack of exposure to the TL (see, e.g., Ellis, 2002).

The role of TL contact for the learning of MWEs in a second language

UBAs to language learning hold that contact with the TL is crucial for the learning of MWEs to take place (e.g. Ellis, 2003; Ellis, Römer and O'Donnell, 2016). In such views, language is learnt through experience with the TL, with the help of generic learning mechanisms which operate on the linguistic input. When it comes to the learning of MWEs in particular, associative learning mechanisms are assumed to help the learner create links between a word sequence and its meaning or function (Ellis, 2003). The more times the learner encounters a word sequence in the linguistic input, the stronger it becomes associated in the learner's mind (Ellis, 2003). While there is indeed empirical evidence from classroom-based research that the chance for an MWE to be learned increases with increased exposure (Webb, Newton and Chang, 2013), this relationship appears to be less straightforward when it comes to MWE learning in a naturalistic setting. The naturalistic learning context is in theory ideal for the development of knowledge of MWEs given the many opportunities it offers for 'input, output, and interaction' in the TL (Pérez-Vidal, 2017, p. 345). Adult L2 learners, however, vary considerably with respect to how much they come into contact with the TL during their stay in the host country (e.g. Mitchell, Tracy-Ventura and McManus, 2017). It could be assumed that higher levels of contact with the TL would lead to higher levels of knowledge of MWEs, yet the empirical evidence is conflicting (e.g. Arvidsson, 2019; Bardovi-Harlig and Bastos, 2011; Schmitt and Redwood, 2011; Taguchi, Li and Xiao, 2013).

To our knowledge, there are two studies which investigate the role of amount of TL contact for the development of MWEs longitudinally (Arvidsson, 2019; Taguchi, Li and Xiao, 2013). They concur in not finding any support for the assumption that amount of TL contact would predict the rate of learning of MWEs in an SA context. In the study by Taguchi, Li and Xiao (2013), the authors investigated if quantity of TL use predicted the development of learners' productive knowledge of formulaic expressions as part of their pragmatic competence. They defined a formulaic expression as 'fixed or semi-fixed syntactic strings whose occurrence is closely bound to specific recurrent situations and communicative functions' (p. 25). The study took place in a Chinese SA context and included thirty-one American participants. The participants performed an oral computerized discourse completion task in L2 Chinese, administered at the beginning and at the end of the semester. By comparing the scores obtained at the two testing times, each participant was given a gain score which represented the development in the ability to produce formulaic expressions. At the end of the semester, the participants also self-reported how many times during the semester they had been exposed to the target situations. Correlation analyses show that frequency of TL exposure was not significantly correlated with gain scores, suggesting that other factors played a role in the learning process. These findings are in line with those reported in Arvidsson (2019), which constitutes the direct background to the study reported in this chapter and which will be discussed subsequently.

Arvidsson (2019): A quantitative study

Our previous study was, to the best of our knowledge, the first to quantitatively investigate the role of quantity of TL contact for the learning of MWEs common in informal conversations, in a naturalistic context. The study followed a pre-test and post-test design and included forty-one Swedish-speaking learners of L2 French, enrolled in a semester-long SA programme in France. MWE knowledge was evaluated at the beginning and at the end of the semester through a modified cloze test, developed and piloted for the study (for a detailed account, see Arvidsson, 2019). The test contained sixty target MWEs and was based on transcriptions of informal spoken conversations from the CLAPI corpus (http://clapi.ish-lyon.cnrs.fr/). The target items had been rated for frequency of occurrence in everyday speech on a scale of 1–3, and all received an average score of 2.5 or more, with an overall mean of 2.74. The test items were presented in their original context (some minor modifications were made to increase intelligibility of the transcriptions) and one of the words of each MWE was replaced by an empty line except for the first letter (for similar MWE test formats, see, e.g., Forsberg Lundell, Lindqvist and Edmonds, 2018; Schmitt et al., 2004). The same test was administered at the beginning and at the end of the semester and a gain score was calculated for each participant by subtracting pre-test scores from post-test scores. There were no ceiling effects and the results suggested important individual variation within the sample with gain scores ranging from 6 to 36 ($M = 17.29$, $SD = 7.59$). The participants also self-reported how often they had engaged in twenty activities in the TL outside of the classroom during their semester in France, through a slightly modified version of the Language Engagement Questionnaire (McManus, Mitchell and Tracy-Ventura, 2014). Response options included 'never', 'rarely', 'a couple times a month', 'a few times a week', 'several times a week' and 'every day', coded as 0–5. A composite score was calculated for each participant representing quantity of TL contact. A regression analysis was conducted with proficiency entered as a control variable (evaluated through LEXTALE_FR, Brysbaert, 2013) which was administered together with the pre-test. The findings showed that the participants' levels of MWE learning varied substantially but that self-reported quantity of TL contact outside of the classroom did not significantly predict gains in MWE knowledge.

In order to further understand the relationship between TL use and the learning of MWEs in a naturalistic context, we conducted a post hoc regression analysis. Given that the targeted MWEs are common in language used in social interaction, it was deemed relevant to explore whether quantity of contact with the TL solely through interactive activities had a significant effect on MWE learning in the given sample. This time, we created a composite score based on ten interactive activities (e.g. taking part in service encounters, engaging in small talk or in longer conversations and interacting through instant messaging). To our surprise, the results from the regression analysis showed that quantity of TL contact in interactive activities did not significantly predict the learners' development of MWE knowledge during the participants' semester abroad. Together, the findings suggest that factors other than sheer quantity of TL contact contributed to the learners' tendency to develop MWEs in the SA context.

Several scholars suggest that it is crucial to consider psychological individual differences (IDs) among adult language learners if we are to better understand what leads to successful L2 learning (e.g. Dewaele, 2009; Dörnyei, 2005; Moyer, 2014). Indeed, some previous qualitative case studies suggest that the learning of MWEs common in academic discourse and the development of an understanding of colloquial phrases appear to relate to motivational factors and to the extent that the learner actively engages in TL activities (Dörnyei, Durow and Zahran, 2004; Kinginger, 2008). These studies are, however, scarce in number. Calls have been made for studies which 'aim at mapping out individual and psychological factors facilitating the acquisition of [MWEs]' (Erman, Forsberg Lundell and Lewis, 2018, p. 116).[1] Given this background, with the aim to complement the findings from our previous quantitative study, we conducted a qualitative follow-up study with a sub-sample of the participants focusing this time on what kind of TL contact and IDs promote the learning of MWEs. Before presenting this study, we will provide a review of the literature on individual differences in L2 learning and use.

Individual differences in L2 learning and use

Individual differences refer to 'dimensions of enduring personal characteristics that are assumed to apply to everybody and on which people differ by degree' (Dörnyei, 2005, p. 4) and are assumed to influence L2 learning at various levels (e.g. Dewaele, 2009; Dörnyei, 2005). IDs are typically categorized into cognitive factors (e.g. aptitude, awareness) and affective or social-psychological factors (e.g. motivation, attitudes, self-efficacy), or into learner-internal and learner-external factors (Dewaele, 2009; Ortega, 2013). Language aptitude is one of the most researched ID factors and while several studies confirm its role for various aspects of adult L2 learning including formulaic language (e.g. Forsberg Lundell and Sandgren, 2013), it is suggested that a constellation of cognitive and affective factors influence learners' tendencies to invest in the language learning process and to benefit from contact with the TL (MacIntyre, 1995; Moyer, 2014). We use the term 'psychological orientation' (Moyer, 2014) to refer to such a constellation of ID factors, which include the tendency to 'notice' (Schmidt, 1990), L2 motivation, self-efficacy and self-regulation. But in what way would these specific IDs affect the learning of MWEs common in conversational discourse in a naturalistic context?

As stated in the previous section, increased levels of TL exposure do not automatically lead the learner to develop his/her knowledge of MWEs. In other words, individuals vary in terms of what they do with the linguistic input they are exposed to (see Moyer, 2014). With respect to picking up MWEs in the input, Ellis (2002) suggests that the learner may have to pay attention to and 'notice' (Schmidt, 1990) a given MWE in the input stream in order for a memory trace to be created and subsequently entrenched (Ellis, 2002). Learners vary in their tendency to pay attention to formal features in the linguistic input (Schmidt, 2012). While language awareness or tendency to 'notice' language forms is certainly difficult to empirically observe within the learner, learner self-reporting on their own tendency to pay attention to a linguistic feature may still be informative (Moyer, 2004).

The extent to which a learner pays attention to the linguistic input is suggested to be strongly linked to motivational factors (Crookes and Schmidt, 1991; Schmidt, 2012). According to Gardner (1988), motivated learners are active learners who engage more in the learning task. Schmidt (2012) contends that 'motivated learners may also try harder and more persistently to understand the significance of noticed language, achieving higher levels of awareness and enhanced learning as a result' (pp. 40–1). Others suggest that active participation in meaningful interaction with L1 speakers of the TL may help orient the L2 user's attention towards language form (see, e.g., Ellis, 2015). It has been observed that SA participants are differentially motivated to learn the language spoken by the TL community during their stay abroad and that motivation underpins their efforts to seek out occasions to use the TL (Isabelli-García, 2006; Jackson, 2017). In fact, learner objectives for going abroad in the first place vary between individuals and do not necessarily primarily include language learning, something which appears to influence behavioural orientations during a sojourn abroad, including investment in the language learning activity (e.g. Coleman, 2015; Jackson, 2017; Kinginger, 2008).

A learner's motivation to learn the TL and to initiate interaction in the TL is also linked to his/her sense of self-efficacy, namely the belief that one is capable of successfully carrying out a given task (Bandura, 1997). A strong sense of self-efficacy helps the learner to approach the task in hand with confidence, to keep focused on the task, to manage failures and to enhance L2 motivation (Dörnyei and Ushioda, 2011; Ehrman, 1996; Mercer and Williams, 2014). Also, a sense of self-efficacy has been shown to help learners initiate contact with TL speakers in the SA context (Jackson, 2017). By contrast, a language learner with a low sense of self-efficacy tends to perceive difficult tasks as threatening (Dörnyei and Ushioda, 2011). In the present context, a strong sense of self-efficacy could potentially help the learner to seek out opportunities to use the TL in social interaction and to focus on the linguistic input while engaging in conversations in the TL, the primary source of input for the kinds of MWEs that are the focus of the current research project. By contrast, a learner with a low sense of self-efficacy may dwell on his/her weaknesses while engaging in verbal communication rather than allocating attentional resources to the word sequences occurring in the linguistic input.

Contemporary ID research acknowledges that IDs are both dynamic and context-dependent (see Dewaele, 2009). At a conceptual level, motivation and perceptions of self-efficacy are subject to fluctuations over time and are conceived as intertwined with the direct environment (Bandura, 1997; Dörnyei and Ushioda, 2011). There are empirical studies from the SA context which have observed how learners' L2 motivation and sense of self-efficacy both affect and are affected by the learner's experience of using the TL and of his/her experience with members of the TL community (e.g. Isabelli-García, 2006; Pellegrino Aveni, 2005). Negative experiences of using the TL seem to affect both motivation and self-perceptions negatively, while positive experiences appear to have the reverse effect, both in the moment and over time (e.g. Isabelli-García, 2006; Pellegrino Aveni, 2005). Overall, learners with an ability to self-regulate such emotional and motivational fluctuations are assumed to be advantaged when it comes to L2 learning (Moyer, 2014; Oxford and Griffiths, 2016; Pérez-Vidal, 2017). Such learners tend take control over their own language learning process both at a micro level (in specific learning situations) and at a macro level (the learning process extended over time), and they tend to use metacognitive and affective strategies in order to achieve a set goal or to realize a desired outcome (e.g. Moyer, 2014; Oxford and Griffiths, 2016).

To sum up, the sojourner's tendency to pick up MWEs from conversational discourse should thus reasonably be promoted by access to rich exposure to the TL in combination with an attentional orientation towards such forms in the input. The extent to which the individual actively engages with the TL and steers his/her attention towards language forms upon exposure relates to a combination of ID factors (here called psychological orientation). The factors outlined are particularly relevant to further understanding of language learning in a naturalistic environment and the tendency to learn MWEs during social interaction in particular, and will therefore be explored in the present study, namely noticing, L2 motivation, self-efficacy and self-regulation.

The study

The purpose of this study is to explore the learning of MWEs occurring in conversational language during study abroad in relation to the learners' TL contact and the ID factors mentioned. The study presents the qualitative component of a mixed-methods project and explores the following research questions:

1. What kind of TL contact promotes the learning of MWEs in an SA context?
2. What psychological orientation seems to promote the learning of MWEs in an SA context?

The study includes case studies of a subset of learners who also participated in the quantitative part described earlier (Arvidsson, 2019). Sampling is a major concern in case-study research (Duff, 2008). Case-study research interested in the association between IDs, learner experiences and language learning often uses an extreme case sampling strategy, where learners are selected for in-depth study based on either their exceptional levels of proficiency in an L2 (for an overview, see Moyer, 2014) or their relatively high rate of L2 development during a stay abroad (typically called 'high gainers') (e.g. Mitchell, McManus and Tracy-Ventura, 2017). Such an approach allows the researcher to describe ID factors and circumstances which are associated with successful L2 learning. However, this approach does not preclude the possibility that less successful learners share similar characteristics and experiences. In order to ensure a more coherent picture, it is useful to compare contrasting cases of learners.

Therefore, the present study includes contrasting cases of learners (cf. Dörnyei, Durow and Zahran, 2004), here referred to as 'high gainers' and 'low gainers' respectively. The high gainers developed their knowledge of MWEs considerably during their semester in France, whereas the low gainers only marginally developed their knowledge of MWEs during the same period of time.

Each case is represented by several participants since this mitigates 'concerns that cases are unique in unforeseen ways' (Duff, 2008, p. 113). The intent was to interview the six individuals who made the most and the least progress as evaluated by the MWE test described in the section 'Arvidsson (2019): A quantitative study'. However, after ranking the participants according to their gain scores, two high gainers occupied rank three. Therefore, it was decided to include four high gainers and three low gainers (cf. Dörnyei, Durow and Zahran, 2004). The sample consists of six females and one male. The gender skewness is representative of the sample as a whole (M = 9, F = 32) and is reported elsewhere in the literature on SA participants in France (Mitchell, 2015).

When post-test data were collected for the preceding quantitative study, the participants were informed that a few individuals would be invited to partake in follow-up interviews. The focal participants responded positively to their invitation. Each interview was carried out individually in a quiet café a few days after the post-test data collection, during the second to last week of their stay abroad (fall 2016). Apart from participating in the pre-test and post-test data collection, the participants had no prior relation to the researcher. Participants were compensated with fifteen euro for their time.

Participants and research context

The seven participants were Swedish students spending one semester in France, all with Swedish as their L1. They were enrolled in an SA programme in France during fall 2016, offered by two Swedish universities. Each programme lasted for sixteen or eighteen weeks, was voluntary and required the same entrance level (corresponding to the B1 level of the Common European Framework of Reference, Council of Europe, 2001). The programme was either part of a bachelor's programme or was taken as an independent university course. Programmes included nine to ten hours of class per week, with modules for grammar, literature, oral communication and French culture and society. Classes were given in a language centre where international students go to study French and were taught by local teachers following the curriculum set by the respective Swedish university. On two occasions during the semester, a home university teacher taught classes on site. Table 10.1 contains information about the participants' background and their test scores from the preceding quantitative study, followed by a short presentation of each of them. Their real names have been replaced with pseudonyms. In Table 10.1, means and standard deviations from the sample of forty-one participants in the preceding study are also presented.

As Table 10.1 shows, the two groups differ in terms of their MWE pre-test scores. Two of the three low gainers scored relatively higher than the high gainers on the MWE test at the beginning of the semester. However, their post-test scores were far from indicating any test ceiling effects which suggests that there was room for them to develop their MWE knowledge considerably more than they did throughout the

Table 10.1 Information about the Participants and Test Scores from the Quantitative Study

Pseudonym	Age	Score Pre-test (max = 60)	Score Post-test (max = 60)	Gain Score	Age of Onset	Number of Years of Previous French Studies
Mean (N = 41)	20.56	21.54	38.83	17.29	12.78	5.38
SD	2.38	8.43	7.28	7.59	2.01	1.69
High gainers						
Elsa	19	14	50	36	13	4
Sarah	29	15	42	27	12	5
Alma	20	16	41	25	12	6
Gustaf	26	13	38	25	12	6
Low gainers						
Nova	19	26	36	10	12	6
Linn	19	35	43	8	13	5
Louise	21	15	21	6	11	6

Pre-test, post-test = modified cloze test targeting MWEs, gain score = pre-test score–post-test.

semester. In the following subsections, we present the participants and their living situation during the semester in France, firstly in the case of the high gainers, followed then by the low gainers.

The high gainers

Elsa finished high school in Sweden in June before going to France where she shared an apartment with another Swedish woman and a French man who was rarely at home due to frequent travelling for work. Sarah was enrolled in a bachelor's programme in political science at home. She initially rented a room from a French family but after a month, as already planned ahead of time, she moved into her own studio where she stayed for the rest of the semester. Alma spent the semester before going to France abroad volunteering for an international organization. In France, she shared an apartment with other Swedish women. Gustaf was enrolled in an engineering programme at home and in France, and he lived by himself in a studio.

The low gainers

Nova graduated from high school a year before going to France, during which she worked in a café. In France, she shared an apartment with a Swedish friend and former colleague from the café. Linn had just finished high school a few months before going to France. She lived alone in a studio during her semester in France. Louise was enrolled in a bachelor's programme (not language related) in Sweden. In France, she shared an apartment with another Swedish woman.

Interview

Semi-structured interviews were chosen as the interview type for the study. This allows us to elicit comparable data between the participants by using an interview script and to ask follow-up questions when deemed relevant to the purpose of the study. The interview script (see Appendix) was constructed with the literature review presented in 'Individual differences in L2 learning and use' in mind. It included questions about the participants' engagement with TL activities, their individual experiences and orientations including objectives, behaviours, thoughts, feelings and reactions in relation to L2 learning and use and their SA experiences in general. Also, they were asked to comment on their perceptions of the previously administered test. Follow-up questions were asked in order to invite the participant to clarify, elaborate or comment on his/her preceding speech turn. Each interview lasted between 30 and 55 minutes and was carried out in Swedish. The variable length reflects participants' varying tendency to elaborate on the topics covered and to initiate their own speech turns. The participants appeared eager to share their thoughts and experiences, and the rapport between the researcher and each participant was relaxed. The interviews were recorded with an iPhone 6 and a Dictaphone.

Data analysis

The interviews were transcribed in Microsoft Word and a thematic analysis was carried out, following the steps presented by Braun and Clark (2006, p. 87). The data were analysed and coded with the help of the concepts introduced in the literature review presented earlier. This involved both descriptive coding ('TL contact') and interpretative coding ('noticing', 'L2 motivation', 'sense of self-efficacy' and 'self-regulation') (Miles and Huberman, 1994). In a first step, themes (patterns) were identified for each individual (e.g. 'high sense of self-efficacy in relation to TL use' or 'other main SA objective apart from language learning'). In a second step, themes were identified for the high gainers and low gainers respectively. The emerging themes relating to the respective case-participants are presented in the following section. The analysis was organized in Microsoft Excel. The analysis was a back-and-forth process, where data were revised and recoded until a point of saturation was reached. The analysis of individual experiences and psychological orientations is based on participants' own statements and testimonies and not on field observations or any other behavioural assessments. The quotes included in the case presentations were translated from Swedish to English by the author and the translations were double-checked by a second researcher.

Findings

In this section, we will present the findings from each of the studied cases separately, starting with the high gainers. The findings relate to the kind of TL contact that the focal participants had during their semester in France and to their psychological orientation, for which the following ID factors were investigated: noticing, L2 motivation, self-efficacy and self-regulation.

The case of high gainers

The high gainers' contact with the TL

The interview data reveal that all high gainers regularly and consistently used French in service encounters and with teachers at school but that they had limited contact with the TL through social interaction, with the exception of Elsa. Indeed, three high gainers (Sarah, Alma and Gustaf) formed social networks including co-nationals exclusively which, according to them, explained why their access to TL interactions outside of the classroom was limited. In this way, they mainly came into contact with the TL through their studies, and through brief verbal exchanges in the supermarket and in stores, when ordering at cafés and restaurants and when soliciting strangers to ask for directions or for information. Despite their limited access to social interaction in French, they expressed having strategically and consciously created and benefited from opportunities for TL contact. Sarah watched a lot of TV and films in French, with French subtitles, an activity which provided her with regular exposure to social interaction through media representations. Also, at cafés she enjoyed eavesdropping on conversations ('at cafés when people speak French you can eavesdrop, I really enjoy that'). Alma declares having occasionally interacted with her Swedish-speaking peers in French ('we occasionally decided that now we are gonna speak French for about ten minutes').

Occasionally, Gustaf carried out short conversations in French in bars about everyday matters such as football games or someone's everyday occupation. Elsa stood out from the other high gainers with respect to the nature of her contact with the TL. She gained access to a French-speaking social network by joining a local sports team that she met with three nights a week. This gave her frequent and regular opportunities to engage in social interaction in the TL with speakers of the TL, both during the sport activity per se and through conversations taking place before and after training, as well as during social gatherings with the team members ('it's mainly with them that I have really used French regularly').

The high gainers' psychological orientation

A few common themes emerge with respect to the high gainers. They seem to have drawn on psychological orientations conducive to sustaining behaviours and which appear to have promoted their high levels of MWE learning. The high gainers appeared to be motivated and self-regulated individuals with a sense of self-efficacy in relation to TL use. Learning French was a clear objective for their stay abroad, but which did not exclude other purposes. Elsa went to France to learn the language and to gain a new life experience ('to have a good semester [...] and to focus on learning the language'). Sarah went to France to develop her linguistic competence and to gain an experience which would allow her to distinguish herself in relation to her peers ('get better at French, above all [...] and to stand out'). Alma had always had a desire to learn French and considered it useful for her future international career ('I have [...] always wanted to learn French [...] and later I would like to work with international issues'). Gustaf declared going to France to combine learning French for future career reasons with the experience of living in a warmer climate.

Their reported consistent efforts to engage with the language learning task inside and outside of the classroom suggest that they were able to maintain their motivation throughout the semester, despite certain motivational fluctuations acknowledged by some of them (e.g. Gustaf: 'it may have fluctuated a bit but it has never, my motivation to learn French has never really disappeared').

Their self-regulatory abilities are evidenced by their tendency to take control of their own learning situation. For example, despite an expressed difficulty and limited efforts to gain access to social networks including host members (except for Elsa), they manifested strategic and self-initiated behaviours by consciously creating occasions to use French. For example, Gustaf struck up conversations solely to have the opportunity to speak French and consciously took advantage of such occasions to learn more French ('let's take advantage of the fact that I get to learn some French'). Alma set clear goals to use French in some way every day ('in the beginning I formulated the goal to at least do something every day'). This involved asking questions or ordering in French in various daily situations ('whether it is asking for something in the supermarket, like "where do I find this?" or getting a coffee or something'). Sarah constantly sought out opportunities throughout the semester to use the TL on a daily basis, in all service situations, at the supermarket, in cafés, and watched TV shows only in French ('I have only watched stuff in French actually'). As mentioned earlier, Elsa joined a sports team where French was the medium of communication. She developed friendships with team members, and they met both during and outside of training several times a week throughout the semester. In addition to such out-of-class activities, these individuals reported having benefited greatly from listening to the teachers in class, all in all reflecting a tendency to actively engage with the TL. These individual initiatives to use French also reflect a sense of self-efficacy, as well as their tendency to hold conversations in the TL despite the communicative challenges experienced. Their experiences of using French in social interaction suggest nonetheless that this task was not easy, evoking some frustration or difficulties, such as not knowing how to express themselves (e.g. Alma: 'you feel that you can't really express what you want [...] and that makes it hard to be yourself as well'). However, these challenges did not discourage them from insisting on sustaining conversations in French (e.g. Sarah: 'I usually keep going in French,' Alma: 'sometimes we have persisted on responding in French'), or at least trying to do so (Gustaf: 'I guess I try', Elsa: 'lately, I've tried my best anyways'), nor from seeking out further occasions for TL use even after any difficult experiences (e.g. Alma towards the end of the semester sought to make contact with French-speaking peers by putting up contact ads at a university in town).

Finally, these high gainers reported having learned MWEs by paying attention to French speakers' ways of expression. Sarah increasingly paid attention to how French speakers expressed themselves and had strategically looked up expressions she was not familiar with ('and with time I feel that I have started noticing more and more "okey, now she said this and that" and you start picking up things in another way as you start getting used to it', 'almost every time when I have looked something up in the dictionary, it has been an everyday or colloquial expression'). Alma and Gustaf indicated noticing recurrent expressions (Alma: 'you notice what is common to say', Gustaf: 'well I have noticed if something is used very often'). Alma reported having memorized expressions that she had noticed in the input whose meaning she would later look up ('and then I have heard them say something and I have gone like "what is it they say all the time?" and then I have checked it up and you learn like that'). Finally, Elsa reported paying attention to linguistic forms when listening to others and reported trying to memorize what French speakers said in order to expand her own repertoire ('What are they saying and how do they say that, things like that, I think about that a lot I think', 'well you try to remember things so that you can use it yourself later'). She had also understood the usefulness of these expressions ('when you want to say something you try to construct your phrases yourself, and they are like "yeah, I don't know if I understand you," because it is just not the way it is said in French').

The case of low gainers

The low gainers' contact with the TL

The qualitative data revealed that the low gainers came into relatively regular contact with the TL mainly through service encounters (in supermarkets, cafés and restaurants) and course work. In addition, Nova sporadically spoke some French with locals during a couple of dates and in bars but mainly at the beginning of the semester. At home, the TV was sometimes on in the background while cooking. Linn sporadically interacted in French with her Romanian yoga teacher and with a young French-speaking man that she had met at a political gathering and with whom she went for walks in the city a couple of times after that ('we met three times after that'). Louise explicitly said that her TL contact other than course work was restricted (Interviewer: 'How much have you used French outside of class?', Louise: 'no well, not much at all actually, unfortunately'), such as in cafés and when greeting the other gym members when entering the gym ('in cafés and such of course', 'well I guess some people at the gym say hi'). In general, however, their contact with the TL through social interaction was relatively limited, which they attributed to the fact that their social network consisted of Swedish-speaking peers or to a lack of personal initiative (e.g. Nova: 'my friends here are Swedish', Interviewer: 'And why do you think that is?', Louise: 'well, on myself, that it wasn't as easy as I thought, you really have to take initiatives yourself').

The low gainers' psychological orientation

A few common themes emerge with respect to the low gainers' psychological orientations. Language learning was not necessarily their primary motivation for enrolling in the SA programme. Nova went to France to get a break from her life back home ('I was ready for a break'). She also found studying French useful for a possible future career in law. For Linn, enrolling in the SA programme was a last-minute choice which sounded appealing with the objective to relax after having worked hard in high school ('it sounded exciting', 'one reason to come here was also to just let go of pressure and to work on like taking it easy'). Louise expressed a love for France but maintained that the primary objective for her stay in France was personal ('because I love France [...] but perhaps more for the personal experience than to learn French').

Their reported behavioural patterns during the sojourn also suggest a relatively low or fluctuating motivation to engage in the language learning task. Apart from a few sporadic self-initiated opportunities to use the TL in social interaction, their active engagement with the TL was limited or fluctuated highly. For example, Nova declared not having been very ambitious in relation to her peers ('I haven't been the most ambitious one in my class'). She reflected a relatively passive stance in relation to language learning ('partly I have been pretty lazy', 'I have rather had the approach "I'll see where it goes"'). Nova set up a couple of dates with locals early on in the semester with the purpose to speak French but declared that her efforts to create opportunities to speak French then ceased ('I made more of an effort to start with than later on'). Louise clearly stated that she needed a break from home after having suffered a difficult academic setback during the preceding semester when her bachelor's thesis was failed ('after the examination I found I didn't pass'). This experience had a negative effect on her self-confidence and her ability to learn ('it was a slap in the face and I feel that my brain took a hit from that, eh, and I feel that it has made it slower [...] I have felt pretty dunce'). In France, she had not engaged in any of the activities she had anticipated ('I was going to speak a lot of French' and 'buy French newspapers [...] but I still haven't done that'). While she gladly greeted other members at her local gym she reported lacking the self-confidence needed to create additional occasions to interact in French ('you need to commit yourself [...] and I haven't really had the self-confidence to do that').

Linn declared having dwelled on what her main objective really was: language learning or living a personal experience and this ambivalence led her to not knowing where to invest her efforts and energy ('one thing that I think has been tough for me is that I haven't really known whether my objective was to learn French or to get time for myself, and not really knowing how to use my energy'). She did, however, make sporadic efforts to speak French towards the second half of the semester. For instance, Linn attended a local political meeting with a group of other Swedes. However, she stated that the fact that they went together made her comfortable but also reduced her initiative to take advantage of the opportunity to speak French ('we were mainly listening', 'the inconvenience and the advantage, that we went all together, is that it made me comfortable but it was also easier not to talk much'). She also joined a local yoga studio where she spoke French to her yoga teacher who, according to her, only spoke minimal French and therefore understood what it was like to use another language ('so she speaks French, but only minimally, but for some reason it is easier to speak to her because she knows what it is like to learn a language'). In the case of Linn and Louise, a relatively limited sense of self-efficacy thus appears to have hindered them from initiating and carrying out conversations in French.

When they did use French in social interaction, the low gainers all appear to have been occupied by reflections on their projected self-image or their perceived inabilities to communicate. While Nova experienced using French in a positive way, she reported finding it frustrating not being self-confident in her French-speaking skills and embarrassing not to speak French very well ('I am pretty spoiled being confident in English [...] while in French, I don't have that confidence at all', 'I have felt it is a bit embarrassing to come here and speak a language that you don't speak well'). She often switched to English during conversations, a language she felt more comfortable with ('It often turns out being a mix, French as far as possible but then I switch to English when I don't understand'). Louise reported feeling limited and a bit stupid when not being able to express herself in conversations ('you feel very limited and you feel a bit stupid'). According to her, this was frustrating and reduced her self-confidence, leading her to withdraw from the conversations. During our interview, Linn elaborated upon the somewhat stressful and destabilizing experience of using French in social situations which made it difficult to present a fair image of herself ('to speak [...] it is a stressful situation', 'not to be able to express your personality, I mean you can't express yourself in a language you can't handle [...] and that means that you both experience the painful feelings related to that at the same time as you have the pressure of speaking'). She declared that interactions in service situations often made her uncomfortable and those situations tended to decrease her self-confidence, at least in the beginning of the semester ('service encounters have most often made me uncomfortable', 'to start with [...] they made me feel worse').

Linn, Nova and Louise all seemed aware that the data elicitation test used in the study targeted everyday expressions, yet Nova and Linn both held that their semester in France did not promote their learning of such expressions. Nova declared: 'I think you have to spend a lot more time with French people to adopt (their ways of expression).' Linn, who had relatively high levels of MWE knowledge already at the start of the semester, believed she had not developed her everyday French to the same extent during the current stay in France as during her prior language trip to France, when she had engaged more closely and frequently with informal spoken French:

> Sure now I may know more about grammar now than back then but those weeks, there were students from all over Europe and even all over the world and I spent a lot of time with a girl from the Czech Republic, and we both spoke pretty bad French, but I even so started getting pretty fluent, more than I did this time, and I think I spoke more freely than I do now [...] and back then we had a teacher who used every day French to a larger extent than they do here.

Louise stated having noticed how the French speakers frequently used two specific expressions ('yes like *ça marche* eh and *ce n'est pas grave*, those you hear a lot'), but when talking about her experience with the rest of the MWE test, she declared having had difficulties ('well my brain kind of just stopped, I couldn't think of a word for each letter there').

Discussion

This study explored what kind of TL contact and psychological orientations promote the learning of MWEs in an SA context by contrasting cases of learners who developed their MWE knowledge to different extents during their semester abroad. The findings suggest that the high gainers engaged in TL-mediated activities relatively frequently throughout the semester but that their TL contact did not necessarily include frequent social interaction other than service encounters. The learner who represented the highest levels of MWE learning, Elsa, clearly illustrates the value of engaging in meaningful interaction with L1 speakers (Ellis, 2015). She gained access to frequent and regular interaction in French through a sports team including locals and developed her knowledge of MWEs considerably during her semester in France. However, the findings also suggest that learners can compensate for a relative lack of engagement in the TL community by engaging in other TL activities such as TV viewing and overhearing others' conversations in cafés, which appeared to be a valuable source of input for some of the high gainers, as reported elsewhere in the literature (Kinginger, 2008).

Interestingly, apart from Elsa's rich experiences with the TL, no clear-cut distinction emerged between the high versus low gainers in terms of patterns of TL contact. The high gainers, however, obviously benefited from their contact with the TL to a greater extent than the low gainers in terms of MWE learning, suggesting that learners need to actively engage with the input to which they are exposed. This brings us to the learners' psychological orientations.

The high gainers in this study shared a clear psychological orientation towards language and language learning. Language learning was their primary objective for going abroad. This motivational orientation in combination with self-regulatory capabilities and a relatively strong sense of self-efficacy may have helped them sustain behaviours conducive to MWE learning. Self-efficacy beliefs help the individual to initiate conversations in the TL and to stay focused on the task in hand (Dörnyei and Ushioda, 2011; Jackson, 2017). It is possible that their sense of self-efficacy helped them allocate attentional resources to register MWEs in the linguistic input (Ellis, 2002). While difficult to prove, the high gainers did report a tendency to 'notice' how L1 speakers of French expressed themselves (Schmidt, 1990). MWE learning thus appears to have been promoted by an attentional orientation towards linguistic forms during exposure (Schmidt, 1990, 2012), seemingly made possible by a certain sense of self-efficacy, a clear orientation towards language learning in combination with self-regulatory capacities (Moyer, 2004, 2014; Oxford and Griffiths, 2016).

The low gainers' psychological orientations were somewhat different to those of the high gainers. One difference pertained to their overall motivation for being abroad which may explain why they did not take advantage of the contact they had with the TL to the same extent as the high gainers in this respect, by not being as 'engaged' or oriented towards the TL during exposure (Crookes and Schmidt, 1991; Gardner, 1988; Moyer, 2004, 2014; Schmidt, 2012). The low gainers reported how their experience of TL use in social interaction was associated with perceived insufficient capabilities to speak French or with a perceived inability to project an accurate self-image while interacting. This could have influenced the extent to which they could focus their attention on language form.

That two of the low gainers had higher initial levels of MWE knowledge than the high gainers could possibly also have influenced their MWE development. Knowledge of a certain number of MWEs may be enough to meet the communicative needs of learners in a given context, and the learner might need to gain new experiences of social interaction in a variety of settings and be communicatively challenged in order to develop MWE knowledge further. Such an interpretation would align with communicative and usage-based approaches to L2 learning, where real communication needs are assumed to push L2 development further and where experience with the language is assumed to shape the linguistic repertoire (Ellis, 2015; Richards, 2006). For example, the learner may have to participate in more extended and more varied social interactions to experience the need to organize one's speech turns or to express stance for which MWEs such as *en gros* ('basically') and *à mon avis* ('in my opinion') are useful (targeted items in the MWE test are described in the section 'Arvidsson (2019): A quantitative study').

The findings of this qualitative study confirm and complement the findings from the quantitative part of the research project (Arvidsson, 2019), in that they suggest that TL contact alone was not enough to drive all participants' MWE knowledge forward. This does not contradict the assumption that TL exposure is necessary for MWEs to be learned (Ellis, 2002, 2003) but corroborates that psychological IDs are at play in adult L2 acquisition in a naturalistic environment (e.g. Dewaele, 2009; Dörnyei, 2005; Moyer, 2014). Also, the findings support the idea that a cluster of factors rather than one factor alone conspire to influence adult L2 learning in a naturalistic environment (Crookes and Schmidt, 1991; Gardner, 1988; MacIntyre, 1995; Moyer, 2014). While it may ultimately be the case, as Ellis (2015, p. 49) suggests, that 'what is attended is the focus of learning, and so attention controls the acquisition of language itself', the tendency to notice the forms available in the linguistic input appears to interact with other psychological factors, as suggested by the data. The learner's L2 motivation, his/her sense of self-efficacy and ability to self-regulate the language learning process seem to be intertwined with each other and to underpin the learner's ability to pick up MWEs in the input stream, an observation which both supports and adds to the empirical evidence available (e.g. Dörnyei, Durow and Zahran, 2004; Isabelli-García, 2006; Jackson, 2017; Mitchell, Tracy-Ventura and McManus, 2017; Moyer, 2004; Pellegrino Aveni, 2005).

Future studies could longitudinally investigate how the development of MWE knowledge interacts with the learners' communicative needs and the development of other L2 abilities to better understand the learning of MWE from a developmental perspective. Also, future research could continue to explore how ID factors interact with the learner's engagement with the TL. As Moyer (2004, p. 32) rightly points out, it is an empirical challenge to research learners' actual engagement with the TL (as opposed to TL exposure and contact at a more general level), but this could be tentatively explored by inviting learners to comment on their own experiences of engaging in different TL tasks and activities (e.g. conversations, TV viewing, reading) in terms of their attentional focus and awareness of language forms and their motivation to successfully carry out the task, combined with individual interviews about the learning process at large.

The study has some implications for language learning in an SA context. It shows that in order to develop knowledge of MWEs used in informal conversations, and which are considered highly useful for communicative purposes, TL exposure is also not sufficient by itself. Rather, the learner needs to actively engage with the input to which (s)he is exposed. A clear objective to make progress in the TL, sustained motivation, linguistic confidence and an ability to self-regulate motivations and emotions appear to underlie behaviours conducive to MWE learning over time. As noted by Mitchell,

Tracy-Ventura and McManus (2017, p. 211), a common desire among SA participants is to develop their 'mastery of idiomaticity', for which knowledge of MWEs is essential. On this count, the findings from the present study are informative for future SA participants themselves and for other language learners learning a new language in the TL setting. By being aware of the possibilities and limitations of TL exposure, and by setting specific goals for their stay abroad and developing strategies to achieve these goals, they may be better prepared to optimally benefit from the input they will receive abroad. These insights are also valuable to SA practitioners. For example, a pre-departure preparatory course could be designed and offered to SA participants, where students are informed about and invited to reflect upon the role of individual initiative for successful learning in the SA context.

Conclusion and limitations

The study contributes to second language acquisition research into multiword phenomena by exploring what factors promote the learning of MWEs in L2 French in an SA context. MWEs are multiword form-meaning mappings and the current study contributes specifically by focusing on the learning of such MWEs which are frequently used in everyday informal social interaction. The chapter has presented the qualitative findings from a mixed-methods project and was based on follow-up interviews with contrasting case-study learners, who had developed their knowledge of MWEs to differing degrees during a semester in France, as shown in a preceding quantitative study (Arvidsson, 2019). The qualitative findings supported the quantitative findings in that contact with the TL alone did not guarantee the learning of MWEs during the stay abroad. To develop one's knowledge repertoire of MWEs, relatively regular and frequent TL contact appears to be an obligatory yet not sufficient condition. In addition, the learning of MWEs appears to be facilitated by a number of psychological individual differences which include an attentional and behavioural orientation to the TL, motivation, self-efficacy and self-regulation. These findings also contribute to the increasing body of literature on individual variation in L2 learning in SA by adding to the diversity of linguistic features investigated.

The present study has its limitations. It is based on findings from a small sample of SA participants which limits the possibility to draw general conclusions. Also, the findings are based on the participants' own accounts of their experiences, which are naturally shaped by their selective memory and their own attributions (Jackson, 2017). Moreover, one single interview only allows us to graze the surface of the sojourners' lived experiences abroad. Finally, further studies would benefit from the development of instruments which provide even more precise information on sojourners' TL contact while abroad.

Note

1   The authors use the term *MWSs*, which is an abbreviation of multiword structures (Erman, Forsberg Lundell and Lewis, 2018).

References

Arvidsson, K. (2019), 'Quantity of Target Language Contact in Study Abroad and Knowledge of Multiword Expressions: A Usage-based Approach to L2 Development', *Study Abroad Research in Second Language Acquisition and International Education*, 4 (2), 145–67.

Bandura, A. (1997), *Self-efficacy: The Exercise of Control*, Basingstoke: W. H. Freeman.

Bardovi-Harlig, K., and Bastos, M. T. (2011), 'Proficiency, Length of Stay, and Intensity of Interaction and the Acquisition of Conventional Expressions in L2 Pragmatics', *Intercultural Pragmatics*, 8 (3), 347–84.

Braun, V., and Clarke, V. (2006), 'Using Thematic Analysis in Psychology', *Qualitative Research in Psychology*, 3 (2), 77–101.

Brysbaert, M. (2013), 'Lextale_FR A Fast, Free, and Efficient Test to Measure Language Proficiency in French', *Psychologica Belgica*, 53 (1), 23–37.

CLAPI (n.d.). Available online at http://clapi.icar.cnrs.fr (accessed 25 July 2015).

Coleman, J. (2015), 'Social Circles during Residence Abroad: What Students Do, and Who With', in R. Mitchell, N. Tracy-Ventura, and K. McManus (eds.), *Social Interaction, Identity and Language Learning during Residence Abroad*, 33–52. Available online at http://www.eurosla.org/ (accessed 26 February 2016).

Coulmas, F. (1981), *Conversational Routine: Explorations in Standardized Communication Situations and Prepatterned Speech*, The Hague: Mouton.

Council of Europe (2001), *Common European Framework of Reference for Languages: Learning, Teaching, Assessment*, Cambridge: Press Syndicate of the University of Cambridge.

Crookes, G., and Schmidt, R. W. (1991), 'Motivation: Reopening the Research Agenda', *Language Learning*, 41 (4), 469–512.

Dewaele, J.-M. (2009), 'Individual Differences in Second Language Acquisition', in W. C. Ritchie, and T. K. Bhatia (eds.), *The New Handbook of Second Language Acquisition*, 623–46, Bingley, UK: Emerald.

Dörnyei, Z. (2005), *The Psychology of the Language Learner*, New York/Abingdon: Routledge.

Dörnyei, Z., and Ushioda, E. (2011), *Teaching and Researching: Motivation*, Harlow, England: Longman/Pearson.

Dörnyei, Z., Durow, V., and Zahran, K. (2004), 'Individual Differences and Their Effects on Formulaic Sequence Acquisition', in N. Schmitt (ed.), *Formulaic Sequences: Acquisition, Processing and Use*, 87–106, Philadelphia: John Benjamins.

Duff, P. A. (2008), *Case Study Research in Applied Linguistics*, New York/Abingdon: Lawrence Erlbaum Associates.

Ehrman, M. E. (1996), *Understanding Second Language Acquisition*, Oxford: Oxford University Press.

Ellis, N. C. (2002), 'Frequency Effects in Language Processing: A Review with Implications for Theories of Implicit and Explicit Language Acquisition', *Studies in Second Language Acquisition*, 24 (2), 143–88.

Ellis, N. C. (2003), 'Constructions, Chunking, and Connectionism: The Emergence of Second Language Structure', in C. J. Doughty, and M. H. Long (eds.), *The Handbook of Second Language Acquisition*, 63–103, Oxford: Blackwell.

Ellis, N. C. (2015), 'Cognitive and Social Aspects of Learning from Usage', in T. Cadierno, and S. W. Eskildsen (eds.), *Usage-based Perspectives on Second Language Learning*, 49–73, Berlin: De Gruyter Mouton.

Ellis, N. C., Römer, U., and O'Donnell, M. B. (2016), 'Constructions and Usage-based Approaches to Language Acquisition', *Language Learning*, 66, 23–44.

Erman, B., Forsberg Lundell, F., and Lewis, M. (2016), 'Formulaic Language in Advanced Second Language Acquisition and Use', in K. Hyltenstam (ed.), *Advanced Proficiency and Exceptional Ability in Second Languages*, 111–48, Boston: De Gruyter Mouton.

Erman, B., Forsberg Lundell, F., and Lewis, M. (2018), 'Formulaic Language in Advanced Long-residency L2 Speakers', in K. Hyltenstam, I. Bartning, and L. Fant (eds.), *High-Level Language Proficiency in Second Language and Multilingual Contexts*, 96–119, Cambridge: Cambridge University Press.

Forsberg Lundell, F., and Sandgren, M. (2013), 'High-level Proficiency in Late L2 Acquisition Relationships between Collocational Production', in G. Granena, and M. Long (eds.), *Sensitive Periods, Language Aptitude, and Ultimate L2 Attainment*, 231–55, Amsterdam: John Benjamins.

Forsberg Lundell, F., Lindqvist, C., and Edmonds, A. (2018), 'Productive Collocation Knowledge at Advanced CEFR Levels: Evidence from the Development of a Test for Advanced L2 French', *Canadian Modern Language Review*, 74 (4), 627–49.

Gardner, R. C. (1988), 'The Socio-educational Model of Second-language Learning: Assumptions, Findings, and Issues', *Language Learning*, 38, 101–26.

Goldberg, A. E. (2003), 'Constructions: A New Theoretical Approach to Language', *Trends in Cognitive Sciences*, 7 (5), 219–24.

Isabelli-García, C. (2006), 'Study Abroad Social Networks, Motivation and Attitudes: Implications for Second Language Acquisition', in M. A. DuFon, and E. Churchill (eds.), *Language Learners in Study Abroad Contexts*, 231–58, Clevedon, England: Multilingual Matters.

Jackson, J. (2017), 'The Personal, Linguistic, and Intercultural Development of Chinese Sojourners in an English-speaking Country', *Study Abroad Research in Second Language Acquisition and International Education*, 2 (1), 80–106.

Kinginger, C. (2008), 'Language Learning in Study Abroad: Case Studies of Americans in France', *The Modern Language Journal*, 92 (1), 1–124.

Langacker, R. W. (1987), *Foundations of Cognitive Grammar: Vol. 1. Theoretical Prerequisites*, Stanford, CA: Stanford University Press.

MacIntyre, P. (1995), 'How Does Anxiety Affect Second Language Learning? A Reply to Sparks and Ganschow', *Modern Language Journal*, 79, 90–9.

Martinez, R., and Schmitt, N. (2012), 'A Phrasal Expression List', *Applied Linguistics*, 33 (3), 299–320.

McManus, K., Mitchell, R., and Tracy-Ventura, N. (2014), 'Understanding Insertion and Integration in a Study Abroad Context: The Case of English-speaking Sojourners in France', *Revue Française de Linguistique Appliquée*, 19 (2), 97–116.

Mercer, S., and Williams, M. (2014), 'Concluding Reflections', in S. Mercer, and M. Williams (eds.), *Multiple Perspectives on the Self in SLA*, 177–85, Bristol: Multilingual Matters.

Miles, M. B., and Huberman, A. M. (1994), *Qualitative Data Analysis: An Expanded Sourcebook* (2nd ed.), Thousand Oaks, CA: Sage.

Mitchell, R. (2015), 'The Development of Social Relations during Residence Abroad', *Innovation in Language Learning and Teaching*, 9 (1), 22–33.

Mitchell, R., Tracy-Ventura, N., and McManus, K. (2017), *Anglophone Students Abroad: Identity, Social Relationships, and Language Learning*, Abingdon/New York: Taylor & Francis.

Moyer, A. (2004), *Age, Accent, and Experience in Second Language Acquisition: An Integrated Approach to Critical Period Inquiry*, Clevedon: Multilingual Matters.

Moyer, A. (2014), 'Exceptional Outcomes in L2 Phonology: The Critical Factors of Learner Engagement and Self-regulation', *Applied Linguistics*, 35 (4), 418–40.

Myles, F., and Cordier, C. (2017), 'Formulaic Sequence (FS) Cannot Be an Umbrella Term in SLA: Focusing on Psycholinguistic FSs and Their Identification', *Studies in Second Language Acquisition*, 39 (1), 3–28.

Ortega, L. (2013), *Understanding Second Language Acquisition*, New York: Routledge.

Oxford, R. L., and Griffiths, C. (2016), *Teaching and Researching Language Learning Strategies: Self-Regulation in Context* (2nd ed.), London/New York: Taylor and Francis.

Pellegrino Aveni, V. (2005), *Study Abroad and Second Language Use*, Cambridge: Cambridge University Press.

Pérez-Vidal, C. (2017), Study Abroad and ISLA. *The Routledge Handbook of Instructed Second Language Acquisition*, 339–60, New York: Routledge.

Richards, J. C. (2006), *Communicative Language Teaching Today*, New York: Cambridge University Press.

Schmidt, R. W. (1990), 'The Role of Consciousness in Second Language Learning', *Applied Linguistics*, 11 (2), 129–58.

Schmidt, R. W. (2012), 'Attention, Awareness, and Individual Differences in Language Learning', in W. M. Chan, K. N. Chin, S. K. Bhatt, and I. Walker (eds.), *Perspectives on Individual Characteristics and Foreign Language Education*, 27–50, Berlin: De Gruyter Mouton.

Schmitt, N., Dörnyei, Z., Adolphs, S., and Durow, V. (2004), 'Knowledge and Acquisition of Formulaic Sequences', in N. Schmitt (ed.), *Formulaic Sequences: Acquisition, Processing and Use*, 55–86, Philadelphia: John Benjamins.

Schmitt, N., and Redwood, S. (2011), 'Learner Knowledge of Phrasal Verbs: A Corpus-informed Study', in F. Meunier, G. Gilquin, and M. Paquot (eds.), *A Taste for Corpora. A Tribute to Professor Sylviane Granger*, 173–208, Amsterdam/Philadelphia: John Benjamins.

Smiskova-Gustafsson, H. (2013), 'Chunks in L2 Development: A Usage-based Perspective', Doctoral Dissertation, University of Groningen, Retrieved from https://www.rug.nl/research/portal/files/14408764/H_Gustafsson_Dissertation.pdf

Szudarski, P. (2017), 'Learning and Teaching L2 Collocations: Insights from Research', *TESL Canada Journal*, 34 (3), 205–16.

Taguchi, N., Li, S., and Xiao, F. (2013), 'Production of Formulaic Expressions in L2 Chinese: A Developmental Investigation in a Study Abroad Context', *Chinese as a Second Language Research*, 2 (1), 23–58.

Tomasello, M. (2000), 'First Steps toward a Usage-based Theory of Language Acquisition', *Cognitive Linguistics*, 11 (1/2), 61–82.

Webb, S., Newton, J., and Chang, A. (2013), 'Incidental Learning of Collocation', *Language Learning*, 63 (1), 91–120.

Wray, A. (2002), *Formulaic Language and the Lexicon*, Cambridge: Cambridge University Press.

Appendix. Interview script

1. Can you please describe a regular day here in CITY?
2. Please describe your living arrangement.
3. With whom have you spent your time throughout the semester? How did you meet?
4. Have you had an extra job?

5. Can you please describe a regular weekend here in CITY?
6. What were your hopes and expectations with respect to your semester in CITY before coming here?
7. Would you say that the semester has corresponded to your expectations? (If not, in what ways?)
8. What made you choose to study French in France?
9. What were you doing at home before coming here?
10. Will you continue to study French after your semester here or to use French in any other way?
11. Do you have any regrets with respect to your semester in CITY? What would you recommend other students who will go to CITY?
12. In what situations have you used French outside of class?
13. How often have you used French outside of class? Why do you think that is?
14. How have you experienced using French in these situations?
15. How do you react when the occasion to speak French presents itself? Can you give an example?
16. What has been the most challenging in terms of learning and using French?
17. Do you feel like you have actively created occasions to speak French?
18. Can you recall any situation when you did not know how to express yourself in French to make yourself understood? How did you react? How did you solve the situation?
19. Would you say you have been eager to meet French people?
20. How would you say you have adapted to life here in France?
21. Have you experienced any differences between everyday life in Sweden and France? Can you give an example?
22. Do you feel like you have developed on a personal level during your semester in France?
23. How would you say your French has developed? What about your ability to speak French?
24. Let us have a look at the test you took both at the beginning and at the end of your semester here in CITY. What would you say this test targeted? Do you have the impression of having made progress? According to you, why is that? (How do you think you have learned these expressions?)
25. Is there anything else you would like to share?

11

When in one's new country: Examining native-like selections in English at home and abroad

Victoria Zaytseva,[1] Imma Miralpeix[2] and Carmen Pérez-Vidal[1]
[1]*Universitat Pompeu Fabra,* [2]*Universitat de Barcelona*

Introduction

Although the study of formulaic language has a long research tradition in the field of second language acquisition (SLA) (see, for instance, Pawley and Syder, 1983), the past few decades have witnessed an increasing interest in examining the use of formulas by learners of second languages (L2) (Foster, 2009; Foster, Bolibaugh and Kotula, 2014; Wray, 2002), which seems to be a potentially promising area of inquiry in applied linguistics (Schmitt, 2010). Native speaker studies assessing formulaic sequences have confirmed that both spoken and written language contains a substantial amount of fixed expressions (e.g. memorized phrases, chunks or collocations), which are stored in memory as single whole items rather than constructed spontaneously, and that the use of these formulas is a key area distinguishing native from non-native production (Erman and Warren, 2000; Foster, 2001).

One fundamental indicator of L2 performance is precisely the mastery of such naturally sounding word combinations versus awkward collocations. These common word combinations which native speakers (NSs) often use and which make learners' speech more fluent are known as 'native-like selections' (NLS), as coined by Pawley and Syder (1983). Learning these combinations is primarily based on learners' exposure to the L2 in use (i.e. linguistic input received) since formulaic language is acquired through experience with the language (Ellis, 2014, 2017). As such, context of learning is paramount: contextualized encounters with this vocabulary take place more often in natural settings than in the classroom. While an early start in an immersion setting has been found to be crucial in the acquisition of NLS (Foster, Bolibaugh and Kotula, 2014), the development of this ability is also tightly linked to sociocultural adaptation (Dörnyei, Durow and Zahran, 2004), which is fostered during residence abroad where the target language (TL) is widely spoken.

The present study investigates the influence of two different learning environments, a stay abroad (SA) period following formal instruction (FI) at home (AH), on the acquisition of NLS by thirty advanced Catalan/Spanish-speaking learners of English. Our primary goal is to evaluate learner NLS ability in English over time, following time in each learning context, FI and SA, as they are experienced one after the other, and in two different production modes: writing and speech. Additionally, the study aims to determine whether improvement in NLS knowledge goes hand in hand with improvement in quantitative lexical metrics (e.g. lexical diversity, sophistication, accuracy). Given that most SLA research has focused on studying vocabulary size, richness or sophistication in terms of individual words and that there is a shortage of studies which look at how these words work in combination (Foster, 2009), focusing on the detail of L2 idiomatic expressions (or lack thereof) may provide new insights into overall L2 lexical competence and put flesh on the conventional quantitative lexical measures. In the following section, we discuss the relevance of formulaic language in language use and review the literature that has considered the development of L2 idiomaticity in different contexts of acquisition.

Formulaic language and study abroad

It is generally acknowledged that the use of NLS (most frequently operationalized as collocations) belongs to the later stages of L2 development. Nevertheless, collocational errors are abundant in L2 writing and speech even at advanced levels, generally resulting from cross-linguistic interference from either the L1 or other second languages (Howarth, 1998; Nesselhauf, 2005). In terms of writing, learner output systematically deviates from native-speaking baseline standards in misuse and underuse of conventionalized forms (Altenberg and Granger, 2001; Granger, 1998; Howarth, 1998; Nesselhauf, 2005; Yorio, 1980), overemphasizes vague uses (e.g. 'be', 'have', 'take') at the expense of more specific forms (Vedder and Benigno, 2016) and lacks specificity (Crossley and McNamara, 2009; Hinkel, 2003; Linnarud, 1986; Silva, 1993). In terms of speech, learners tend to overuse dysfluency markers, such as filled pauses and hesitation phenomena, and produce incorrect combinations even with high-frequency vocabulary ('to make a favour') (Vedder and Benigno, 2016). While there is agreement that 'any analysis of students' speech or writing shows a lack of [...] collocational competence' (Hill, 2000, p. 49) and that 'mastery of formulaic language takes a long time to acquire' (Schmitt, 2010, p. 145), little is known about the acquisition of formulas in different learning environments. While it appears that some dysfluency phenomena can be overcome and replaced by formulaic expressions with exposure and interaction in the TL community (Adolphs and Durow, 2004; Foster, 2001; Trenchs-Parera, 2009), formal classroom instruction at home, on the contrary, does not appear to be an environment rich enough to trigger idiomatic language or build native-like word association networks (Boers and Lindstromberg, 2009; Eyckmans, Boers and Stengers, 2007; Forsberg, 2010).

In light of this, it is interesting to review the existing research that has considered the impact of learning environment, in particular SA, on the development of L2 NLS use. Early studies from the 1980s and 1990s showed that SA learners, compared to their AH peers, improved in the area of fluency, thanks to their ability to sound more natural in the L2 (Möhle and Raupach, 1983; Regan, 1998), and that the significant gains in fluency were also associated with the learners making greater use of formulaic language in combination with enhanced speech rate and reduced hesitation (Regan, 1998; Towell, Hawkins and Bazergui, 1996). Marriott (1995) and Siegal (1995) also found a greater number of formulaic expressions in SA learners, suggesting that these, and not syntactic knowledge, accounted for growth in L2 overall morphosyntactic complexity. As Foster, Bolibaugh and Kotula (2014, p. 105) argued, these findings broadly point to lexical organization of the formulaic language kind as the main area of benefit for L2 learners, suggesting that 'context can significantly influence acquisition of L2 lexical knowledge'.

Foster (2009) investigated progress in productive vocabulary knowledge among L1 and L2 users of English both quantitatively, using the D measure of lexical diversity, and qualitatively, providing an account of learners' NLS in comparison with the NSs' preferred expressions. Results showed that the L2 learners studying abroad framed their speech in more native-like ways than their counterparts learning English in an AH environment. The SA learners used more narrowly defined lexical choices (e.g. 'notice', 'pay attention', 'explain', 'realize', 'cycle', 'ride') instead of broad general vocabulary (e.g. 'see', 'say', 'understand', 'come', 'go'), more colloquialisms (e.g. 'bike' for 'bicycle', 'kid' for 'boy', 'chat' for 'talk') and target-like collocational phrasing (e.g. 'go for/on a picnic' instead of 'go to a/the picnic'). In a subsequent study, Foster, Bolibaugh and Kotula (2014) presented a similar analysis, this time tapping into L2 receptive knowledge of NLS, and found that an early age of exposure to the L2 in an immersion situation was particularly conducive to development of nativelikeness.

Foster's findings were in line with those reported by Siyanova and Schmitt (2008) examining native and non-native collocational knowledge. According to their results, 'extended stays in an L2-speaking environment lead to a more native-like idiomaticity' (p. 447), as participants who had spent a year abroad in an English-speaking country showed significantly better intuitions concerning collocations than those who had never been abroad. The authors concluded that whether it is shorter or longer than a year, a prolonged stay in the L2 country can help learners become more native-like in their perception of collocations than learners without any L2 natural exposure during an SA exchange. It should be noted, however, that learners' receptive knowledge of collocations did not extend to better production of collocations, a finding that echoes other work on this topic, such as Nesselhauf (2005, p. 236) and Yorio (1980), who note that accuracy of collocation improves only slightly with time spent in the TL country.

This study builds on such existing work (Foster, 2009; Foster, Bolibaugh and Kotula, 2014; Siyanova and Schmitt, 2008) by investigating to what extent learners acquire productive knowledge of NLS in English in an SA context, preceded by an FI context, along with examining how NLS knowledge develops in both writing and speech modalities. To our knowledge, no prior investigation has been conducted with such an approach while focusing on both written and oral production of NLS, which is also complemented by several quantitative measures that help describe learners' lexical development.

Study

Research aims

The study reported here is part of the SALA project based in Barcelona, which examines the effects of two learning contexts, FI and SA (the latter within the European Erasmus framework), on a full range of language skills among advanced learners of English (see Mora and Valls-Ferrer, 2012; Trenchs-Parera, 2009; Pérez-Vidal, 2014, for a full description of the project). In this chapter, we aim to investigate the corresponding effects of a period spent abroad, preceded by a period of classroom instruction, on learners' use of NLS in both writing and speech as well as on the learners' quantitative lexical abilities. For this purpose, we analysed learners' oral and written lexical choices, longitudinally, after experiencing both learning contexts, FI and SA, and in comparison with native-speaker baseline performance. In so doing, we aim to address the following research questions.

1. Does learners' knowledge of NLS in writing and speech improve over time, in an SA learning context, preceded by an FI context, to approximate native-like language at any point during the observation period?
2. To what extent does this approximation correspond to growth (if any) in learners' quantitative lexical measures, during SA, in contrast with the preceding FI period?

Participants, data collection and tasks

The participants in this study were Spanish/Catalan learners of English ($n = 30$); twenty-four were female and six male. They were undergraduate students with an advanced level of English,[1] pursuing a language specialization degree at a university in Barcelona. They ranged in age between seventeen and twenty-one at the beginning of the study, with the majority (93.3 per cent) having entered the degree at the age of seventeen to eighteen. During the second year of their studies, students were required to spend three months in an English-speaking country as a compulsory requirement of their university curriculum within the Erasmus mobility scheme (see Pérez-Vidal, 2014, for a detailed description of the programme). For baseline data, NSs of English ($n = 27$) from the United States (fifteen), the UK (six) and Ireland (four) were also recruited in the study. They were undergraduate students (77.8 per cent female) on an exchange programme at different Spanish universities and were highly comparable to the learners in terms of age and education. It should be noted that the use of NSs as the golden measure of L2 development (Cook, 1999; Ortega, 2014) has been extensively discouraged in SLA research. This is a position we share, as the inclusion of NSs in our study was used only as a reference point with the expectation that baseline data may provide special insight into L2 development across time and in the absence of a better means of comparison with learners at an already advanced level of proficiency.

The data collection took place longitudinally during a fifteen-month period, over two academic years. The first data collection occurred at time 1 (T1) upon the students' enrolment in the programme; then at time 2 (T2) following a six-month period of

Table 11.1 Testing Times*

	Academic Year 1			Academic Year 2		
Trimester	1	2	3	1	2	3
Context		FI		SA		
Testing times	T1	T2		T3		

* Adapted from Pérez-Vidal (2014)

FI – eighty hours – at their home university and before SA; and finally at time 3 (T3) after the students' return from their three-month SA exchange in an English-speaking country. Following this repeated-measures design, T1 helped to establish the learners' initial level of English, while T2 served as both a post-test for T1 and a pre-test for T3, with T3 being a post-test for T2. Table 11.1 presents the research design reflecting the three (T1, T2 and T3) testing times.

Two tasks were used to gather the participants' writing and speech samples: an argumentative essay and a semi-guided interview. Students were asked to write a text in response to the following prompt:

> Someone who moves to a foreign country should always adopt the customs and way of life of his/her new country rather than holding on to his/her own customs.

To this end, participants were given a double-sided A4 sheet of paper and were allowed 30 minutes to write the composition by hand without using any external resources or dictionaries. Although the maximum number of words was not specified in the instructions, none of the final drafts examined here exceeded a single double-sided sheet. The decision to analyse NLS knowledge in free written expression was made in light of prior studies which find written compositions to be sufficiently complex to discriminate between different proficiency levels and highly reliable for assessment in higher education (Laufer, 1998; Sasaki, 2009). In order to avoid possible variation in vocabulary use, the same prompt was maintained at each testing time since changes in topic have been reported to influence L2 written narrative and result in uncontrolled variation in word choice (Laufer, 1998).

The oral task was a semi-guided interview, in which students were asked to act as both interviewers and interviewees. They were randomly assigned 'Student A' and 'Student B' roles and were given a list of questions on the topic: 'University life'. First, student A asked student B the questions one at a time and then they switched roles (see Appendix for the list of questions used in the interview). The oral interviews were recorded digitally in a quiet place and lasted approximately five minutes. In order to ensure the quality of the digital recordings, a research assistant was present as an observer and only intervened to inform the test-takers of the approaching time limit or solve any technical problem. Participants were instructed to perform the interview as if the researcher were not there, making for a relaxed atmosphere and a balanced interaction. The rationale for asking students to discuss their life at university was that of topic familiarity since our goal was to elicit speech data as natural and close to real life as possible, and speaking about something familiar in an L2 (e.g. personal experiences) generally entails more extensive production preventing the speaker from running out of ideas (Foster and Skehan, 1996; Skehan and Foster, 1997). The whole corpus resulted in a total of 115 oral interviews (90 by the NNSs and 25 by the NSs) and 117 written compositions (90 by the NNSs and 27 by the NSs). These samples were transcribed following CHAT transcription conventions of the CLAN programme (MacWhinney, 2000), comprising a full corpus of 27,774 words for the written compositions and 30,370 words for the interviews.

Data analysis

In order to explore learners' idiomatic ability when speaking and writing (i.e. whether they tend to use word combinations that their NS counterparts use at any point over the observation period), we looked for NLS in the data. NLS can be simple collocations ('make a difference'), whole utterances ('it goes without saying') or more complex syntactic frameworks ('I'm so glad you could bring Harry') whose paraphrased grammatical equivalents often lead to unnatural usages ('the fact that Harry could be brought by you causes me to be so glad').

First of all, following Foster (2009), we looked for common 'frames' (narrative events) in the data. Unlike the study by Foster, in which the lexical choices were extracted from a controlled task (cartoon picture prompts), with learners describing exactly the same action, both our oral and written tasks were characterized by a high degree of freedom. For example, while most learners brought up immigration and racial issues in response to the essay statement (especially before SA), the NSs related the topic to their own experiences living and studying abroad in Spain, which then made the search for similar narrative events less straightforward. Similarly, certain interview questions were too specific and at times encouraged participants to recount anecdotes, yielding as a consequence a number of diverse responses. Therefore, instead of six frames as in Foster's data, we found a total of ten frames in our data (five for each task), for example: 'meeting new people', 'setting expectations' or 'adapting to a new culture'. We then compiled for each frame an exhaustive data-driven list of phrases and sentences used in each frame at each testing time and looked for the similarities and differences between learners at the three testing times and the NSs. For example, in the frame 'making friends' we saw development in the choice of the NLS (collocation in this case) across testing times:

T1: 'I have done one small group of friends'
T2: 'I did here make friends'
T3: 'I've made a lot of friends'
NS: 'I have made many wonderful friends'

And in the frame 'adapting to a new culture' participants used 'adapt to' at T3 (as the NSs did) instead of 'adopt to' or 'adapt', as in the previous testing times:

T1: 'To adopt yourself to'
T2: 'To adapt his new conditions'
T3: 'To adapt themselves to new customs'
NS: 'Adapting to customs'

Inter-rater reliability analysis was conducted on 10 per cent of randomly selected texts using the Intraclass Correlation Coefficient (ICC) for average measures, with a two-way fixed effects model and the confidence interval set at .95. It was found that inter-rater reliability was acceptable, at .809, indicating that coding criteria were applied consistently across raters. As a result, we were able to locate a handful of comparable word choices across the data and extract some general observations that will be considered in the next section.

As for the quantitative lexical measures, the written and spoken samples were coded for a variety of variables: lexical diversity (measured through Guiraud's index, 'GI'), which estimates the variety of vocabulary and avoidance of repetition in a given text by dividing the number of word types by the square root of tokens, and lexical sophistication or use of advanced vocabulary (measured through Academic Word List 'AWL' and the least frequent words in English '+2k'); adjective, adverb, noun and verb density ('Adj/w', 'Adv/w', 'N/w', 'V/w'), measuring information density in each word class (total number of adjectives per word, etc.); and lexical accuracy or vocabulary errors per word ('VE/w') together with spelling errors ('SpE/w' in writing) (for more details, see Zaytseva (2016) and Zaytseva, Miralpeix and Pérez-Vidal (2019)).

Results

In order to consider RQ1, which addresses the development of learners' NLS knowledge in writing and speech over time, and after either FI or SA, we compared the learners' word choices at each testing time (T1, T2 and T3) with those of the NSs when describing the same event in their written compositions and oral interviews. To arrive at a more manageable overview of the analysis, we distinguished between gradual approximation to NS usage (longitudinal development of NLS), context-specific approximation in FI and SA respectively (context-specific NLS, occurring after either FI or SA) and lack of changes at any point over the observation period. In what follows, we present the analysis of written production followed by that of the oral, detailing the most representative examples for each case.

Written production: Longitudinal changes in NLS

Looking at the lexical choices in the learners' essays over time, one of the most visible changes that can be observed is a gradual increase in the use of impersonal forms. As shown in Table 11.2, learners make more use of the 'it'-cleft construction, mostly based on the 'it + copula be + adjective' pattern at T2 and T3 than at T1, suggesting that both contexts seem to be equally beneficial for the acquisition of generality, a feature that is typical of academic writing and also highly frequent in the NS corpus.

Table 11.2 Frequency of Use of Impersonal Forms in Written Production

Written Production		Number of Uses			
	Impersonal Forms	T1	T2	T3	NSs
It + copula be + adj. (important, essential, vital, etc.)		23	34	35	52
Use of the pronoun 'one'		3	4	8	48

Table 11.3 Excerpts from Learners' and NSs' Written Compositions Illustrating the Use of Impersonal Forms

T1	T2	T3	NSs
'it is important not to forget your own customs ...'	'it is very important to get used to their customs ...'	'it is impossible to forget one's culture ...'	'it is important to not lose sight of one's heritage'
'you shouldn't forget your own customs'	'one cannot forget his origins ...'	'one has to know the new culture ...'	'one should make an effort to keep an open mind ...'

Likewise, by the end of the study learners rely more on the pronoun 'one'. Although the pronoun 'one' cannot be considered part of formulaic knowledge, we decided to include it because it was the most common substitute for personal pronouns ('I', 'you', 'he') in general statements in the NSs' texts and also became relatively more frequent in the NNS corpus after the SA experience.

Although in both cases (especially with the reference to the pronoun 'one') NSs make substantially wider use of impersonal language, overall the learners' essays give the impression of being more formal by the end of the observation period. Table 11.3 illustrates these examples.

Written production: Context-specific changes in NLS

As for the approximation to NS usage specifically after each of the two learning periods (FI and SA), we found no remarkable patterns for FI: it appears that learners made more frequent use of the collocation 'hold onto customs/habits/roots' at T2 than at T1 or T3, although the number of incorrect uses, either through producing the base verb 'hold' without the required preposition/particle (e.g. 'hold their customs and way of life') or by selecting a wrong preposition (e.g. 'hold with our own customs', 'holding to your habits'), was equally high at all times (see Table 11.4 for the frequency of correct and incorrect uses). Taking into account that the full form of the phrasal verb 'hold onto' was actually used in the prompt, we cannot infer that more accurate usage was due to learners' better knowledge of this compound as a result of FI in the classroom.

Regarding SA, the most noteworthy NLS were found in the use of adverbs modifying adjectives. At T3, learners incorporated into their lexicon a higher number of adverbs ending in '-ly', used for emphasis or to moderate and/or intensify adjectives (e.g. 'really difficult', 'entirely different'), similar to NS usage (see Table 11.5).

Table 11.4 Frequency of Correct and Incorrect Uses of 'Hold onto Customs' in Written Production

Written Production		Number of Uses			
	Hold onto Customs (Roots, Habits)	T1	T2	T3	NSs
Correct usage		1	7	4	13
Incorrect usage*		9	11	11	0

*Due to either (1) incomplete form (e.g. 'hold' or 'hold on') or (2) used in combination with the wrong preposition (e.g. 'hold with', 'hold to', among others).

Table 11.5 Frequency of Use of Adverbs Modifying Adjectives in Written Production

Written Production		Number of Uses			
	Adverbs Modifying Adjectives	T1	T2	T3	NSs
'-ly' adv. + adj. (e.g. 'really difficult', 'entirely different')		8	6	20	20

Table 11.6 Examples of Adverbs Modifying Adjectives in Learner and NS Written Compositions

T1	T2	T3	NSs
Really difficult	Really substantial	Really hard	Entirely different
Really interested	Really different	Completely different	Seemingly disparate
Really interested	Really significant	Exactly the same	Undoubtedly difficult
Really important	Really difficult	Equally valid	Vaguely familiar
Really important	Completely adapted	Extremely attached	Perfectly natural
Highly important	Completely changed	Strongly important	Extremely profitable

As shown in Tables 11.5 and 11.6, not only did the learners rely more on modifying adverbs after SA, the range of adverbs used was also more extensive (no longer limited to the forms 'really' and 'completely', but involving other variants such as 'equally', 'extremely' or 'strongly' and thus resembling NS patterns).

Written production: Lack of changes

Despite the longitudinal and context-specific approximations to NS selections described earlier, there is evidence that the learners tended to overuse basic vocabulary, in contrast to the NSs. To illustrate, learners were more likely to select high-frequency topic-related verbs such as 'lose' and 'forget' (with twenty-eight uses even at T3), unlike NSs, whose choices were rich in demanding more low-frequency variants (e.g. 'discard', 'disregard', 'forego'). Table 11.7 summarizes these selections.

Similarly, when describing the process of integration within their new host community in the SA context, learners showed a clear preference for the verb 'accept', while most NSs made use of a large set of synonyms instead (e.g. 'embrace', 'immerse', 'adjust', 'assimilate', 'adhere' and 'absorb'), as seen in Table 11.8.

Table 11.7 Frequency of Topic-related Verbs in Written Production I

Written Production	Number of Uses			
Topic-related Verbs I	T1	T2	T3	NSs
Lose (identity, culture, customs, roots)	6	9	8	4
Forget (culture, customs, roots)	16	7	20	6
Give up (culture, customs, beliefs)	0	0	1	5
Abandon (culture, customs, values)	2	3	1	3
Refuse (culture, customs, past)	0	1	3	0
Reject (customs, country)	0	0	1	1
Leave (customs, culture) (behind)	6	3	4	2
Leave (customs) apart	1	1	0	0
Quit (way of life)	1	0	0	0
Drop, discard, disregard, forego, surrender, take away, terminate, negate (customs, roots)	0	0	0	8

Table 11.8 Frequency of Topic-related Verbs in Written Production II

Written Production	Number of Uses			
Topic-related Verbs II	T1	T2	T3	NSs
Embrace (customs, culture)	0	1	0	6
Accept (customs, traditions)	4	1	7	0
Immerse in (the new culture)	1	0	0	6
Follow (some of the local customs)	0	2	1	2
Settle into (a different way of life)	0	0	1	2
Adjust to (local customs)	0	0	0	5
Assimilate into (a new country)	0	0	0	2
Adhere to (new customs)	0	0	0	2
Absorb (the new culture)	0	0	0	2
Accommodate (all aspects of one's customs)	0	0	0	1

Table 11.9 Frequency of Use of 'Another' and 'New' as Examples of L1 Transfer in Written Production

Written Production	Number of Uses			
Another vs New	T1	T2	T3	NSs
Move to another country[2]	16	22	15	3
Move to a new country	4	3	4	18

Another example where learners systematically differed from NSs may be reflective of language transfer from the L1 to the L2 (in this case, from Spanish/Catalan into English). For instance, when paraphrasing the idea of going abroad, most learners felt more inclined to use the determiner 'another', producing word strings like 'move to another country'. The NSs, by contrast, were most likely to prefer the adjective 'new' over 'another', as in 'move to a new country'. The explanation for these differences may lie in the learners translating literally from Catalan/Spanish *anar a un altre país/ir a otro país*, where using 'new' instead of 'another', while not ungrammatical, is less common. As we can see in Table 11.9, the use of 'another' becomes slightly less frequent at T3, while for the NS group it is practically non-existent (with only three uses).

Oral production: Longitudinal changes in NLS

Turning to the analysis of NLS in oral production, our observation is that the learners gradually approached NS usage as they used fewer words and collocations involving literal translation from their L1 or involving deceptive cognates (false friends). Examples of such selections are displayed in Table 11.10.

In Table 11.10, we can see that the learners progressively decreased their use of the false friend 'career' meaning 'university degree' (*carrera* in Spanish/Catalan), replacing it with its true equivalents (e.g. 'degree', 'programme', 'major'). In a similar vein, learners collocated the noun 'lunch' with 'have' instead of 'do' at T3, gaining in accuracy especially after SA. It is interesting to note that NS selections were more narrowly defined than those of the learners, as they resort to the verbs 'pack' or 'bring in' specifying the type of food they usually eat during their lunch break (see Appendix for the list of questions used in the oral interview).

Another example of learners dealing with L1 transfer relates to the verbs 'do' versus 'make' and 'meet' versus 'know' (see Table 11.11). While the NSs limited their choices to the collocations 'make friends' and 'meet people' when asked about their social life on campus, the learners kept mixing 'make' with 'do' (as in 'do friends') except at T2

Table 11.10 Frequency of Use of Deceptive Cognates and Literal Translation from L1 in Oral Production

Oral Production		Number of Uses			
	Cognates/L1 Transfer	T1	T2	T3	NSs
Career (instead of degree)		10	5	0	0
Degree		9	6	8	2
Programme		0	1	0	2
Major		0	0	0	1
To lunch/do the lunch (instead of have lunch)		5	1	0	0
Have lunch		7	6	15	0
Pack/bring (in) one's own food, lunch, sandwich		1	0	0	11

Table 11.11 Frequency of Use of L1 Transfer in Oral Production

Oral Production		Number of Uses			
	L1 Transfer II	T1	T2	T3	NSs
Make friends (acquaintances)		9	8	7	12
Meet friends		3	3	2	1
Do friends		2	0	3	0
Get to know one's friends		0	0	1	0
Meet people (kids, classmates)		16	12	11	9
Know people		2	3	1	0
Come across some people		0	0	1	0

and 'meet' with 'know' (as in 'know people'). While this can be explained by a strong influence of the Catalan/Spanish single verb *fer/hacer* for both 'make' and 'do' and a single verb *conèixer/conocer* for both 'meet' and 'know', it is interesting to note the two rather complex constructions that emerged at T3: 'get to know' and 'come across'. Although there is just one token of each of these verbs, their presence should not be disregarded.

Oral production: Context-specific changes in NLS

As for the movement towards NS selections specifically after FI, we did not find any noteworthy instances at T2 where learners framed their speech in more native-like ways. Conversely, the SA context enabled learners to acquire greater idiomaticity in terms of lexicalized phrases functioning as pause fillers or through emphasis expressed by the use of adverbs, similar to what we have observed in their written productions, thereby adjusting their speech to NS patterns.

For instance, as can be seen in Table 11.12, learners were likely to select considerably more idiomatic fillers such as 'I'd say' or 'I mean' at T3 than at T1 or T2, approaching NS usage. Also, there seemed to be a tendency at T3 for some learners to make more use of adverbs of emphasis ('really', 'quite', 'particularly'), collocating them with 'like' and 'enjoy' rather than simply producing 'I like' and thus moving in the direction of NS choices.

Considering that the learners at T3 used a greater number of adverbs ending in '-ly' than at T1 or T2 in their writing, and that the range of these adverbs was also much more diverse, we also examined the adverbs in their speech. Table 11.13 and Figure 11.1 present the number of the different adverbs used in oral production in detail. As can be seen, the total number of '-ly' adverbs approached NS values at T3 (with eighty-three uses), pointing to SA as the context that was very likely to induce these changes. Similarly, the learners exhibited an increasing range of adverbs at T3, with a greater diversity of use reflecting NS patterns.

Examining Native-Like Selections in English 223

Table 11.12 Frequency of Use of Emphasis in Oral Production

Oral Production		Number of Uses			
	Pause Fillers and Emphasis	T1	T2	T3	NSs
I would say/I'd say		1	1	6	12
I mean		1	2	14	6
I really (quite, particularly) like/enjoy …		3	1	6	14
I like …		54	50	48	22

Table 11.13 Frequency of Use of Emphasis through '-ly' Adverbs in Oral Production

Oral Production		Number of Uses			
	'-ly' Adverbs	T1	T2	T3	NSs
Really, basically, actually, usually, etc.		64	79	83	119

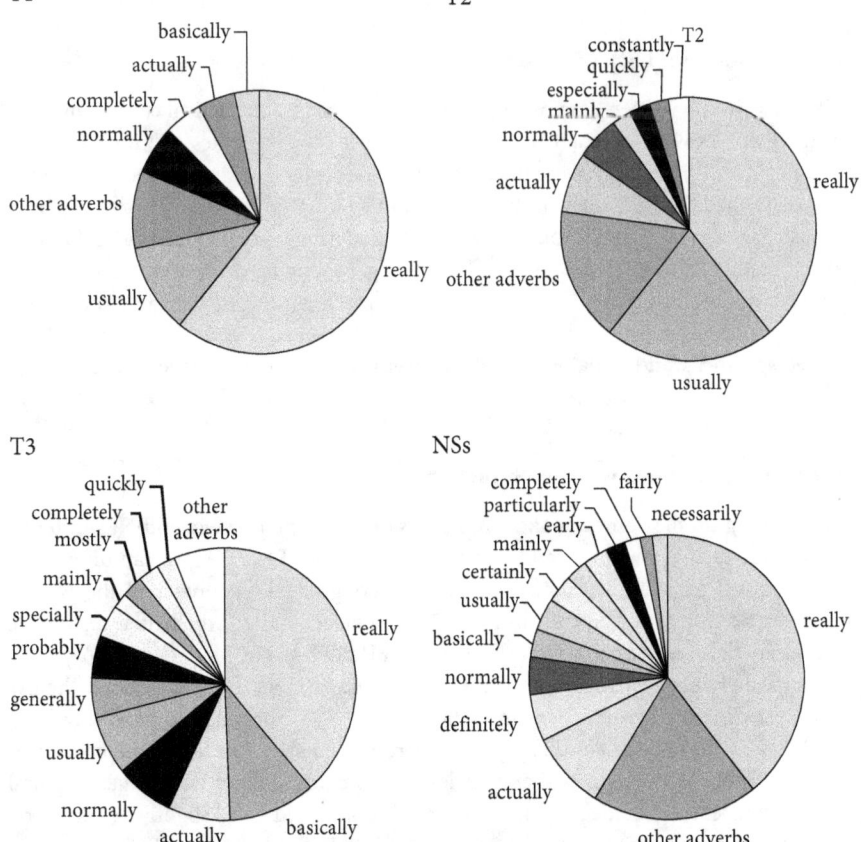

Figure 11.1 Proportion of Different Adverbs Used in Oral Production.[3]

Table 11.14 Frequency of Use of Delexicalized Verbs in Oral Production

Oral Production		Number of Uses			
	Delexicalized Verbs	T1	T2	T3	NSs
Do (a lot of, more …) work		4	5	6	8
Do a lot of study(ing)		0	0	0	4
Work (more, harder, at home …)		7	12	12	2
Study (more, a lot …)		10	15	11	7

Table 11.15 Frequency of Use of Specific Verb Combinations in Oral Production

Oral Production		Number of Uses			
	Specificity	T1	T2	T3	NSs
Do homework		2	9	8	3
Do/have/write papers, assignments, projects, readings …		2	1	1	8

Oral production: Lack of changes

Finally, as in the written data, we also found evidence that the lexical choices of some of the learners were resistant to change at all three testing times. Compared to NS use, for instance, learners were likely to select the verbs 'work' and 'study', while the NSs combined the verb 'do' with the nouns 'work' and 'study', producing delexicalized phrasings such as 'do some work' or 'do a lot of study(ing)' (see Table 11.14).[4] NSs were also more likely to select specific vocabulary (e.g. producing collocations like 'writing papers', 'researching books', 'doing projects/research/readings', 'get the assignments done', etc., when describing their study habits). Learners' lexical choices, on the contrary, lacked specificity and remained somewhat vague across time (e.g. the collocation 'do homework' was overused after both FI and SA, as shown in Table 11.15).

Written and oral production: Summary

In summing up the contrasts and similarities between the learners and NSs in terms of NLS for each production mode, and as a function of FI or SA, we can offer a few observations. In written production, the learners gradually approached the NSs in their use of impersonal forms and gained greater generality, which is a distinctive characteristic of academic writing, after both FI and SA. For its part, the SA period was especially beneficial for the development of intensifiers, as seen through the use of adverbs modifying adjectives in alignment with NS norms. In general, however, the learners did not expand their lexical repertoire to native-like levels and continued to select more frequent and therefore less specific vocabulary. With regard to oral production, learners made more accurate word choices and relied slightly less on literal translations from their L1, especially in terms of false friends, after both FI and SA. They also showed greater idiomaticity by using more lexicalized fillers and diverse adverbs, particularly after SA. Despite these changes, the learners avoided the use of collocations with delexicalized verbs and overused more general lexical items, unlike the NSs. In the following section, we present the results of the quantitative lexical measures.

Quantitative lexical measures

In order to address RQ2 concerning the learners' approximation to native-like standards in terms of quantitative lexical measures (diversity, sophistication, density and accuracy), we conducted a series of independent samples t-tests between the learners' scores at each testing time (T1, T2 and T3) and the scores of the NSs (see the descriptive statistics in Tables 11.16 and 11.17 and the inferential analyses in Tables 11.18 and 11.19).

Table 11.16 Descriptive Statistics for Written Lexical Proficiency: Mean Scores Obtained at T1, T2 and T3 for Learners ($n = 30$) and NSs ($n = 27$)

Written Production		T1	T2	T3	NSs
Diversity	GI	7.44 (0.77)	7.11 (0.82)	7.87 (0.71)	8.01 (0.87)
Sophistication	AWL	3.47 (1.71)	3.36 (1.79)	4.05 (2.00)	4.94 (1.98)
	+2k	1.06 (0.81)	0.88 (0.85)	1.11 (1.09)	2.85 (1.78)
Density	Adj/w	6.94 (2.19)	7.69 (2.06)	6.96 (1.73)	9.04 (2.23)
	Adv/w	4.02 (1.61)	4.18 (1.70)	4.98 (1.84)	4.45 (1.55)
	N/w	17.79 (3.04)	17.17 (2.84)	16.19 (2.82)	18.80 (3.02)
	V/w	11.72 (2.13)	11.87 (1.85)	12.59 (2.04)	12.11 (1.88)
Accuracy	LexE/w	2.28 (1.50)	1.88 (0.85)	1.40 (0.98)	0.07 (0.15)
	SpE/w	0.76 (0.63)	0.87 (0.79)	0.69 (0.88)	0.34 (0.42)

Table 11.17 Descriptive Statistics for Oral Lexical Proficiency: Mean Scores Obtained at T1, T2 and T3 for Learners ($n = 30$) and NSs ($n = 25$)

Oral Production		T1	T2	T3	NSs
Diversity	GI	6.78 (0.74)	6.83 (0.62)	6.81 (0.59)	7.57 (0.85)
Sophistication	AWL	0.98 (0.65)	1.11 (0.82)	1.13 (0.70)	1.94 (1.17)
	+2k	1.25 (0.97)	1.81 (1.01)	1.28 (0.68)	2.49 (0.99)
Density	Adj/w	5.59 (1.68)	5.33 (1.89)	5.48 (1.53)	6.06 (1.98)
	Adv/w	6.24 (2.40)	6.47 (1.37)	7.84 (1.83)	8.19 (1.80)
	N/w	12.12 (2.65)	12.83 (2.08)	11.74 (1.89)	15.10 (2.00)
	V/w	10.78 (1.76)	10.36 (1.82)	10.54 (2.01)	10.03 (1.98)
Accuracy	LexE/w	1.72 (1.00)	1.30 (0.80)	0.86 (0.71)	0.06 (0.17)

Table 11.18 Independent Samples *t*-Tests Comparing the NNS Written Lexical Mean Scores to Those of the NSs at T1, T2 and T3

	T1			T2			T3		
Measure	t	df	p	t	df	P	t	df	p
GI	−2.587	55	**.012**	−4.011	55	**<.001**	−.637	55	.527
AWL	−3.013	55	**.004**	−3.159	55	**.003**	−1.684	55	.098
+2k	−4.800	35.6	**<.001**	−5.257	36.4	**<.001**	−4.502	55	**<.001**
Adj/w	−3.561	55	**.001**	−2.369	55	**.021**	−3.943	55	**<.001**
Adv/w	−1.020	55	.312	−.621	55	.537	1.160	55	.251
N/w	−2.447	55	**.014**	−2.099	55	**.040**	−3372	55	**<.001**
V/w	−.714	55	.478	−.477	55	.635	.930	55	.357
VE/w	8.047	29.7	**<.001**	11.499	31.1	**<.001**	7.371	30.6	**<.001**
SpE/w	2.911	55	**.005**	3.213	45.3	**.002**	1.961	42.6	.056

Note: Bold values indicate significance. Shaded cells refer to the learner values that converged with NS values over time.

Table 11.19 Independent Samples *t*-Tests Comparing the NNS Oral Lexical Mean Scores to Those of the NSs at T1, T2 and T3

	T1			T2			T3		
Measure	t	df	p	t	df	P	t	df	p
GI	−3.709	53	**<.001**	−3.729	53	**<.001**	−3.913	53	**<.001**
AWL	−3.664	36.1	**.001**	−3.000	41.7	**.005**	−3.026	37.8	**.004**
+2k	−4.668	53	**<.001**	−2.472	53	**.017**	−5.183	41.2	**<.001**
Adj/w	−.953	53	.345	−1.407	53	.165	−1.234	53	.223
Adv/w	−3.351	53	**.001**	−4.004	53	**<.001**	−.707	53	.483
N/w	−4.618	53	**<.001**	−4.101	53	**<.001**	−6.383	53	**<.001**
V/w	−1.503	53	.139	.645	53	.521	.954	53	.344
VE/w	8.918	31	**<.001**	8.307	32.2	**<.001**	5.961	33	**<.001**

Note: Bold values indicate significance. Shaded cells refer to the learner values that converged with NS values over time.

In written production, *t*-test results revealed that the learners converged with the baseline data on three measures representing three domains: the Guiraud's Index (GI) of lexical diversity, the academic vocabulary (AWL) of lexical sophistication and the number of spelling errors (SpE/w) as part of lexical accuracy. This NS–NNS convergence to a no longer significant level occurred at T3 (and not at T2), suggesting that the SA period was more beneficial than FI at home for these areas in particular.

In oral production, *t*-tests results revealed fewer changes in learner approximation towards native-like standards as compared to the written mode. The only growth towards NS usage was observed for adverb density (Adv/w), which approached NS values at T3 to a level that it was no longer statistically distinguishable from the NS pattern. In other words, the proportion of adverbs in learner speech was the only measure that reflected target-like behaviour after the SA experience.

Discussion

The overarching goal of this study was to evaluate the development of written and oral NLS ability in English among advanced Catalan/Spanish learners during an SA period preceded by FI in their home university. Having compiled an exhaustive account of the similarities and differences between the learner and NS groups, we were able to extract a few key observations for each production mode respectively.

In written production, we noted a slight gradual tendency from T1 to T3 whereby the learners produced increasingly more general statements by the end of the study through 'it'-cleft constructions or the use of the pronoun 'one'. Yet, NS usage of these features was far more frequent than that of the learners even at T3. Given that 'it'-cleft is considered to be an advanced construction that marks the text for a formal register (McCarthy, 1994), and that the frequency rates of 'it'-cleft in academic writing are particularly low in L2 texts (Hinkel, 2003), we were provided with further evidence that learners were writing more idiomatic and native-like texts. As for context-specific NLS, our results confirm that during the SA period the participants made progress in their writing by incorporating more idiomatic intensifiers through the use of adverbs modifying adjectives (e.g. 'really hard', 'completely different'), thereby adjusting their expressiveness to a NS pattern. Such findings confirm that naturalistic exposure to language such as through SA enables learners to sound more natural (Foster, 2009; Möhle and Raupach, 1983). Despite this improvement, however, the learners consistently relied on a rather restricted lexical repertoire and tended to overuse basic vocabulary (e.g. 'forget-lose', 'accept-follow') unlike the NSs, whose choices were more elaborate and consisted of rarer word types with numerous alternative variants (e.g. 'discard-forego', 'embrace-adjust'). This was consistent with previous research that has pointed to lexical sophistication as a key difference between L1 and L2 writing (Hinkel, 2003; Silva, 1993).

In oral production, our results show that the learners' word choices approached native-like usage gradually in terms of foregoing deceptive cognates or false friends (e.g. 'career' instead of 'degree') after both FI and SA compared to at the outset of the study. This observation corroborated Horst and Collins's (2006) finding that overreliance on cognates to compensate for lexical gaps is less prevalent with greater proficiency. The learners also showed signs of improvement in terms of collocational accuracy and relied less on L1 transfer (e.g. 'do lunch' instead of 'have lunch'), although they continued mixing up the verbs 'do' and 'make' (as in 'do friends') up until T3. Regarding context-specific NLS, we found that the learners' speech was richer in lexicalized fillers (e.g. 'I'd say' or 'I mean') and target-like adverbs (e.g. 'really', 'actually', 'basically') after SA compared to after FI, moving in the direction of NS choices. This finding fits well with the work of Regan (1995) and Möhle and Raupach (1983), in which SA was found to propel greater production of lexical fillers and enhanced L2 fluency, replacing hesitations with formulaic expressions. Using the same interview as ours, Trenchs-Parera (2009) also obtained similar results in terms of lexical fillers and reported a greater flow of L2 discourse upon her learners' return from a sojourn abroad. Notwithstanding these examples of approximation to target-like norms, the learners' productive lexical range was comparatively small and consisted largely of high-frequency general vocabulary even after SA, in line with previous literature on proficient L2 learners. Although referring to writing skills, Hinkel's (2003, p. 276) observation that 'texts written by NNSs frequently rely on a limited lexical repertoire that results in vague and less sophisticated prose relative to that of NSs' seems to hold true in this case.

The study has also considered how the learners converged towards baseline values on quantitative lexical measures (e.g. diversity, sophistication). The learners' written production showed an approximation towards target-like norms in lexical diversity (GI), academic vocabulary (AWL) and spelling accuracy (SpE/w), after the SA period but not after FI. In view of ample evidence that L2 writing often shows less lexical specificity, diversity and sophistication than L1 writing (Crossley and McNamara, 2009; Hinkel, 2003; Linnarud, 1986; Silva, 1993), the convergence with NSs indicated that spending three months overseas had resulted in an enriched and more native-like lexicon. Likewise, in oral production, the NS–NNS convergence took place after SA and predominantly affected adverb density. Our finding can also be related to a preliminary study by Trenchs-Parera (2009) as part of the SALA project, where the author examined dysfluency phenomena and reported significant growth in lexical fillers after SA, leading to lexically richer and more fluent L2 speech. It is important to note that the lexical fillers included in her study consisted of lexicalized phrases (e.g. 'it's like', 'you know', 'I don't know', 'and stuff') and single words (e.g. 'well', 'so', 'like'); the latter mainly composed of adverbs (e.g. 'well', 'so', 'like'). According to the author, lexical fillers acted as helpful crutches in oral production, as happens with formulaic speech in language, and their growth could be associated with general growth in the lexical repertoire reported in other SA studies (Milton and Meara, 1995). This observation is very likely to do justice to what we found in qualitative comparisons of NS–NNS output, in which the learners' speech exhibited an increasing number and range of adverbs after the SA experience, moving towards native-like patterns.

Conclusion

The present study investigated longitudinal changes in the NLS ability of advanced learners of English across learning contexts in both FI and SA and across both spoken and written production. Considering that SLA research underlines that the capacity to select the right words and expressions in ways preferred by native speakers is an integral component of fluent language production, our study can be seen as a useful contribution to the analysis of formulaic language in English. This has been examined in a specific learning context, SA, considered a naturalistic environment in which learners may avail themselves of ample opportunities for interacting through the TL, preceded by an FI context, in which interaction is much more limited in terms of quantity and quality. Our findings seem to suggest that it is the combination of both learning environments, FI and SA, which appears to be beneficial for learners' NLS knowledge, reminding us of the 'Combination and Complementarity of Contexts Hypothesis' (see DeKeyser, 2007; Pérez-Vidal, 2014, p. 30), where 'the different types of practice [...], in combination, make for enhanced linguistic benefits'.

Indeed, once the SA period was over, in written production, the learners achieved greater impersonality and generality, typical of academic writing. In oral production, they relied less on false friends and used lexicalized fillers and adverbs, also corroborated by statistical results, especially after SA. At the other end of the spectrum, the learners did not expand their lexical repertoire to native-like standards and continued to select less specific vocabulary and to produce some incorrect combinations (e.g. 'make friends' vs 'do friends'). However, in light of previous research (Altenberg and Granger, 2001) suggesting that EFL learners experience great difficulty even with high-frequency verbs ('make', for example), they should not be regarded in negative terms, but rather the opposite. They are instances of risk-taking and linguistic experimentation (Howarth, 1998; Vedder and Benigno, 2016), which may take greater time than a three-month stay abroad to be fully acquired.

Acknowledgements

This work was supported by the Spanish Ministry of Economy and Competitiveness (grant number FFI2013-48640-C2-1-P), the Agencia Universitària de Recerca (AGAUR) in Catalonia (grant number 2014 SGR 1563) and a three-year doctoral scholarship (grant number FI-DGR 2013). The authors are also very much indebted to all the members of the SALA team and the informants who over the years have participated in the SALA project, making this research possible.

Notes

1. Participants were officially required to have an upper-intermediate level in English (B2 in the Common European Framework of Reference, CEFR) upon university entrance.
2. Other verbs such as 'immigrate', 'emigrate', 'live', 'study', 'stay' collocating with 'to/in another/a new country' were also found in the data and, therefore, are included in the list.
3. 'Other adverbs' refer to the adverbs that were used only once in each group. They were mostly low-frequency adverbs ('deeply', 'slowly', 'individually', 'firstly', 'academically', 'hopefully', 'barely', etc.).
4. Delexicalized phrasings refer to the semantically depleted word: for example, saying 'have something to eat/drink' or 'have a swim' instead of the single forms 'eat/drink' or 'swim' (as in Foster, 2009, p. 101).
5. Here the name of the university, which was specified in the original interview question, has been substituted with 'this university'.

References

Adolphs, S., and Durow, V. (2004), 'Social-cultural Integration and the Development of Formulaic Sequences', in N. Schmitt (ed.), *Formulaic Sequences*, 107–26, Amsterdam: John Benjamins.

Altenberg, B., and Granger, S. (2001), 'The Grammatical and Lexical Patterning of MAKE in Native and Non-native Student Writing', *Applied Linguistics*, 22 (2), 173–95.

Boers, F., and Lindstromberg, S. (2009), *Optimizing a Lexical Approach to Instructed Second Language Acquisition*, Basingstoke: Palgrave Macmillan.

Cook, V. (1999), 'Going beyond the Native Speaker in Language Teaching', *TESOL Quarterly*, 33 (2), 185–210.

Crossley, S. A., and McNamara, D. S. (2009), 'Computational Assessment of Lexical Differences in L1 and L2 Writing', *Journal of Second Language Writing*, 18, 119–35.

DeKeyser, R. (2007), 'Study Abroad as Foreign Language Practice', in R. DeKeyser (ed.), *Practice in a Second Language: Perspectives from Applied Linguistics and Cognitive Psychology*, 208–26, Cambridge: Cambridge University Press.

Dörnyei, Z., Durow, V., and Zahran, K. (2004), 'Individual Differences and Their Effect on Formulaic Sequence Acquisition', in N. Schmitt (ed.), *Formulaic Sequences*, 87–106, Amsterdam: John Benjamins.

Ellis, N. (2017), 'Cognition, Corpora and Computing: Triangulating Research in Usage-based Language Learning', *Language Learning*, 67 (1), 40–65.

Ellis, N., and Wulff. (2014), 'Usage-based Approaches to SLA', in B. Van Patten and J. Williams (eds.), *Theories in Second Language Acquisition: An Introduction* (2nd ed.), 75–93, New York: Routledge.

Erman, B., and Warren, B. (2000), 'The Idiom Principle and the Open Choice Principle', *Text*, 20 (1), 29–62.

Eyckmans, J., Boers, F., and Stengers, H. (2007), 'Identifying Chunks: Who Can See the Wood for the Trees?', *Language Forum*, 33, 85–100.

Forsberg, F. (2010), 'Using Conventional Sequences in L2 French', *International Review of Applied Linguistics*, 48, 25–51.

Foster, P. (2001), 'Rules and Routines: A Consideration of Their Role in the Task-based Language Production of Native and Non-native speakers', in M. Bygate, P. Skehan, and M. Swain (eds.), *Researching Pedagogic Tasks: Second Language Learning, Teaching, and Testing*, 75–94, Harlow: Longman.

Foster, P. (2009), 'Lexical Diversity and Native-like Selection: The Bonus of Studying Abroad', in B. Richards, H. Daller, D. Malvern, P. M. Meara, J. Milton, and J. Treffers-Daller (eds.), *Vocabulary Studies in First and Second Language Acquisition*, 91–106, Hampshire: Palgrave Macmillan.

Foster, P., and Skehan, P. (1996), 'The Influence of Planning on Performance in Task-based Learning', *Studies in Second Language Acquisition*, 18 (3), 299–324.

Foster, P., Bolibaugh, C., and Kotula, A. (2014), 'Knowledge of Nativelike Selections in a L2: The Influence of Exposure, Memory, Age of Onset, and Motivation in Foreign Language and Immersion Settings', *Studies in Second Language Acquisition*, 36 (1), 101–32.

Granger, S. (1998), *Learner English on Computer*, London: Longman.

Hill, J. (2000), 'Revising Priorities: From Grammatical Failure to Collocational Success', in M. Lewis (ed.), *Teaching Collocation: Further Developments in the Lexical Approach*, 88–117, Hove: LTP.

Hinkel, E. (2003), 'Simplicity without Elegance: Features of Sentences in L1 and L2 Academic Texts', *TESOL Quarterly*, 37 (2), 275–302.

Horst, M., and Collins, L. (2006), 'From *Faible* to Strong: How Does Their Vocabulary Grow?', *The Canadian Modern Language Review*, 63 (1), 83–106.

Howarth, P. (1998), 'The Phraseology of Learners' Academic Writing', in A. P. Cowie (ed.), *Phraseology: Theory, Analysis, and Applications*, 161–86, Oxford: Oxford University Press.

Laufer, B. (1998), 'The Development of Passive and Active Vocabulary in a Second Language: Same or Different?', *Applied Linguistics*, 19 (2), 255–71.

Linnarud, M. (1986), *Lexis in Composition: A Performance Analysis of Swedish Learners' Written English*, Lund, Sweden: Gleerup.

MacWhinney, B. (2000), *The CHILDES Project: Tools for Analyzing Talk* (3rd ed.), Mahwah: Lawrence Erlbaum Associates.

Marriot, H. (1995), 'Acquisition of Politeness Patterns by Exchange Students in Japan', in B. F. Freed (ed.), *Second Language Acquisition in a Study Abroad Context*, 197–224, Amsterdam: John Benjamins.

McCarthy, M. (1994), 'It, This, and That', in M. Coulthard (ed.), *Advances in Written Text Analysis*, 266–75, New York: Routledge.

Milton, J., and Meara, P. M. (1995), 'How Periods Abroad Affect Vocabulary Growth in a Foreign Language', *ITL Review of Applied Linguistics*, 107/108, 17–34.

Möhle, D., and Raupach, M. (1983), *Planen in der Fremdsprache: Analyse von Lernersprache Französisch*, Bern: Peter Lang.

Mora, J. C., and Valls-Ferrer, M. (2012), 'Oral Fluency, Accuracy, and Complexity in Formal Instruction and Study Abroad Learning Contexts', *TESOL Quarterly*, 46 (4), 610–41.

Nesselhauf, N. (2005), *Collocations in a Learner Corpus*, Amsterdam: Benjamins.

Ortega, L. (2014), 'Ways Forward for a Bi/multilingual Turn in SLA', in S. May (ed.), *The Multilingual Turn: Implications for SLA, TESOL and Bilingual Education*, 32–53, Oxford: Routledge.

Pawley, A., and Syder, F. H. (1983), 'Two Puzzles for Linguistic Theory: Nativelike Selection and Nativelike Fluency', in J. C. Richards, and R. W. Schmidt (eds.), *Language and Communication*, 191–225, London: Longman.

Pérez-Vidal, C. (2014), 'Study Abroad and Formal Instruction Contrasted: The SALA Project', in C. Pérez-Vidal (ed.), *Language Acquisition in Study Abroad and Formal Instruction Contexts*, 17–59, Amsterdam/Philadelphia: John Benjamins.

Regan, V. (1995), 'The Acquisition of Sociolinguistic Native Speaker Norms: Effects of a Year Abroad on Second Language Learners of French', in B. F. Freed (ed.), *Second Language Acquisition in a Study Abroad Context*, 245–68, Amsterdam: John Benjamins.

Regan, V. (1998), 'Sociolinguistics and Language Learning in a Study Abroad Context', *Frontiers*, 4, 61–90.

Sasaki, M. (2009), 'Changes in English as a Foreign Language Students' Writing over 3.5 Years: A Socio-cognitive Account', in R. Manchón (ed.), *Writing in Foreign Language Contexts: Learning, Teaching and Research*, 49–76, Clevedon: Multilingual Matters.

Schmitt, N. (2010), *Researching Vocabulary: A Vocabulary Research Manual*, Basingstoke: Palgrave Macmillan.

Siegal, M. (1995), 'Individual Differences and Study Abroad: Women Learning Japanese in Japan', in B. F. Freed (ed.), *Second Language Acquisition in a Study Abroad Context*, 225–44, Amsterdam: John Benjamins.

Silva, T. (1993), 'Toward an Understanding of the Distinct Nature of L2 Writing: The ESL Research and Its Implications', *TESOL Quarterly*, 27 (4), 657–77.

Siyanova, A., and Schmitt, N. (2008), 'L2 Learner Production and Processing of Collocation: A Multi-study Perspective', *The Canadian Modern Language Review*, 64 (3), 429–58.

Skehan, P., and Foster, P. (1997), 'Task Type and Task Processing Conditions as Influences on Foreign Language Performance', *Language Teaching Research*, 1 (3), 185–211.

Towell, R., Hawkins, R., and Bazergui, N. (1996), 'The Development of Fluency in Advanced Learners of French', *Applied Linguistics*, 17, 84–119.

Trenchs-Parera, M. (2009), 'Effects of Formal Instruction and a Stay Abroad on the Acquisition of Native-like Oral Fluency', *The Canadian Modern Language Review*, 65 (3), 365–93.

Vedder, I., and Benigno, V. (2016), 'Lexical Richness and Collocational Competence in Second-language Writing', *International Review of Applied Linguistics*, 54 (1), 23–42.

Wray, A. (2002), *Formulaic Language and the Lexicon*, Cambridge: Cambridge University Press.

Yorio, C. A. (1980), 'Conventionalized Language Forms and the Development of Communicative Competence', *TESOL Quarterly*, 14 (4), 433–42.

Zaytseva, V. (2016), 'Vocabulary Acquisition in Study Abroad and Formal Instruction: An Investigation on Oral and Written Lexical Development', PhD dissertation, Universitat Pompeu Fabra, Barcelona.

Zaytseva, V., Miralpeix, I., and Pérez-Vidal, C. (2019), 'ESL Written Development at Home and Abroad: Taking a Closer Look at Vocabulary', *International Journal of Bilingual Education and Bilingualism*. online.

Appendix. Oral interview questions

Student A asks student B:

1. Why did you choose [this university][5] as the university where you wanted to study?
2. How do you like your classes so far and why?
3. Which classes do you enjoy the most and why?
4. Has it been easy to make friends here?
5. Tell us about either a very good experience or a very bad experience that you have had at the university.
6. How similar and how different is your university life from what you expected it to be like?
7. How similar and how different are your study habits now from what they were like in high school?

Student B asks student A:

1. Have you made any good friends at the university yet? If yes, what are they like? If no, why do you think you haven't?
2. How different is your university life from your high school life?
3. How do you like the library? How often do you go there? What resources do you usually use?
4. What advantages and disadvantages do you see in the location of [this university] building?
5. What do you normally do for lunch during school days?
6. What do your friends and family think of your future profession as a translator and interpreter?
7. What do you think of the requirement at [this university] of having to study abroad?

12

The role of transparency in grammatical gender marking among stay abroad learners of Spanish and French

Amanda Edmonds and Aarnes Gudmestad
Université Paul-Valéry Montpellier 3/Virginia Polytechnic Institute and State University

Introduction

Within the field of second language acquisition (SLA), much research has been dedicated to documenting linguistic gains in an additional language (AL) after a period spent in a target language (TL) community. This research makes clear that linguistic gains do not always follow from a stay abroad (Llanes, 2011) and that when gains are observed, they may be unevenly distributed across skills (DeKeyser, 2007; Kinginger, 2009). Whereas numerous studies have documented gains in general speaking skills and in fluency, it has been suggested that grammatical competence does not always show clear benefits from a stay abroad. This finding may be the result of the learning context, with some scholars suggesting that the stay abroad context may focus learners' attention more strongly on, for example, pragmatic competence, while relegating grammatical accuracy to a secondary role (e.g. Charkova and Halliday, 2011). However, the lack of conclusive evidence of grammatical gains may also simply reflect the fact that grammatical competence covers a wide variety of structures. Although subsumed under the label 'grammar', structures differ with respect to many factors, including their frequency, salience and transparency. These factors may favour or hinder learning in different contexts and may help explain the variety of findings regarding the development of grammatical competence in connection with a stay abroad (see Howard and Schwieter, 2018, for a recent review).

As pointed out by DeKeyser (2014), research on linguistic gains in stay abroad research has tended to focus on either the general (e.g. grammatical correctness on the whole) or the specific (e.g. expression of past tense) and has provided detailed descriptions of how learners' language systems change over the course of a stay abroad. Such descriptions are valuable, although DeKeyser suggests that the stay abroad context may also serve as an excellent testing ground for certain psycholinguistic processes (involved in skill development). In his view, for such tests to be relevant, the researcher needs to identify 'variables that distinguish different learning problems while still maintaining a certain level of generalizability' (p. 320). In the current study, we aim to investigate one potential learnability issue, namely how formal transparency of a grammatical structure may impact its development in a stay abroad context. To do so, we focus on grammatical gender-marking behaviour in AL Spanish and French. The gender-marking systems in these two related languages share many characteristics, although it is widely accepted that the Spanish system is the more transparent one (see, e.g., Monner et al., 2013). Following authors such as Eichler, Jansen and Müller (2013), Kupisch, Müller and Cantone (2002), Monner et al. (2013) and Halberstadt, Valdés Kroff and Dussias (2018), we use the term 'transparency' to refer to the reliability of gender cues, both on nouns and on modifiers. Under this definition, transparency is the property of a language system, and systems with more reliable and systematic mappings between forms and grammatical categories are considered more transparent than systems with less reliable mappings. Given that the stay abroad is generally expected to involve increased contact with the TL, we may expect that learners of a more transparent gender-marking system like AL Spanish make greater gains because the input they come in contact with should provide reliable cues as to gender marking. However, it may also be the case that a more transparent system is already learnable from classroom input and that it is learners of less transparent gender-marking systems, such as AL French, that show the most benefit from a stay abroad. We thus aim to compare how university learners in the UK specializing in Spanish or French express gender marking in written argumentative essays and how their gender-marking behaviour may evolve over a period of twenty-one months, including a nine-month period spent in a TL environment.

Previous research

We begin by reviewing research conducted on the development of grammatical competence during a stay abroad. We then present the grammatical gender systems of Spanish and French, highlighting how the two systems differ in terms of transparency. We end with a brief overview of AL research that has examined the acquisition of grammatical gender in Spanish and French.

Development of grammatical competence during a stay abroad

As observed by Llanes (2011, p. 193), previous research on the development of grammatical competence during a stay abroad 'presents conflicting results'. This inconsistency may be, at least in part, due to the fact that the operationalization of grammatical competence has differed from study to study, with some researchers adopting global measures and others restricting their focus to a single morphosyntactic phenomenon. Among those having used global measures is Collentine (2004). In this study, he compared American university students studying Spanish in an at-home and in a stay abroad context by analysing their grammatical accuracy in oral proficiency interviews conducted at the beginning and end of one semester. He coded seventeen different measures, including grammatical gender, and found a significant advantage for stay abroad learners only with respect to the expression of tense. As concerns gender, mean differences between pre-test and post-test scores were low for both the at-home and stay abroad learners. The development of grammatical competence was also investigated using a global definition in Freed, So and Lazar (2003) for AL French and in Pérez-Vidal and Juan-Garau (2009) and Llanes, Tragant and Serrano (2012) for AL English. In each of these three studies the focus was on written production, and no significant evidence of improvement in grammatical accuracy was documented over the course of a stay abroad.

Stay abroad research having focused on one or a small number of components of grammatical competence is exemplified by Howard's work on the acquisition of the temporal-aspectual system in AL French by Irish university learners, some of whom had spent an academic year abroad. In an investigation of past-tense marking, Howard (2001) found that a stay abroad had a significantly positive impact on learners' ability to mark perfectivity and imperfectivity in the past. In Howard (2012a), the focus was on development in the expression of future, conditional and subjunctive verb forms. The frequency and distribution of such forms taken from sociolinguistic interviews were examined, revealing an increase in use on the part of stay abroad learners (as compared to at-home learners) only with respect to the past conditional and the periphrastic future. Godfrey, Treacy and Tarone (2014) examined how the writing of four stay abroad learners and four domestic learners of AL French changed over the course of a semester. To investigate accuracy, the authors focused on grammatical gender marking and found that the four stay abroad learners made almost four times more errors at the beginning of the semester than at the end, whereas the domestic students only showed a slight decrease in non-targetlike use over the course of the study.

Taken together, previous research does not show a consistent advantage for the stay abroad context in terms of development of grammatical accuracy, whether global or specific measures are used, although much individual variation is apparent (see Howard, 2012b). DeKeyser (2007) suggests that this variability in outcomes may be due to a host of different factors, including the length of stay abroad, the students' proficiency pre-departure and the fact that learners are engaged in different amounts (and types) of language practice while abroad. In the current study, our aim is to contribute to this set of research by examining how students specializing in either Spanish or French evolve in the expression of gender marking in written production over the course of an academic year spent in a TL community.

Grammatical gender in Spanish and French

Spanish and French are both Romance languages, and their grammatical gender systems share several characteristics. All nouns in both languages are either masculine or feminine, and in both Spanish (Plann, 1979, p. 126) and in French (Surridge and Lessard, 1984, p. 46), masculine nouns occur more often. In both languages, a subset of nouns has semantic (or biological) gender, such that *girl* is feminine in both Spanish (*chica*) and French (*fille*), whereas *boy* is masculine (Spanish: *chico*; French: *garçon*). However, most nouns show grammatical gender, and their meaning does not predict their gender. In addition, in both languages, nominal modifiers such as determiners and adjectives are required to show gender agreement with the noun that they modify, as illustrated in (1):

(1) a. Spanish: *la*$_{fem}$ *casa*$_{fem}$ *nueva*$_{fem}$; French: *la*$_{fem}$ *maison*$_{fem}$ *neuve*$_{fem}$
'the new house'
  b. Spanish: *un*$_{masc}$ *apartamento*$_{masc}$ *nuevo*$_{masc}$; French: *un*$_{masc}$ *appartement*$_{masc}$ *neuf*$_{masc}$
'a new apartment'

There are, however, differences between the two systems. For example, it has been suggested that gender marking in Spanish is more transparent than gender marking in French (Eichler, Jansen and Müller, 2013; Kupisch, Müller and Cantone, 2002; Monner et al., 2013; Nelson, 2005). In the research on grammatical gender marking, the notion of transparency has generally been used to describe the availability of gender-assignment cues, meaning that systems are considered to be transparent if the gender of a noun is strongly predictable from the shape of the noun: 'Transparently-marked nouns exhibit a high correspondence between their noun endings and their grammatical gender category' (Halberstadt, Valdés Kroff and Dussias, 2018, pp. 8–9). In the case of Spanish and French, these phonemic cues are noun endings that are associated with one of the two genders. Although such endings are available in both languages, the correspondence between noun ending and gender is more straightforward in Spanish (Monner et al., 2013). Indeed, according to Teschner and Russell (1984), the majority of Spanish nouns ends in one of six phonemes – [a], [d], [o], [e], [l] and [r] – each of which is strongly predictive of one of the two genders. Whereas at least 90 per cent of all Spanish nouns ending in [a] and [d] are feminine, 89 per cent of nouns ending in [o], [e], [l] and [r] are masculine. Of these endings, final -a (for feminine) and final -o (for masculine) are considered canonical (see examples in (1)), although there are 'deceptive' nouns with a final -o or a final -a whose gender is the opposite of what one would expect (e.g. *moto*$_{fem}$ 'motorcycle' and *día*$_{masc}$ 'day'). In French, certain phonological and orthographic endings are also strongly associated with one of the two genders (Lyster, 2006; Tucker, Lambert and Rigault, 1977), but French has no equivalent to the canonical endings in Spanish. Moreover, the diversity of endings is greater in French than in Spanish (Eichler, Jansen and Müller, 2013, pp. 555–6), and a lower percentage of total nouns is considered to have a predictive ending.

In addition, the two systems differ with respect to the marking of gender on determiners and adjectives, and we suggest that this difference also contributes to making the gender cues in Spanish more transparent than in French. In both systems, certain determiners and adjectives are invariable, meaning that the same form is used with both feminine and masculine nouns. In these cases, we can also talk about non-overt gender, as the invariable modifier shows no outward sign of gender marking. Whereas in Spanish, certain adjectives (e.g. *difícil* 'difficult') and possessive determiners (*mi* 'my', *tu* 'your', *su* 'his/her' or 'your') are invariable, the list of invariable modifiers is much longer in French and includes most plural determiners (e.g. *les* 'the', *des* 'some'), certain possessive determiners (e.g. *leur* 'their', *notre* 'our', *votre* 'your') and the majority of adjectives (see Boloh and Ibernon, 2010, p. 7: *sympa* 'nice', *propre* 'clean'). Furthermore, with French vowel-initial nouns, an even greater proportion of modifiers does not show overt gender marking, due to phenomena such as elision of the vowel of the definite article (*l'examen*$_{masc}$ 'the exam', *l'étude*$_{fem}$ 'the study'). Ayoun (2010, p. 132) examined a corpus of written French press and found that only 50.24 per cent of 5,016 determiner phrases were accompanied by at least one modifier on which gender was overtly marked. For written Spanish, we know of no previous research having addressed this question, but given the differences in the two gender-marking systems, we anticipate that a greater percentage of determiner phrases would include at least one variable modifier.[1]

We have suggested that the Spanish gender-marking system provides more reliable cues to gender assignment and that differences in the realization of gender marking on modifiers in the two languages mean that there should be a greater number of instances of overt gender marking in Spanish than in French. These two features lead us to consider the Spanish system to be more transparent than the French one. We expect the greater transparency of gender marking in Spanish to reduce the learnability issue of acquiring this system, a position which is consistent with current usage-based informed approaches to studying language acquisition. Indeed, Ellis, Römer and O'Donnell (2016) have convincingly demonstrated that language learners and native speakers alike are sensitive to characteristics of the input, including the reliability of cues to form-meaning mapping, the frequency of constructions and saliency.

SLA findings on grammatical gender in Spanish and French

The acquisition of grammatical gender in an AL has been the subject of extensive research in the field of SLA using diverse methodological approaches (e.g. error analysis, online processing measures, event-related potentials). In our review, we concentrate on those studies having examined how learners of Spanish or French mark gender when they express themselves in their AL, be it in writing or in speaking. Findings from these studies reveal three tendencies that are common to examinations of both Spanish and French, as well as several findings that are language-specific.

The first common finding concerns the importance of noun gender. It has generally been found that learners of Spanish and French tend to be more targetlike with masculine nouns, which means that most instances of non-targetlike use stem from the masculine forms of determiners and adjectives being used with feminine nouns (for Spanish, see Finnemann, 1992; Gudmestad, Edmonds, and Metzger, 2019; Schlig, 2003; White et al., 2004; for French, see Bartning, 2000; Dewaele and Véronique, 2001; Edmonds and Gudmestad, 2018; Harley, 1979). Furthermore, in both Spanish (Alarcón, 2010; White et al., 2004) and French (Holmes and Dejean de la Bâtie, 1999), researchers have suggested that the masculine form of modifiers may be treated as the default by learners. The second finding common to the two languages concerns the fact that learners tend to be more targetlike on determiners than they are on adjectives (Spanish: Alarcón, 2010; Bruhn de Garavito and White, 2002; Fernández García, 1999; Gudmestad et al., 2019; White et al., 2004; French: Ayoun, 2007; Bartning, 2000;

Dewaele and Véronique, 2001; Granfeldt, 2005; Harley, 1979). Finally, Finnemann (1992) and Gudmestad, Edmonds and Metzger (2019) for Spanish and Edmonds and Gudmestad (2018) and Holmes and Dejean de la Bâtie (1999) for French have suggested that targetlike use of gender marking may depend on the distance between the noun and its modifiers, with greater distance leading to greater processing difficulty or memory demands.

In addition to these shared trends, we note several language-specific observations. Starting with Spanish, researchers have found that learners are sensitive to noun endings when speaking in Spanish, meaning that targetlike use appears to be in part determined by the ending of the noun (Alarcón, 2011; Fernández García, 1999; Gudmestad, Edmonds and Metzger, 2019; Isabelli-García, 2010).[2] There is also evidence from the literature on AL Spanish that learners are more targetlike when marking gender on nouns with semantic (or biological) gender than on those with grammatical gender (e.g. Alarcón, 2010) and that learners of Spanish are more targetlike in marking gender with singular versus plural nouns (Finnemann, 1992). In research on the acquisition of French, Dewaele (2015) found that learners at certain proficiency levels were more targetlike in marking gender with consonant-initial (vs vowel-initial) nouns.

Thus, the research on the acquisition of AL Spanish and French has found that the factors of noun gender, modifier type and distance may influence how learners of these two languages mark gender when they speak or write in similar manners. In addition, patterns specific to both Spanish and French have been uncovered and concern how noun endings, noun class (grammatical vs semantic gender), noun number and the initial phoneme of the noun may influence gender marking. This brings us to our own project, in which we investigate how these different factors may influence learners' gender-marking behaviour in their written production. We have chosen to investigate development for AL Spanish and AL French during a stay abroad experience in a single investigation to gain insight into the potential impact of the transparency of grammatical gender cues on the expression of gender in a written task. We expect greater transparency of the grammatical gender-marking system to lead to greater targetlike behaviour. The role of the stay abroad experience, however, remains an open question. Indeed, the stay abroad, with the potential to offer both more – and more varied – input than the classroom setting may prove to be particularly beneficial for the acquisition of a transparent system (given clear, reliable cues to grammatical gender categories in the input). It may also be the case that the stay abroad is less impactful in the learning of a transparent system and that the input and interactions involved in a stay abroad show a greater influence in the learning of a less transparent system.

The current study

In the present study, we contribute to research on the development of grammatical competence during a stay abroad with an investigation of the development of gender-marking behaviour. By focusing on two language systems that differ with respect to the transparency of gender marking – AL Spanish (the more transparent system) and AL French (the less transparent one) – we aim to build on observations of a single, morphosyntactic phenomenon by addressing the more general role played by transparency in the development of grammatical competence in connection with a stay abroad. The research question that guided this study was: In what ways do specialists in Spanish or French at a UK university show similar and language-specific patterns of gender marking in written production before, during and after a stay abroad?

The corpus

The dataset is drawn from the LANGSNAP corpus, which contains data for twenty-seven learners of Spanish and twenty-nine learners of French, all of whom were enrolled in their second year of university study as language majors in the UK at the outset of the project (see Mitchell, Tracy-Ventura and McManus, 2017).[3] For the purposes of the current analysis, data from the first twenty learners of Spanish and French have been analysed. Details concerning this subset of the corpus, including a measure of global AL proficiency at the outset of the project (elicited imitation score),[4] are presented in Table 12.1. Looking at the full set of background information, it is clear that the two groups show differences in, for example, the proportion of women versus men (75 per cent of the Spanish sample is made up of women, 90 per cent in the French sample) and the time spent studying the language in question (5.3 years on average for Spanish versus 10.45 years on average for French). Moreover, the number of students engaged in each of the three placement types while abroad differed somewhat between the two groups: exchange students (nine in the Spanish group, five in the French group), teaching assistants (nine among the Spanish learners, twelve for the French) and

Table 12.1 Background Information on Participants

Characteristics	Spanish	French
Age	$M = 20.8$, $SD = 1.16$ (range: 20–25)	$M = 20$, $SD = 0.38$ (range: 19–21)
Sex	15 women, 5 men	18 women, 2 men
Years spent studying	$M = 5.3$, $SD = 3$ (range: 2–14)	$M = 10.45$, $SD = 2.3$ (range: 6–20)
Elicited imitation score	$M = 85.3$, $SD = 9.7$ (range: 59–108 points)	$M = 59.25$, $SD = 14.6$ (range: 36–97 points)
Type of placement	Exchange student: $n = 9$ Teaching assistant: $n = 9$ Workplace intern: $n = 2$	Exchange student: $n = 5$ Teaching assistant: $n = 12$ Workplace intern: $n = 3$
Country of placement	Spain = 15 Mexico = 5	France = 20
Other languages studied at university	French = 12 German = 3 English = 2 Italian = 1	Spanish = 3 German = 3 Chinese = 1 Italian = 1

workplace interns (two students specializing in Spanish and three in French). However, the two groups are matched in their academic profiles: all learners have completed their second year at the same university as a language major and were preparing to go abroad for the obligatory year-abroad experience at the outset of the project.

Data were collected from the participants on six occasions, spanning twenty-one months: at the end of their second year of university studies (before the departure for their stay abroad), three times in the following year during their year abroad and twice after their return to the UK. On each of these six occasions, participants completed two oral tasks (an interview and a picture-narration task) and wrote an argumentative essay of approximately 200 words. In the current study, we examine the argumentative essays written at three data-collection points: before the learners went abroad (pre-stay), one year later after the learners had spent approximately nine months in their stay abroad community (in-stay) and at the final data-collection period, twenty-one months after the beginning of the project and approximately eight months after learners' return to the UK (post-stay). The same prompt was used for the pre-stay and the in-stay essays: Do you believe homosexual couples have the right to get married and adopt children? At post-stay, the prompt asked participants to write about whether they thought that in order to encourage people to eat in a healthy manner, sugary beverages and fatty foods should be taxed.

Data coding

Every instance of a determiner (e.g. definite and indefinite article, possessive, demonstrative, interrogative, indefinite determiner) or adjective modifying a referent was identified, for a total of 3,008 tokens in Spanish and 3,059 in French. For the analysis of grammatical gender marking, we removed all instances of invariable modifiers from the dataset, leaving us with 2,323 analysable tokens in Spanish and 1,601 in French.[5] Examples from the Spanish dataset are provided in (2a, b) and for French in (2c, d):

(2) a. *el tema de la adopción es más polémico* (Participant 169, in-stay)
   'the$_{masc}$ theme$_{masc}$ of the$_{fem}$ adoption$_{fem}$ is more controversial$_{masc}$'
   b. *comprar la comida más saludable porque es menos caro* (Participant 151, post-stay)
   'to buy the$_{fem}$ food$_{fem}$ more healthy$_{masc/fem}$ because it's less expensive$_{masc}$'
   c. *vivre ma vie* (Participant 120, post-stay)
   'to live my$_{fem}$ life$_{fem}$'
   d. *ce serait un bonne idée* (Participant 116, post-stay)
   'it would be a$_{masc}$ good$_{fem}$ idea$_{fem}$'

Each token was coded for the dependent variable (targetlikeness of gender marking), as well as for participant (included in our analyses as a random effect). Additionally, tokens were coded for independent variables that we analysed as fixed effects and that were taken from the literature on gender marking (see Table 12.2 for a full list). Seven variables were coded for in both the Spanish and the French data. These include the time at which the token was written, the gender of the noun, the type of modifier (adjective or determiner), the distance (in syllables) between the noun and the modifier, noun number (singular or plural), noun class (semantic vs grammatical gender) and finally the frequency of the noun. It is only this final factor that was not mentioned in the review of previous research, as it has not received much attention in production studies (cf. Gudmestad et al., 2019). However, Surridge and Lessard (1984) found that learners of French were more targetlike in assigning gender to more frequent nouns in an experimental task. For this reason, we include in our own analysis the variable of noun frequency. Frequency per one million words for each noun is taken from either the *Corpus del español* (Davies, 2016) or the book portion of the Lexique 3.8 database (New et al., 2007).

In addition to these seven factors, we included five language-specific variables. In Spanish, the factor noun ending coded four categories: (a) masculine nouns ending in -o and feminine ones ending in -a were coded as having a 'canonical -o/-a' ending, (b) 'deceptive -o/-a' nouns were those whose -o or -a ending did not match the canonical gender, (c) 'predictive' refers to any other nominal ending strongly associated with a gender, following Teschner and Russell (1984), and (d) all remaining nouns fell into the 'other' category. Noun ending was also coded for in French, but as there is less consensus in the literature as to how to operationalize this variable, we created three variables: (a) phonological ending was coded through 'noun-final phoneme', as research has suggested that masculine nouns tend to end in vowels, whereas feminine ones end in consonants (see Tucker, Lambert and Rigault, 1977); (b) orthographic ending was coded with the variable 'noun-final orthographic rhyme', for which we

Table 12.2 Independent Variables

Language	Variable	Categories or Description
Spanish/French	Time	Pre-stay, in-stay, post-stay
	Noun gender	Feminine, masculine
	Modifier type	Adjective, determiner
	Syllable distance	# of syllables between the noun and modifier (continuous)
	Noun number	Singular, plural
	Noun class	Grammatical, semantic
	Noun log-frequency (language)	Log of the # of occurrence per 1 million words of a noun (continuous)
Spanish	Noun ending	Canonical -o/-a, deceptive -o/-a, predictive endings (e.g. -tad/-dad), other
French	Noun-final phoneme	Consonant, vowel
	Noun-final orthographic rhyme	Not predictive, predictive
	Noun derivational morphology	Absent, present
	Noun-initial phoneme	Consonant, vowel

Note: We analysed the log of noun frequency in order to account for the skew in the distribution of frequency scores.

used Lyster's (2006) identification of noun endings that are predictive of one gender in at least 89 per cent of cases in order to code nouns as either predictive or not predictive; and (c) following Surridge (1989), the presence or absence of derivational morphology was coded for. Finally, given evidence that the initial phoneme of the noun may impact gender-marking behaviour in French, each French token was coded for whether its initial phoneme was a consonant or a vowel (Dewaele, 2015).

Data analysis

The data analysis proceeded in two steps. First, the rates of targetlike gender marking in pre-stay, in-stay and post-stay essays were calculated. These rates are presented using boxplots with an overlay showing the data points for each individual, thus allowing us to observe group and individual trends. Second, mixed-effects regressions including participant as a random effect were conducted using the statistical package R. This was done in order to identify the factors that simultaneously influence how each group of learners marks gender, how these factors may change across time and how the models may look similar or different in the two languages. Factors that were not significant were removed, and models were rerun. After having obtained models with only significant main effects, we then tested for strong interactions (i.e. interactions between two significant main effects). Finally, we calculated the Bayesian Information Criterion (BIC) for each model in order to determine whether it provided a good fit for the dataset. The presentation of the results in the following section will be divided into two parts: results for Spanish and results for French. Each part will begin with a presentation of the targetlike rates of use and will be followed by the mixed-effects regression model. Details concerning the random effect of participant are provided in the Appendix.

Results for Spanish

The evolution in the group average and individual rates of targetlike use over time for Spanish is presented in Figure 12.1. In this figure, each dot represents the mean rate of targetlike use for one individual at a given point in time. The group average is represented with a diamond to the right of centre of each boxplot; standard deviations are given with the arrows above and below the diamond. It is clear that the twenty learners are overall highly targetlike in marking gender in their essays before going abroad: the group average is 95.93 per cent targetlike gender marking, with only one participant showing a score below 90 per cent (Participant 157 is targetlike in 76.92 per cent of contexts). Seven individuals are fully targetlike in these first essays. One year later, the group average has increased slightly to 97.16 per cent, and the standard deviation has decreased; at this point, all participants are 90 per cent targetlike or greater, with half of the twenty learners achieving 100 per cent targetlike use. The average group rate of targetlike use at post-stay is similar to that found for in-stay: 97.12 per cent. The range of scores obtained by the group has not changed since in-stay, although the group median (shown with the bold horizontal line) has decreased.

Of the eight fixed effects explored, two were found to be non-significant and were, thus, removed from the model: noun class and noun log-frequency (language). The final mixed-effects regression analysis of the Spanish data identified six significant fixed effects and no strong interactions (Table 12.3). For both the dependent variable and the categorical fixed effects, one category was identified as the reference point, and the other categories were compared against this reference point. The reference point for the dependent variable was targetlike use, whereas the reference points for the independent variables are given in Table 12.3. Note that syllable distance has no reference point, as it is a continuous factor. Table 12.3 also provides the parameter estimates for each significant effect. A positive parameter estimate indicates that there was an increase in the log odds of targetlike use compared to the reference point. For example, the factor of noun gender has a significant positive parameter estimate, indicating that the log odds of marking gender in a targetlike manner are higher with masculine nouns than they are with the reference point (feminine nouns). This group of learners also had significantly greater odds of being targetlike in gender marking at post-stay (vs pre-stay), on singular (vs on plural) nouns and on determiners (as opposed to on adjectives).

Two significant factors show negative parameter estimates: syllable distance and noun ending. For the continuous factor of syllable distance, this finding indicates that as more syllables intervene between the modifier and the noun, the log odds of targetlike use decrease. As for noun ending, only one of the three comparisons was found to be significant: these learners were significantly less likely to mark gender in a targetlike manner with deceptive -o/-a nouns compared to canonical -o/-a nouns. The comparisons between canonical -o/-a nouns and both predictive and other nouns were not significant. We assessed the fit of the overall model with the BIC. For this measure, the final model (Table 12.3) is compared to the null model using their log-likelihood. The model with a lower value is considered a better fit, with a difference of at least ten points taken to indicate strong evidence in favour of the model with the lower value. The BIC for our final model was clearly lower (619.3) than the value obtained for the null model (642.84).

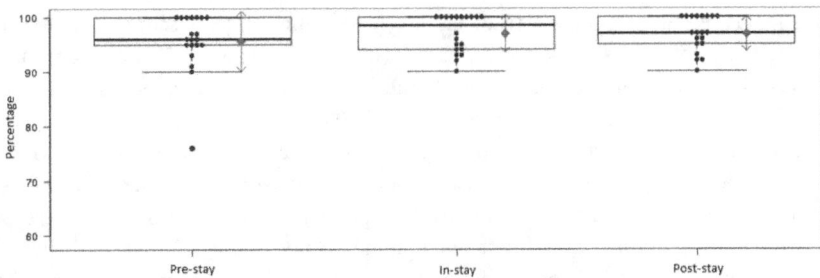

Figure 12.1 Targetlike Rates of Use for Individuals and the Group (Spanish Dataset).

Table 12.3 Mixed-effects Regression Model for Spanish Data

Factors	Parameter Estimate	Standard Error	z-Value	p-Value	Confidence Intervals	
					Lower	Upper
Intercept	1.55794	.32674	4.768	1.86e-06***	.9301	2.2320
Time (ref point: pre-stay)						
In-stay	.55383	.31071	1.782	.074678	−.0547	1.1809
Post-stay	.67911	.31032	2.188	.028639*	.0707	1.3041
Noun gender (ref point: feminine)						
masculine	1.44773	.31108	4.654	3.26e-06***	.8539	2.0921
Syllable distance	−.11772	.03251	−3.621	.000293***	−.1838	−.0538
Noun number (ref point: plural)						
singular	1.08973	.26984	4.038	5.38e-05***	.5614	1.6324
Modifier type (ref point: adjective)						
determiner	1.29414	.27030	4.788	1.69e-06***	.7620	1.8354
Noun ending (ref point: canonical -o/-a)						
deceptive -o/-a	−2.67451	.48324	−5.535	3.12e-08***	−3.6205	−1.6905
predictive	−.31925	.39737	−.803	.421733	−1.0677	.5216
other	−.34363	.35539	−.967	.333582	−1.0179	.3983

Note: *$p < .05$, ***$p < .001$

Results for French

As is evident in Figure 12.2, the learners of French also show improvement over time. At pre-stay, 81.81 per cent of all instances of gender marking in the essays are targetlike, an average that rises to 87.73 per cent one year later. The gains observed between pre-stay and in-stay appear to be maintained after the learners' return to the UK, with a group average of 87.19 per cent targetlike use at post-stay. Variability of scores among individuals learning French is relatively large, with the range of scores obtained in the French data increasing between pre-stay (68.42 per cent and 95.24 per cent) and in-stay (59.46 per cent and 100 per cent). The range that can be observed at post-stay resembles findings for in-stay: 62.5 per cent and 100 per cent.

Using a mixed-effects regression, we explored eleven fixed effects, of which the following eight were not significant: modifier type, noun number, noun class, noun log-frequency (language), noun-initial phoneme and the three manners of operationalizing noun ending (noun-final phoneme, noun-final orthographic rhyme, noun derivational morphology). These factors were removed from the model. The final mixed-effects regression model identified three significant main effects (noun

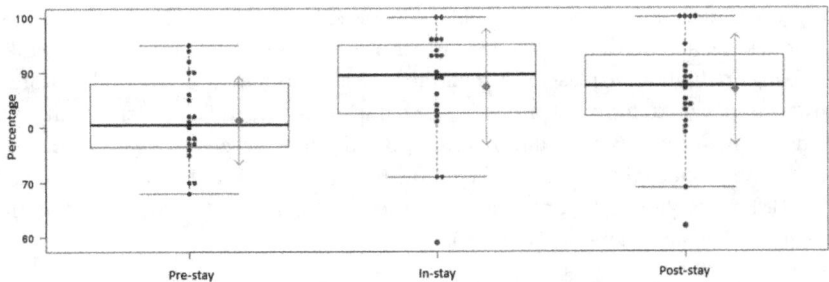

Figure 12.2 Targetlike Rates of Use for Individuals and the Group (French Dataset).

Table 12.4 Mixed-effects Regression Model for French Data

Factors	Parameter Estimate	Standard Error	z-Value	p-Value	Confidence Intervals	
					Lower	Upper
Intercept	.97944	.19200	5.101	3.37e-07***	.6051	1.3681
Time (ref point: pre-stay)						
In-stay	.71843	.24437	2.940	.003283**	.2414	1.2048
Post-stay	1.08923	.24380	4.468	7.91e-06***	.6143	1.5758
Noun gender (ref point: feminine)						
masculine	1.32607	.26341	5.034	4.80e-07***	.8160	1.8560
Syllable distance	−.20831	.05551	−3.752	.000175***	−.3238	−.1035
Noun gender × Time (ref point: feminine × pre-stay)						
masculine × in-stay	−.60299	.37057	−1.627	.103694	−1.3370	.1251
masculine × post-stay	−1.40024	.36532	−3.833	.000127***	−2.1263	−.6852
Noun gender × syllable distance	.19971	.08192	2.438	.014770*	.0492	.3761

Note: * $p<.05$, ** $p<.01$, *** $p<.001$

gender, syllable distance, time) and two significant strong interactions (noun gender × time and noun gender × syllable distance). Starting with the three main effects, we find that the learners of French are significantly more likely to mark gender in a targetlike fashion on masculine (vs feminine) nouns and their log odds of targetlike use decrease as the distance between the noun and modifier increases. As concerns time, a significant improvement in targetlike use was seen between pre-stay and in-stay, as well as between pre-stay and post-stay.

The significant interaction between noun gender and time reflects the fact that the greater likelihood of targetlike behaviour on masculine nouns (vs feminine ones) decreases from pre- to post-stay. This means that the effect of noun gender is stronger at pre-stay than it is at post-stay. The noun gender × syllable distance interaction indicates that as a modifier is situated farther from the noun, the log odds of targetlike marking are higher for masculine than they are for feminine nouns. In other words, distance appears to have a stronger negative impact on targetlike gender marking for feminine nouns versus masculine ones. Finally, in order to evaluate the fit of our final model, we calculated the BIC for the model presented in Table 12.4 and for the null model. Results showed that the BIC was lower for our model (1304.2) than the BIC calculated for the null model (1321.59).

Discussion

We begin by addressing the research question that guided this study and by connecting our findings to previous research. We then consider the potential role of transparency in understanding the findings from the current analysis.

Using targetlike rates of use and mixed-effects regression models, we set out to identify in what ways specialists of Spanish or French at a UK university show similar and language-specific patterns of gender marking in written production before, during and after a stay abroad. Beginning with similarities, the analysis revealed that gender marking in the argumentative essays had significantly improved between pre-stay and post-stay for learners of both AL Spanish and French. Two previous studies – Collentine (2004) and Godfrey, Treacy and Tarone (2014) – also reported on rates of targetlike gender marking: whereas Collentine found no significant change in the oral production of his learners of Spanish who had spent a semester abroad, Godfrey, Treacy and Tarone documented a dramatic decline in non-targetlike marking of grammatical gender in written French after a semester in France. Because the studies presented by Collentine and Godfrey, Treacy and Tarone, as well as that in the current chapter adopted different designs (in terms of length of stay, modality and potentially initial proficiency), these seemingly contradictory findings will need to be explored in future research. Continuing with similarities, the gender-marking behaviour of the learners of both languages was found to be significantly characterized by two of the same linguistic factors: noun gender and syllable distance. In the case of noun gender, learners of both languages were more likely to be targetlike on masculine (vs feminine) nouns. This finding adds further support to the already robust finding that most instances of non-targetlike gender marking in AL Spanish and in AL French involve the use of masculine modifiers with feminine nouns (Bartning, 2000; Dewaele and Véronique, 2001; Edmonds and Gudmestad, 2018; Finnemann, 1992; Gudmestad, Edmonds and Metzger, 2019; Harley, 1979; Schlig, 2003; White et al., 2004). It is of note that masculine nouns outnumber feminine ones in both Spanish and French. When combined with the current and past findings, this may suggest that learners tend to overuse modifiers marked for the most frequent noun gender (masculine, in the case of Spanish and French). As for syllable distance, log odds of targetlike gender marking decreased as the distance between the noun and the modifier increased in both languages. A handful of previous studies have shown (Edmonds and Gudmestad, 2018; Gudmestad, Edmonds and Metzger, 2019) or suggested (Finnemann, 1992; Holmes and Dejean de la Bâtie, 1999) that the distance between a noun and its modifier may significantly affect gender marking on the latter. The current findings provide additional empirical evidence for the importance of this factor for both AL Spanish and French. Given that the significance of this variable is thought to reflect greater processing difficulty and/or memory demands associated with long(er) distance agreement, we would expect syllable distance to be significant for gender marking across different ALs and to potentially be sensitive to individual differences such as working memory. Verification of these possibilities is left to future research.

In addition to the three similarities detailed in the preceding paragraph, our analysis revealed numerous differences in gender-marking behaviour in AL Spanish and French. In the remainder of this section, we focus on three of those differences that we feel may relate to the construct of transparency, namely the rates of targetlike use, the importance of noun ending and the significance of modifier type. Beginning with the rates of targetlike use, the learners of Spanish are, as a whole, more targetlike than the learners of French. The group average at pre-stay for the Spanish learners is already at 95.93 per cent, whereas the learners of French are only at 81.81 per cent. There is also clearly less intra-individual variability in the Spanish group than in the French one, as evidenced by the lower standard deviations for the Spanish learners. Moreover, it is only among the Spanish learners that the standard deviations become smaller over time, suggesting a reduction in variability as a result of the stay abroad. Taken together, the learners of the more transparent system have outperformed the learners of the less transparent one. This finding, which replicates (with actual learners) what Monner et al. (2013) found using computational modelling, is consistent with the idea that a strong and reliable mapping between form and gender category, as is found in Spanish gender marking, should be picked up on by learners (Ellis, Römer and O'Donnell, 2016). It is thus logical that the more transparent system should lead to greater targetlike behaviour. It is interesting that despite having learned Spanish for an average of 5.3 years (opposed to 10.45 for the average length of study for AL French in this project), the AL Spanish group already has a better command of grammatical gender marking in written production than their AL French counterparts before the stay abroad. This finding may suggest that classroom input can be sufficient for high rates of targetlike use with transparent grammatical gender-marking systems.

The second result that we suggest can be linked to the greater transparency of grammatical gender in Spanish versus French is the significance of noun ending in the Spanish (but not the French) model. This is because noun ending is a more reliable cue to noun gender in Spanish (Monner et al., 2013) than it is in French. In the current data, the Spanish learners were significantly more likely to be targetlike on nouns with a canonical -o/-a ending than on deceptive -o/-a words. This finding highlights the fact that these learners have picked up on the fact that -o and -a are strongly associated with masculine and feminine genders, respectively, and that these learners have the tendency to overgeneralize this strong association to deceptive -o/-a nouns. The analysis of the French data suggests that noun ending (which we operationalized in three different ways) is not significantly influencing their gender-marking behaviour. This may reflect the fact that the French learners have not detected that certain noun endings can be used as cues to noun gender. It is expected that such detection would be more challenging in a less transparent system.

Table 12.5 Proportion of Modifiers Marked Overtly for Gender

	Spanish		French	
Modifier Type	n	%	n	%
Determiners	1,737/1,883	92.2	982/2,188	44.9
Adjectives	586/1,146	51.1	619/907	68.2

For the final observation (concerning the variable of modifier type), we are interested in how the two languages differ in the overt (vs invariable or non-overt) expression of gender. As discussed earlier, both Spanish and French have determiners and adjectives that do not show overt gender marking, although there are many more such modifiers in French. This is clear within our own dataset: whereas 77.2 per cent (2,323/3,008) of all tokens in Spanish involved modifiers that showed overt gender, only 52.3 per cent (1,601/3,059) of French tokens did. Globally, this means that learners of Spanish have more occasions than learners of French to mark gender overtly and, we presume, to encounter overt gender marking in the input (cf. Ayoun, 2010, for French). More specifically with respect to modifier type, it is instructive to examine the proportion of determiners and modifiers in the current corpus that showed overt gender marking in Spanish and in French (Table 12.5).

The usage profiles shown in this table are appreciably different. In Spanish, the vast majority – 92.2 per cent – of all determiners written by the twenty learners involved overt marking of gender, whereas only a little more than half of all adjectives did. In French, the tendency is inversed, and the gap is smaller: 44.9 per cent of all determiners in the learners' essays necessitated an overt marking of gender, whereas 68.2 per cent of adjectives did. To come back to transparency, the distribution of data in Table 12.5 suggests that gender may be more overtly (and, thus, transparently) marked on determiners than on adjectives in Spanish, a pattern that does not obtain in French. We suggest that this stark difference between determiners and adjectives may be reflected in the significance of modifier type in the Spanish data, where it was found that learners were more likely to be targetlike precisely on the category of modifier (i.e. determiners) with which overt gender marking was highly frequent.

Conclusion

We investigated how twenty learners of AL Spanish and twenty learners of AL French develop their gender-marking behaviour over a period of twenty-one months, including a nine-month stay in a TL community. We examined learners of Spanish and French in a single study because the gender-marking systems of these two languages show many similarities but are different in terms of transparency. We were interested in how the difference in transparency may lead to different developmental patterns during a stay abroad. Results from our analysis reveal that learners of both languages showed gains after their stay abroad and that gender-marking behaviour was influenced by noun gender and syllable distance for both languages. Numerous differences were also identified, three of which we suggested may reflect the difference in transparency between the two systems, giving an advantage to the more transparent system (Spanish, in this case). We have suggested that the greater transparency of the Spanish gender-marking system is a characteristic that allows learners both to more easily detect the mapping of nouns to gender categories (because of the greater reliability of cue-interpretation distribution) and to engage in more practice (because a greater proportion of modifiers – particularly determiners – requires overt gender marking). However, the high level of targetlike use among the AL Spanish learners before leaving for their year abroad has led us to suggest that classroom input and use of Spanish appears to have been sufficient for attaining high rates of targetlike use in at least written grammatical gender marking. With the AL French learners, on the other hand, we see a greater increase in targetlike rates of use (made possible because they began at lower levels than their AL Spanish counterparts) and, importantly, one interaction with time (noun gender × time). This interaction shows that the factor of noun gender significantly changes with respect to its influence on how these learners express gender marking over time, suggesting that the stay abroad has impacted the way in which the gender of the noun influences gender-marking behaviour. More specifically, the gap between targetlike use on masculine versus feminine nouns at pre-stay has been almost erased at post-stay. These findings indicate that the stay abroad has been particularly beneficial both in increasing overall targetlike rates of use and in overcoming the difference in gender marking with masculine versus feminine nouns in the less transparent AL French system. Future research would do well to investigate whether other instances of less transparent systems show particular benefit from the stay abroad experience.

Notes

1. An anonymous reviewer brought up the possibility that the difference in gender marking in Spanish and French may also be explained with reference to vowel harmony, insofar as the canonical endings for Spanish nouns (-o/-a) are also the endings used to indicate gender on many modifiers. Although an intriguing suggestion, it is not clear how such an account would explain transparency between other endings (e.g. [d] and [l] in Spanish) and gender marking.
2. Sensitivity to noun ending has also been found for AL French, although these studies have not examined production, instead Hardison (1992) asked learners how they made gender-assignment decisions and Holmes and Dejean de la Bâtie (1999) tested sensitivity to noun endings using nonce words.
3. The corpus is available at http://langsnap.soton.ac.uk/.
4. There is a difference in the elicited imitation scores obtained by the learners of Spanish versus those of French. However, it should be pointed out that these measures were developed and validated using tests of concurrent validity, meaning that correlations were run to ensure that scores obtained on this task correlated with scores obtained on other tasks (in the same language) thought to measure the same construct (see Tracy-Ventura et al., 2014, for the development of the French

    test; Ortega, 2000, for Spanish). This means that it is not possible to conclude that participants obtaining the same numerical score on the two different versions actually have comparable levels of proficiency in those two languages.
5   For a separate analysis of the French dataset and further details concerning specificities of the coding, see Edmonds and Gudmestad (2018); for an analysis of the full Spanish dataset (written and oral data), see Gudmestad et al. (2019).

References

Alarcón, I. (2010), 'Gender Assignment and Agreement in L2 Spanish: The Effects of Morphological Marking, Animacy, and Gender', *Studies in Hispanic and Lusophone Linguistics*, 3, 267–99.

Alarcón, I. (2011), 'Spanish Gender Agreement under Complete and Incomplete Acquisition: Early and Late Bilinguals' Linguistic Behavior within the Noun Phrase', *Bilingualism, Language and Cognition*, 14 (3), 332–50.

Ayoun, D. (2007), 'The Second Language Acquisition of Grammatical Gender and Agreement', in D. Ayoun (ed.), *French Applied Linguistics*, 130–70, Amsterdam: Benjamins.

Ayoun, D. (2010), 'Corpus Data: Shedding the Light on French Grammatical Gender … or Not', *EUROSLA Yearbook*, 10, 119–41.

Bartning, I. (2000), 'Gender Agreement in L2 French: Pre-advanced vs. Advanced Learners', *Studia Linguistica*, 54, 225–37.

Boloh, Y., and Ibernon, L. (2010), 'Gender Attribution and Gender Agreement in 4- to 10-year-old French Children', *Cognitive Development*, 25, 1–25.

Bruhn de Garavito, J., and White, L. (2002), 'The Second Language Acquisition of Spanish DPs: The Status of Grammatical Features', in A. T. Pérez-Leroux, and J. M. Liceras (eds.), *The Acquisition of Spanish Morphosyntax: The L1/L2 Connection*, 143–60, New York: Bilingual Press.

Charkova, K. D., and Halliday, L. J. (2011), 'Second- and Foreign-language Variation in Tense Backshifting in Indirect Reported Speech', *Studies in Second Language Acquisition*, 33, 1–32.

Collentine, J. (2004), 'The Effects of Learning Contexts on Morphosyntactic and Lexical Development', *Studies in Second Language Acquisition*, 26, 227–48.

Davies, M. (2016), 'Corpus del Español: Two Billion Words, 21 Countries'. Available online at www.corpusdelespanol.org/web-dial/.

DeKeyser, R. (2007), 'Study Abroad as Foreign Language Practice', in R. DeKeyser (ed.), *Practice in a Second Language: Perspectives from Applied Linguistics and Cognitive Psychology*, 208–26, Cambridge: Cambridge University Press.

DeKeyser, R. (2014), 'Research on Language Development during Study Abroad: Methodological Considerations and Future Perspectives', in C. Pérez-Vidal (ed.), *Language Acquisition in Study Abroad and Formal Instruction Contexts*, 313–25, Amsterdam: Benjamins.

Dewaele, J.-M. (2015), 'Gender Errors in French Interlanguage: The Effects of Initial Consonant versus Initial Vowel of the Head Noun', *Arborescences: Revue d'Etudes Françaises*, 5, 7–27.

Dewaele, J.-M., and Véronique, D. (2001), 'Gender Assignment and Gender Agreement in Advanced French Interlanguage: A Cross-sectional Study', *Bilingualism: Language and Cognition*, 4, 275–97.

Edmonds, A., and Gudmestad, A. (2018), 'Gender Marking in Written L2 French: Before, during, and after Residence Abroad', *Study Abroad Research in Second Language Acquisition and International Education*, 3 (1), 59–82.

Eichler, N., Jansen, V., and Müller, N. (2013), 'Gender Acquisition in Bilingual Children: French-German, Italian-German, Spanish-German, and Italian-French', *International Journal of Bilingualism*, 17 (5), 550–572.

Ellis, N. C., Römer, U., and O'Donnell, M. B. (2016), *Usage-based Approaches to Language Acquisition and Processing: Cognitive and Corpus Investigations of Construction Grammar*, Malden, MA: Wiley.

Fernández García, M. (1999), 'Patterns of Gender Agreement in the Speech of Second Language Learners', in J. Gutiérrez-Rexach, and F. Martínez-Gil (eds.), *Advances in Hispanic Linguistics: Papers from the 2nd Hispanic Linguistics Symposium*, 3–15, Somerville, MA: Cascadilla Press.

Finnemann, M. D. (1992), 'Learning Agreement in the Noun Phrase: The Strategies of Three First-year Spanish Students', *International Review of Applied Linguistics in Teaching*, 30 (2), 121–36.

Freed, B., So, S., and Lazar, N. A. (2003), 'Language Learning Abroad: How Do Gains in Written Fluency Compare with Gains in Oral Fluency in French as a Second Language?', *ADFL Bulletin*, 3, 34–40.

Godfrey, L., Treacy, C., and Tarone, E. (2014), 'Change in French Second Language Writing in Study Abroad and Domestic Contexts', *Foreign Language Annals*, 47 (1), 48–65.

Granfeldt, J. (2005), 'The Development of Gender Attribution and Gender Concord in French: A Comparison of Bilingual First and Second Language Learners', in J.-M. Dewaele (ed.), *Focus on French as a Foreign Language: Multidisciplinary Approaches*, 164–90, Clevedon: Multilingual Matters.

Gudmestad, A., Edmonds, A., and Metzger, T. (2019), 'Using Variationism and Learner Corpus Research to Investigate Grammatical Gender Marking', *Language Learning*, 69 (4), 911–42.

Halberstadt, L., Valdés Kroff, J. R., and Dussias, P. E. (2018), 'Grammatical Gender Processing in L2 Speakers of Spanish: The Role of Cognate Status and Gender Transparency', *Journal of Second Language Studies*, 1 (1), 5–30.

Hardison, D. M. (1992), 'Acquisition of Grammatical Gender in French: L2 Learner Accuracy and Strategies', *The Canadian Modern Language Review*, 48, 292–306.

Harley, B. (1979), 'French Gender "Rules" in the Speech of English-dominant, French-dominant, and Monolingual French Speaking Children', *Working Papers in Bilingualism*, 19, 129–56.

Holmes, V. M., and Dejean de la Bâtie, B. (1999), 'Assignment of Grammatical Gender by Native Speakers and Foreign Learners of French', *Applied Psycholinguistics*, 20, 479–506.

Howard, M. (2001), 'The Effects of Study Abroad on the L2 Learner's Structural Skills: Evidence from Advanced Learners of French', *Eurosla Yearbook*, 1, 123–41.

Howard, M. (2012a), 'From Tense and Aspect to Modality: The Acquisition of Future, Conditional and Subjunctive Morphology in L2 French. A Preliminary Study', *Cahiers Chronos*, 24, 201–23.

Howard, M. (2012b), 'The Advanced Learner's Sociolinguistic Profile: On Issues of Individual Differences, Second Language Exposure Conditions, and Type of Sociolinguistic Variable', *The Modern Language Journal*, 96 (1), 20–33.

Howard, M., and Schwieter, J. W. (2018), 'The Development of Second Language Grammar in a Study Abroad Context', in C. Sanz, and A. Morales-Front (eds.), *The*

Routledge Handbook of Study Abroad Research and Practice, 135–48, New York, NY: Routledge.

Isabelli-García, C. (2010), 'Acquisition of Spanish Gender Agreement in Two Learning Contexts: Study Abroad and at Home', *Foreign Language Annals*, 43 (2), 289–303.

Kinginger, C. (2009), *Language Learning and Study Abroad: A Critical Reading of Research*, Basingstoke: Palgrave Macmillan.

Kupisch, T., Müller, N., and Cantone, K. F. (2002), 'Gender in Monolingual and Bilingual First Language Acquisition: Comparing Italian and French', *Lingue e Linguaggio*, 1, 107–49.

Llanes, À. (2011), 'The Many Faces of Study Abroad: An Update on the Research on L2 Gains Emerged during a Study Abroad Experience', *International Journal of Multilingualism*, 8 (3), 189–215.

Llanes, À., Tragant, E., and Serrano, R. (2012), 'The Role of Individual Differences in a Study Abroad Experience: The Case of Erasmus Students', *International Journal of Multilingualism*, 9 (3), 318–42.

Lyster, R. (2006), 'Predictability in French Gender Attribution: A Corpus Analysis', *Journal of French Language Studies*, 16, 69–92.

Mitchell, R., Tracy-Ventura, N., and McManus, K. (2017), *Anglophone Students Abroad: Identity, Social Relationships, and Language Learning*, London: Routledge.

Monner, D., Vatz, K., Morini, G., Hwang, S.-O., and DeKeyser, R. (2013), 'A Neural Network Model of the Effects of Entrenchment and Memory Development on Grammatical Gender Learning', *Bilingualism: Language and Cognition*, 16 (2), 246–65.

Nelson, D. (2005), 'French Gender Assignment Revisited', *Word*, 56, 19–38.

New, B., Brysbaert, M., Veronis, J., and Pallier, C. (2007), 'The Use of Film Subtitles to Estimate Word Frequencies', *Applied Psycholinguistics*, 28, 661–77.

Ortega, L. (2000), 'Understanding Syntactic Complexity: The Measurement of Change in the Syntax of Instructed L2 Spanish Learners', unpublished doctoral dissertation, University of Hawai'i at Manoa.

Pérez-Vidal, C., and Juan-Garau, M. (2009), 'The Effect of Study Abroad (SA) on Written Performance', *EUROSLA Yearbook*, 9, 269–95.

Plann, S. (1979), "Morphological Problems in the Acquisition of Spanish in an Immersion Classroom', in R. W. Andersen (ed.), *The Acquisition and Use of Spanish and English as First and Second Languages*, 120–32, Washington, DC: TESOL.

Schlig, C. (2003), 'Analysis of Agreement Errors Made by Third-year Students', *Hispania*, 86 (2), 312–19.

Surridge, M. E. (1989), 'Le Genre Grammatical en Français Fondamental: Données de Base pour l'Enseignement et l'Apprentissage', *La Revue Canadienne des Langues Vivantes*, 45, 664–74.

Surridge, M. E., and Lessard, G. (1984), 'Pour une Prise de Conscience du Genre Grammatical', *La Revue Canadienne des Langues Vivantes*, 41, 44–52.

Teschner, R. V., and Russell, W. M. (1984), 'The Gender Patterns of Spanish Nouns: An Inverse Dictionary-based Analysis', *Hispanic Linguistics*, 1, 115–32.

Tracy-Ventura, N., McManus, K., Norris, J., and Ortega, L. (2014), 'Repeat as Much as You Can: Elicited Imitation as a Measure of Oral Proficiency in L2 French', in P. Leclercq, A. Edmonds, and H. Hilton (eds.), *Measuring L2 Proficiency: Perspectives from SLA*, Bristol, UK: Multilingual Matters.

Tucker, R., Lambert, W. E., and Rigault, A. (1977), *The French Speaker's Skill with Grammatical Gender: An Example of Rule-governed Behavior*, Paris: Mouton.

White, L., Valenzuela, E., Kozlowska-Macgregor, M., and Leung, Y.-K. I. (2004), 'Gender and Number Agreement in Nonnative Spanish', *Applied Psycholinguistics*, 25, 105–33.

Appendix. Participant random effect

Spanish		French	
Participant	Intercept	Participant	Intercept
150	.0618	100	.3278
151	−.1648	101	.3346
152	−.0744	102	.2771
155	.4010	104	.1617
156	−.0759	105	−.0520
157	−.7053	106	−.7003
158	.1859	107	−.3881
160	.2389	108	.6723
161	−.1277	109	−.2873
162	.5849	110	.2178
163	−.2335	111	−.4467
164	.2589	112	.0644
165	−.1028	113	−.3161
166	−.2765	114	−.1643
167	−.3577	115	−.2814
168	−.3994	116	−.2111
169	.0692	117	.2859
170	.0158	118	−.1932
171	.2682	119	.0858
172	.01890	120	.3293

Index

accommodation 5–7, 22, 92–3, 101, 104–5, 108–9
accuracy 5, 40–4, 77–8, 212, 227
adolescents 2, 3, 91, 101–9
affordances 168
age 3, 6–7, 150, 156, 160, 213
agency 7, 150–2, 165–7, 169–70, 174, 176–7, 180–1
at-home learning 35, 40–3, 70, 152, 211–12, 226, 235
attention 193–194, 200–1, 204–6. *See also* noticing
attitudes 5–6, 52, 115, 122, 176
autonomy 149–52, 154, 158

beliefs 49–55, 132, 153, 160–1, 180, 204
Bologna process 18

communities of practice 167, 171
complexity 5, 77, 132, 213
confidence 138, 175, 202, 205
context 165, 167–8
cultural empathy 34–5, 38, 42–4
cultural intelligence 122–3, 125
culture shock 54, 91, 101

European Credit Transfer System (ECTS) 18, 20, 142
emotional intelligence 33, 35, 38, 42, 44
Erasmus 1, 3, 4, 6, 15–27, 94–5, 173
　Erasmus Charter for Higher Education 20–1
experiential learning 118–19, 140
extraversion 34–6, 38, 41–4

feedback 94, 101
fluency 3, 5, 40–4, 56, 77, 213
formulaic language 8, 189, 191, 211–30

gender 160, 166–7
gender marking 8, 235–49

grammar 5, 7, 35, 56, 177, 233
　grammatical skills 3, 233, 234

home stay 7, 35, 78, 92–3, 98, 107. *See also* residence
host family 4, 76, 93–4, 102, 170. *See also* home stay

identity 3, 5–7, 91, 117, 125, 165–83
　European 26
idiomaticity 212, 224
IEREST Project 117, 119–20, 182
impersonal language 218, 224
individual differences 34, 62, 160, 193–206, 247. *See also* individual variation
individual factors 2, 5, 7, 155
individual variation (variability) 5, 124, 189, 192, 206, 235, 247
input 5–7, 35, 69, 71, 77, 81, 84, 92, 152, 168, 190, 191–4, 201, 204–5, 211, 234, 237–9
instruction (instructed learning) 5, 101–2, 141, 145–6, 211–13, 226
integration 4, 15–16, 20, 22, 26, 72, 97, 103, 105
　host family 94
　reintegration 3
interaction 5, 35, 61–3, 69, 73, 84, 92, 94–5, 105, 115–16, 123, 131–2, 138, 152, 194, 199–202, 238
intercultural awareness 96–7, 107, 109, 120, 145, 182
intercultural communication 25
　adjustment 44
　exchange 22
intercultural competence 76, 91, 96–7, 107, 10
intercultural development 35–6, 63, 115–17, 124–6, 128–32, 146
intercultural education 16, 143

language contact 4–5, 7, 69–84, 95, 100, 191, 198, 201, 206, 234. *See also* language engagement
  interactive 73, 76
  L1 70, 73–4
  out-of-class 70, 75–6, 80
  virtual 73–4
Language Contact Profile 7, 70–1, 74–7
language engagement 35, 202. *See also* language contact
LANGSNAP Project 239
learning agreement 20
learning strategies 150–1, 160
legislation 15–27
length of stay (duration) 3, 25, 34, 37, 80, 235
lexis 3, 40–1, 56, 74, 77–8, 116, 177, 213
  vocabulary size 124
lingua franca 92, 96, 98, 104–5, 175
linguistic development 2, 6–7, 35, 71, 125
  and language contact 69, 74–5, 84
  linguistic gains 3, 34, 62, 233
  and L2 use 45
  and personality 36
listening 39, 40, 57–9, 61, 71, 76–7

marketing 4, 6, 49–53, 60–4
mentoring 4–5, 7, 137–46. *See also* training
  intercultural 137–8
MILSA Project (Mentoring Intercultural Learning through Study Abroad) 139–41, 143
motivation 73, 131–2, 204–6
  and attention 194, 198–200
  and autonomy 153
  intrinsic 142
  and oral development 76
  and self-regulation 150–1
multilingualism 165, 172
multiword expressions 189–206

noticing 193–4, 198, 200, 204–5. *See also* attention

open-mindedness 35, 38, 43, 44

pedagogical intervention 116–18, 122, 124, 130, 138
personality 5–6, 33–8, 41–5, 93, 97, 153
plurilingual identities 7, 165–83
  plurilingualism 172, 178
post-structuralism 166, 180
practice 105, 229, 235
pragmatic competence 5, 78, 122, 124, 168
  and formulaic language 191
  and identity 171
  and language contact 80
preparation 4, 5, 7, 20, 63, 153
pronunciation 5, 40, 56, 75

reading 39, 40, 57–9, 61, 71, 76
residence 4, 7, 23, 25, 153

SALA Project 214
saliency 233, 237
Study Abroad Language Support App (SALSA) 116, 132
self-efficacy 5, 50–3, 60–5, 132, 198–9, 204–6
  and motivation 194–5
self-regulation 5, 7, 132, 149–61, 165, 195, 198–200, 204–6
short-term study abroad 3, 36, 55, 91–2, 102, 107
social networks 4–5, 45, 78–83, 91, 94–5, 101, 105, 138, 167, 199–201
  development 34–7, 122
  formation 126, 128–9, 131
  measures of 71–3
social network analysis 81, 168
sociolinguistic competence 5, 80
speaking 35, 39–42, 57–9, 61, 76
Study Abroad Social Interaction Questionnaire (SASIQ) 7, 71, 78

technology 115–16
  and mentoring 139, 141, 143, 146
  online language contact 74
  and self-regulation 150–1, 154–5, 157–8, 161
training 6, 109, 131. *See also* mentoring
transfer (crosslinguistic / L1) 212, 221, 227
transparency 233–4, 236, 238–9, 247–8
translanguaging 170–1, 175–6, 178, 180–1

usage-based approaches 237

vocabulary. *See* lexis

willingness to communicate 153, 160–1
writing 39–40, 57–8, 60–1, 128, 212, 229
   and language contact 76

www.ingramcontent.com/pod-product-compliance
Lightning Source LLC
Chambersburg PA
CBHW072133290426
44111CB00012B/1868